Grammar – Discourse – Context

Diskursmuster
Discourse Patterns

Edited by
Beatrix Busse and Ingo H. Warnke

Volume 23

Grammar Discourse Context

Grammar and Usage in Language Variation and Change

Edited by
Kristin Bech and Ruth Möhlig-Falke

DE GRUYTER

ISBN 978-3-11-077811-3
e-ISBN (PDF) 978-3-11-068256-4
e-ISBN (EPUB) 978-3-11-068266-3

Library of Congress Control Number: 2019956277

Bibliografische Information der Deutschen Nationalbibliothek
The Deutsche Nationalbibliothek lists this publication in the Deutsche Nationalbibliografie;
detailed bibliographic data are available on the Internet at http://dnb.dnb.de.

© 2021 Walter de Gruyter GmbH, Berlin/Boston
This volume is text- and page-identical with the hardback published in 2019.
Printing and binding: CPI books GmbH, Leck

www.degruyter.com

Contents

List of tables and figures —— VII

Ruth Möhlig-Falke and Kristin Bech
Grammar – discourse – context: Grammatical variation and change and the usage-based perspective —— 1

Kristin Bech
Contextualizing Old English noun phrases —— 15

Bettelou Los and Thijs Lubbers
Syntax, text type, genre and authorial voice in Old English: A data-driven approach —— 49

Belén Méndez-Naya
The intensifier system of the *Ormulum* and the interplay of micro-level and macro-level contexts in linguistic change —— 93

Lynn Anthonissen
Constructional change across the lifespan: The nominative and infinitive in early modern writers —— 125

Ruth Möhlig-Falke
Contextualizing dual-form adverbs in the *Old Bailey Corpus*: An assessment of semantic, pragmatic, and sociolinguistic factors —— 157

Dagmar Haumann and Kristin Killie
Bridging contexts in the reanalysis of *naturally* as a sentence adverb: A corpus study —— 191

Reijirou Shibasaki
From parataxis to amalgamation: The emergence of the sentence-final *is all* construction in the history of American English —— 221

Elena Seoane
The role of context in the entrenchment of new grammatical markers in World Englishes —— 249

Martin Konvička
Paradigms, host classes, and ancillariness: A comparison of three approaches to grammatical status —— 277

Hendrik De Smet
The motivated unmotivated: Variation, function and context —— 305

María José López-Couso
Grammar in context: On the role of hypercharacterization in language variation and change —— 333

List of contributors —— 365

Index —— 367

List of tables and figures

Tables

Tab. 2.1: Properties of weak and strong adjectives according to Fischer (2001, 2001, 2006, 2012) —— 22
Tab. 2.2: Properties of prenominal and postnominal adjectives according to Haumann (2003, 2010) —— 22
Tab. 3.1: Characteristics of sample set of early (o2) and late (o3/4) OE texts —— 56
Tab. 3.2: Lexical 4-grams of Gregory's *Dialogues* and Ælfric's *Lives of Saints* —— 58
Tab. 3.3: Lexical 4-grams of Ælfric's and Wulfstan's homilies —— 61
Tab. 3.4: Early verbs and style, from Pintzuk (1999: 208) —— 63
Tab. 3.5: Significant POS trigrams in the "Scripture" cluster —— 75
Tab. 3.6: Significant POS trigrams in the "Histories" cluster —— 77
Tab. 3.7: Significant POS trigrams of the "Centre" cluster —— 80
Tab. 3.8: POS-tag trigrams in narratives: Gregory's *Dialogues* and Ælfric's *Lives of Saints* —— 82
Tab. 3.9: POS-tag trigrams in homilies: Ælfric's *Catholic Homilies I* and Wulfstan's *Homilies* —— 84
Tab. 4.1: Top intensifiers in the history of English —— 97
Tab. 4.2: Intensifiers in the *Ormulum* (time-depth) —— 102
Tab. 4.3: Development of *swipe* based on Méndez-Naya (2003) —— 112
Tab. 5.1: Sample of first-generation EMMA authors, attestations of NCIs —— 140
Tab. 6.1: Numbers of occurrences for the individual search items as adverbs and predicative adjectives —— 163
Tab. 6.2: Distribution of different types of orientation over adverbial zero- and -LY-forms found in the OBC between 1730 and 1913 —— 174
Tab. 7.1: The distribution of *naturally* in copular *be* sentences —— 205
Tab. 7.2: *Naturally* as sentence adverb and narrow scope adverb across distributional classes —— 207
Tab. 8.1: The distributional pattern of the three constructions in CLMETEV —— 235
Tab. 8.2: The distributional pattern of the three constructions in BYU-BNC and COCA —— 236
Tab. 8.3: The distributional pattern of *,/Ø is all* in COCA —— 236
Tab. 8.4: The survey results of the sentence-final *is all* construction in GloWbE —— 247
Tab. 8.5: The survey results of the sentence-final *is all* construction in The TV Corpus —— 247
Tab. 8.6: The survey results of the sentence-final *is all* construction in The Movie Corpus —— 247
Tab. 9.1: Form and regional distribution of the verbs expressing perfect meaning —— 255
Tab. 9.2: Number and percentage of adverbial absence and presence by geographical variety —— 257
Tab. 9.3: Distribution of contexts with adverbial support per verbal form in all varieties —— 258
Tab. 9.4: Distribution of adverbials per lexical verb —— 259
Tab. 9.5: Distribution of adverbials according to context polarity —— 260
Tab. 9.6: Proportion of forms with adverbial support per mode —— 261
Tab. 9.7: Subtypes of perfect meaning in BrE and L2 varieties —— 262

Tab. 9.8: Summary of the estimated linear effects for model 1 together with Odds Ratio (OR) and 95% Confidence Intervals (CI) for the estimated OR —— 266
Tab. 12.1: Polyfunctionality of Old English adverbial subordinators —— 340

Figures

Fig. 3.1: Rowprincipal asymmetric CA of POS-unigrams in the OE sample —— 69
Fig. 3.2: Rowprincipal asymmetric CA of POS-trigrams of the OE sample, 1st slice, 100+ occurrences —— 74
Fig. 3.3: Close-up of Quadrant 1 of figure 3.1 —— 75
Fig. 3.4: Close-up of Quadrant 2 of figure 3.1 —— 77
Fig. 3.5: Close-up of Quadrant 3 of figure 3.1 —— 79
Fig. 3.6: Close-up of the centre of figure 3.1 —— 79
Fig. 4.1: Inventory and distribution of intensifiers in the PPCME2 sample of the *Ormulum* —— 100
Fig. 4.2: Major Middle English intensifiers —— 106
Fig. 4.3: *Swiþe, full, rihht* in the PPCME2 sample of the *Ormulum* —— 108
Fig. 5.1: Symmetric biplot of John Owen's dataset —— 143
Fig. 5.2: Asymmetric biplot of John Owen's dataset —— 144
Fig. 5.3: Proportion of modalized/evidential uses across the lifespan —— 146
Fig. 5.4: Proportion of modalized/evidential uses for *say* and all other PCU verbs (Fuller) —— 149
Fig. 6.1: Chronological distribution of adverbial and adjectival uses for the investigated items in the OBC —— 168
Fig. 6.2: Adverbial zero-forms (top) and -LY-forms (bottom) found in the OBC between 1730 and 1913 —— 169
Fig. 6.3: Distribution of -LY-forms and zero-forms across female and male speakers —— 183
Fig. 6.4: Distribution of -LY-forms and zero-forms across different social/occupational classes —— 184
Fig. 7.1: The structure of the clause —— 203
Fig. 7.2: The positions of EvidP and ByNatureP —— 204
Fig. 7.3: The diachronic trajectory of *naturally* as sentence adverb and narrow scope adverb in copular *be* sentences —— 206
Fig. 8.1: Amalgamation of paratactic sentences —— 230
Fig. 8.2: The diachronic distribution of the *is all* constructions in COHA —— 233
Fig. 9.1: Developmental phase of the L2s under study according to Schneider's (2003, 2007) Dynamic Model —— 253
Fig. 9.2: Presence of adverbial per variety —— 257
Fig. 9.3: Distribution (percentages) of adverbial support per meaning and variety —— 263
Fig. 9.4: Percentage of adverbial support per register —— 264
Fig. 11.1: Emotion adjectives and their PP-complements in Present-day English (BNC) —— 320
Fig. 11.2: The PP-complements of *disappointed* over time (HC) —— 324
Fig. 12.1: Distribution of the overlap deictic, double-locative overlap deictic, and existential constructions in the prose texts of the Old and Early Middle English sections of the *Helsinki Corpus* —— 358

Ruth Möhlig-Falke and Kristin Bech
Grammar – discourse – context

Grammatical variation and change and the usage-based perspective

1 Some thoughts about the relationship between grammar, discourse, and context

> [... G]rammar is predominantly about the coherence relations between the proposition (clause) and the wider communicative context, be it the current text, face-to-face speech situation and, within the latter, the speaker-hearer interaction. Our traditional structuralist methodology of examining – or experimenting with – isolated clauses has tended to obscure what grammar actually does. [... G]rammar has little to do with atomic verbal clauses (proposition), but rather with their discourse context – i.e. the communicative function. (Givón 2018 [1979]: 35)

The present volume is concerned with the relationship between grammar and discourse and the issue how grammar is shaped by language use in context, in a synchronic as well as in a diachronic perspective. Our focus is on the English language, but in describing grammatical phenomena of English, several of the contributions to this volume discuss methodological or theoretical issues that have a wider implication for linguistics in general. The topic of this volume is the outcome of two conference workshops convened by us at ISLE4 in Poznan in 2016, and at ICAME 38 in Prague in 2017.[1]

Grammar in linguistics is commonly understood with reference to morphological and syntactic patterns, which are (a) perceivable and linguistically describable as regularly recurring sequences of specific types of morphosyntactically marked content and function words in linguistic performance, and which (b)

---

[1] The workshops had the titles "Grammar – discourse – context: Widening the horizon for a theory of grammatical change" (ISLE 4, 18 September 2016), and "Back to text – Contextualizing corpus data in historical and variationist English linguistics" (ICAME 38, 24 May 2017).

Ruth Möhlig-Falke, Heidelberg University, English Department, Heidelberg, Germany, ruth.moehlig@as.uni-heidelberg.de
Kristin Bech, University of Oslo, Department of Literature, Area Studies and European Languages, Oslo, Norway, kristin.bech@ilos.uio.no

https://doi.org/10.1515/9783110682564-001

reflect more abstract cognitive structures – schemata, rules, or principles – that are stored in speakers' memories as part of their linguistic competence, and govern the formation of complex words, phrases, clauses, and sentences in speech production. Disregarding for the moment the, in parts vast, discrepancies between different theories of grammar,[2] a commonality between all of them is the assumption that the concrete grammatical patterns visible in linguistic performance reflect some kind of abstract knowledge about the "well-formedness" of utterances on the part of speakers.

From a functionalist perspective, such as is voiced by Givón (2018 [1979]: 35) in the introductory quote, grammar is, however, more than just a set of abstract patterns or rules determining "well-formedness": grammatical structures are meaningful, or functional, in and of themselves. Following this view, grammar may be described as a structural code that is used as an instrument for coding communicative function (Givón 2018 [1979]: 33; see also Strauss et al. 2018), involving the four major coding devices of morphology, intonation (on word-level and clause-level), rhythm (e.g. pace, lengths, pauses), and sequential order of words or morphemes (Givón (2018 [1979]: 34).

This view of grammar is also inherent in cognitive and usage-based linguistics (e.g. Langacker 2000; Taylor 2002; Halliday and Matthiessen 2004; Croft and Cruse 2004; Bybee 2010), which have come to play an increasingly important role in current linguistic thinking, including the study of variational and diachronic linguistics. Cognitive linguistics goes even further than defining grammar as a structural code for communicative function by claiming that "grammar is conceptualization" (Langacker, quoted in Croft and Cruse 2004: 3; see also Langacker 2008: 3–4). Grammar is seen as symbolic and recognized to play a crucial role in the way human beings conceptualize, or make sense of, their experience

---

[2] Such discrepancies concern, for instance, the question whether the very general structural principles that are universally found in the languages world-wide are domain-specific, belonging to an innate language component in human beings' brains (e.g. Chomsky 1972, 1981, 1986; Radford 1988: 34–38; cf. Schlobinski 2003), or whether our knowledge of grammar emerges in interplay with other domain-general learning mechanisms in the process of language acquisition (e.g. Hopper 1988; Langacker 2000, 2008; Tomasello 2003; Bybee 2010; Edwardes 2010; see also Piatelli-Palmarini 1980); further, the question whether grammatical knowledge is different from or the same in kind to lexical knowledge, i.e. likewise symbolic but with a different degree of abstractness (e.g. Langacker 2000, 2008; Taylor 2002; Croft and Cruse 2004); or whether sentences and utterances are construed with grammatical structures as templates into which the words are simply inserted following a "slot-and-filler principle", or whether speakers make use of chunks of lexical and grammatical items that are memorized as such, following a so-called "idiom principle" (e.g. Gleason 1965; Sinclair 1991, 2004; Hoey 2005; Bybee and Beckner 2015; see also Green 2017).

with the world and how they organize this knowledge in their minds. The categories and structures shaping this knowledge of language and "the world" are "built up from our cognition of specific utterances on specific occasions of use" (Croft and Cruse 2004: 4), which reflects a usage-based view of language acquisition (e.g. Tomasello 2003; see also Taylor 2002: 27–28; Hopper 1987, 1988; Bybee 2006, 2010). Different languages may reflect different cultural conceptualizations of "the world" (e.g. Palmer 1996, Sharifian 2015) and thus synchronic variability and diachronic change are not only inherent in grammar but also meaningful with respect to both the mental organization of knowledge in speakers' minds and the communicative and interactive functions which language serves in different societies.

In order to do justice to the functionalist, symbolic, and usage-based view of grammar and language, linguistic analyses need to interpret language data in their discourse context (see Givón 2018 [1979]: 35, quoted initially). In pragmatics, *discourse* is usually understood as language in the contexts of its use and above the level of the sentence, taking recourse to the systems of knowledge and beliefs, social practices and the socially recognizable identities involved in it (e.g. Blommaert 2005; van Dijk 2008, 2014; Flowerdew 2014). As Blommaert (2005) notes,

> [d]iscourse is language in action [... It] comprises all forms of meaningful semiotic human activity seen in connection with social, cultural, and historical patterns and developments of use. [...] What is traditionally understood by language is but one manifestation of it; all kinds of semiotic 'flagging' performed by means of objects, attributes, or activities can and should also be included for they usually constitute the 'action' part of language-in-action. (Blommaert 2005: 2–3)

Pragmatic discourse analysis is accordingly interested in "what happens when people draw on the knowledge they have about language, knowledge based on their memories of things they have said, heard, seen, or written before, to do things in the world: exchange information, express feelings, make things happen, create beauty, entertain themselves and others, and so on." (Johnstone 2008: 3). As Johnstone (2008) further points out, discourse is both the source of this knowledge about language and the result of it. Thus, the pragmatic linguistic concept of *discourse* is interconnected with Foucault's (1972) social-philosophical concept of *discourses*, which are

> [...] conventional ways of talking that both create and are created by conventional ways of thinking. These linked ways of talking and thinking constitute ideologies (sets of interrelated ideas) and serve to circulate power in society. In other words, "discourses" in this sense involve patterns of belief and habitual action as well as patterns of language. [...] Discourses, in their linguistic aspect, are conventionalized sets of choices for discourse, or talk. (Johnstone 2008: 3).

In the light of this, linguistics in general, but especially diachronic and historical linguistics, is faced with the challenge of finding ways of incorporating as much of the discourse context into their analyses as possible. The different facets of discourse *context* may be summarized as follows (based on Wodak 2014):

On the micro-level:
1) the immediate surrounding text of the communicative event in question, i.e. what has also been called *co-text* (see Halliday and Hasan 1985);
2) a) the intertextual and interdiscursive relationship between utterances, texts, genres, and discourses;
   b) the intertextual and interdiscursive relationship between spoken and/or written texts and other modes of communication (e.g. pictures, colours, fonts, scripts);
   c) the intertextual and interdiscursive relationship between different varieties and languages that are part of the "world of discourse";

and on the macro-level:
3) the extralinguistic social, environmental variables and institutional frames of a specific "context of situation", including multilingual and multicultural settings; and
4) the broader sociopolitical and historical context that discursive practices are embedded in and related to.

Looking at the influence of context on processes of grammatical variation and change, context on the micro-level of analysis further includes:
5) the structural context provided by the language system, i.e. the system of interdepencies between lexemes (semantic fields, cognitive domains, collocations, etc.) and grammatical patterns and constructions (Fischer 2007: 116, Möhlig-Falke 2012: 24) which form the linguistic input and underlying cognitive structures (mental grammars) of speakers at any historical stage of the language.

Especially in historical linguistics, the issue of "context" and "contextualizing" becomes even more pressing because – naturally – native-speaker knowledge of historical stages of a language, such as of Old, Middle, Early Modern and Late Modern English up to the early 20th century, can only be accessed indirectly. Hence, what constitutes "normal" or "canonical" grammatical usage, for instance with respect to word order, and what is a deviation from it for stylistic reasons, carrying some special communicative function, often requires a very close look into the discourse context. The inclusion of this aspect of context follows

Halliday's systemic view which states that "meaning is choice", i.e. in construing their utterances, speakers choose linguistic patterns from a range of options, and they usually do so for a specific communicative purpose, which may be semantically, discourse-structurally, sociopragmatically, or stylistically motivated (Halliday 1977). Processes of grammatical change may be closely intertwined with lexical semantics and discourse structure, and several grammatical changes may interact (e.g. Bech and Eide 2014; Möhlig-Falke 2012, 2017; Petré 2014, 2015). There is a dynamic interaction between *discourse* and *discourses*, the interlocutors involved in them, and the grammatical context (see Flowerdew 2014: 4–5; Duranti and Goodwin 1992: 31).

Further, which level(s) of context are selected to be relevant in a given analysis depends on the researcher, on the goals of the analysis and the (theoretical and methodological) context of the study. Context is thus also *construed* by analysts in their work (Flowerdew 2014: 6). Researchers themselves are part of the context and may influence the outcome of their research by the way they form hypotheses on the basis of the theoretical frameworks they follow and by making "judicious decisions about what to include and how far to go" (Baker 2014, quoted from Flowerdew 2014: 6). Therefore, context also comprises

6) the construal of those aspects of context which the researcher considers to be relevant, accounting for his/her theoretical background and assumptions, hypotheses and goals of research.

The role of context for the interpretation of linguistic utterances and successful communication by means of language has long been acknowledged in linguistics, being a prime object of study in pragmatics, discourse analysis, anthropological and cultural linguistics, for instance. Interpretation on the basis of contextual clues has also been shown to play a central role in the process of language acquisition and language evolution, being vital for the human capacity of intention reading (Tomasello 1999, 2014). Sense-making with the help of context is furthermore the essence of analogical reasoning, i.e. the human capacity of forming links between categories on the basis of shared similarities while ignoring small differences (Fischer 2018; see also Paul 1909; Gentner and Namy 2006). Analogy is also an essential part of productively extending our expressive powers by metonymization and metaphorization (e.g. Traugott and Dasher 2005). Context, contextual knowledge, and contextual clues are thus central to making sense of "the world" and to communicate about it by means of language.[3]

However, these general insights into the centrality of the discourse context for language usage and cognition have not yet been fully integrated into the investigation of processes of language variation and change, and particularly of grammatical change. Placing one's focus on the investigation of discourse means that the clear distinctions between the different structuralist levels of linguistic description, such as phonology, morphology, syntax, semantics, and pragmatics, become blurred – distinctions on which many of our methodological tools of variational and diachronic linguistic analysis still rest. Our structuralist heritage, useful as it is for tearing apart the complexity of language to break it down to its essentials, has for a long time favoured de-contextualized analytical perspectives on contemporary and historical language use as well as on the mechanisms and processes guiding variation and change over time (see also Givón 2018 [1979]: 35, quoted above). What happens if we take these theoretical notions seriously and try to implement them in our investigations, both with respect to the questions we ask, the data we use (e.g. concordances retrieved from large corpora vs. full texts or longer text passages, digitized texts vs. printed facsimiles vs. manuscripts), and the methodologies we apply in trying to answer these questions, and in explaining grammatical variation and change *in its discourse context*? The task of implementing such an approach is challenging, and we can only proceed to it step by step, especially if we include the objective to be able to model mechanisms and processes of language variation and change, such as, for instance, diffusion, analogy, reanalysis, and (inter)subjectification in processes of grammaticalization (e.g. De Smet 2009, 2013; López-Couso 2010; Traugott 2010, Los 2012; Bisang 2016; Fischer 2018).

One way to approach this task is to focus on the different aspects of *context*, as outlined above, and to investigate the influence of (selected levels of) context on processes of grammatical variation and change qualitatively to see what their inclusion adds to our knowledge and understanding of causes and mechanisms of grammatical variation and change.

---

[3] See also the theory of frame knowledge, or semantic frames (e.g. Fillmore 1976, 1982; Goffman 1986 [1974]; Ziem 2014) and Konerding (2008) on the relation between discourse and knowledge frames.

2 About the contributions

The contributions to this volume treat the relationship between grammar, discourse, and context from various perspectives – theoretical, methodological, and with respect to diachronicity. **Kristin Bech**'s contribution (pp. 15–48) focuses on the structure of noun phrases in Old English and demonstrates that theoretical generalizations found in the literature on Old English syntax often do not hold when verified with empirical contextualized data, i.e. noun phrases within their immediate micro-level context (or co-text). By the example of noun phrases with present participle modifiers in pre- and postnominal position in the Old English translation of *Cura Pastoralis* compared with its Latin source text, she further reveals that postnominal position of a present participle modifier was used systematically "to convey meaning which would otherwise be obscured if prenominal position had been mandatory. In other words, although postnominal position was rare in Old English, it was used productively and for specific purposes" (Bech, this volume, p. 46). Thus, contextualizing syntactic data both on the micro- as well as on the macro-contextual level is necessary to understand the kind of synchronic syntactic variation found in historical data.

The contribution by **Bettelou Los** and **Thijs Lubbers** (pp. 49–92) also investigates Old English syntax in what they call a corpus-based, data-driven, and quantitative stylometric approach including n-grams on the basis of morphological tags. The major methodological challenge they face is what has been called the "Fish fork" by Stubbs (2005: 6), i.e. the fact that "working (by necessity) from a pre-determined set of assumptions about what constitute relevant linguistic features means that such investigations may well uncover high frequencies of these features, but that such findings can be unsatisfactory because they are unsurprising" (Los and Lubbers, this volume, p. 55). Developing an exploratory methodology including lexical trigramming, POS-tag n-gramming, and feeding the latter into correspondence analyses, as well as philologically informed interpretation of the data, they manage to visualize, or model, textual and stylistic differences that correspond with genre, register, text type, and authorial style.

Belén Méndez-Naya's article (pp. 93–124) moves further into the Early Middle English period of English language history, which is still underrepresented in the research literature due to the scarcity of sources, although it has been found to be a crucial period for the development of the English language particularly with respect to its morphosyntactic system (e.g. Kroch and Taylor 1997; Trips 2002; Los 2009). Méndez-Naya investigates the configuration and grammaticalization development of the Early Middle English intensifier system by focusing on a single text, the late 12th-century *Ormulum*. She undertakes an in-depth exploration of the effects of the micro-level linguistic context on the one hand, identifying bridging contexts for newly arising degree interpretations, and the macro-level context of language contact with Old Norse on the other, demonstrating that norsification both affects the inventory of intensifiers itself as well as frequency and distribution of individual items.

Lynn Anthonissen (pp. 125–156) investigates the passive nominative and infinitive (NCI) construction in Early Modern English with the aim of exploring whether constructional syntactic change is possible within the adult lifespan of individual speakers, for

> [i]f we are serious about the cognitive commitment, research on language (change) as an abstract structure must be complemented by research on variation and change in the linguistic individual. As pointed out by Schmid and Mantlik (2015) and De Smet (2016), variation in language use reflects differences in how language is cognitively represented. Therefore, "any patterns or tendencies found in this variation may reveal something about the organization of mental representation" (De Smet 2016: 251), and, I would add, possibly also about the extent to which the adult mind can adapt to ongoing linguistic change. (Anthonissen, this volume, p. 127f.).

The study analyzes language data by four authors included in the EMMA corpus (*Early Modern Multiloquent Authors*, Petré et al. 2019) with respect to the micro-level semantic and pragmatic contexts of use. It reveals not only considerable variation in the use of NCIs by these authors throughout their lifetime, but also finds non-random patterns in that individual authors exhibit linear trends of semasiological change in the NCI construction that persist into old age. She thus demonstrates how functionally determined variation in the language usage of individuals is connected with more general processes of diachronic change.

Ruth Möhlig-Falke's article (pp. 157–190) investigates dual-form adverbs in the 18th and 19th century by using data from the *Old Bailey Corpus* 2.0. The study explores variable adverb marking in order to explain why these adverbs may appear with and without the adverbial suffix *-ly* in similar syntactic environments at a time when *-ly*-marking for adverbs becomes the preferred choice in standardized contexts. By close contextual analysis on the micro-level as well as by taking the systemic context of the categories of adjective as against adverb into account, she demonstrates how variable adverb marking is mainly due to the general fuzziness of the category boundary between adjective and adverb in English, the adverbs' highly context-sensitive interpretation, and their differences in semantic-pragmatic orientation – i.e. variation in *-ly*-marking is largely functionally determined rather than in free variation.

The contribution by **Dagmar Haumann** and **Kristin Killie** (pp. 191–220) focuses on the concept of "bridging context" in the syntactic reanalysis of the sentence adverb *naturally* between the late 16th to late 19th century, bridging contexts being micro-level co(n)texts in which both an old and a new analysis are possible (e.g. Heine 2002). The authors find that the reanalysis of narrow scope *naturally* as an evidential adverb depends on a variety of interacting factors, with syntax playing the central role by determining the contexts in which a reanalysis is possible, i.e. in clauses that project a ForceP specified for assertive illocutionary force. By micro-level co(n)textual analysis they further show that reanalysis may be lexically, pragmatically, and contextually constrained even if it is licensed by the syntax, thus emphasizing the importance of multifactorial analysis for phenomena representing bridging contexts.

Reijirou Shibasaki (pp. 221–247) investigates the grammaticalization process of the sentence-final *is all*-construction from independent clause to an amalgamated discourse marker with summarizing function in 19th- and 20th-century American English. Based on a large number of different corpora, he shows how this amalgamation process proceeds over different genres and registers and depends on the specifiable linear sequence of clauses in particular pragmatic conditions, i.e. on co-text. His study thus supports the assumption of Systemic Functional Grammar that "a lexical or grammatical item can be properly construed only in a given stretch of discourse" (Shibasaki, this volume, p. 224). Shibasaki also discusses how the construction has begun to spread to other varieties of English, and can be expected to spread further, since new pragmatic markers travel quickly (Mair 2009; Aijmer 2013). Hence language-external factors also play a role in the diffusion of linguistic structures.

Elena Seoane's contribution (pp. 249–276) is concerned with the role of contextual features in the consolidation of the adverbs *just*, *(n)ever* and *yet* as perfect markers in World Englishes. Based on a meticulous qualitative and quantitative analysis of data from the *International Corpus of English* (ICE), the author shows the complex interplay of structural and contextual factors interacting to shape grammatical variation, only partially confirming Miller's (2000) and Brown and Miller's (2017) hypothesis on the entrenchment of the investigated adverbials as perfect markers. Findings concern the alleged spread to L2-varieties of English, the semantically and pragmatically differing functions of *just*, *(n)ever*, and *yet*, as well as the relative insignificance of spoken as against written mode in their distribution. She thus demonstrates the importance of combining quantitative analyses with contextually informed qualitative assessment of the data.

Martin Konvička (pp. 277–304) presents a theoretical assessment of three different functionalist approaches to the issue of grammatical status, i.e. to the question which factors and properties give a linguistic element its grammatical rather than lexical status, which is crucial within a theory of grammaticalization.

The author works out the similarities and differences between the three existing models proposed by Himmelmann (1992), Diewald (2011), and Boye and Harder (2012), focusing on the principles employed as well as on how the three models approach the question of grammatical gradability. In mapping both the advantages and disadvantages of the extant models he further works out the points of convergence that may be profitable for future research.

Hendrik De Smet (pp. 305–331) also focuses on a theoretical topic by approaching the issue of motivation in linguistic variation and how this is interpreted in the two large strands of variationist linguistics on the one hand, and functional linguistics on the other. While variation is seen as "natural and common" in variationist linguistics, Functionalists "assume that [it] is anomalous" (De Smet, this volume, p. 305), this having different implications for the respective understanding of language change. In a case study of hypervariation in the prepositional complements of emotion adjectives, he demonstrates, by analyzing them in their broader grammatical context, that both views may be reconciled: variation "arises because grammars offer multiple near-equivalent solutions to the same coding problem" (De Smet, this volume, p. 327), since having an abundance of solutions may offer an advantage in efficiently coding and communicating experience. Furthermore, "many linguistic subsystems are parasitic on their elements' core functions" (De Smet, this volume, p. 328) and available form-function mappings originally developed for spatial relations may be less than optimal for coding the causes of emotional states. Hence, synchronic variation and even hypervariation may be communicatively and functionally motivated, this in turn opening a better understanding for the motivations underlying diachronic language change.

The final contribution by **María José López-Couso** (pp. 333–364) also treats a theoretical topic by focusing on hypercharacterization in language variation and change, i.e. the fact that languages accumulate apparently redundant linguistic material in category marking. In three in-depth case studies of syntactic hypercharacterization in the history of English (strengthened adverbial subordinators, pronoun resumption in extraction contexts, and "double-locative overlap constructions" with *there*), the author demonstrates that hypercharacterized forms and constructions resulting from accretion are more than superfluous and functionless material but may in fact be seen to realize important functions in the respective linguistic systems at the communicative level as well as at the level of grammatical structure and "can be plausibly explained as the result of predictable language change – as well as language variation – phenomena" (López-Couso, this volume, p. 360).

3 Final remarks

Although working against a wide range of different theoretical and methodological backgrounds, as well as having different research aims and foci, all of the contributions to this volume subscribe to a usage-based view of language variation and change, taking up the challenge of contextualization. The contributions show how important it is to integrate contextual information to various degrees in the investigation of processes of grammatical variation and change at any stage of language history, depending on the availability of sources on whose basis contextualization is possible. In the long run, it may be useful to combine such investigations, which take grammatical patterns in their context of use as their starting point, with approaches that consider historical discourses in their own right and identify interacting patterns of language variability and change emerging from the discourse itself, i.e. combine the historical, variationist, and diachronic linguistic perspective with modern discourse analysis, and take texts and discourses as a starting point (e.g. Johnstone 2008; Landwehr 2008). However challenging, such a task might be a logical next step in usage-based diachronic linguistics. With this volume, we would like to open the floor for an exploration of (more) contextualized approaches to grammatical variation and change, with the perspective to expand on this both theoretically and methodologically.

References

Aijmer, Karin. 2013. *Understanding pragmatic markers*. Edinburgh: Edinburgh University Press.
Baker, Paul. 2014. Considering context when analysing representations of gender and sexuality: A case study. In John Flowerdew (ed.), *Discourse in context*, 27–48. London: Bloomsbury.
Bech, Kristin & Kristine Eide (eds.). 2014. *Information structure and syntactic change in Germanic and Romance languages*. Amsterdam: John Benjamins.
Bisang, Walter. 2016. Linguistic change in grammar. In Keith Allan (ed.), *The Routledge handbook of linguistics*, 366–384. Oxford: Routledge.
Blommaert, Jan. 2005. *Discourse. A critical introduction*. Cambridge: Cambridge University Press.
Boye, Kasper & Peter Harder. 2012. A usage-based theory of grammatical status and grammaticalization. *Language* 88 (1). 1–44.
Brown, Keith & Jim Miller. 2017. *A critical account of English syntax*. Edinburgh: Edinburgh University Press.
Bybee, Joan. 2006. From usage to grammar. The mind's response to repetition. *Language* 82 (4). 711–733.
Bybee, Joan. 2010. *Language, usage and cognition*. Cambridge: Cambridge University Press.

Bybee, Joan & Clay Beckner. 2015. Usage-Based Theory. In Bernd Heine and Heiko Narrog (eds.), *The Oxford handbook of linguistic analysis*. 2nd edn., 827–856. Oxford & New York: Oxford University Press.

Chomsky, Noam. 1972. *Language and mind*. Rev. and enlarged edn. New York: Harcourt Brace Jovanovich.

Chomsky, Noam. 1981. *Lectures on government and binding*. Dordrecht: Foris.

Chomsky, Noam. 1986. *Knowledge of language: Its nature, origin, and use*. New York: Praeger.

Croft, William & D. Alan Cruse. 2004. *Cognitive Linguistics*. Cambridge: Cambridge University Press.

De Smet, Hendrik. 2009. Analysing reanalysis. *Lingua* 119. 1728–1755.

De Smet, Hendrik. 2013. *Spreading patterns. Diffusional change in the English system of complementation*. Oxford & New York: Oxford University Press.

De Smet, Hendrik. 2016. The roots of *ruthless*: Individual variation as a window on mental representation. *International Journal of Corpus Linguistics* 21 (2). 250–271.

Diewald, Gabriele. 2011. Grammaticalization and pragmaticalization. In Bernd Heine & Heiko Narrog (eds.), *The Oxford handbook of grammaticalization*, 450–461. Oxford: Oxford University Press.

Dijk, Teun A. van 2008. *Discourse and context. A sociocognitive approach*. Cambridge: Cambridge University Press.

Dijk, Teun A. van. 2014. *Discourse and knowledge. A sociocognitive approach*. Cambridge: Cambridge University Press.

Duranti, Alessandro & Charles Goodwin. 1992. *Rethinking context: Language as an interactive phenomenon*. Cambridge: Cambridge University Press.

Edwardes, Martin. 2010. *The origins of grammar. An anthropological perspective*. London: Continuum.

Fillmore, J. Charles. 1976. Frame semantics and the nature of language. *Annals of the New York Academy of Sciences: Conference on the origin and development of language and speech* 280. 20–32.

Fillmore, J. Charles. 1982. Frame semantics. In Linguistic Society of Korea (ed.), *Linguistics in the morning calm*, 111–138. Seoul: Hanshin.

Fischer, Olga. 2007. *Morphosyntactic change. Functional and formal Perspectives*. Oxford & New York: Oxford University Press.

Fischer, Olga. 2018. Analogy: Its role in language learning, categorization, and in models of language change such as grammaticalization and constructionalization. In Sylvie Hancil, Tine Breban & José Vincente Lozano (eds.), *New trends in grammaticalization and language change*, 75–104. Amsterdam: John Benjamins.

Flowerdew, John. 2014. Introduction: Discourse in context. In John Flowerdew (ed.), *Discourse in context*, 1–26. London: Bloomsbury.

Foucault, Michel. 1972. *The archaeology of knowledge*. Translated from French by A. M. Sheridan Smith. New York: Pantheon Books.

Gentner, Dedre & Laura L. Namy 2006. Analogical processes in language learning. *Current Directions in Psychological Science* 15 (6). 297–301.

Givón, Talmy. 2018 [1979]. *On understanding grammar*. 2nd rev. edn. Amsterdam: John Benjamins.

Gleason, Henry A. 1965. *An introduction to descriptive linguistics*. Rev. edn. New York: Holt, Rinehart and Winston.

Goffman, Erving. 1986 [1974]. *Frame analysis: An essay on the organization of experience*. New York: Harper & Row.

Green, Clarence. 2017. Usage-based linguistics and the magic number four. *Cognitive Linguistics* 28 (2). 209–237.
Halliday, Michael A.K. 1977. Text as semantic choice in social contexts. In Teun A. van Dijk & Janoš S. Petöfi (eds.), *Grammars and descriptions*, 176–226. Berlin: Walter de Gruyter.
Halliday, Michael A.K. & Ruqaiya Hasan. 1985. *Language, context and text: Aspects of language in a social-semiotic perspective*. 2nd edn. Geelong, Australia: Deakin University Press.
Halliday, Michael A. K. & Christian M. I. M. Matthiesen. 2004. *An introduction to Functional Grammar*. 3rd edn. London: Arnold.
Heine, Bernd. 2002. On the role of context in grammaticalization. In Ilse Wischer & Gabriele Diewald (eds.), *New reflections on grammaticalization. International Symposium, Potsdam, 17–19 June, 1991*, 83–101. Amsterdam: John Benjamins.
Himmelmann, Nikolaus P. 1992. *Grammaticalization and grammar*. Köln: Universität zu Köln.
Hoey, Michael. 2005. *Lexical priming: A new theory of words and language*. London: Routledge.
Hopper, Paul J. 1987. Emergent grammar. In Joe Aske, Natasha Beery, Laura Michaelis & Hana Filip (eds.), *Berkeley Linguistics Society. Proceedings of the thirteenth annual meeting, February 14–16, 1987: General session and parasession on grammar and cognition*, 139–157. Berkeley, CA: Berkeley Linguistics Society.
Hopper, Paul J. 1988. Emergent grammar and the a priori grammar postulate. In Deborah Tannen (ed.), *Linguistics in context: Connecting observation and understanding. Lectures from the 1985 LSA/TESOL and NEH Institutes*, 117–134. Norwood, NJ: Ablex.
Johnstone, Barbara. 2008. *Discourse Analysis*. 2nd edn. Malden, MA: Blackwell.
Konerding, Klaus-Peter. 2008. Diskurse, Topik, Deutungsmuster – Zur Komplementarität, Konvergenz und Explikation sprach-, kultur- und sozialwissenschaftlicher Zugänge zur Diskursanalyse auf der Grundlage kollektiven Wissens. In Ingo Warnke & Jürgen Spitzmüller (eds.), *Methoden der Diskurslinguistik: Sprachwissenschaftliche Zugänge zur Transtextuellen Ebene*, 117–150. Berlin & New York: Walter de Gruyter.
Kroch, Anthony & Ann Taylor. 1997. Verb movement in Old and Middle English: Dialect variation and language contact. In Ans van Kemenade & Nigel Vincent (eds.), *Parameters of morphosyntactic change*, 297–325. Cambridge: Cambridge University Press.
Landwehr, Achim. 2008. *Historische Diskursanalyse*. Frankfurt & New York: Campus.
Langacker, Ronald W. 2000. *Grammar and conceptualization*. Berlin & New York: Mouton de Gruyter.
Langacker, Ronald W. 2008. *Cognitive grammar. A basic introduction*. Oxford & New York: Oxford University Press.
López-Couso, María José. 2010. Subjectification and intersubjectification. In Andreas H. Jucker & Irma Taavitsainen (eds.), *Historical pragmatics*, 127–163. Berlin & New York: Mouton de Gruyter.
Los, Bettelou. 2009. The consequences of the loss of verb-second in English: information structure and syntax in interaction. *English Language and Linguistics* 13. 97–125.
Los, Bettelou. 2012. New perspectives, theories and methods: Generative approaches to English historical linguistics. In Alex Bergs & Laurel Brinton (eds.), *Historical linguistics of English* (HSK 34.2), 1613–1631. Berlin: Mouton de Gruyter.
Mair, Christian. 2009. Corpus linguistics meets sociolinguistics. In Antoinette Renouf & Andrew Kehoe (eds.), *Corpus linguistics: Refinements and reassessments*, 7–32. Amsterdam: Rodopi.
Miller, Jim. 2000. The perfect in spoken and written English. *Transactions of the Philological Society* 98 (2). 323–352.

Möhlig-Falke, Ruth. 2012. *The early English impersonal construction. An analysis of verbal and constructional meaning*. Oxford & New York: Oxford University Press.

Möhlig-Falke, Ruth. 2017. Contexts and conditions of grammatical change: The loss of the English impersonal construction in Middle English. In Tanja Rütten (ed.), *Focus on the philologist's dilemma*, special issue *Anglistik* 28 (1). 87–110.

Palmer, Gary B. 1996. *Toward a theory of cultural linguistics*. Austin, TX: University of Texas Press.

Paul, Hermann. 1909. *Prinzipien der Sprachgeschichte*. 4th edn. Halle: Niemeyer.

Petré, Peter. 2014. *Constructions and environments. Copular, passive, and related constructions in Old and Middle English*. Oxford & New York: Oxford University Press.

Petré, Peter. 2015. What grammar reveals about sex and death: interdisciplinary applications of corpus-based studies. *Digital scholarship in the humanities* 30 (3). 371–387.

Petré, Peter, Lynn Anthonissen, Sara Budts, Enrique Manjavacas, Emma-Louise Silva, William Standing & Odile A. O. Strik. 2019. Early Modern Multiloquent Authors (EMMA): Designing a large-scale corpus of individuals' languages. *ICAME Journal* 43. 83–122.

Piatelli-Palmarini, Massimo (ed.). 1980. *Language and learning: The debate between Jean Piaget and Noam Chomsky*. London: Routledge and Kegan Paul.

Radford, Andrew. 1988. *Transformational grammar. A first course*. Cambridge: Cambridge University Press.

Schlobinski, Peter. 2003. *Grammatikmodelle. Positionen und Perspektiven*. Wiesbaden: Westdeutscher Verlag.

Schmid, Hans-Jörg & Annette Mantlik. 2015. Entrenchment in historical corpora? Reconstructing dead authors' minds from their usage profiles. *Anglia* 133 (4). 583–623.

Sharifian, Farzad. 2015. Cultural linguistics. In Farzad Sharifian (ed.), *The Routledge handbook of language and culture*, 473–492. London: Routledge.

Sinclair, John. 1991. *Corpus, concordance, collocation*. Oxford: Oxford University Press.

Sinclair, John. 2004. *Trust the text. Language, corpus and discourse*. London & New York: Routledge.

Strauss, Susan, Parastou Feiz & Xuehua Xiang. 2018. *Grammar, meaning, and concepts. A discourse-based approach to English grammar*. London & New York: Routledge.

Stubbs. 2005. Conrad in the computer. Examples of quantitative stylistic methods. *Language and Literature* 14 (1). 5–24.

Taylor, John R. 2002. *Cognitive grammar*. Oxford & New York: Oxford University Press.

Tomasello, Michael. 1999. *The cultural origins of human cognition*. Cambridge, MA: Harvard University Press.

Tomasello, Michael. 2003. *Constructing a language: A usage-based theory of language acquisition*. Cambridge, MA: Harvard University Press.

Tomasello, Michael. 2014. *A natural history of human thinking*. Cambridge, MA: Harvard University Press.

Traugott, Elizabeth C. & Dasher, Richard B. 2005. *Regularity in semantic change*. Cambridge: Cambridge University Press.

Traugott, Elizabeth C. 2010. Grammaticalization. In Andreas H. Jucker & Irma Taavitsainen (eds.), *Historical pragmatics*, 97–126. Berlin: Mouton de Gruyter.

Trips, Carola. 2002. *From OV to VO in Early Middle English*. Amsterdam: John Benjamins.

Wodak, Ruth. 2014. Discourse in politics. In John Flowerdew (ed.), *Discourse in context*, 321–346. London: Bloomsbury.

Ziem, Alexander. 2014. *Frames of understanding in text and discourse: Theoretical foundations and descriptive applications*. Amsterdam: John Benjamins.

Kristin Bech
Contextualizing Old English noun phrases

Abstract: This three-part study considers adjectival modification in Old English noun phrases from a micro-level perspective. In the first part, I outline and discuss Fischer's (2000, 2001, 2006, 2012) and Haumann's (2003, 2010) academic exchange on the topic. Fischer's proposal is that there is a relation between adjective position on the one hand, and definiteness, declension and linear iconicity on the other, while Haumann proposes that pre- or postnominal position follows from interpretive contrasts, such as attribution vs. predication, individual-level vs. stage-level reading, given vs. new information, and restrictive vs. non-restrictive modification. In the second part, I carry out a close reading of noun phrases taken from two Old English texts, *Cura Pastoralis* and the *West-Saxon Gospels*, focusing on constructions with conjoined adjectival modification. I show that neither Fischer's nor Haumann's generalizations can account for the distribution. Finally, in the third part of the study, I turn to noun phrases containing prenominal or postnominal adjectival present participles in *Cura Pastoralis*. Here the focus is on the intertextual relation between the original Latin text and the translation into Old English, which sheds light on noun phrase structure.

1 Introduction

As is well known, Old English clausal word order is more flexible than that of Present-day English, and much research has been devoted to understanding the mechanisms of clausal word order variation and word order development in English. On the phrase level as well, Old English displays more variation than Present-day English does, but, with some notable exceptions (Fischer 2000, 2001, 2006, 2012; Haumann 2003, 2010; Pysz 2009; Sampson 2010; Grabski 2017), phrasal word order is less well studied than clausal word order. In the first two parts of the study, I will consider some of the more well-known work on noun phrase word order in Old English, in light of examples from two Old English texts: the Old English translation of Gregory's *Cura Pastoralis*, and the *West-Saxon Gospels*. The focus will be on two constructions with conjoined adjectival

Kristin Bech, University of Oslo, Department of Literature, Area Studies and European Languages, Oslo, Norway, kristin.bech@ilos.uio.no

modification, namely constructions of the type A-*and*-A-N (1) and A-N-*and*-A (2). In the first type, both adjectives are prenominal, while in the second, one adjective is postnominal. These particular constructions were chosen because Fischer and Haumann would analyze them differently, as will be discussed below.

(1) unwærlicu & giemeleaslicu spræc (cocura:15.89.7.571)
    unguarded and careless speech

(2) wac reod & idel (cocura:42.306.2.2044)
    weak reed and useless

The final part of the study deals with adjectival present participles in prenominal or postnominal position, as in (3) and (4), and the relation between the Latin text and the Old English translation.

(3) ða synna weaxende (cocura:17.123.15.834)
    the sins increasing

(4) ðæt irsigende mod (cocura:10.63.11.400)
    the angry mind

2 Background

2.1 Two positions on adjective position

In this section, I outline the exchange that took place between Fischer and Haumann in a series of four articles by Fischer (2000, 2001, 2006, 2012) and two by Haumann (2003, 2010).

Until Fischer started looking into adjective positioning in Old English, no one had paid it much systematic attention, except to note that adjectives can occur both pre- and postnominally. Mitchell (1985), mentions it, of course, but focuses on description and classification. He says, however, that it is unclear whether postnominal adjectives are used attributively, predicatively or as appositions, and that possible reasons for postposition may be emphasis, rhythm, or style (Mitchell 1985 i: §160, §172). Sørensen (1956, in Fischer 2000: 162) suggests that constructions with flanked adjectives, i.e. adjective – noun – adjective, are due to immaturity in the writing style, to the effect that postnominal adjectives are "afterthoughts". Spamer (1979) proposes that weak adjectives are actually what he calls "adjuncts", i.e. not adjectives at all diachronically, but substantives, while strongly inflected adjectives are the real adjectives, which explains the distribution.

Against this rather meagre background, Fischer (2000) takes on the task of disentangling the positional distribution of adjectives in Old English. She is also inspired by work on other languages, such as Modern Greek (Stavrou 1996) and Italian (Vincent 1986). Bolinger's (1952 [1972], 1967) proposal that linear modification determines adjective positioning in Present-day English and Spanish also comes to play a central role in her argumentation. According to Bolinger (1952: 1118), a hearer continuously readjusts the interpretation of an utterance as new elements are added to it by the speaker. The semantic range of the first word is at its fullest, and is then narrowed down as elements are added. This is the basis for the idea of linear modification. Bolinger (1952) considers adjectives specifically and seeks a pattern for adjective position in Present-day English that accords with his proposed principle of linear modification, especially as regards the difference between prenominal and postnominal position, e.g. *the navigable river* vs. *the river navigable*. He suggests that postnominal adjectives are similar to participles and adverbs in referring to some transitory state, a certain detachability from the noun. There is also some implication of newness. Prenominal adjectives, on the other hand, are non-verbal elements that represent a fixed, characterizing quality (1952: 1134–1136; 1967: 7–12). Bolinger (1967) discusses the functional difference between attributive and predicative modification, pointing out the shortcomings of the traditional relative clause transformation in accounting for attributive adjectives. Instead he suggests two solutions, of which the first, concerning *be* predications, is of particular relevance for the present paper. According to Bolinger (1967), there are two kinds of *be* predications. The one underlying attributives is of a non-temporary or customary aspectual type, and it contrasts with the temporary aspectual type of *be* predication (Bolinger 1967: 12–14).

Already in the first article on the topic, Fischer (2000) sets forth the proposal that she holds to throughout her work on adjectives, namely that strong adjectives are used predicatively, and that they convey additional and new information (see section 2.2 for further discussion of terminology). This applies whether the adjective follows a copula verb or whether it is a "secondary predicate", like an object complement. She follows Spamer (1979) in calling weak adjectives "adjunctive", but this is abandoned in later work. The main point, however, is that weak prenominal adjectives convey given information and qualify nouns in such a way that the nouns are turned into a different category, a new compound noun (cf. Spamer's [1979] view that weak adjectives are substantives diachronically, so that a combination of weak adjective and noun would form a compound). Postnominal strong adjectives, on the other hand, are more verbal in character and express a non-inherent quality of the noun (Fischer 2000: 170). Fischer links this to the observation that Old English adjectives are non-recursive; i.e. they do not occur together without being linked by *and*. Strong adjectives are non-recursive because they are predicative, and such adjectives are parallel and not hierarchically ordered. Weak adjectives are non-recursive because they form compounds with the noun (Fischer 2000: 171). There are some counterexamples, however, which Fischer comments on (Fischer 2000: 171–174; see also Bech 2017 for a discussion and comparison with Old Norwegian). What Fischer does not do in the 2000 article is comment on the fact that prenominal adjectives can also be strong; she simply says that the natural position for predicative adjectives is postnominal, while the natural position for weak adjectives is prenominal (Fischer 2000: 170). The issue of strong prenominal adjectives is, however, taken up in an article that appeared a year later. In her 2001 article, Fischer clarifies her theoretical position, which is based on Hopper and Thompson's (1984: 747–748; see also Fischer 2001: 254) stance that language should be considered in its "natural functional context" and that there is a perceptual basis for the cognitive strategies underlying grammar. Again inspired by Bolinger (1952, 1967; see also Fischer 2001: 254–255), Fischer suggests that the ordering of elements, in this case adjectives in relation to the head noun, is perceptually, or iconically, motivated. In other words, form and meaning are connected in the sense that the position in a sequence determines meaning. In particular, postnominal strong adjectives are rhematic and close to the verbal category (Fischer 2001: 257), while weak prenominal adjectives are thematic, close to the nominal category, and change the noun into a new noun token (Fischer 2001: 258). At this point the question arises as to what to do about strong *prenominal* adjectives, and Fischer suggests that they, too, are predicative and rhematic, but that this is shown not through linear iconicity, but through phonological iconicity; i.e. prenominal strong adjectives were presumably stressed (Fischer 2001: 257, 271).[1] The fact that strong adjectives occur both pre- and postnominally in Old English is a problem for her generalization, as will be discussed below. The rest of this article is about presenting evidence for the verbal nature of strong adjectives, during which she makes a number of interesting observations concerning which types of adjectives occur where.

To sum up so far: Fischer (2000, 2001) suggests that strong adjectives in Old English, whether they occur before or after the noun, are predicative, rhematic

---

[1] Fischer uses the word "presumably" because stress, particularly of certain words, is speculation for which it is very difficult to find evidence in historical texts, as Fischer also acknowledges (Fischer 2001: 271). Nevertheless, the generalization she proposes is partly based on the assumption that certain adjectives were stressed.

and convey new information. Weak adjectives are thematic and convey given information.

Enter Haumann (2003). She proposes a uniform analysis, couched within the Minimalist framework, for postnominal *and*-adjective constructions in which the second adjective is or is not preceded by a determiner, as in (5) and (6), respectively.

(5) *Se leofa cuma & se lufiendleca* (cobede 4:3.266.9.2707)
 the dear.WK stranger and the lovely.WK (cf. Haumann 2003: 63, her (17b))

(6) *seftne drenc & swetne* (coboeth:39.132.6.2623)
 soft.STR drink and sweet.STR (cf. Haumann 2003: 63, her (16b))

The proposal is that these *and*-adjective constructions, regardless of whether the second adjective is preceded by a determiner (5) or not (6), are not instances of ambilateral adjectives, but rather of DP coordination with an empty nominal element, *pro*, in the second conjunct (Haumann 2003: 58). Haumann points out that Fischer's analysis of strong prenominal adjectives as predicative is problematic (Haumann 2003: 60) and adopts a different stance, namely that prenominal adjectives are attributive and postnominal adjectives (i.e. where no conjunction precedes the adjective) are predicative, regardless of inflection (Haumann 2003: 63). This is further discussed in her 2010 article, which we will return to below.

As regards the postnominal *and*-adjective construction, Haumann's suggestion is that the second adjective in such constructions is neither attributive nor predicative with respect to the preceding noun, but that it is an attributive adjective to a phonetically empty head, *pro* (Haumann 2003: 65), and she compares this construction to the Present-day English construction with *one* (Haumann 2003: 77–80).[2]

---

[2] Haumann does not consider examples like (i) and (ii), in which there are similar or identical adjectives in pre- and postnominal position, but they may be an argument against her analysis. She would analyze (i) to have a *pro*, and thus to mean 'the evil generation and the adulterous one', while (ii) would simply be 'this adulterous and sinful generation', but it is not clear that there is a semantic difference here that would warrant two different syntactic analyses.
(i) *seo yfele cneoryss & unrihthæmende* (cowsgosp, Mt: 16.4.1077)
 the evil.WK generation and adulterous.WK
 Vulgate: generatio mala et adultera
(ii) *þisre unrihthæmedan & synfulran cneorisse* (cowsgosp, Mk: 8.38.2821)
 this adulterous.WK and sinful.WK generation
 Vulgate: generatione ista adultera et peccatrice

Fischer (2006) deals with adjective position in Middle English, but the article merits mention here because she also provides further information about how she sees the relation between adjective position and meaning in Old English by introducing some additional terminology. She upholds the distinction between strong pre- and postnominal adjectives conveying new information, and weak adjectives conveying given information, but she also says that she uses terms such as given/new, theme/rheme, topic/focus, topic/comment in a general sense. Although she recognizes that the terms are not synonyms, she ignores the differences and focuses on the shared characteristics: given/theme/topic mean that the element is non-salient and adds least to the communication. New/rheme/comment/focus mean that the element is salient and adds extra information (Fischer 2006: 256). She also says that "postposed adjectives are generally rhematic, while thematic adjectives are placed early in the NP" (Fischer 2006: 256). Note that she specifically does not say that preposed adjectives are thematic – since preposed adjectives can also be strong, and hence rhematic. Furthermore, rhematic (i.e. strong) adjectives are non-restrictive and predicative, and thematic (i.e. weak) adjectives are restrictive and attributive (see section 2.2 for further discussion of terminology).

Haumann (2010) argues against Fischer, and proposes that position rather than inflection determines the meaning of adnominal adjectives. Prenominal adjectives, whether weak or strong, are attributive, given, non-restrictive and have an individual-level reading, while postnominal adjectives are predicative, new, restrictive and have a stage-level reading. According to Haumann (2010: 62), following Bolinger (1952), an attributive adjective helps to identify the referent of the noun, whereas a predicative adjective assigns a property to the noun. Furthermore, these terms are closely related to the distinction between given and new information, but given and new are not defined other than to say that weak adjectives are given and strong adjectives are new, which is in line with what Fischer also claims. A third distinction Haumann (2010: 63) uses is between individual-level vs. stage-level reading, where the former means that the adjective describes an inherent or enduring property, and the latter means that the adjective describes an accidental or temporary property. Finally, Haumann (2010: 64) mentions the distinction between non-restrictive and restrictive reading, which she links to contrast. Non-restrictive adjectives characterize the referents in a non-contrastive manner, whereas restrictive adjectives "identify a particular referent from a set of entities that contrast with respect to the property they denote" (2010: 64) (see discussion in section 2.2).

Recall that Haumann (2003) claimed that postnominal *and*-constructions (of the kind adjective–noun–*and*–adjective, cf. (5) and (6)) are not ambilateral, which means that adjectives in such constructions are always prenominal, either to a noun or to *pro*, and hence attributive. The 2010 article, in addition to discussing single prenominal and postnominal adjectives, also discusses flanked constructions, i.e. instances where there is an adjective on either side of the noun, but without *and*, as in (7).

(7) ænne   sweartne   deofol   ormætne   (coaelive [Martin]:1182.6755)
    a   black.STR   devil   immense.STR

In this kind of construction, the prenominal and the postnominal adjectives would have fundamentally different properties, according to Haumann, with the prenominal one, *sweartne*, being attributive (given, individual-level, non-restrictive) and the postnominal one, *ormætne*, being predicative (new, stage-level, restrictive). Already at this point we begin to see some problems, because the adjectives in (7) do not differ along these parameters. For example, it is not the case that 'black' and 'immense' contrast in the sense that 'black' conveys given information and 'immense' conveys new information (Saint Martin comes into a room and sees an immense black devil sitting on somebody's back). Both adjectives also have an individual-level reading (the devil is inherently big and immense), and they are both non-restrictive. Consider also (8), where *niwe* is prenominal in one noun phrase and postnominal in the other. As such they should have completely different properties with respect to e.g. givenness and restrictiveness in Haumann's generalization. But the context is that elderly priests get a new cape and a new wollen robe every year, so *niwe* cannot possibly have different properties in the two positions in (8).

(8) [niwe   cæppan]   &   [wyllene   reaf   niwe]   (cochdrul:39.1.546)
    [new.STR   cape]   and   [woollen.STR   robe   new.STR]

Fischer (2012) is a reply to Haumann (2003, 2010), in which she points out some problems with Haumann's proposal, both in relation to empirical facts and to interpretation (Fischer 2012: 253). Fischer again states that her position is that adjectives could have an attributive or predicative function in Old English, and that this was indicated both through morphology (weak and strong inflection) and by position (Fischer 2012: 253). The paper further deals with the issue of "sloppy" versus "strict" identity, i.e. whether the adjectives in *and*-adjective constructions refer to the same referent or to two different referents. She also discusses the development of constructions with *one* in English, with reference to Haumann's

(2003) *pro* analysis, and concludes, *pace* Haumann, that it is not possible to subsume all instances of the *and*-construction under one analysis (Fischer 2012: 278).

Fischer's and Haumann's generalizations are summarized in table 2.1 and table 2.2, respectively:

Tab. 2.1: Properties of weak and strong adjectives according to Fischer (2001, 2001, 2006, 2012)[3,4]

Weak adjectives (prenominal)	Strong adjectives (pre- and postnominal)
attributive	predicative
given/theme/topic	new/rheme/focus/comment
restrictive	non-restrictive

Tab. 2.2: Properties of prenominal and postnominal adjectives according to Haumann (2003, 2010). The table is slightly adapted from Haumann (2010: 70)[5]

Prenominal adjectives (weak and strong) incl. all adjectives in *and*-constructions	Postnominal adjectives (strong)
attributive	predicative
given	new
individual-level reading	stage-level reading
non-restrictive	restrictive

For Fischer, weak vs. strong inflection is the main parameter determining meaning. She says that position also plays a role, but since she does not distinguish

---

[3] An important point for Fischer is that weak adjectives cannot be modified by an adverb in Old English. Where Present-day English allows *the very old man*, Old English does not allow **se swiðe ealde.*WK *man* 'the very old man'. The adverb can only be used with strong adjectives: *se wæs swiðe eald.*STR *man* 'he was (a) very old man'. According to Fischer (2001: 261), this testifies to the verbal and predicative nature of strong adjectives. I will not consider this further here, as it is not relevant for the present discussion.

[4] In her first articles (Fischer 2000, 2001), Fischer mentions adjectives expressing inherent quality vs. temporary state (cf. Haumann's individual-level and stage-level), but this is not mentioned in later articles (Fischer 2006, 2012), so I have not included it as part of her generalization.

[5] Haumann, too, mentions degree modifiers in her table (Haumann 2010: 70), but I have not included them here, since their distribution is an empirical fact and not something to be tested.

clearly between strong pre- and postnominal adjectives, the main parameter is in fact inflection. For Haumann, on the other hand, meaning is related to position only. Hence strong prenominals pattern with weak prenominals, and not with strong postnominals. Postnominal adjectives in *and*-constructions are taken to be prenominal adjectives to a *pro* element.

2.2 Some terminological issues

A problem with both Fischer's and Haumann's proposals is that the terms used are not well defined, and partly overlap, which makes it difficult to evaluate claims about the relation between inflection, meaning and position. Below I comment on some of the terminological issues.

2.2.1 Terminology: Attributive versus predicative

The formal structural distinction between attributive and predicative adjectives in Present-day English is usually taken to be that attributive adjectives are noun phrase constituents, modify nominals and occur prenominally, whereas predicative adjectives characterize a noun phrase that is a separate clause element, and follow a copula verb or are in secondary predication as object predicatives (Biber et al. 1999: 505; Quirk et al. 1985: 417). In order to account for adjective distribution in Old English noun phrases, both Fischer and Haumann expand the definitions into the semantic and functional domains.

As mentioned in section 2.1, Fischer's main proposal is that strong adjectives are "functionally predicative" (Fischer 2012: 256), i.e. they get a predicative reading also when they are grammatically attributive. As regards definitions, she says that a predicative adjective 1) conveys additional and new information (Fischer 2000: 170), and 2) is used rhematically (which is the same as conveying new information, according to Fischer), and forms a separate constituent (Fischer 2012: 252). Furthermore, strong adjectives are closer to the verbal than the nominal pole (Fischer 2001: 259–270). In other words, predicativity is defined in terms of some of the other properties in her generalization (see table 2.1), which creates a methodological problem if one wishes to test the predictions empirically.

Haumann (2010) suggests that since Old English postnominal adjectives, like adjectives following a copula, inflect strong, postnominal adjectives must be predicative. Prenominal weak adjectives are "generally held" to be attributive (Haumann 2010: 61), presumably both because of their position and because they occur in definite constructions. There is a thus clear "division of labour" between weak prenominals and strong postnominals (2010: 66). However, that leaves the strong prenominal adjectives, and here Haumann finds that they pattern with weak prenominal adjectives as regards semantic and functional properties (Haumann 2010: 66–69).

In other words, Fischer, for whom inflection is the main criterion distinguishing attributive and predicative adjectives, has to explain how strong *prenominal* adjectives can be predicative in her generalization, since that is an unexpected position for predicatives with respect to linear iconicity. As we have seen, her explanation has to do with phonological stress. Haumann, on the other hand, for whom position is the main criterion, has to explain how *strong* prenominal adjectives can be attributive in her generalization, since strong adjectives are initially defined as predicative. Her explanation is functional.

What this amounts to is that whether an element is attributive or predicative is not something that can be tested in itself through analysis of examples, since it firstly depends on inflection or position, which is observable and does not require testing, and, secondly and crucially, on how the noun phrases are analyzed according to the other properties in the generalizations that Fischer and Haumann propose. In my analysis of data in section 3, I will therefore focus on these other properties, to which we now turn.

2.2.2 Terminology: Given versus new

Givenness can be defined in different ways. It can refer to shared knowledge in the sense that the speaker assumes that the information conveyed is present in the listener's mental world (Clark and Haviland 1977: 4); it can refer to cognitive status in the sense that given information is assumed to be present in the consciousness of the addressee at the time of utterance (Chafe 1976: 30); or it can refer to what is predictable or recoverable from the preceding context (Kuno 1978: 282–283).[6] It has also been shown that given and new information are not clear dichotomies, but occur in degrees; some information can for example be inferable, either textually or situationally (Prince 1981; Lambrecht 1994: 100; Haug 2011). Furthermore, givenness can be specified lexically, or through grammatical devices such as deaccentuation, ordering and deletion (Krifka 2007: 37). Though there is some degree of overlap in practice (a given element can be a topic, for example), the distinction between given and new information should be distinguished from topic–comment and focus–background. Givenness has to do with the information-structural

---

6 See Petrova and Solf (2009) for a good overview and discussion.

status of sentence constituents in the discourse, and it overlaps with the theme–rheme distinction in the Prague School tradition as represented by Firbas (1966: 240). Topic–comment refers to the predicational division of an utterance into starting point and comment, and focus–background are terms used to signal communicative weight or relevance (Petrova and Solf 2009: 133).

Both Fischer and Haumann list givenness as a property of adjectives, but as mentioned in section 2.1, Fischer does not define givenness, other than to say that she uses terms like given/theme/topic and new/rheme/focus/comment loosely to mean approximately the same thing. To Fischer it seems to boil down to *salience*, i.e. which elements add least and most to the advancing process of communication (Fischer 2006: 256; Fischer and van der Wurff 2006: 122). However, she seems to find the terms theme/rheme particularly useful, because those are linked to position, with postposed adjectives being rhematic, and thematic adjectives being preposed (Fischer 2006: 256). This lumping together of terminology again makes it difficult to test the generalization empirically, since there is not necessarily overlap between the terms, as mentioned above, and as Fischer acknowledges (Fischer 2006: 256).

Haumann does not define givenness either, but relates it to the distinction between attribution and predication, and to weak and strong inflection. Weak adjectives must be given, since they occur within definite, thematic nominal expressions, and strong adjectives convey new or additional information (Haumann 2010: 62). In actual analysis of historical texts, givenness is usually taken to be related to the textual context, so that given information refers to something that has been mentioned before in the text, while new information has not been mentioned before (see e.g. Haug 2011). From some of the examples Haumann provides, it is difficult to see how this might work in practice. For example, she says that in (9), the weak adjective *deadan* 'dead' is an attribute, and thus given information. But in the context of the text, *deadan* must be new information, since the woman carrying her son is clearly introduced here. Hence, her son must be new information as well, including the fact that he is dead.[7]

---

7 Another issue related to givenness that neither Fischer nor Haumann mentions is that the term is usually used for referents: it is the referent of the noun that is taken to be given or new, not just the adjective. Adjectives modify nouns, and are therefore less likely to occur more than once. A sequence like *Jenny bought a red dress. She wore the red dress to school. There she spilled ink on her red dress* is unlikely. Rather, the story would probably go as follows: *Jenny bought a red dress. She wore the dress/it to school. There she spilled ink on it.* In this sequence it makes sense to say that *a red dress* is new information, and *the dress* and *it* are given information, referring

(9) sum   wif   bær   hire dædan sunu ongean þone halgan
     some   woman carried her   dead   sun   towards the   holy
     Libertinum
     Libertinum

(Haumann 2010: 62, her example (25b))

For the purpose of my analysis of the examples in section 3, I will use the term "given information" to refer to elements that are mentioned in the previous textual context or are inferable from the context, irrespective of the distance between the first occurrence and later occurrences. "New information" is information that is new in the context or cannot be inferred from the context. This is not necessarily unproblematic either, because there is also the issue of when a constituent goes from given information to given information that is inactive and needs to be reactivated. In addition, direct speech constitutes its own discourse universe within a text, and noun phrases can be non-specific and generic as well (see e.g. Bech 2014). However, since the point here is to consider Fischer's and Haumann's proposals in relatively broad terms, the simple definition will suffice.

2.2.3 Terminology: Individual-level versus stage-level interpretation

Haumann in particular distinguishes between individual-level (inherent, enduring) versus stage-level (accidental, temporary) properties of an adjective (Haumann 2010: 63).[8] Weak and strong prenominal adjectives get an individual-level reading, while strong postnominal adjectives get a stage-level reading. Haumann provides some examples, but considering that almost all Old English adjectives (ca. 96%, see Bech et al. 2016) are prenominal, we would not expect them all to have an individual-level interpretation. It is also not difficult to find postnominal adjectives that clearly have an individual-level meaning, e.g. *hwetstan bradne* 'whetstone broad – broad whetstone' (*Lacnunga*). This is an example of a noun that is unchangeable, and Haumann does not discuss whether the distinction between individual-level and stage-level is relevant for such noun phrases, or only for concrete, changeable entities. The distinction may furthermore be obscured

---

back to *a red dress*. To define an adjective by itself as new information would not be particularly useful, except in cases of contrast (*Jenny bought a red and a blue dress*).
8 Fischer also does so in the early articles (Fischer 2000, 2001), with reference to inherent vs. incidental properties, but she abandons this in later work.

with certain non-concrete nouns if the noun itself has a temporal/eventive/stative interpretation, e.g. *will*, *understanding* (see examples (13) and (14)). Another example of a postnominal adjective with individual-level reading is *sum lytel cniht sweart* 'a little boy black – a little black boy' (*Martyrology III*), which refers to a little black demon.

In general, the distinction between individual-level and stage-level is not difficult to apply in practice, but it may not be relevant for all types of noun phrases.

2.2.4 Terminology: Restrictive versus non-restrictive

The concept of restrictivity is much discussed in semantics (see e.g. Pfaff 2015: 12 and the references therein; Pfaff 2017; Fabricius-Hansen ms). The standard definition is that a restrictive modifier "denotes a subset of the denotation of the head noun" (Fabricius-Hansen ms: 2), i.e. picks a referent out of a set and narrows the set of potential referents, whereas a non-restrictive modifier "does not constrain the denotation of the modified DP as compared to the host DP" (Fabricius-Hansen ms: 2). The discussion of restrictivity includes issues such as non-restrictivity vs. not-restrictivity, i.e. whether the absence of restrictivity is just that (not restrictive) or a property in itself (non-restrictive) (Pfaff 2015: 13); non-restrictive vs. non-restricting modifiers, i.e. modifiers that are restrictive by default may be used non-restrictively, and this is termed "non-restricting" (Fabricius-Hansen ms. 23 referring to Leffel 2014); the difference between non-restrictive and appositive modifiers (Pfaff 2015, 2017), and issues to do with compositionality and formalization (Pfaff 2015; Fabricius-Hansen ms).

Both Fischer and Haumann distinguish between restrictive and non-restrictive adjectives. Fischer briefly mentions contrast in connection with restrictive interpretation (Fischer 2001: 256), but otherwise assumes that the distinction is obvious. Haumann defines restrictive–non-restrictive on the basis of contrast, saying that weak adjectives "do not identify a particular referent from among a set of entities that contrast with respect to the property denoted by the modifier" (Haumann 2010: 64). They are non-restrictive, characterizing elements, while strong postnominal adjectives do, and are therefore restrictive, identifying elements. Strong prenominal adjectives pattern with weak adjectives (Haumann 2010: 68). However, some of the examples given do not provide unambiguous evidence for this. For example, in (10), Haumann finds that *unendurable* must be restrictive because we can imagine that it contrasts with *endurable* tortures.

(10)   &   wende   þæt   hit   hel   wære   be
        and   imagined that   it   hell   was   from

      ðam   tintregum unaræfnendlicum ic   oft   sæcgan herde
      the   tortures   unendurable   I   often say   heard

'I imagined that it was hell by the unendurable tortures I often heard about' (Haumann 2010: 64, her example (31a))

This seems far-fetched, because tortures are by definition rather unendurable, and there is no mention of endurable tortures in the text (*Bede*) either. In other words, it is not the case that the set of referents of 'tortures' is reduced by the addition of the adjective, hence it is not used restrictively.

In the following, I will adhere to the basic definition of restrictivity: a restrictive modifier denotes a subset of the denotation of the head noun, while a non-restrictive modifier does not, but rather adds information about the head noun.

3 Testing Fischer's and Haumann's generalizations

3.1 Data and method

In addition to the issues having to do with terminology, what is missing in both Fischer's and Haumann's works is a systematic analysis of data according to the parameters they set up. For example, if it is the case that weak adjectives are attributive, thematic and restrictive, and strong adjectives are predicative, rhematic and non-restrictive, as is Fischer's stance (see table 2.1), the next step would be to take weak and strong adjectives and analyze them according to these criteria. Haumann focuses on position, distinguishing between prenominal and postnominal adjectives, but although she refers to work in which the predominance of prenominal modifiers is acknowledged (Haumann 2010: 53), she does not specify that postnominal adjectives are in fact rare in Old English, compared to prenominal adjectives. Both Fischer and Haumann give the impression that strong postnominal adjectives are a frequent and regular feature of Old English, but this is not the case.

The present study is not a quantitative study either, apart from some comments on the general distribution. Instead, I will contextualize Old English noun phrases by carrying out a close reading of some examples in their expanded context. In the first part, I take two texts in which there is an approximately equal number of A-*and*-A-N constructions and A-N-*and*-A constructions in each text, and I consider how these are distributed contextually. I searched for the constructions in the *York-Toronto-Helsinki Corpus of Parsed Old English Prose* (YCOE, Taylor et al. 2003) and found two texts in which there was a reasonably even distribution of the two constructions, namely *Cura Pastoralis* and the *West-Saxon Gospels*. *Cura Pastoralis* contained nine examples of the A-*and*-A-N construction and seven examples of the A-N-*and*-A construction, while the corresponding numbers for the *West-Saxon Gospels* were six and eight, respectively. The query gave a few more examples, but they were constructions in which the referent was clearly not the same for the adjectives, of the type "good men and evil". These were disregarded.

Cura Pastoralis 'Pastoral Care' is a religious treatise translated from Latin as part of King Alfred's translation programme, possibly by the king himself, who writes about it in a preface, in which he famously says that he sometimes translates word by word and sometimes according to the sense. *Cura Pastoralis* exists in two contemporary manuscripts, Hatton 20 and Cotton Tiberius B.xi, of which Hatton is the most complete. The YCOE has both and I made the searches in the Hatton version.

The *West-Saxon Gospels* exists in several manuscripts, and the one in the YCOE, Cambridge, Corpus Christi College 140, is from the 11th century. The gospels are translated from Latin, and the translation is expected to be more conservative than the *Cura Pastoralis* translation, since this is the Scriptures.

3.2 Noun phrases in *Cura Pastoralis* and the *West-Saxon Gospels*

Below I present some of the A-*and*-A-N, and A-N-*and*-A phrases I found in *Cura Pastoralis* and the *West Saxon Gospels*, with the aim to evaluate possible reasons for position in light of Fischer's and Haumann's criteria and predictions about adjective meaning. I also include the Latin original, in order to consider possible influence for adjective position from the source language. The translations of the *Cura Pastoralis* examples into Present-day English are from the edition in which the Old English text occurs (Sweet 1871). The Latin versions are from Judic et al.'s edition (1992) and I have marked the Latin equivalent of the Old English noun phrase in italics. The translations of the examples from the *West-Saxon Gospels* are from King James' Authorized Version of the Bible (1611). The examples are marked in boldface in the textual context. For reasons of space, I do not provide glosses for the whole context, only an idiomatic translation, since the most important aspect to consider here is the way in which the examples interact with the textual context.

3.2.1 Cura Pastoralis

Example (11) has two coordinated adjectives preceding the noun, and here it should be pointed out that Sweet, after commenting on the independence of the Old English translators with respect to the Latin model, specifically brings up the Old English use of synonyms: "The anxiety to bring out the meaning of the Latin as vividly as possible is strikingly shown in the frequent rendering of a single Latin words by two English ones of practically identical or similar meaning" (Sweet 1871: xli). This strategy is also evident in the noun phrases, where, as we shall see, Old English usually has two adjectives where Latin has one (see also Grabski 2017: 140–141).

(11) *unwærlicu   &   giemeleaslicu spræc*   (cocura:15.89.7.571)
 unguarded.STR and careless.STR   speaking

> Latin: Nam sicut *incauta loquutio* in errorem pertrahit [...] (Judic et al. 1992: 186, 188). The Latin has one prenominal adjective, *incauta*, which can mean both 'unguarded' and 'careless'.
>
> Context: The example occurs in a chapter about how the teacher should take care how he speaks, so as not to be overly talkative or overly silent. I include the chapter heading for this example, since the text from which the example is extracted occurs right below the heading.
>
> *Hu se lareow sceal bion gesceadwis on his swigean & nytwyrðe on his wordum.*
>
> *Sie se lariow gemetfæsð & gescadwis & nyttwyrðe on his wordum, ðætte he ne suigige ðæs ðe nyttwyrðe sie to sprecanne, ne ðæt ne sprece ðæt he suigigean scyle. Forðæm sua sua **unwærlicu & giemeleaslicu spræc** menn dweleð, sua eac sio ungemetgode suige ðæs lareowes on gedwolan gebrin(g)ð ða ðe he læran meahte, gif he sprecende beon wolde.*
>
> How the teacher must be discreet in his silence and useful in his words.
>
> Let the teacher be moderate and discreet and useful in his words, lest he keep unsaid what is useful to speak, or speak what ought to be kept silent. For as **unguarded and careless speaking** leads men astray, so the

excessive silence of the teacher leads into error those whom he might teach if he were willing to speak (Sweet 1871: 88).

Since these are strong prenominals, Fischer predicts that they should convey new information and be non-restrictive, and thus be functionally predicative. But *unwærlicu & giemeleaslicu* 'unguarded and careless' contrasts with *gemetfæsð & gescadwis & nyttwyrðe* 'moderate and discreet and useful', and the unguardedness of speech is also inferred from the immediately preceding clause, where "speak what ought to be kept silent" is mentioned. In other words, the adjectives do not convey new information, and they are restrictive, as they denote a subset of the denotation of the head noun: it is about the kind of speech that is unguarded and careless. Hence these adjectives are not functionally predicative in Fischer's definition.

According to Haumann, prenominal adjectives should be attributive, given, non-restrictive and get an individual-level reading. For Haumann, it is position that determines whether an adjective is attributive or predicative, so the adjectives in (11) would by definition be attributive. As regards givenness, a curious thing in Haumann's 2010 article is that she says that weak prenominal adjectives are given because they occur in definite expressions (Haumann 2010: 62), whereas strong prenominal adjectives "do not convey new information" (Haumann 2010: 68). It is unclear whether she by this actually means that they convey given information or that they are just "not new". The wording is not explained. In any case, it can be argued that *unwærlicu & giemeleaslicu spræc* is inferred, and hence it may at least be said that the information is "not (brand) new", so that this feature is in line with what Haumann's generalization would predict. As regards a possible individual-level (i.e. inherent, enduring) reading, speaking is not inherently unguarded and careless, and as regards restrictiveness, the adjectives are not non-restrictive as predicted by Haumann, but restrictive, as we saw above. We can therefore conclude that for example (11), neither Fischer's nor Haumann's generalization can be successfully applied.

Let us look at a similar example, but with the conjunction and one adjective placed postnominally. Like (11), which functions as subject of the sentence, (12) is also an argument, a direct object.

(12) *unnytlicu   ðing   &   unalifedu*   (cocura:37.265.7.1722)
     useless.STR   things   and   unlawful.STR

Latin: [...] ut audenter *illicita* committat (Judic et al. 1992: 336). The Latin has a substantival adjective, *illicita*, which means 'unlawful things'.

Context: The topic of the chapter is that man should do good for the love of doing good and not for fear of punishment.

Se ðe for ðæm anum god deð ðæt he sumre ðreaunge yfel him ondrætt, se wilnað ðætte nan ðing ne sie ðe he him ondrædan ðyrfe, ðæt he ðy orsorglicor dyrre don **unnytlicu ðing & unalifedu.**

He who only does good because he fears the evil of some correction, wishes not to have cause to fear anything, that he may the more carelessly dare to do **useless and unlawful things** (Sweet 1871: 254).

For Fischer, there should be no difference in reading between the adjectives in (11) and the adjectives in (12). Recall that although the principle of iconicity is important in her scheme, i.e. the order of elements plays a role with respect to interpretation, she is not able to account for any difference between strong prenominal and strong postnominal adjectives, other than to say that strong prenominal adjectives are functionally predicative not because of position, but because of "phonological iconicity", namely stress. As regards the given–new distinction, we could perhaps concede that *unnytlicu* 'useless' and *unalifedu* 'unlawful' convey new information, since those adjectives are not used previously in the chapter. However, the chapter is about good versus evil or sinful actions, so it could be argued that the writer does not assume that the concepts 'useless' and 'unlawful' will be completely new to the reader. It would perhaps be possible to argue for a focus reading in the sense that there is a contrast involved between good actions and bad actions, so that the adjectives become particularly salient, which seems to be Fischer's preferred overarching term (see section 2.1), but the contrast also precludes a non-restrictive reading. 'Useless' and 'unlawful' limit the reference of the noun here, which is a feature of restrictive adjectives. In addition, it is hard to see how the adjectives can be separate constituents conveying additional information, which is a part of Fischer's definition of functional predicativity.

For Haumann as well, (11) and (12) should get identical readings: semantically an A-*and*-A-N construction is the same as an A-N-*and*-A construction, since the postnominal adjective in the latter is actually an attributive adjective to a *pro*. Hence, both adjectives in (12) should be given, individual-level, and non-restrictive. However, the same comments apply here as to example (11): "things" are not inherently useless and unlawful, i.e. the adjectives do not receive an individual-level reading, and it might be added that the nature of the semantically underspecified noun (*ðing* 'things') makes it difficult to assign such labels at all. Also, these adjectives are restrictive, not non-restrictive as predicted by the scheme.

We might also recall the Old English translator's tendency to produce two adjectives where the Latin original only has one adjective, or sometimes none at all, so the question is to which extent adjective position is stylistically determined in this text, since the order is apparently not caused by a wish on the part of the translator to stay close to the original text.

Below are two more examples from *Cura Pastoralis*, again one A-*and*-A-N construction (13) and one A-N-*and*-A construction (14).

(13) hal   &   good   andgiet   (cocura:36.261.22.1708)
     sound.STR and   good.STR   understanding

> Latin: Aut quis *sana intellegentia* de percussione sua ingratus exsistit [...] (Judic et al. 1992: 332). The Latin has one postnominal adjective, *intellegentia*.
>
> Context: This occurs at the very end of a chapter that is about how the healthy should be admonished in one way, and the unhealthy in another, and how the sick should remember that Christ himself had to suffer bodily pain and even death.
>
> *Forhwy [ðonne] sceal ænigum menn ðyncan to rcðc oððe to unieðe ðæt he Godes suingellan geðafige for his yfelum dædum, nu God self sua fela yfeles geðafode, sua sua we ær cuædon, for moncynne? Hwa sceal ðonne, ðara ðe* **hal & good andgiet** *hæbbe, Gode unðoncfull beon, forðæm, ðeah he hine for his synnum suinge, nu se ne for butan suingellan of ðys middangearde se ðe butan ælcre synne wæs & giet is?*
>
> Why, then, shall it seem to any man too severe or hard to endure the castigation of God for his evil deeds, since God himself, as we said above, suffered so much evil for mankind? Who, then, who has **a sound and good understanding**, ought to be unthankful to God, because, although he chastise him for his sins, he did not depart without stripes from this world, who was, and still is, without any sin? (Sweet 1871: 261).

Here it might be argued that *hal & good* 'sound and good' are new in the context, since those specific adjectives have not been mentioned before. However, the idea of having a good understanding occurs several times in the chapter; a few pages earlier it says that (in the Present-day English translation) "[t]he sick are also to be admonished to understand how great a gift of God the troubles of the flesh are for them" (Sweet 1871: 257). Hence, the "sound and good understanding" can at least be said to relate to the topic of the chapter. The adjectives are also restrictive, which is not what Fischer predicts for strong adjectives. Consequently, they cannot be "functionally predicative" in her definition.

According to Haumann's generalization, the adjectives should be attributive and given, so in that sense she is closer to the mark with respect to this particular example. As regards individual- vs. stage-level reading, this type of noun does not easily lend itself to that classification, since on the one hand "understanding" cannot be said to be inherently sound and good, and on the other hand it would be odd to think of it as temporarily sound and good. Finally, the adjectives are restrictive, which is the opposite of what Haumann predicts for prenominal adjectives. "Sound and good" are identifying elements here, since understanding can be unsound and poor.

(14) clænes   willan   &   goodes   (cocura:46.349.2.2355)
      pure.STR   will   and   good.STR

> Latin: Quae autem desursum est sapientia primum quidem pudica est, deinde pacifica. Pudica uidelicet, quia caste intellegit [...] (Judic et al. 1992: 404). Here the Old English translation is very free – *Pudica uidelicet, quia caste intellegit* means 'That is, pure, since (it) understands virtuously'. The Old English text is expanded in relation to the Latin here, which is not surprising, as it seems to have been the strategy of the translator(s) to make sure the readers got the point. Hence *clænes willan and godes* does not have an equivalent in the Latin.
>
> Context: We are still dealing with admonitions, and this example occurs in the middle of a chapter about how the peaceful should be admonished in one way and the quarrelsome in another.
>
> *Ac se se ðe of Gode cymð, he bið godes willan and gesibsum. Ðæt is ðonne ðæt he sie **clænes willan & goodes**, ðæt he clænlice & ryhtwislice ongiete ðæt ðæt he ongiete.*
>
> '[...] But that which comes from God is of good will and peaceful.' Being of **pure and good will**, is purely and righteously understanding what he understands (Sweet 1871: 348).

Since these are strong adjectives, they should be functionally predicative according to Fischer, which entails salience (rhematicity, newness) and non-restrictiveness. Here, *clænes willan & goodes* 'pure and good will' is an elaboration on *godes willan and gesibsum* 'good will and peaceful' in the immediately preceding sentence, which quotes something the apostle James said. One adjective is given in the context, and the other is new, but it can perhaps be argued that they are particularly salient in the sense that it is the adjectives that contribute the most important information. It is also possible to assign a non-restrictive reading to them, by which the will is characterized as pure and good ("when your will is pure and good, you can understand [...]"), hence the adjectives do not denote a subset of the denotation of the noun. So, for this particular example, Fischer's generalization works fairly well.

Haumann's scheme predicts that these adjectives should be attributive, given, individual-level, and non-restrictive, and again it is difficult to get a good fit. As mentioned, one of the adjectives, *goodes* 'good', is given in the immediately preceding context, while the other one, *clænes* 'clean' is new. The difference between individual-level and stage-level reading is obscured with non-concrete nouns of this type: it is difficult to think of *willan* 'will' in terms of a distinction between inherently pure and good or temporarily pure and good. The adjectives may, however, get a non-restrictive reading, as predicted by the generalization.

The examples discussed so far make it clear that Fischer's and Haumann's schemes cannot easily be applied in practice. Part of the problem is the lack of clear definitions, and this lack of clarity perhaps happens because they know what they want to find and therefore make links that may not be well motivated. In addition, some of the features of their schemes are defined on the basis of other features, which makes empirical testing challenging.

3.2.2 The *West-Saxon Gospels*

We turn to a different type of text, the *West Saxon Gospels*. As might be expected of a Bible text, the translation is more conservative in the sense that if there are two adjectives in the Latin, the Old English version also has two adjectives, but usually not in the same order as in the Latin.

Examples (15) and (16) are vocatives, and therefore the adjectives are inflected weak. But as we see, the adjectives can occur both pre- and postnominally.

(15) ge   ungeleaffulle &   þwyre   cneores   (cowsgosp,Mt:17.17.1151)
    you   faithless.WK   and perverse.WK   generation

Vulgate: *o generatio incredula et perversa*[9]

Đa andswarode he him, Eala **ge ungeleaffulle & þwyre cneores**, *hu lange beo ic mid eow; Hu lange forbere ic eow.*

Then Jesus answered and said, O faithless and perverse generation, how long shall I be with you? how long shall I suffer you? (King James, Matthew 17:17).

---

[9] This is verse 16 in the Vulgate.

(16) þu   goda   þeow   &   getrywa   (cowsgosp,Mt:25.21.1760)
    you   good.WK   servant and true.WK

Vulgate: euge *bone serve et fidelis*

*Ða cwæþ hys hlaford to hym, beo bliþe, **þu goda þeow & getrywa***

His lord said unto him, Well done, thou good and faithful servant (King James, Matthew 25:21)

According to Fischer's inflectional criteria, weak prenominal adjectives should be attributive, given/thematic/topical, and restrictive. Vocatives are of course special constructions, since it can be assumed that if you address someone directly, the information you convey about them will not be new to them. Whether the information is topical is a matter of discussion. Example (15) is from Matthew chapter 17, and in the previous chapter Jesus also speaks of "a wicked and adulterous generation" (Matthew 16:4). In that sense, the not so admirable qualities of that particular generation are a topic, but there are forty verses between the two mentions. As regards restrictiveness, it is also a matter of interpretation. Perhaps there is an implicit contrast to a faithful and pure generation in the sense that the generation mentioned is unusual, in which case a restrictive reading is possible, which is what Fischer predicts for weak adjectives. But a reading according to which *ungeleaffulle & þwyre* 'faithless and perverse' is characterizing, and hence non-restrictive, as Haumann predicts for prenominal adjectives, is more likely. The adjectives do not pick out this generation with the properties faithless and perverse from among a set of generations. As regards Haumann's distinction between individual-level reading for prenominal adjectives and stage-level reading for postnominal adjectives, it might be argued that "faithless and perverse" is meant to be conveyed as an inherent and enduring characteristic of that particular generation. So, for the weak prenominals, some features of both Fischer's and Haumann's schemes can be applied, but they do not work consistently.

Example (16) is also a vocative, but this time with one postnominal adjective, as in the Latin version. Fischer (2001: 265–266) briefly comments on postnominal weak adjectives, saying that the reason why they are weak is that they do not convey new information; in other words, inflection is based on givenness. This means that all adjectives that do not convey new information should be weak, which we have seen in previous examples is not the case. The adjectives *goda* 'good' and *getrywa* 'faithful' are given in the sense that the servant is characterized through direct speech; i.e. it would presumably not be surprising to the servant to be thus characterized, and the servant's actions previously in the text justify the description. As for Haumann's scheme, the adjectives can receive an individual-level reading (the servant is inherently or enduringly good and faithful), but whether the adjectives are restrictive or non-restrictive is a matter of interpretation, as it was in example (15). Fischer's scheme predicts that they should be restrictive (since they are weak), and Haumann's scheme predicts that they should be non-restrictive (since they are prenominal). "Good" and "faithful" can potentially be seen as characterizing, non-restrictive elements. However, Matthew chapter 25 is about good servants versus bad servants, so there is a contrast in the story, which points to a restrictive reading whereby the adjectives denote a subset of servants, though it is possible that the contrast is not expressed in the direct speech aimed at the servants.

Let us consider a few more examples. Example (17) is similar to (16) in word choice, but it is not a vocative, so the adjectives have strong inflection. While chapter 25, from which (16) is taken, presents a parable which illustrates the difference between good servants and wicked servants, the chapter before it, chapter 24, gives the first mention of "faithful and wise servant" (17). So here the information is new in a sense, but the verses leading up to it are an admonition that man should be prepared for the coming of the Lord, because no one knows the hour. Thus, one would do well to be a good servant, i.e. be prepared for the day of judgement, since evil servants "shall be cut asunder'" and "there shall be weeping and gnashing of teeth" (Matthew 24:51). In other words, the topic of the chapter is faithfulness towards God. This is why it is problematic to conflate e.g. "given" and "topic", as they do not mean the same thing (see also Lambrecht 1994: 160–165). Furthermore, for Fischer, the adjectives in (17) should be completely different in meaning than the adjectives in (16). For example, (16) should be given and restrictive, and thus attributive, since they are weak, and (17) should be new and non-restrictive, and thus functionally predicative, since they are strong. It is difficult to see how the examples differ along these parameters.

For Haumann, the adjectives in (17) should get the same reading as the adjectives in (16), but the same comments apply here as for example (16), though in (17) there is a clearer contrastive reading for the adjectives, since evil servants are mentioned just three verses below. Consequently, the adjectives are probably restrictive rather than non-restrictive, which goes against the prediction of the generalization.

(17) getrywe   &   gleaw   þeow   (cowsgosp,Mt:24.45.1712)
      faithful.STR and   wise.STR   servant

Vulgate: *fidelis servus et prudens*

*Wens þu hwa sy **getrywe & gleaw** þeow þone geset hys hlafurd ofer his hired þæt he him on tide mete sylle?*

Who then is a faithful and wise servant, whom his lord hath made ruler over his household, to give them meat in due season? (King James, Matthew 24:45)

Examples (18) and (19) both have the structure A-N-*and*-A, and here the adjectives occur in noun phrases that function as subject (18) or (apposition to) subject predicative (19) in the sentences.

(18) *ettul mann & windrincende* (cowsgosp,Mt:11.19.688)
gluttonous.STR man and wine-drinking.STR

Vulgate: ecce *homo vorax et potator vini*

*Mannes sunu com etende and dryncynde & hi cweðaþ, her ys **ettul mann & windrincende**, manfulra & synfulra freond;*

The Son of man came eating and drinking, and they say, Behold a man gluttonous, and a winebibber (King James, Matthew 11:19)

(19) *god wer & rihtwis* (cowsgosp,Lk:23.50.5631)
good.STR man and righteous.STR

Vulgate: *vir bonus et iustus*

*& þa an man on naman Iosep, se wæs gerefa **god wer & rihtwis***

And, behold, there was a man named Joseph, a counsellor; and he was a good man, and a just (King James, Luke 23:50)

In both (18) and (19), the information conveyed by the adjectives can really be said to give new information about the referents, and they are non-restrictive, as they point to a specific person which has unique reference. The man (Jesus) is gluttonous and he is a winebibber; the man (Joseph) was good and he was righteous. Consequently, for these examples, both with strong adjectives, Fischer's generalization would work, but Haumann's would not work completely, as it predicts given information for the adjectives. However, individual-level readings of the adjectives are possible here, and the adjectives are non-restrictive.

The discussion of the examples above has illustrated the problems with Fischer's and Haumann's schemes for the analysis of adjective meaning in Old English, related to inflection and position: the results of the empirical analysis are not consistent. Old English adjectives seem to resist generalizations that operate with a list of "either – or" features that are supposed to be applicable to all instances, and they are elusive as concerns the reasons for placement. After a thorough empirical study, Grabski (2017: 168–169) ends up suggesting that A-N-

and-A order, not A-*and*-A-N, is the default order when there are two adjectival modifiers, and that the reason is a preference for splitting heavy groups.[10] Here Grabski is in line with Mitchell (1985), who sees it as "one of the characteristic tendencies of the language" (Mitchell 1985 i: §1472), and not a feature that is due to emphasis or specific stylistic considerations. Grabski furthermore finds that there is a marked difference between noun phrases with several modifiers and noun phrases with one modifier. While the postposition of a modifier in complex constructions is due to a wish to avoid heavy groups, postposition in noun phrases with a single adjective or participle is correlated with the "verbal" nature of the modifier (Grabski 2017: 109). We now turn to the latter construction.

4 Noun phrases in context: Postnominal present participles

According to Grabski (2017: 52–53), "verbal" modifiers are 1) adverb-like adjectives, most notably the ones ending in -*weard*, such as *norðeweardum* 'northwards', which have an adverbial interpretation, 2) adjectives governing complements, 3) stage-level adjectives, i.e. adjectives referring to incidental, non-inherent properties, and 4) participles. However, while postnominal position accommodates verbal elements, prenominal position is not restricted to non-verbal elements (Grabski 2017: 171). In other words, non-verbal elements occur prenominally, while verbal elements occur both pre- and postnominally. In this section, I consider adjectival present participles, which are prototypically "verbal" elements, i.e. the adjective derives from a verb, and the question that arises is the following: if verbal elements can occur both pre- and postnominally, what determines position? Here, the focus will be on contextualization in relation to the Latin original text.

I turned to one of the two texts under consideration here, namely *Cura Pastoralis*, and queried for all prenominal and postnominal present participles, i.e. present participles that have been annotated as belonging to the noun phrase. In *Cura*, there are 28 prenominal and six postnominal present participles. YCOE as a whole has 889 prenominal present participles and 59 postnominal ones, so the proportion of postnominal present participles is slightly higher in *Cura* (17.6%) than in all of YCOE (6.2%). In general, prenominal present participles greatly

---

[10] Grabski (2017: 169) also finds that definiteness is not a relevant parameter in accounting for the word order of noun phrases with adjectival modification.

outnumber postnominal ones, which is as expected since prenominal position is the default position when there is just one modifier in the noun phrase. The question is how the variation arises that after all exists in Old English.

In section 4.1, I present all the six examples in which there is a postnominal present participle, and consider those with reference to the Latin text, and in section 4.2, some of the noun phrases with a prenominal present participle are exemplified. The discussion will show that, with one exception, the Old English postnominal present participles do not have a present participle counterpart in the Latin text, while the prenominal present participles generally do. Hence, postnominal modification was a native, productive pattern used for a specific purpose.

4.1 Postnominal present participles

(20) ða   synna   weaxænde   (cocura:17.123.15.834)
     the sins   increasing

Context:
Sua sua sio wund wile toberan, gif hio ne bið gewriðen mid wræde, sua willað **ða synna weaxænde** *toflowan, gif hie ne beoð gebundne hwilum mid stræclice lareowdome.*

As the wound is sure to swell unless bound with a bandage, so will sins increase and spread unless sometimes bound with rigorous discipline (Sweet 1871: 123)

The translation is relatively free here, as the Latin text says that the hardness of the bandage prevents the wound (i.e. a metaphor for sins) from flowing (in different directions) to such an extent that it causes death: [...] *ne plaga usque ad interitum diffluat, si hanc districtionis seueritas non coartat* (Judic et al. 1992: 214).

An Old English construction with coordination would be possible: *sua willað ða synna weaxan and toflowan* (see Sweet's translation into Present-day English), but Alfred chose to translate it with a construction that may be thought of as subordination: the sins do not increase and flow in different directions; they increase *as* they flow in different directions. A similar construction is seen in (21).

(21) se   lareow   ieldende   (cocura:21.153.5.1039)
     the teacher   delaying

Context:
Ac ðonne **se lareow ieldende** secð ðone timan ðe he his hieremenn sidelice on ðreatigean mæge, ðonne bið hit swutol ðæt he bierð on his geðylde ða byrðenne hira scylda.

But when the teacher delays, and watches for a suitable opportunity of reproving his subjects, it is evident that he bears in his patience the burden of their sins (Sweet 1871: 152)

The Latin text has a passive construction: *Sed cum tempus subditis ad correptionem quaeritur* (Judic et al. 1992: 240), which reads 'When the time is sought for the rebuke of (his) subjects'. This kind of construction cannot easily be transferred into Old English, so the translator opts for a more straightforward active sentence. However, instead of coordinating the verbs: *Ac ðonne se lareow ieldeð and secð* (see also Sweet's Present-day English translation), he chooses a present participle instead, rendering a construction that can be interpreted as subordinate: But when the teacher, delaying, seeks the time [...] The participle clearly has an adverbial meaning, since it is linked to the action of the main verb. In both (20) and (21) the present participle, though (annotated as) part of the noun phrase, is connected to another verbal action.

Examples (22) and (23) are similar in having a present participle that is immediately followed by the verb *cwæð* 'said':

(22) Dryhten   ðreatigende   (cocura:43.315.23.2116)
     Lord   rebuking

Context:
Ac us is suiðe geornlice to gehieranne hwæt **Dryhten ðreatigende** cuæð to Iudeum ðurh Sacharias ðone witgan;

But we must listen attentively to what the Lord said, rebuking the Jews through Zachariah the prophet (Sweet 1871: 315)

Latin: [...] Dominus redarguit, dicens [...] (Judic et al. 1992: 378)
       [...] Lord rebukes, saying [...]

(23) Dryhten   siofigende   (cocura:48.369.4.2483)
     Lord   lamenting

Context:
Be ðæm **Dryhten siofigende** cwæð ðurh Ossei ðone witgan

Of which the Lord spoke sadly through the prophet Hosea (Sweet 1871: 368)

> Latin: [...] Dominus queritur, dicens [...] (Judic et al. 1992: 422)
> [...] Lord laments, saying [...]

The interesting feature here is that Latin and Old English do the opposite: in Latin there is a finite verb (*redarguit* (22), *queritur* (23)) followed by the present participle *dicens*. So why does the translator not render the Old English as [...] *hwæt Dryhten ðreatað/ðreatode, cweðende* [...] 'what the Lord rebukes/rebuked, saying', or *Be ðæm Dryhten siofað/siofode, cweðende* [...] 'Of which the Lord laments/lamented, saying'?

It seems that these alternatives would be unidiomatic in Old English. A corpus search in YCOE of all instances of the present participle *cweðende* (with spelling variations) shows that *cweðende* usually occurs with the adverb *þus*: *þus cweðende* 'thus saying', followed immediately by the direct speech. This is not possible in (22) and (23), as the clause contains other elements which have to be accommodated. A reordering of the sentence elements would make the sentences more cumbersome than in the chosen translation. Again, it would be possible to coordinate the verbs: [...] *Dryhten ðreatode and cwæð* [...] 'the Lord rebuked and said', but then the embedding of the action would be lost: the Lord rebukes the Jews through his utterance, and the Lord laments through his words.

Interestingly, Sweet's Present-day English translation retains a present participle in (22), but the ordering is different, such that the non-finite verb (*rebuking*) becomes a part of a non-finite subordinate clause. In (23), Sweet actually renders the present participle as the adverb *sadly*, which also testifies to the adverbial nature of the original participle.

The noun phrases we have considered so far have all been in the nominative case, and therefore it is not possible to determine whether the participles have case endings, since the case ending and the participle ending would be identical. In (24), the noun phrase is in the accusative case, see the inflectional ending *-ne* in *fleondne*.

(24) *Loth   fleondne*   (cocura:51.399.14.2718)
    Lot   fleeing

Context:

Sio Segor gehælde **Loth fleondne**

Zoar saved Lot, when a fugitive (Sweet 1871: 398)

There is no equivalent in the Latin text, so this is an elaboration by the translator. Sweet's translation renders *fleondne* as a verbless adverbial clause, and it is clear that even in the Old English noun phrase, *fleondne* has a temporal adverbial meaning.

The final example is (25), and the only example in which there is actually a present participle in the Latin text: [...] *mens* [...] *dormiens* [...] 'mind sleeping' (Judic et al. 1992: 490). As with the previous examples, it is possible to assign an adverbial meaning to the participle: the mind is wounded *while* asleep.

(25) ðæt   mod   slæpende   (cocura:56.431.18.3041)
     the   mind   sleeping

Context:
*Swa bið **ðæt mod slæpende** gewundad swa hit ne gefret, ðonne hit bið to gimeleas his agenra ðearfa.*

The mind is so wounded while asleep as not to feel it, when it is too heedless of its own wants (Sweet 1871: 430)

In contrast to the postnominal present participles, the Old English prenominal present participles usually have an equivalent in Latin, either a present participle, or a nominalized adjective that is translated into Old English by means of a present participle and a noun.[11] A few examples are given in section 4.2.

4.2 Prenominal present participles

(26) ðæm **weldondum** monnum   (cocura:17.107.5.700)
     Direct transl.: the **well-doing** men
     Sweet: the well-doers   (Sweet 1871: 106)
     Latin: *bene **agentibus***   (Judic et al. 1992: 116)

(27) ðæs **flowendan** welan   (cocura:8.55.7.339)
     Direct transl.: the **flowing** wealth
     Sweet: abundant wealth   (Sweet 1871: 54)
     Latin: ***affluentium** abundantia*   (Judic et al. 1992: 156)

---

11 An example of the latter is the nominalized adjective *reptilium* (genitive plural) which is translated as *eallra creopendra wuhta* 'of all creeping creatures' (e.g. cocura:21.153.21.1049). The noun *reptile* did not enter English until the 14th century, according to the *Oxford English Dictionary*, and the adjective *reptile*, now rare, even later.

(28) ða **biernendan** ceastre (Sodoman) (cocura:51.397.32.2708))
 Direct transl.: the **burning** city (of Sodom)
 Sweet: the **burning** city (of Sodom) (Sweet 1871: 396)
 Latin: ***ardentem*** Sodoman (Judic et al. 1992: 452)

These examples show that, unlike the postnominal present participles, the prenominal ones are used to modify the head noun, so although participles are "verbal" by definition, they act more like adjectives in prenominal position. The postnominal participles, on the other hand, are adverbial in meaning. There is thus a continuum along which participles contained in noun phrases can be more or less adjectival and more or less verbal.

Mitchell (1985 i: §975–982, §1434–1436), recognizing the difficulty of determining the function of present participles, very tentatively (Mitchell 1985 i: §977) operates with a category of participles that he calls "appositive", which includes participles that are equivalent to an adverbial clause (Mitchell: 1985 i: §975). Some of the examples he adduces seem to be similar to the kind seen in (21)–(25), but most of them are constructions in which the elements are paratactically joined (see Mitchell's definition of apposition in 1985 i: §1428). The user manual of the YCOE corpus (Taylor et al. 2003) would call phrases of the latter type, i.e. phrases containing a participle head that is not part of the main verb sequence, "participle phrases" and, like Mitchell, Taylor et al. comment on the difficulty of distinguishing between the different functions of these.[12] The participles under consideration in this study have all been annotated as part of the noun phrase, but it nevertheless seems clear that in postnominal position they can be interpreted to have an adverbial meaning.

In any case, it seems clear that in *Cura Pastoralis*, at least, grammar, discourse and context all play a role when it comes to the position of present participles. The translator has to find ways to convey the meaning of the Latin text, and Alfred, whose prose is sometimes regarded as somewhat pedestrian compared to the more careful stylist Ælfric, should perhaps be given some credit for actually handling the translation well. Not only does he use the possibilities of the Old English grammatical system creatively in creating layers of embedding; he also has a good grasp of the discourse situation as conveyed by the original Latin text, and manages to transmit it to an Anglo-Saxon audience.

---

12 Cf. entry under "Participle Phrases (PTP)" at http://www users.york.ac.uk/~lang22/YCOE/doc/annotation/YcoeRefToc.htm

What also becomes clear from studying examples in their expanded context is that the older stages of English should be investigated in the context of textual transmission. In this case, it means considering the relation between the source text and the translation. The electronic corpus with its query possibilities is invaluable in giving us easy access to different constructions, but the context can tell us why they are used.

5 Conclusion

This study had three aims: the first was to describe in some detail two opposing generalizations concerning adjective placement in Old English, namely those by Fischer (2000, 2001, 2006, 2012), and Haumann (2003, 2010). According to Fischer, adjective inflection (strong vs. weak) is what determines adjective meaning, with strong adjectives being functionally predicative (new/rhematic/focused, non-restrictive), and weak adjectives being attributive (given/thematic/topical, restrictive). Haumann's proposal is that adjective meaning is dependent on position only: postnominal adjectives are predicative (new, restrictive, and receive a stage-level reading), while prenominal adjectives are attributive (given, non-restrictive, and receive a stage-level reading).

Following a review and discussion of Fischer's and Haumann's schemes for interpreting adjectival modifiers in noun phrases, with particular attention given to terminological issues, the second aim was to consider a number of examples in context, more specifically constructions with conjoined adjectives where either both adjectives occur prenominally (A-*and*-A-N), or one adjective occurs postnominally (A-N-*and*-A). The study showed that neither Fischer's nor Haumann's generalization can fully account for adjective position in Old English. Grabski (2017) suggests that A-N-*and*-A is the default pattern for such complex constructions, and relates it to a tendency to avoid heavy clusters of elements, as also noted by Mitchell (1985), and this seems to be the case.

The third aim of the study was to delve into noun phrases containing present participle modifiers. In constructions with just one modifier, prenominal position is the default position in Old English, and Grabski (2017) suggests that postnominal position is due to the modifier being "verbal". However, prenominal position is not excluded for "verbal" modifiers, so the question was what determines position for a prototypical "verbal" modifier such as a participle. I conducted a detailed analysis of present participle modifiers in noun phrases in *Cura Pastoralis*, and it transpired that postnominal position was used if the present participle conveyed adverbial meaning, and thus was more verbal than adjectival on the continuum, while prenominal position was used if the present participle was less verbal and more adjectival. An interesting finding was that where *Cura* had a postnominal present participle, there was, with one exception, no participle in the Latin original, while a prenominal present participle in *Cura* was retrievable from the Latin text. This means that the translator used the grammatical possibilities available in Old English to convey meaning which would otherwise be obscured if prenominal position had been mandatory. In other words, although postnominal position was rare in Old English, it was used productively and for specific purposes.

The present study was intended and carried out as a close study of noun phrases in context, and it was shown that context, both textual and intertextual, matters in accounting for the distribution of elements within noun phrases. More work remains in which larger empirical samples of translated and non-translated texts should be taken into account and compared to other old Germanic languages, which eventually leads to the issue of whether it is possible to provide a principled theoretical account for noun phrase structure in Old English and related languages.

References

Bech, Kristin. 2014. Non-specificity and genericity in information structure annotation. In Kari E. Haugland, Kevin McCafferty & Kristian Rusten (eds.), *'Ye whom the charms of grammar please'. Studies in English language history in honour of Leiv Egil Breivik*, 273–297. Oxford: Peter Lang.

Bech, Kristin. 2017. Old English and Old Norwegian noun phrases with two attributive adjectives. *Bergen Language and Linguistics Studies* (BeLLS) 8. 1–18.

Bech, Kristin, Hannah Booth, Kersti Börjars, Tine Breban, Svetlana Petrova, George Walkden & Sheila Watts. 2016. Modifiers in early Germanic: A comparative corpus study. Presentation at *Grammar and Corpora 2016*, 9–11 November, Mannheim.

Biber, Douglas, Stig Johansson, Geoffrey Leech, Susan Conrad & Edward Finegan. 1999. *Longman grammar of spoken and written English*. London: Longman.

Bolinger, Dwight. 1952 [1972]. Linear modification. *PMLA (Publications of the Modern Language Association of America)* 67. 1117–1144. Excerpts reprinted in Fred Householder (ed.), *Syntactic theory. 1. Structuralist*, 31–50. Harmondsworth: Penguin.

Bolinger 1967. Adjectives in English: Attribution and predication. *Lingua* 18. 1–34.

Chafe, Wallace. 1976. Givenness, contrastiveness, definiteness, subjects, topics, and point of view. In Charles N. Li (ed.), *Subject and topic*, 25–55. New York: Academic Press.

Clark, Herbert H. & Susan E. Haviland. 1977. Comprehension and the given-new contrast. In Roy O. Freedle (ed.), *Discourse production and comprehension*, 1–40. Hillsdale, NJ: Lawrence Erlbaum Associates.

Fabricius-Hansen, Cathrine. Ms. (Non)restrictive nominal modification: 'Dogs that bark don't bite' and 'black ravens'. University of Oslo. Draft for Lisa Matthewson, Cécile Meier, Hotze Rullman & Ede Zimmermann (eds.), *The companion to semantics*. Oxford: Wiley, 30 pages.

Firbas, Jan. 1966. On defining the 'theme' in functional sentence analysis. *Travaux Linguistiques de Prague* 1. 267–280.

Fischer, Olga. 2000. The position of the adjective in Old English. In Ricardo Bermúdez-Otero, David Denison, Richard M. Hogg & C. B. McCully (eds.), *Generative theory and corpus studies. A dialogue from 10 ICEHL*, 153–181. Berlin & New York: Mouton de Gruyter.

Fischer, Olga. 2001. The position of the adjective in (old) English from an iconic perspective. In Olga Fischer & Max Nänny (eds.), *The motivated sign. Iconicity in language and literature* 2, 249–276. Amsterdam: John Benjamins.

Fischer, Olga. 2006. On the position of adjectives in Middle English. *English Language and Linguistics* 10 (2). 253–288.

Fischer, Olga. 2012. The status of the postposed '*and*-adjective' construction in Old English: attributive or predicative? In David Denison, Ricardo Bermúdez-Otero, Chris McCully & Emma Moore (eds.), *Analysing older English*, 251–284. Cambridge: Cambridge University Press.

Fischer, Olga & Wim van der Wurff. 2006. Syntax. In Richard Hogg & David Denison (eds.), *A history of the English language*, 109–198. Cambridge: Cambridge University Press.

Grabski, Maciej. 2017. *The position of the adjective in Old English prose. A corpus study*. University of Łódź, PhD dissertation.

Haug, Dag. 2011. Guidelines for annotation of givenness. The PROIEL project. http://folk.uio.no/daghaug/info_guidelines.pdf

Haumann, Dagmar. 2003. The postnominal '*and* adjective' construction in Old English. *English Language and Linguistics* 7 (1). 57–83.

Haumann, Dagmar. 2010. Adnominal adjectives in Old English. *English Language and Linguistics* 14 (1). 53–81.

Hopper, Sandra A. & Paul J. Thompson. 1984. The discourse basis for lexical categories in Universal Grammar. *Language* 60. 703–750.

Judic, Bruno, Floribert Rommel & Charles Morel (eds.), 1992. *Gregoire le Grand: Règle pastorale*, vol. I & II. Sources Chrétiennes N° 381. Paris: Les étitions du Cerf.

Krifka, Manfred. 2007. Basic notions on information structure. In Caroline Féry, Gisbert Fanselow & Manfred Krifka (eds.), *The notions of information structure*, 13–56. Potsdam: Universitätsverlag.

Kuno, Susumo. 1978. Generative discourse analysis in America. In Wolfgang U. Dressler (ed.), *Current trends in textlinguistics*, 275–294. Berlin & New York: De Gruyter.

Lambrecht, Knud. 1994. *Information structure and sentence form: Topic, focus and the mental representations of discourse referents*. Cambridge: Cambridge University Press.

Leffel, Timothy James. 2014. *The semantics of modification: Adjectives, nouns and order*. PhD dissertation, New York University.

Mitchell, Bruce. 1985. *Old English syntax*, vol. I. Oxford: Oxford University Press.

OED = *Oxford English Dictionary online*. http://www.oed.com (last access 28 April 2019)

Petrova, Svetlana & Michael Solf. 2009. On the methods of information-structural analysis in historical texts: A case study on Old High German. In Roland Hinterhölzl & Svetlana Petrova (eds.), *Information structure and language change. New approaches to word order variation in Germanic*, 121–158. Berlin: De Gruyter Mouton.

Pfaff, Alexander Peter. 2015. Adjectival and genitival modification in definite noun phrases in Icelandic. A tale of outsiders and inside jobs. PhD dissertation, UiT The Arctic University of Norway.

Pfaff, Alexander. 2017. Adjectival inflection as a diagnostic for structural position: inside and outside the Icelandic definiteness domain. *Journal of Comparative Germanic Linguistics* 20. 283–322.

Prince, Ellen. 1981. Toward a taxonony of given-new information. In Peter Cole (ed.), *Radical pragmatics*, 223–255. New York: Academic Press.

Pysz, Agnieszka. 2009. *The syntax of prenominal and postnominal adjectives in Old English*. Newcastle: Cambridge Scholars Publishing.

Quirk, Randolph, Sidney Greenbaum, Geoffrey Leech & Jan Svartvik. 1985. *A comprehensive grammar of the English language*. London: Longman.

Sampson, Salena Ann. 2010. *Noun phrase word order variation in Old English verse and prose*. PhD dissertation, Ohio State University.

Sørensen, Knud. 1956. Substantive with two epithets. *English Studies* 37. 261–264.

Spamer, James B. 1979. The development of the definite article in English: A case study of syntactic change. *Glossa* 13. 241–250.

Stavrou, Melita. 1996. Adjectives in Modern Greek: An instance of predication, or an old issue revisited. *Journal of Linguistics* 32. 79–112.

Sweet, Henry (ed.). 1871. *King Alfred's West-Saxon version of Gregory's Pastoral Care*. EETS o.s. 45. London: Trübner & co.

Taylor, Ann, Anthony Warner, Susan Pintzuk & Frank Beths. 2003. *The York-Toronto-Helsinki parsed corpus of Old English prose* (YCOE). Department of Linguistics, University of York. Oxford Text Archive, first edition. (http://www-users.york. ac.uk/~lang22/YcoeHome.htm)

Vincent, Nigel. 1986. La posizione dell'aggettivo in italiano. In Harro Stammerjohann (ed.), *Tema-rema in italiano. Symposium, Frankfurt am Main, 26/27-4-85*, 181–195. Tübingen: Gunter Narr.

Bettelou Los and Thijs Lubbers
Syntax, text type, genre and authorial voice in Old English: A data-driven approach

Abstract: In the course of the 1990s, the Old English part of the Helsinki Corpus was extended and enriched with morphological and syntactic tagging as the result of a number of research projects, before the publication in 2003 of the final version (as Taylor et al. 2003). The nature and the size of extant Old English texts is such that Old English texts can be compared by genre or register (homily versus narrative, metrical versus non-metrical prose, translated versus non-translated prose) and in some cases by author (Wulfstan versus Ælfric). The question posed here is to what extent such quantitative data can inform our qualitative understanding of the language of these texts, and how properties of the grammar in combination with text-type characteristics either constrain or give shape to forms of stylistic variation. The present paper takes advantage particularly of morphological tags to attempt a data-driven, quantitative stylometric approach which includes n-grams on the basis of such tags, as well as visualizations in the form of correspondence analyses. The biggest challenge is how to move beyond the "Fish fork" – to avoid the circular bootstrapping of looking for features that we already know are significant – and to find hitherto unnoticed features that set texts apart, but that are also meaningful in that they increase our understanding of the interaction between the range of options offered by the syntax and the stylistic choices found in individual texts.

1 Introduction

The advent of digital corpora of historical texts in the course of the 1990s made it possible to do large-scale investigations into the word order of Old English (OE). Many of these investigations focused on finding diagnostic evidence for underlying orders. Constructions can be found that appear to demonstrate word orders that do not conform to the pattern of the other West-Germanic languages, offering an explanation for the non-V2, non-OV nature of later Middle English. The fact

---

Bettelou Los, Edinburgh School of Philosophy, Psychology and Language Sciences, Linguistics and English Language, Edinburgh, United Kingdom, b.los@ed.ac.uk
Thijs Lubbers, independent scholar, c/o Bettelou Los

that such investigations tend to be dominated by Ælfric's texts (c. 955–1020) due to their sheer size is usually not regarded as problematic, as his writings are original texts rather than translations. What *is* problematic, perhaps, is that crucial diagnostic constructions tend to be found almost exclusively in Ælfric's work (Koopman 2005) – for instance the stranded prepositions, particles and pronouns found to the right rather than to the left of a verb which is in its basic, rather than a derived, position. The question arises whether such outlier-constructions reflect authentic Old English or whether they are in fact very creative usages that use non-canonical word orders to do a specific job – particularly since detailed studies of Ælfric's work have shown him to be a conscious stylist (Hurt 1972).

One such job can be to fill the requirements of the alliterative metrical style Ælfric employs in his *Lives of Saints* (Skeat 1966 [1881–1900]) and in some of the homilies (Pope 1967–1968). Consider (1):

(1) 7   geseah   þær   standan   ane   atelice   sceade
    and saw   there stand   a   terrible shade

'and saw a terrible ghost standing there'

(ÆLS 31.357)[1]

The canonical order for such Accusative-and-Infinitive (AcI) constructions would be as in (2), with the object (in bold in (1)–(2)) preceding the infinitive:

(2)   7 geseah þær **ane atelice sceade** standan

The non-canonical order in (1), which requires shifting an NP to the right, can be explained by the exigencies of the metre: the canonical order would destroy both the careful spread of the lexical material over two half-lines, with the caesura after *standan*, as well as the alliteration *geseah – standan – sceade*.

Another such job is the use of rhetorical devices in order to express or heighten emphasis. Consider (3), with verbs underlined, *forth* in bold and the objects in small caps:

---

[1] The reference to an Old English text enclosed in brackets follows the system of short titles as employed in Healey and Venezky (1985 [1980]) (in turn based on the system of Mitchell, Ball, and Cameron 1975, 1979). It is identical to the TEI reference in the DOEC (= *Dictionary of Old English Corpus*, also known as the Toronto Corpus), which means that line numbers refer to the beginning of the sentence rather than the line in which the relevant structure occurs.

(3) ac ða apostoli heton   lædan **forð** ÞONE DIACON and ÞÆT CILD
but the apostles commanded lead forth the deacon and the child

forð <u>beran</u> þe ðær acenned wæs
forth carry which there born was

'but the apostles ordered the deacon to be led forth and the child which had been born there to be carried forth'

(ÆCHom II, 38.284.158; Koopman 2005: 57)

Koopman notes that the great majority of postverbal particles in late OE texts are found in the work of Ælfric (38 out of 41), and represent 35% of Ælfric's total use of particles in the texts investigated (Koopman 2005: 58). Postverbal in this context means following a non-finite verb, under the assumption that non-finite verbs, unlike finite verbs, will not have undergone movement. Koopman notes that the non-finite verbs preceding the particles are often part of an AcI-construction and/or part of a coordinate sentence; (3), with its coordinated AcIs, is both. Koopman regards the increase in the frequencies of postverbal pronouns and particles between the early and late texts of his Old English corpus study primarily as reflecting a change in progress, although he speculates that "parallelism" (Koopman 2005: 56) and "stylistic differences" (59) may have played a role. However, a closer look at the context of (3) reveals that the first *forð* 'forth' appears postverbally as part of a particular rhetorical device to emphasize and contrast the non-finite verb: the deacon is an adult and can be *led* forth, while the baby has to be *carried* forth. This is not so much parallelism as its opposite, *chiasmus*, a rhetorical device that juxtaposes structures with mirror-image syntax, V – *forth* – object and object – *forth* – V, here expressing the contrast between these different modes of locomotion.

Ælfric is known to favour chiasmus (Ohkado 2004; Sato 2012). Chiasmus is one of the factors indentified by Ohkado as responsible for the high rate of XP-V orders in the second conjunct of coordinate main clauses, rather than expected V-XP (as the result of V2). An example of the type of construction he is looking for is (4); the order of the second conjunct following *and* 'and' has XP-V order, which is unexpected; we would expect to find V2 in a main clause:

(4) þær-to-geanes <u>gehælde</u> Petrus BLINDE, AND HEALTE, AND
on-the-other-hand healed Peter blind and halt and

DEOFOL-SEOCE, **and** ÐA DEADAN <u>arærde</u>
possessed-of-devils and the dead raised-up

'On the other hand, Peter healed the blind, the halt, and those possessed by devils, and raised up the dead'

(ÆCHom I, 376. 6-7; Ohkado 2004: 169)

Note that here, too, there is chiasmus: *gehælde* – [subject] – object **and** object – *arærde*. Ohkado's quantitative study is inconclusive, not only because of many other confounding factors (which he discusses) but also because achieving chiasmus in OE syntax can be done in so many different ways. The order in (4) could easily be reversed to achieve chiasmus the other way around, i.e. as object–V and V–object, by using a verbal periphrasis in the first conjunct, like *wolde* 'wanted' (given in bold) which would leave a (non-finite) verb in clause-final position (XP-V), and the order in the second conjunct – although, in this context, also non-canonical – would then be V-XP (5):

(5) *þær-to-geanes* **wolde** Petrus BLINDE, AND HEALTE, AND DEOFOL-SEOCE <u>gehældan</u> **and** <u>aræran</u> ÐA DEADAN

Another reason why quantitative word order studies such as Okhado (2004) are unlikely to be revealing is that devices such as parallelism and chiasmus cannot be captured satisfactorily when the scope of the enquiry is the clause (i.e. comparing main clauses to subclauses, and comparing *and*-clauses to non-*and*-clauses) instead of the sentence, or possibly even longer stretches of discourse. Consider (6), with chiasmus and parallelisms marked by underlining for the verbs, small caps for the two parallel NPs of *Man* and *the Devil*, and the two mirrored PPs *by the Devil's wiles* and *by any enticements*, with other structural elements in bold (the conjunctions meaning 'because' and 'but', the use of negation to create pairs like *ofhreow/ne ofhreow* 'pity/did not pity', *wæs/næs* 'was/wasn't') and recte (the *him/he/him/he* sequence, alternately referring to God, Man, God, and the Devil):

(6) (Nevertheless God Almighty grieved about mankind's misery, and thought how he might wrestle his creation away from the power of the devil:)

forði	him	<u>ofhreow</u>	ÞÆS MANNES,		
for that	him	pitied	the man		
forðon ðe he	**wæs**	<u>bepæht</u>	mid ÞÆS DEOFLES	SEARO-CRÆFTUM.
because he	had-been	seduced	by the devil's	wiles

ac	him	*ne*	<u>*ofhreow*</u>	*na*	*ÐÆS DEOFLES HRYRE;*	
but	him	not	pitied	not	the devil's fall	
forðan ðe	he	*næs*		*ÞURH NANE TIHTINGE*		<u>*forlæred*</u> [...]
because	he	had not been		by any enticements		led astray

'The reason that he pitied Man was that he had been seduced by the Devil's wiles; but he did not pity the Devil when he fell, because he had not been led astray by any enticements'

(AnnunciationMaryHom)

Parallelism and chiasmus are distributed over quite an extended passage here, in an a – b – a – b pattern of alternating clauses, and their use is extremely functional in that they help to highlight comparison and contrast: the First Man and the Devil both fell from grace through their own actions, so why did God pity the one and not the other? The answer is that the First Man was not wholly responsible for his actions as he acted on someone else's prompting, whereas the Devil was, as there had not been anyone to tempt him.

In setting up this highly argumentative prose, Ælfric maximizes the word-order options made available to him by Old English syntax: parallelism and chiasmus are constructed on the back of the flexibility of the first position in a V2 (V3)-language like OE, and on the large Middle Field of an OV language. The flexibility of distributing adverbials in the Middle Field, before V, and the Post Field, after V, allows the two PPs *by the Devil's wiles* and *by any enticements* to sit in mirrored positions; the Prefield made available by finite verb movement accommodates the subject and object pronouns in the *him/he/him/he* sequence in the same pre-verbal position, allowing the two parallel NPs of *Man* and *the Devil* to be postverbal.[2] Ælfric's syntax, then, cannot be separated from his style (his own authorial voice), nor from the text types he employs (narrative and logical exposition) and the genre (homilies, saints' lives) in which he writes.

---

[2] Note that *ofhreowan* 'pity' is an impersonal verb, hence the object pronouns in the dative in (6), where the PDE translation has subjects: *him ofhreow* 'he pitied', *him ne ofhreow* 'he did not pity'.

2 Investigating style

The type of quantitative investigations that have been possible since the completion of the YCOE corpus will duly note the frequencies of various word-order patterns, but will fail to pick up on the reason behind the conscious positionings of Ælfric's subjects, objects and adverbials as mirrorings or parallelisms; all of which do not do so much as *reflect* late OE syntax, but rather *exploit* it. Conversely, qualitative studies of Ælfric's works may home in on his lexical choices, the use he made of metre, assonance, alliteration, and paronomasia (Corona 2008) or, indeed, parallelism and chiasmus (Sato 2012), but these remain snapshots of illustrative passages, like our discussions of (4) and (6) above.

With respect to style, discourse and information structure, work that is both quantitative and qualitative in equal measure has been carried out on peak marking and discourse-referent tracking, but, given constraints of time and space, the focus in such studies generally is on pragmatic uses of single elements like *þa* (e.g. Wårvik 1995) or *uton* (Steele 2001) rather than syntax. When faced with the choice of which elements to study, researchers of necessity have to do a bit of bootstrapping to predict which features will be significant – and this selection tends to proceed initially from intuitions and assumptions. While this approach can be fruitful particularly for charting large-scale diachronic developments (e.g. Biber and Finegan 1989, 1997; Pahta and Taavitsainen 2011; Taavitsainen and Pahta 2004), it also presents researchers with a logical dilemma. Stubbs (2005) refers to this as the "Fish Fork", after Fish (1980):

> Either we select a few linguistic features, which we know how to describe, and ignore the rest; or we select features which we already know are important, describe them, and then claim they are important. Since a comprehensive description is impossible, and since there is no way to attach definitive meanings to specific formal features, stylisticians are apparently caught in a logical fork (which I will call the Fish Fork). (Stubbs 2005: 6)

Although Fish's concerns about the relationship between (literary) text and interpretation[3] are somewhat removed from the quantitative linguistic work in diachronic investigations, the logical dilemma is nevertheless valid. Stubb's *Fish*

---

[3] "[T]hese activities [the interpretive work done by the reader] are constitutive to a structure of concerns which is necessarily prior to any examination of formal patterns because it is itself the occasion of their coming into being. The stylisticians proceed as if there were observable facts that could first be described and then interpreted. What I am suggesting is that an interpreting entity, endowed with purposes and concerns, is, by virtue of its very operation, determining what counts as the facts to be observed" (Fish 1980: 94).

fork serves as a warning that working (by necessity) from a pre-determined set of assumptions about what constitute relevant linguistic features means that such investigations may well uncover high frequencies of these features, but that such findings can be unsatisfactory because they are unsurprising. This is where a data-driven, exploratory approach is potentially useful when studying elements at the intersection of style, discourse and syntax.

The challenge of using a quantitative investigation to support a link between non-canonical word orders and conscious stylistic choices is not going to be resolved in this paper. What this paper hopes to do instead is to step back from this arena to see whether pointers for text types, genres and, if at all possible, authorial voice can be found in a purely data-driven stylometric approach, and crucially, how these are realized at the syntactic level. The question we will ask is whether such an approach can circumvent the *Fish fork*, while yielding hitherto unnoticed features that set texts apart but are also meaningful and interpretable. We take advantage of the existence of three resources: (i) the nature and the size of extant Old English texts; (ii) the wonderful resource of the YCOE corpus (Taylor et al. 2003), which has made available a substantial part of these texts as a digitized corpus whose morphological tags will allow us to go beyond the level of the lexicon; and (iii) the availability of open-source software, in this case R (R Core Team 2017), for the processing and statistical analysis of linguistic material.

The paper is structured as follows: section 3 gives an overview of the texts used in this paper; section 4 shows some results from n-gramming (4-grams) at the lexical level, comparing Ælfrician texts with similar text types (narrative and expository) by other authors. In section 5, we will take the n-gramming to a more structural level by n-gramming Part-of-Speech (POS)-tags, first by a correspondence analysis of unigrams (sections 5.2–5.3) and trigrams (sections 5.4–5.5). Correspondence analysis zooms out, which makes it difficult to interpret the results; we will therefore end section 5 by a discussion of POS-tag n-grams by frequency. Section 6 provides some concluding remarks.

3 The texts

The nature and the size of extant Old English texts in YCOE allow us to compare Old English texts by period (early versus late Old English), genre (homilies versus biography/ history), register (metrical versus non-metrical prose, translated versus non-translated prose) and even by author (Wulfstan's homilies versus Ælfric's homilies). In the case of Ælfric, we have texts from a single author spanning different genres. The properties of the sample set we will be using in this paper is given in table 3.1 (details taken from YCOE):

Tab. 3.1: Characteristics of sample set of early (o2) and late (o3/4) OE texts

Text	Period	Genre	Translation	Word count
Ælfric's *Catholic Homilies* I (cocathom1)	o3	Homilies	No	106,173
Ælfric's *Catholic Homilies* II (cocathom2)	o3	Homilies	No	98,583
Ælfric's *Homilies* (coaelhom)	o3	Homilies	No	62,669
Ælfric's *Lives of Saints* (coaelive)	o3	Lives	No	100,193
Ælfric's *Treatise on the Bible* (cootest)	o3	Bible	Yes	59,524
Bede's *History of the English Church* (cobede)	o2	History	Yes	80,767
King Alfred's *Cura Pastoralis* (cocura)	o2	Treatise	Yes	68,556
Gregory's *Dialogues* (cogregdC)	o24	Lives	Yes	91,553
Orosius (coorosiu)	o2	History	Yes	51,020
West-Saxon Gospels (cowsgosp)	o3	Bible	Yes	71,104
Wulfstan's *Homilies* (cowulf)	o34	Homilies	No	28,768

Period labels refer to the Helsinki Corpus subperiods for Old English (Rissanen, Kytö, and Palander-Collin 1993). Relevant here are periods o2 (850–950), o3 (950–1050) and o4 (1050–1150; Kytö 1993). When two periods are listed, the first number points to the period of original composition, while the second number refers to the period of the sampled manuscript in cases where this information is available (e.g. cogregdC is listed as originally composed in subperiod o2, while the manuscript sampled in YCOE stems from subperiod o4). The total word count of the current sample is 818,493 words, and these 11 texts thus cover more than half of the total word count in YCOE (1.5 million words; Taylor et al. 2003). The hypothesis that we want to test is that Ælfric's style is very different from other Old English texts, which explains why he is over-represented in our sample set (his texts make up 55.8% of the ca. 818,000 words). This "Ælfrician universe" of our sample set is not as unrepresentative of the YCOE corpus as might be expected, as Ælfrician texts make up almost a third (31.8%) of the total word count in YCOE.

A final note about spelling: the vast bulk of late Old English is written in the West-Saxon written standard, with remarkably consistent spellings. Prior to lexical n-gramming, some spelling changes had to be made: eths (ð) had to be converted into thorns (þ), merging them with existing thorns; these graphemes do not reflect a phonemic or allophonic difference in Old English and might artificially depress the frequencies of lexical items. Some spelling variation remains, particularly i/y (short vowel as in ylca/ilca 'same'). In addition, the file of *Ælfric's Homilies* (coaelhom) has seen some very light editing, with a duplicate in the text, as well as rhythmic prose sections, deleted.

4 Lexical n-gramming

4.1 Introduction

In data-driven approaches, linguistic features are not predetermined by the analyst, but bubble up in the analysis, so it is the analysis that determines which features and distributions are significant (Stewart 2006: 771). Data-driven studies may include "low-level" features like word length, sentence-length, key word frequency, lexical density (type-token ratio) and punctuation, among others. Finding frequencies of lexical strings of *n* number of words, also known as word n-grams, multi-word units, multi-word expressions, or lexical bundles (e.g. Biber, Conrad, and Cortes 2004), can also be considered a relatively low-level feature, and n-gramming routines have become readily available in online services such as Google n-grams and concordancing software like AntConc. N-gramming is particularly interesting for Present-day English (PDE) in view of claims that Present-day English discourse displays high levels of prefabricated chunks, or "prefabs" (Erman and Warren 2000). Results of such investigations, although usually not predictable at the outset, can be unsurprising in retrospect (an example is the sequence *I grete you well* as the most frequent 4-gram in the Paston letters (Wood 2009: 199–201, 206–207). Unlike investigations into pre-determined linguistic features, and possibly particularly for research into stylistics (cf. the *Fish fork*), lexical n-gramming is not so "liable to miss much of what is going on" (Culpeper and Kytö 2010: 140).

In the following section, we have opted for 4-grams, after some trials with other numbers for n; 4-grams provide a good balance between yielding informative results and reasonable frequencies. For further discussion of these points, see for example Biber, Conrad, and Cortes (2004) and Gries, Newman, and Shaoul (2011).

4.2 Lexical 4-grams of Old English texts

Lexical 4-grams of the plain text files from YCOE (table 3.1) show the top twenty frequencies of two mainly narrative texts (Gregory's *Dialogues* (C) and Ælfric's *Lives of Saints*) side-by-side. These texts are not from the same period (see table 3.1); there is a later revision of Gregory's *Dialogues* (the H manuscript) that is more contemporaneous with Ælfric, but it contains only the first two books rather than the full five, which would bring frequencies down considerably. Although the H manuscript is a conscious reworking of the C text, including its syntax, the evidence for its syntax being more "modern" than that of C is conflicting (see Yerkes 1982; Los 2005 for comparisons between the two versions).

Tab. 3.2: Lexical 4-grams of Gregory's *Dialogues* and Ælfric's *Lives of Saints*

rank	freq	Gregory's *Dialogues*	freq	Ælfric's *Lives of Saints*
1	16	& þa þa he	49	for þan þe he
2	15	þa se godes wer	24	for þan þe hi
3	12	& þa þa se	22	and cwæþ to þam
4	11	& he þa sona	21	and cwæþ þæt he
5	11	to þon þæt he	21	for þan þe se
6	9	eac hit gelamp on	16	swa swa he sylf
7	8	dæge hit gelamp, þæt	14	swa swa se hælend
8	8	hit gelamp sume dæge,	11	swa swa we ær
9	8	sume dæge hit gelamp,	11	ær þan þe he
10	8	þa þa se godes	11	þurh þone halgan gast,
11	7	& he þa se	11	þæt is on englisc,
12	7	þa se halga wer	10	on þære ealdan æ,

rank	freq	Gregory's *Dialogues*	freq	Ælfric's *Lives of Saints*
13	6	on þa ylcan tid	10	swa swa we sædon
14	6	sume dæge, þa þa	10	to þam ecan life,
15	6	to þon þæt hi	10	þa cwæþ to þam
16	5	& þa sona swa	9	be þam þe he
17	5	eac hit gelamp sume	9	on sawle and on
18	5	gelamp sume dæge, þa	9	swa swa us secgaþ
19	5	he þa se godes	8	and se halga gast
20	5	hit gelamp on oþre	8	cwæþ se halga wer

The top twenty 4-grams of Gregory's *Dialogues* give us five fragments of the typical narrative backgrounding sequences *& þa þa he/& þa þa se godes wer/& þa þa se halga wer* 'and then, when he'/'and then, when the man of God'/'and then, when the holy man'. Some of the 4-grams from these sequences overlap with another narrative device, the "reactivation sequence" that employs *þa* 'then' to reactivate/reintroduce an old topic (see e.g. van Kemenade and Los 2006): *& he þa sona/& he þa se halga wer/& he þa se godes wer* 'and he then at once/and he then, [i.e.] the holy man/the man of God.' There are seven 4-grams of the sequences *sume dæge hit gelamp/eac hit gelamp sume dæge þæt* 'one day it happened/ it happened one day that [...]', as well as *hit gelamp on oþre dæge* 'it happened on another day', sequences that have been identified as episode boundary markers in Old English (Brinton 1996: 116–143). In position 18, we see that some of these 4-grams, as well as some instances of *sume dæge, þa þa* 'some day, when' in position 14, will have been part of a variant where the construction includes a backgrounded *þa* 'when' clause: *sume dæge hit gelamp/eac hit gelamp sume dæge þa* 'one day it happened/it happened one day when [...], that [...]', a construction also described by Brinton (1996: 143) as having the function of overtly marking the background (circumstances, causes) of an event. *On þa ylcan tid* 'at that (same) time', in position 13, and *& þa sona swa* 'and then as soon as' in position 16, are similarly recognizable as narrative devices. The remaining 4-grams are two expressions explaining people's reasons for their actions in the form of purpose clauses: *to þon þæt he* 'to that end that he' in position 5 and *to þon þæt hi* 'to that end that they' in position 15. The top twenty n-grams in Gregory's *Dialogues*, then, can all be traced to discourse functions associated with the narrative text type: narrative backgrounding, reactivation sequences, overt circumstance-/cause-marking and purpose clauses explaining (people's) motives.

Ælfric's *Lives of Saints*, although concerned with the same subject matter and text type as Gregory's *Dialogues*, shows an entirely different picture. N-grams like *and cwæþ to þam/þa cwæþ to þam/cwæþ se halga wer* 'and said to the/then said to the/said the holy man' (at rank position 3, 15, and 20, respectively) bring home the fact that there is a lot more direct speech in *Lives of Saints*, which heightens the dramatic effect of the narrative. Some of those n-grams, of course, may also have been part of indirect speech introductions, whose presence is indicated by *and cwæþ þæt he* 'and said that he' in position 4. Another sign of the narrative text type is the sequence *ær þan þe he* 'before he'. There are three *for þan þe* 'because' clauses, in positions 1 (with *he*), 2 (with *they*), and 5 (with *the*). Our first thought might be that Ælfric prefers these clauses to express his protagonists' motives for their actions, where the author of Gregory's *Dialogues* prefers nonfinite Purpose Clauses (more specifically, a subset of Purpose Clauses termed "Rationale Clauses" by Jones 1991), and a closer look confirms that this is true in some cases. The match is not perfect, because Rationale Clauses appear to be more constrained:

(7) Iudas   ða   hine   bewende   and   wan   wið   ða hæðenan
    Judas   then   turned himself   and   fought   against   the heathens

    forðan ðe hi   woldon   awestan   þa   iudeiscan
    because they   wished   to destroy   the   Jews

'Judas then turned back and fought against the heathens, because they wished to destroy the Jews'
(ÆLS [Maccabees] p. 92, l. 385–6)

Hi 'they' refers to the object of the previous clause, and this appears to pose difficulties for using a Purpose Clause as an alternative: **to þon þæt hi mihten awestan þa iudeiscan* 'to that end that they [= the heathens] might destroy the Jews'. What limits their flexibility is the fact that purpose clauses are often "controlled" by the subject of the higher clause (which is why *to*-infinitives are such good alternatives for purpose clauses in Old English; Los 2005: 28–31, 185–189); a 'because' clause is not so constrained.[4] Most of Ælfric's *for þan þe* 'because' clauses, however, are part of exposition rather than an expression of protagonists' motives.

---

4 There are PDE examples of non-controlled Purpose Clauses, both finite or non-finite, in Huddleston and Pullum (2002: 727–729,) however. Note that any difference in control relations between the two types of clauses in Old English would be a further argument in favour of the more independent status of *for þan þe* 'because' clauses, as control indicates dependent status and embedding (Cristofaro 2003).

The fact that Ælfric's *Lives of Saints* contains more exposition than Gregory's *Dialogues* is also reflected in the high frequency of *swa swa* 'as' clauses: rank positions 6, 7, 8, 13 and 18 are all indicative of the frequency of this type of clause. *Þurh þone halgan gast* 'through the Holy Ghost' in 10, *þæt is on englisc* 'that is in English' in 11, *on þære ealdan æ* 'in the old law' in 12 and *to þam ecan life* 'to eternal life' in 14, and possibly *and se halga gast* 'and the Holy Ghost' in 19, are further indications of exposition.

Tab. 3.3: Lexical 4-grams of Ælfric's and Wulfstan's homilies

rank	freq	Ælfric's *Catholic Homilies* I	freq	Wulfstan's *Homilies*
1	69	for þan þe he	15	swa us þearf is
2	45	for þan þe hi	13	utan don swa us
3	22	for þan þe se	12	and we gelyfaþ þæt
4	19	ær þan þe he	11	a butan ende, amen.
5	18	swa swa se apostol	11	don swa us þearf
6	17	for þan þe we	10	ealswa hit æode on
7	16	soþ ic eow secge.	10	furþor sæde ealswa hit
8	14	for þan þe heo	10	gyt isaias furþor sæde
9	14	þan þe he is	10	isaias furþor sæde ealswa
10	12	swa swa he sylf	10	sæde ealswa hit æode
11	11	for þan þe seo	9	soþ is þæt ic
12	11	on ealra worulda woruld.	8	and þonne se sacerd
13	10	se þe leofaþ and	8	gecnawe se þe cunne
14	9	for þan þe ge	8	is þæt ic secge
15	9	for þan þe ic	8	þæt is on englisc
16	9	swa se apostol paulus	7	butan ende amen leofan
17	8	ealra worulda woruld. amen:	7	hit æode on forsyngodre
18	8	for þan þe hit	7	in ealra worulda woruld
19	8	for þan þe on	7	ofer ealle oþre þing
20	8	for þan þe þa	7	on forsyngodre þeode be

Table 3.3 shows the top twenty of Ælfric's and Wulfstan's homilies – same genre, same period, two authors. Note that the focus will be on the position/rank of these 4-grams and not on their absolute frequency, since the word count of these two texts is quite dissimilar: 106,173 vs. 28,768, respectively.

For þan þe 'because' clauses are, once again, thick on the ground in Ælfric, this time dominating the list with 11 appearances; and all 14 cases of *þan þe he is* in position 9 are also part of a *for þan þe*-clause. There are three *swa (swa)* clause fragments (positions 5, 10, and 16). All of these are characteristic of the expository, argumentative text type, and the same goes for *Soþ ic eow secge* 'What I tell you is true' in position 7. *On ealra worulda woruld* (rank 12), and *ealra worulda woruld. amen:* (rank 17) are partly overlapping sequences of minute variations in the string *on ealra worulda woruld a butan ende amen* 'in a world of all worlds always without end, amen' that closes off each homily.

Wulfstan's top twenty reflect various pragmatic devices that have been identified as typical of his style (Green 1995). Pre-eminent is what Green calls "selective inclusiveness", which he describes as "a pragmatic device to approach groups in an audience varying in moral and spiritual commitment and therefore differing in a willingness to subscribe to Wulfstan's teachings" (Green 1995: 114). Positions 1, 2 and 5 contain first-person plural pronouns, an inclusive we that frames indirect speech acts – exhortations in the guise of suggestions and assertions, because it is the business of a homily to persuade the audience to subscribe to its precepts as an act of free will (Green 1995: 125). The remaining we in *and we gelyfaþ þæt* 'and we believe that' in position 3 mostly refers to the homilist himself, whose statements of his own convictions, like *soþ is þæt ic secge* 'what I say is true' (positions 11 and 14), serve "as a way to attain allegiance" (Green 1995: 125). *Utan/uton* 'let us' is part of another favourite ploy in Wulfstan's toolkit (Green 1995: 113 finds 111 occurrences, we find 108).

Many 4-grams are text structuring devices: *þæt is on englisc* 'that is in English' introduces translations of Latin quotations; *gecnawe se (þ/ð)e cunne* 'let him understand it who is able to' is used in all cases to close off a paragraph; *a butan ende amen* 'always without end, Amen' and *in ealra worulda woruld* 'world without end' and in positions 4, 16, and 18 are used to close off homilies, as they also do in those of Ælfric.[5] The remaining 4-grams are used as structuring devices (introducing subsections) in specific homilies: *and (þ/ ð)onne se sacerd* 'and when the priest' in <WHom 8b>, <WHom 8c> (*Baptism*, see Bethurum 1957: 172–184) introduces various procedures; the 4-grams in positions 8, 9, 10, 17 and 20, which all derive from a single sentence that is repeated several times in one particular homily, <WHom 11> (*Isaiah on the Punishment for Sin*, Bethurum 1957: 211–220), introduce various subsections, each discussing a separate sin. *Leofan* in position

---

5 Punctuation marks were ignored in the n-gramming procedure for Wulfstan's *Homilies*, so as to give better results for such a small corpus.

16 is part of the *leofan men* 'dear people' of the next homily, Wulfstan's favourite homily opening.

The high frequency of *for þan þe* 'because' clauses in Ælfric's *Homilies* is responsible for the high frequency of V2-like orders in subclauses noted by Pintzuk (1999: 208, see table 3.4) (we are using labels such as "V2-like" and "early verbs" to avoid committing ourselves to any particular analysis):

Tab. 3.4: Early verbs and style, from Pintzuk (1999: 208)

date	text	main clauses		subclauses	
		N	% V-mvt[6]	N	% early V
884	GregDial (C)	87	83.9	61	52.5
ca1000	GregDial (H)	84	83.3	41	48.8
991	ÆCHom	77	97.4	43	74.4
995	ÆLS	109	90.8	172	58.7

In Pintzuk, these figures are interpreted as evidence of syntactic variation whose changing frequencies gradually morph into "I-medial" syntax as the predominant pattern in Middle English. There is, however, a clear explanation for the spike of main-clause-like subclauses in table 3.4: the predominance of *For þan þe* 'because' clauses in Ælfric, coupled with the fact that such explaining clauses will predominate in this text type (homilies, i.e. exposition). In *for þan þe* 'because' clauses, the finite verb is almost invariably in second place. They are labelled as embedded clauses in the syntactic annotation of YCOE, with some justification, as the presence of the particle *þe* is usually a clear sign of embedding in Old English. *For þan þe* 'because' clauses are well known, however, for their main clause behaviour (Ohkado 2004; van Bergen 2003), which can be understood in terms of Cristofaro's Subordination Deranking Hierarchy (Cristofaro 2003: 229; see also Hooper and Thompson 1973; Givón 1990: 528–530); reason clauses are assertions, and the parameter assertion versus non-assertion is a powerful driver of what kind of information is expressed by main, and what by subordinate clauses. The behaviour of 'because' clauses in Present-day English – as in their ability to be followed by a tag-question – similarly belies their formal status of subordinate clause (Chafe 1984: 439, quoted in Cristofaro 2003: 35). The other driver of main versus subclause systems is grounding, with main clauses

---

6 Verb movement.

expressing foregrounded events and subclauses backgrounded events; in terms of Segmented Discourse Representation Theory, for instance (Asher and Lascarides 2003; Asher and Vieu 2005), coordinating and subordinating discourse relations are aligned with foregrounded and backgrounded information, respectively; as reason clauses, and explanations in general, represent subordinating discourse relations, they can be expected to align themselves with subordinate rather than main clauses from this perspective. The 74.4% of subclauses with early verbs in table 3.4, then, is not a case of random syntactic variation but the result of a link between a particular clause type – the reason clause – and a particular genre. It also suggests that the scenario of syntactic drift as presented in Pintzuk (1999) is not necessarily the best interpretation of these frequencies, as we may need to take into account to what extent such findings are driven by the distribution of text types of the surviving texts.

Wulfstan's top twenty does not show much overlap with Ælfric's language, and this does not appear to be due to the different sizes of their respective corpora, or to the fact that Ælfric's favourite, the *for þan þe* 'because' clause, surfaces as a joined unit *forþan* instead of the two units *for* and *þan* in Bethurum's edition of Wulfstan. Wulfstan's homilies contain 20 *forþan þe/forþam þe* clauses, a much lower frequency than found in Ælfric's texts (see next section for numbers). Instead, Wulfstan's rhetorical toolkit can be described in terms of pragmatic devices (e.g. Green 1995), while Ælfric's expository style appears to be primarily one of reasoning and argumentation – an appeal to intellect rather than to emotions.

The quantitative patterns of lexical 4-grams, then, can be instructive in pointing to stylistic preferences, and help to distinguish between authors or text types. They also bring home the fact that much of the language used is imposed by the text type, which is in turn constrained by genre.

5 POS-tag n-gramming and Correspondence Analysis

5.1 Introduction

Analysis using n-grams is taken to another level if what is n-grammed are not the lexical items of a text corpus but their parts-of-speech (POS) tags (e.g. Ernestus, van Mulken, and Baayen 2006). This procedure involves first enriching texts with POS tags (or retrieving POS-tagged files from a tagged corpus, as in the current study) and then stripping lexical content, leaving only a string of POS tags per file. POS-tag n-grams, also POS grams, can be revealing of underlying structure and are therefore particularly promising for stylistic investigations, both for authorship analysis, genre classification and similar tasks (for an overview, see Lubbers 2017: 113–116). An example of such a procedure for an authorship study of historical texts is Tyrkkö (2013), in which the author presents hierarchical clustering as a useful tool for the historical linguist faced with the task of providing evidence for authorship identification using clusters of POS frequencies in Early Modern English medical texts.

Unlike most authorship studies, however, where any stylometric differences in frequencies tend to be attributed to individual style, a diachronic investigation such as the current one, which does not have identification as its goal, needs further analysis and interpretation of quantitative findings to make a satisfactory contribution (note that Tyrkkö 2013 also takes into account sub-genres and formulaic style conventions). The current study begins to address the problem, noted by various researchers in the stylometrics community (e.g. Burrows 1987; Forsyth 1995; Stamou 2008), that many authorship disambiguation tasks attempt to tackle problematic cases without a thorough overview of the uncontested contextual stylometric "profiles" of genres or historical periods in which such problems are situated. In turn, our main challenge here is finding the right balance between providing enough quantitative data while simultaneously offering an interpretation of results.

In addition, although more advanced computational methods are available, both in terms of n-gramming and statistical processing, the risk is that such methods will make interpreting the results even harder. This is why we have opted to use correspondence analysis, a statistical method with a high degree of intuitive value due to its focus on visual inspection, as a starting point for exploration of the linguistic data.

The correspondence analysis relies on the tag-set of the YCOE corpus rather than an informed choice of any particular POS tagger, which means that we cannot present the analysis as "purely data-driven": the tag-set represents a layer of linguistic interpretation. The YCOE tag-set is quite straightforward, although there are a few decisions that are not mainstream, like labelling *þa* 'when' a preposition (but see the treatment of prepositions and conjunctions in Huddleston and Pullum's [2002] *Cambridge Grammar*). The impact of the labelling choices only becomes clear after the correspondence analysis is performed and the task of interpreting the results begins. This process can still be instructive, as it deepens our insight into the impact of the tag-set labels on the results, as we will see below.

The input to our first attempt were 4-grams taken from YCOE POS files, stripped of lexical content. The n-gramming was carried out in R using the RWeka package (Hornik et al. 2007). We decided to retain punctuation; punctuation, even though largely editor-driven, may give clues about clause-beginnings and endings, which can be syntactically significant. In line with the YCOE tagging distinction between sentence-medial and sentence-final punctuation, full stops (PUSF; p̲unctuation, s̲entence-f̲inal) were distinguished from commas, colons and semi-colons (PUSM).

As a rough guide to the labels referred to in the sections below, FW stands for Foreign Word (i.e. Latin quotations within the OE text); CONJ stands for coordinating conjunction, predominantly 'and', PRO for personal pronoun, POS (instead of PRO$ in YCOE) for possessive pronoun, and ADV^T for temporal adverb, e.g. þa, þonne 'then'. Other frequent labels are N (common noun, sg. or pl.), ADJ (adjective), D (determiner, excluding possessive pronouns and quantifiers), and strings starting with V: verbs other than HAVE (HV), BE (BE), 'other auxiliary' (AX) or modal (MD). After a number of trials, we decided to retain a small number of lexical items because they were informative with respect to syntactic structure: þæt/ðæt for the subordinating conjunction 'that', þa for the subordinating conjunction 'when', and gif for 'if', as well as some prepositions. Without these modifications, sentence medial *for þan þe* and *to þon þæt* clauses would be subsumed in the same string [PUSM P D^I C], and we felt on the basis of the results of the lexical n-gramming in the previous section that distinguishing between reason clauses and purpose clauses might yield better results.

One last point to take on board is that the frequencies of the resulting POS grams are much higher than the lexical n-grams above: frequencies of part-of-speech categories will be higher than frequencies of individual lexical items (compare e.g. the tables in the previous section to those in section 5.6). The samples used in the correspondence analysis would be too small for a lexical analysis, but they are large enough for a POS-tag analysis.

5.2 Correspondence analysis: POS unigrams

Ernestus et al. (2006) and Baayen (2008) use a dataset of syntactic tag n-grams of Old French manuscripts for a number of exploratory statistical procedures to study register and diachronic variation, including correspondence analysis (CA). These studies illustrate how such methods may be effectively put to use when embarking on a qualitative investigation of prevalent syntactic clusters in (historical) texts (see also Baayen, van Halteren, and Tweedie 1996).

Like the better-known Principal Component Analysis (PCA) technique, corresponddence analysis is a multivariate statistical method for dimension reduction. Specifically developed for frequency counts, correspondence analysis may uncover important associations between variables by creating two- or three-dimensional plots from often complex and high-dimensional datasets, such as the rows and columns of a spreadsheet. The technique has a wide range of applications, from corpus linguistics (Tummers et al. 2012; Tummers et al. 2014) and forensic linguistics (see Bécue-Bertaut et al. 2014) to studies in chemistry, ecology, marketing and tourism (see Beh and Lombardo 2014 for an overview). Like Baayen (2008), we subject our dataset to a (simple) CA to study the relationship between texts and POS tags in our dataset.

The data matrices we are using here contain a row for every POS tag, with the columns containing the frequencies of POS tags in a particular text. If we regard every row or column in that data matrix as one "dimension", our data matrices can be said to be "high-dimensional". The purpose of a correspondence analysis is (1) to reduce that dimensionality by decomposing the complexity of the dataset and drawing new dimensions that retain most of the (important) information in the dataset, and (2) to display the results graphically using a two- or three-dimensional plot, with the two or three "latent" dimensions that account for most of the variation in a given data set as the plot axes. The idea is to reduce the number of dimensions while retaining as much information about the essential associations between rows and columns as possible. We will not dwell on the underlying statistical metrics here unless absolutely necessary, since our focus in the current paper is on the qualitative interpretation of the output of these procedures.[7] The interested linguistic reader is referred to Glynn (2014), Greenacre (1984, 2010, 2017), and Beh and Lombardo (2014) for more details on the methodology.

In a correspondence plot, the visual component of a correspondence analysis, both the rows and columns appear as data points which are positioned according to coordinates on new, latent dimensions. In the plots below, the labels of the axes show the two "principal" dimensions, with percentages to indicate how much of the variation found in the dataset (in terms of the differences in POS-tag frequencies between text samples) is accounted for by each dimension. For the plots in this paper, we make use of "rowprincipal mapping". In a rowprincipal map, the columns (texts) are positioned as extreme points in the plot, and the rows (POS tags) are projected according to how much they are "attracted" to these extremes based on their relative distribution in the entire sample corpus. Data points for rows (POS tags) that appear close to data points for columns (texts)

---

[7] The plots and data supporting section 5 that could not be included for reasons of space can be accessed at the following stable URL: <http://datashare.is.ed.ac.uk/handle/10283/2912>. These online plots have the advantage that they can be enlarged to view more detail (unlike the plot in figure 3.1). This repository also includes the full output, the data set and a step-by-step guide to (re)producing the data and the CA plots.

represent associations that are statistically more likely (Agresti 2002: 384). POS tags that appear close to other POS tags in the plot indicate that the frequency distributions across texts is similar.

This type of rowprincipal asymmetrically scaled mapping refers to plots where the procedure for "stretching" out the data points preserves (dis)similarities, such that the distances between the rows (the POS tags, in our case) and columns (the texts) can be interpreted in the same way that the row-to-row and column-to-column distances are compared. To achieve this, either the rows or the columns of the data matrix have to be plotted with principal coordinates, while the other set is projected in standard coordinates (hence the label "rowprincipal", which indicates that in the current case the rows are in principal coordinates). This straightforwardly interpretable relationship between row and column points makes asymmetric plots suitable for explorations like ours, as we are interested in the relative distances between texts and POS tags. The downside of the stretching of asymmetric plots is that the data points can easily crowd each other out (see Greenacre 2017: 70–71), as figure 3.1 below demonstrates. We will therefore also show zoomed-in sections, in which more detail is visible, in section 5.5.

Using the package *ca* (Nenadić and Greenacre 2007) available for *R*, a first correspondence analysis was performed on frequencies of single POS tags (POS unigrams), while retaining some lexical information. The correspondence plot in figure 3.1 below (unigrams in blue, filenames/source texts in red) is based on frequencies for all POS tags in the sample set in table 3.2. Due to text size differences, we used standardized counts per POS unigram (n per 1,000 tokens).

Not only because of our interest in the stylistic characteristics of Ælfric's particular use of grammar, but also due to the fact that his output contributes considerably to the total of extant Old English prose texts, Ælfric's texts make up 55.4% of the total word count of all the Old English texts in table 3.1. As a result, the correspondence analysis will in a sense tend to take his texts as the "norm", and measure how, and how much, the other texts differ from him. This is why texts near the centre of the plot in figure 3.1 are all Ælfric's: (below the horizontal axis, from left to right) the metrical homilies, *Catholic Homilies I*, *Catholic Homilies II*, and *Lives of Saints*. The impenetrable cluster of blue POS tags surrounding these texts are shared by many other sources in our corpus in considerable quantities, so these tags do not help us when we want to distinguish between texts. (Note that the tags in this region are most indicative of the "profile" of the sample corpus as a whole, however.) The remaining text by Ælfric, his *Treatise on the Bible*, appears at the bottom of the plot, as does the *West-Saxon Gospels*. The blue POS tags that appear in this region are particularly associated with these two texts. In the top half of the plot, but spread out along the horizontal axis from left to right, we find the remaining texts in our sample set: Wulfstan's *Homilies, Cura Pastoralis*, Gregory's *Dialogues*, Bede's *History of the English Church* and *Orosius*.

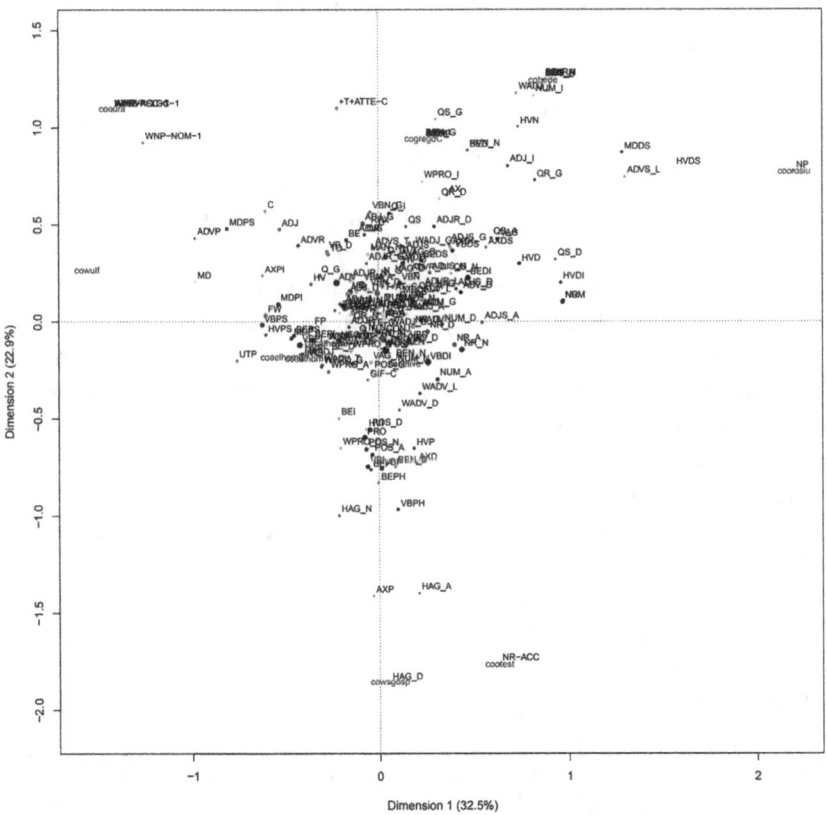

Fig. 3.1: Rowprincipal asymmetric CA of POS-unigrams in the OE sample

5.3 Interpretation of the dimensions

The horizontal and vertical lines through the middle of figure 3.1 denote the two "dimensions" that the correspondence analysis has identified as explaining most of the variation in the data. The contribution of each dimension, termed its "principal inertia" (or *eigenvalue*), reflects how much each dimension accounts for the differences between the rows and the columns in the matrix, calculated as chi-squared distances. In the plot in figure 3.1, these two plotted dimensions together account for 55.4% of the variation in the data: the horizontal dimension,

dimension 1, accounts for 32.5%, and the vertical dimension, dimension 2, accounts for 22.9%. Just over half of the distributional complexity in the sample can be captured in these two dimensions, therefore, but what does it tell us?

Where Ælfric's *Treatise on the Bible* and the *West-Saxon Gospels* appear at the bottom of the plot, we find texts such as Bede's *History*, Gregory's *Dialogues*, *Cura Pastoralis* and *Orosius* at the top; this means that they have been identified as markedly different from Ælfric's *Treatise on the Bible* and *West-Saxon Gospels* on dimension 2. Among themselves, these texts in the top-half differ on dimension 1: while *Orosius* appears in the righthand domain of this dimension, the text closest to the *Cura Pastoralis* in the lefthand domain is Wulfstan's *Homilies*.

Inspection of the underlying data on which the plot is drawn may provide some pointers as to which texts and POS unigrams are of particular importance for our interpretation of this visualization. With 190 unigram tags found in the corpus (this number includes tags with case labels), we take 53 permille as our cut-off point in the corresponddence analysis data (i.e. the point that determines whether any POS tag makes a significant contribution in terms of variation: 100/190=0.53).[8] This cut-off point identifies the following POS tags as making a significant contribution to dimension 1, either on the righthand side (positive x-axis coordinates) or on the lefthand side (negative x-axis coordinates, indicated by (-)):

- VBDI (past tense, indicative)
- VBPI (-) (present tense, indicative)
- NR_N (proper name, nominative)
- BEDI (BE, past tense, indicative)
- VBPS (present tense, subjunctive)
- NR (names without any further case specification, usually foreign personal names and place names)
- NUM (numeral)

For the second dimension, we find only tags with a negative sign (i.e. below the horizon in the plot) to have a large enough contribution on the vertical axis:
- PRO (-) (pronouns ambiguous as to case, so mostly datives and accusatives),
- VBI (-) (imperative)
- VBP (-) (past tense, ambiguous as to mood, so 1st and 3rd person singular or indistinct *-an* endings for the plural)

---

[8] This number is based on the notion that under a purely random distribution, each POS-tag row would be expected to contribute .53% to inertia (see Bendixen 1996: 28).

It is particularly these tags which may provide an interpretation of dimensions 1 and 2 in the plot (see below).

With respect to the texts, the cut-off point for significant contributions is 9% (=100/11). On dimension 1, seven texts have contributions greater than 9%: Ælfric's *Metrical Homilies* (-), his *Treatise on the Bible*, his *Catholic Homilies* I (-), Wulfstan's *Homilies* (-), King Alfred's *Cura Pastoralis* (-), Orosius and Bede's *History of the English Church*. The question for this dimension is therefore: what connects *Treatise on the Bible*, *Orosius* and Bede's *History* on the one hand, and Ælfric's *Metrical Homilies*, his *Catholic Homilies*, Wulfstan's *Homilies* and *Cura Pastoralis* on the other hand? Are we looking at translated versus original texts (although *Cura Pastoralis* will then be the odd one out)? Both Gregory's *Dialogues* and Ælfric's *Lives of Saints*, categorized as "Lives" in table 3.1, occur with somewhat similar coordinates on dimension 1 (40 and 33, respectively), an intermediate position between homilies and narrative, but they differ greatly in terms of dimension 2 since their coordinates take opposite signs on this axis (it may be observed, however, that we already noted various marked differences between these texts in the previous sections). *West-Saxon Gospels* is also close to these tags in terms of dimension 1, with a similar coordinate on dimension 1 (10), but this text has a highly negative value on dimension 2 (-320; note that all these values are in permille), and appears here together with Ælfric's *Treatise on the Bible*. The most likely interpretation for dimension 1 seems to be narrative versus exposition: the higher frequencies of past tenses and names can be identified as typical of narratives, as can numerals, which appear in time adverbials that place narrative events.

On dimension 2, there are also seven texts with a significant contribution (9%<): Ælfric's *Treatise on the Bible* (-), Wulfstan's *Homilies*, *Cura Pastoralis*, *Orosius*, Gregory's *Dialogues*, Bede's *History* and the *West-Saxon Gospels* (-). For this dimension, the question is: what connects Ælfric's *Treatise on the Bible* and the *West-Saxon Gospels*, as opposed to Wulfstan's *Homilies*, *Cura Pastoralis*, *Orosius*, Gregory's *Dialogues* and Bede's *History*? Are we looking at Bible translations versus everything else? We will see below that the answer might have to do with the fact that the text type of the Bible translations is wholly narrative, unmixed with exposition, so that the typical narrative features also shared by other texts are not swamped out by expository features.

An additional, or perhaps alternative, interpretation of dimension 2 might take into account the variable time, since all texts composed in the o2 subperiod are seen to appear with high positive coordinates in the plot: Bede's *History*, *Cura Pastoralis*, *Orosius* and Gregory's *Dialogues* (note that MS C hails from subperiod o4, but that its original date of composition is listed as o2). Such an interpretation would certainly work for samples drawn from this earlier subperiod, but is more difficult to maintain for texts appearing at the other end of the dimension, primarily the *West-Saxon Gospels* and Ælfric's *Treatise on the Bible*, since these are strictly speaking not the texts with the latest dates of composition in the entire sample. An account in terms of translations versus original prose must also be discarded, since translated texts are found both near the top of the plot (corresponding to the four texts from subperiod o2/o24), while the other translated texts, the Bible translations Ælfric's *Treatise on the Bible* and the *West-Saxon Gospels*, appear at the bottom end of the dimension. These findings will have to be explained by a more fine-grained interpretation based on grammatical/morphological features. We will see in the next section that such an interpretation is supported by a correspondence analysis of POS trigrams.

5.4 Correspondence analysis: POS trigrams

This section discusses an exploration in strings of three consecutive POS tags (i.e. trigrams) rather than unigrams. Data in the form of strings of POS tags will show considerable overlap and duplication: trigramming a string of data *abcdefgh* will yield *abc – bcd – cde – def – efg – fgh* as output. However, where the single elements *c*, *d*, *e* and *f* in the data string each appear in three different trigrams, so that their occurrences are in effect multiplied by 3, *b* and *g* are multiplied by 2, and *a* and *h* are not multiplied at all (i.e. they occur only in one single trigram).[9] This is why the sample size needs to be controlled, as even minor differences in text size would skew a comparison of the texts when creating a standardized or relative frequency. Since our sample size differs considerably (see table 3.1), a correspondence analysis on trigrams was carried out on only the first 25,000 tokens of every text sample in our YCOE selection. To check whether this sampling was representtative, an additional correspondence analysis on POS trigrams of all 25,000 token slices available in our corpus was conducted, which confirmed that our method of sampling would not be affected by random skewing because of text-internal subject matter, lists of headings, text openings or closings, etc.; some of the plots which illustrate this point can be found in the permanent data repository that accompanies this paper, as described in footnote 7. In addition to this slicing procedure, we based our CA only on POS-tag trigrams that have a total frequency 100 or more occurrences in the corpus as a whole.

---

[9] Again, n-gram generation was carried out in *R* using the package *Rweka* (Hornik et al. 2007).

5.5 Interpreting the dimensions

The CA on these POS-tag trigrams indicates that the first two dimensions account for 43.1% of the data. This is lower than the figure of 55.4% of the Unigram CA in the previous section, which means that the variation in the data is not as easily captured in a low-dimensional model (this is confirmed by the fact that the first six dimensions in the Unigram CA account for 94% of all the variation, whereas they only account for 86.7% in the Trigram CA). However, since the data matrix on which this CA is based is much larger – 11 texts by 190 POS tags in the previous CA, and for the current CA 11 texts by 349 POS trigrams with an absolute frequency of 100 or more occurrences in the sample corpus – it should not come as a total surprise that the model has a slightly poorer fit.

The Trigram CA plot in figure 3.2 below shows that the *West-Saxon Gospels* and Ælfric's *Treatise on the Bible* again appear quite close together, but now on the left-hand side of the plot, while other texts generally appear to the right of the vertical axis. The only exception is Ælfric's *Lives of Saints*, which appears on the left – here too, as in the unigram plot of figure 3.1, this text, out of all other sample texts, is closest to this "scriptural cluster". With the homiletic texts (both Ælfric and Wulfstan) and the *Orosius* intermediaries on the horizontal axis, the other end of the dimension is populated by Gregory's *Dialogues*, Bede's *History* and *Cura Pastoralis*. It seems as if, at least in terms of position of sample texts, what appeared in the previous CA plot as the vertical axis is now the main dimension in the current plot. Because the method positions axes according to contributions to total inertia (primary contributor horizontally, secondary contributor vertically), this indicates that what was the "Bible v. Everything else" dimension in the unigram data seems to be the most important carrier of information in the trigram data. The second dimension seems to point to the homilies versus other texts (but notice the positioning of the biographies *Lives of Saints* and Gregory's *Dialogues*).

The two dimensions visible in the plot show a densely populated centre (mainly Ælfric's works as his writings are our "corpus world"), and three reasonably populated quadrants. The main distinguishing POS trigrams appear in table 3.5. Although the overall picture of text clusterings in both plots – the unigram plot of figure 3.1, and the trigram plot of figure 3.2 – is similar, it is easier to make sense of the trigrams than the unigrams found near the texts in these plots: average POS frequencies only give a general overview of frequent POS used, but trigrams give a feel for frequent grammatical patterns/chunks. This is why we discuss these findings using three separate sectors of the plot.

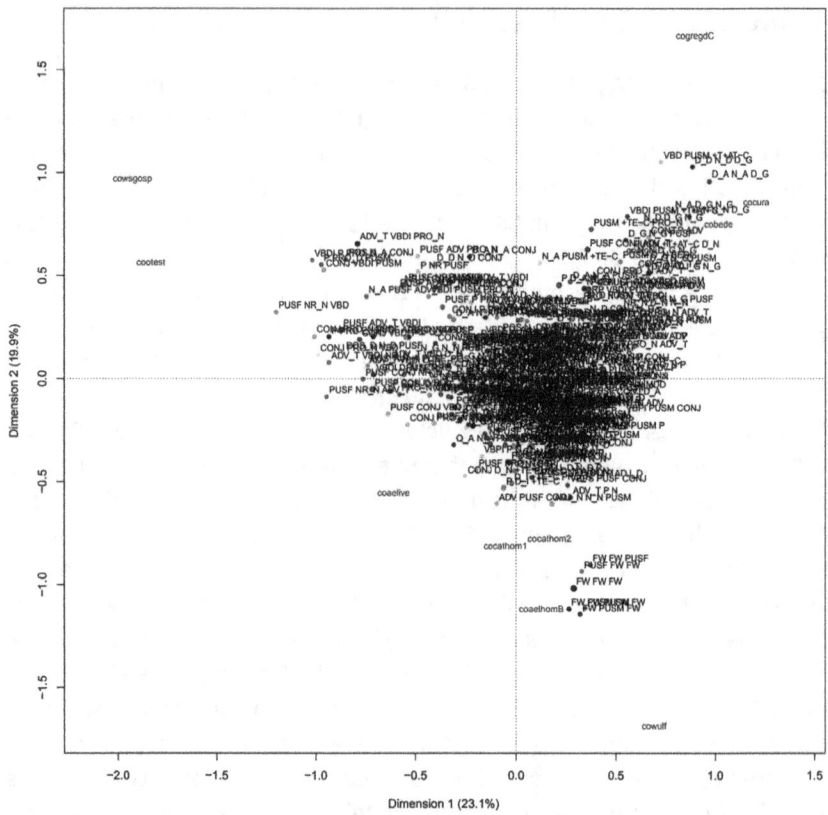

Fig. 3.2: Rowprincipal asymmetric CA of POS-trigrams of the OE sample, 1st slice, 100+ occurrences

Interpreting quadrants in the plot. Quadrant 1: The Bible translations

This quadrant (see figure 3.3 below) shows many foregrounded main clauses expressing narrative events: *þa* 'then' + verb (=V2). VBD and VBDI are past tense verbs, in the indicative: "then came X", "then happened Y". The coordinating conjunction *and* is also much to the fore. Subject pronouns are thick on the ground: these are the characters in the narrative that build long "chains" of pronouns referring to the main protagonists. All these characteristics are highly indicative of the narrative text type. Texts in the other quadrants contain these trigrams as well – it is just that the texts in this quadrant have so little exposition that the narrative features become prominent.

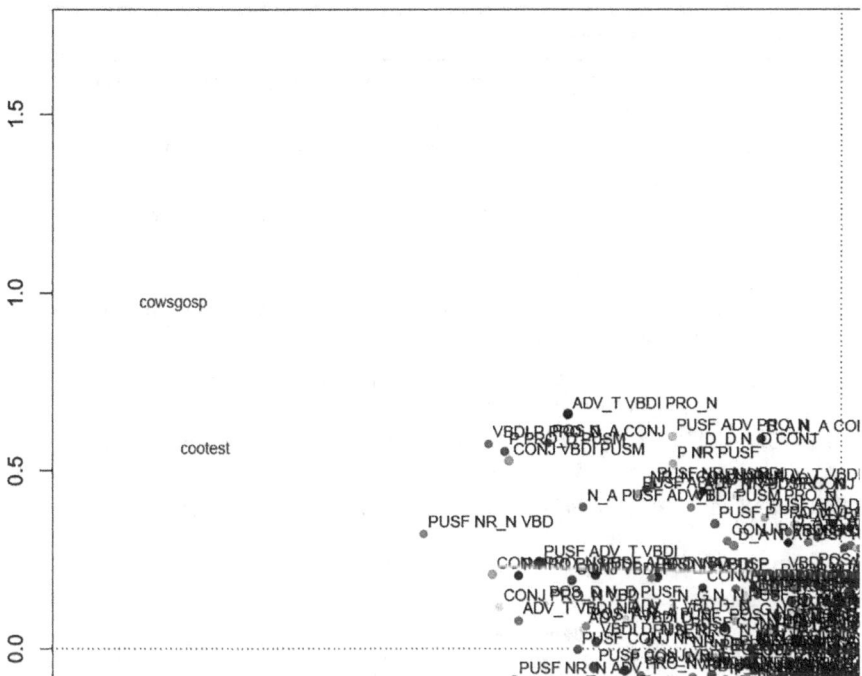

Fig. 3.3: Close-up of Quadrant 1 of figure 3.1

Tab. 3.5: Significant POS trigrams in the "Scripture" cluster

Quadrant 1: Bible	Examples
ADV^T VBDI D^N	þa_ADV^T comon_VBDI þa_D^N tungolwitegan fram eastdæle to Hierusalem (cowsgosp Mt:2.1.64) then came the astrologers from the east to Jerusalem
ADV^T VBD D^N	And þa_ADV^T genealæhte_VBD se_D^N Costnind (cowsgosp Mt:4.3.164) and then approached the Tempter
PUSF ADV^T VBD	._PUSF þa_ADV^T gebrohte_VBD se Deofol hine on þa halgan ceastre (cowsgosp Mt:4.5.167) . Then brought the Devil him into the holy city
PUSF ADV^T VBDI	._PUSF þa_ADV^T com_VBDI þær ren & mycele flod (cowsgosp Mt:7.25.395) . Then came there rain and a great flood
N^A PUSF ADV^T	Adam soðlice ne gemette ða gyt nanne fultume his gelican_N^A ._PUSF Ða_ADV^T sende God slæp on Adam (cootest Gen: 2.20.107–21.108)

Quadrant 1: Bible	Examples
	Adam truly hadn't met yet any helpmeet as his equal. Then sent God sleep on Adam [...]
ADV^T VBDI NR^N	Đa_ADV^T aras_VBDI Iosep_NR^N of swefene (cowsgosp Mt:1.24.57) Then arose Joseph from sleep
PRO^N VBDI P	he_PRO^N cwæð_VBDI to_P him, La næddrena cyn (cowsgosp Mt:3.7.135) He said to them, Lo, breed of vipers
CONJ PRO^N VBD	And_CONJ he_PRO^N asende_VBD hi to Bethlem (cowsgosp Mt:2.8.77) And he sent them to Bethlehem
CONJ PRO^N VBDI	&_CONJ hi_PRO^N andettan_VBDI hyra synna. (cowsgosp Mt:3.6.134) And they confessed their sins.
CONJ VBDI P	&_CONJ com_VBDI on_P Israhelaland. (cowsgosp Mt:2.21.118) and arrived in Israel.
PUSF PRO^N VBD	._PUSF He_PRO^N gemiltsude_VBD soðlice þære menigeo (cowsgosp Mt:9.36.576) . He took pity truly on the multitude
PUSF NR^N VBDI	God_NR^N cwæð_VBDI ða: Gewurðe leoht (cootest Gen:1.3.6) God said then: Let it be light

Quadrant 2: the Histories cluster

Bede's *History*, *Cura Pastoralis*, *Orosius*, and the outlier Gregory's *Dialogues* (see figure 3.4 below): PPs and DPs – pinpointing details about time and place, as well as restrictively postmodifying nouns in the introduction of the many characters that histories require – predominate to such an extent that they overwhelm the purely narrative characteristics that these texts will also contain. The numbers of verbal tags are low in this quadrant because they are swamped out by nominal constructions (i.e. clauses are full of nested PPs and DPs). Note also the genitive postmodification [D^G ADJ^G N^G] – some of these will have been produced by the need for pinpointing and identifying entities, but we will see that others are nominalizations; we will discuss these in more detail in the next section.

Syntax, text type, genre and authorial voice in Old English — 77

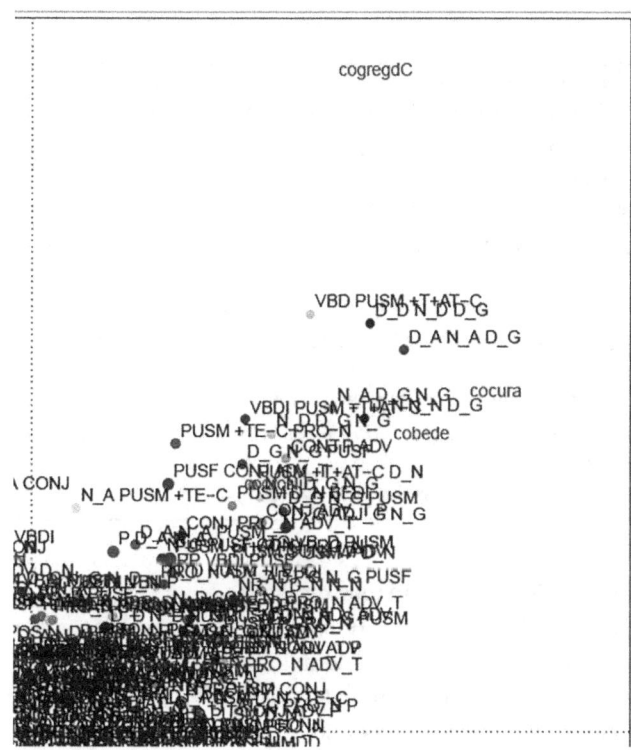

Fig. 3.4: Close-up of Quadrant 2 of figure 3.1

Tab. 3.6: Significant POS trigrams in the "Histories" cluster

Quadrant 2	Examples
P D^D N^D	þæt hi ne ablunnen fram_P þam_D^D gewinne_N^D (cobede, BedeHead:1.10.1.26) that they did not flinch from the battle
P D^A N^A	seo cyrice on Breotene hwæthwugu fæc sibbe hæfde, oð_P ða_D^A tide_N^A þæs Arrianiscan gedwolan (cobede BedeHead:1.6.19.9) the church in Britain for a time had peace, until the time of the Aryan heresy
D^G ADJ^G N^G	seo cyrice on Breotene hwæthwugu fæc sibbe hæfde, oð ða tide þæs_D^G Arrianiscan_ADJ^G gedwolan_N^G (cobede BedeHead:1.6.19.9) the church in Britain for a time had peace, until the time of the Aryan heresy
D^D N^D N^N	ðære_D^D tide_N^D blodlæs_N^N eow wære swiðe frecenlic (cobede,Bede_5:3.392.14.3904) bloodletting at that time would be very dangerous to you

Quadrant 2	Examples
PUSF P D^D	._PUSF *In*_P *þam*_D^D *worldscyrum we beoð ful oft genyded þæt* [...] (cogregdC GDPref 1:3.7.8) In worldly affairs we are very often compelled to [...]
P D^N N^N	*ða*_P *se*_D^N *Hælend*_N^N *ðæt ongeat, ða becierde he hie* (cocura CP:3.33.15.152) When the Saviour perceived that, then he converted them
D^D N^D PUSM	*Se naht freomlices ongan on þære*_D^D *cynewisan*_N^D ,_PUSM (cobede Bede_1:3.30.28.246) He began nothing profitable in the state
C D^N N^N	*þæt*_C *se*_D^N *dema*_N^N *butan ðenunge abad on þære ceastre.* (cobede Bede_1:7.38.10.315) so that the ruler was left in the city without a retinue.
CONJ P ADV	*Oðþe*_CONJ *æfter*_P *hu*_ADV *micelre tide mot heo in circan gongan?* (cobede Bede_1:16.74.12.687) or after how long [after childbirth] may she go to church?

Quadrant 3: The Homiletic region and Centre (bottom-half)

In quadrant 3 (see figure 3.5 below), near the Homiletic region, there is a clear cluster of trigrams characterized by tag clusters containing foreign words (FW), particularly in combination with punctuation tags: FW-FW-FW; FW-FW-PUSF; PUSF-FW-FW; FW-PUSM-FW. As the direction of points indicates, this cluster is primarily relevant for Wulfstan's *Homilies*, and to a certain extent also for Ælfric's supplemental homilies (coaelhom), where Ælfric uses short Latin quotes to structure his exegetical texts.

Centre (see figure 3.6 below): the more dense cluster of points closer to the centre of the plot, where Ælfric's work is concentrated (remember that his work is the "norm" in these correspondence analyses because it makes up more than half of the texts), contains POS trigrams that can be characterized as containing tags for adjectives in various case forms and coordinating conjunctions (CONJ). These trigrams are part of the expository genre (adjectives are evaluative) and add to the didactic flavour of the texts. Quantifiers – *little, much, all, some, many,* including negative quantifiers *no/none* etc. – are also much to the fore, as expected in exposition.

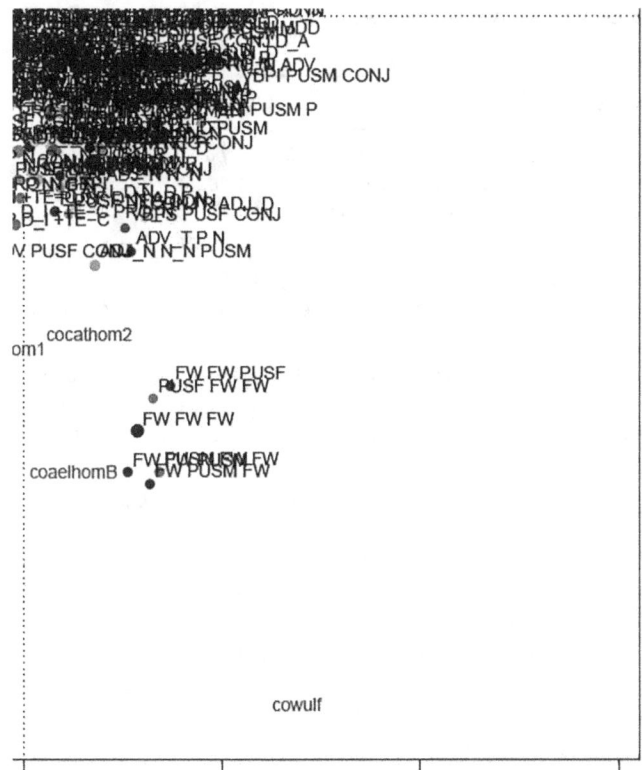

Fig. 3.5: Close-up of Quadrant 3 of figure 3.1

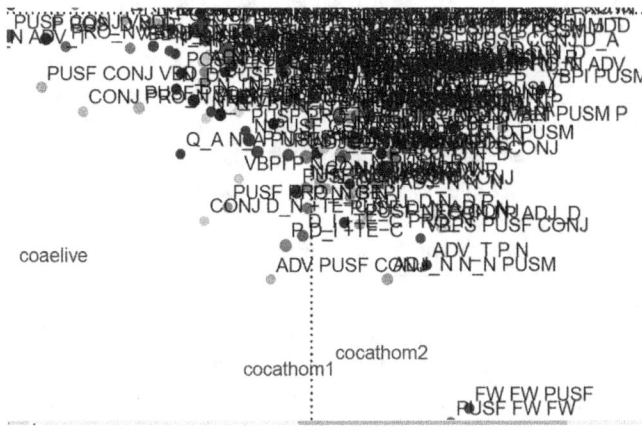

Fig. 3.6: Close-up of the centre of figure 3.1

Tab. 3.7: Significant POS trigrams of the "Centre" cluster

Centre	Examples
ADJ^A N^A CONJ	*Menigfealde*_ADJ^A *earfoðnysse*_N^A *&*_CONJ *hospas*_N^A *wolde gehwa eaðelice forberan* (cocathom1 ÆCHom I,3:204.180.616) Many hardships and insults would each gladly bear
ADJ^D N^D CONJ	*þæt hy ænig man to swicollice ne bepæhte mid leaslicre*_ADJ^D *lare*_N^D *&*_CONJ *mid egeslican gylpe* (cowulf,WHom_2:37.25) that they should not tempt any man too deceitfully with false doctrine and with terrible arrogance
ADJ^G N^G PUSF	*Sy wuldor Gode on heannyssum, & on eorðan sib mannum, þam ðe beoð godes*_ADJ^G *willan*_N^G *.*_PUSF (cocathom1,ÆCHom_I,_2:191.27.331) Glory be to God on high and on earth peace be to men, those who are of good will
ADJ^G N^G PUSM	*Forðam þonne wyrð ehtnes grimlic & sorhlic cristenes*_ADJ^G *folces*_N^G *,*_PUSM (cowulf WHom_2:52.34) On that account arose a grim and sorrowful persecution of Christ's people
CONJ POS N^A	*and*_CONJ *his*_PRO *muð*_N^A *ne ondyde, swa swa lamb deð þonne hit man scyrð* (cocathom2 ÆCHomII, 1:8.191.169) and does not open his mouth, like a lamb does when people shear it
CONJ POS N^N	*ac*_CONJ *heora*_PRO *blod*_N^N *is heora lif.* (cocathom1 ÆCHomI, 1:182.106.106) but their blood is their life
CONJ P POS	*&*_CONJ *ðurh*_P *heora*_PRO *yfel gecnawan mæg* (cowulf WHom 1b:12.6) and through their evil may know'
CONJ P PRO^N	*and*_CONJ *buton*_P *he*_PRO^N *soð God wære, noldon ða englas him ðenian* (ÆCHom1_T02160006600,271.129) and unless he were the true God, the angels would not serve him
Q^A D^A N^A	*he let faran hæþenne here & forhergian eall*_Q^A *þæt*_D^A *land*_N^A (cowulf WHom 6:115.316) He let go a heathen army and (let it) harry all the land
Q N PUSF	*ðu heolde minne lichaman wið ælcere*_Q *besmitennysse*_N *.*_PUSF (cocathom1 ÆCHom I, 4:215.259.867) You will protect my body from any defilement

Overall, the correspondence analysis grouped texts together in a coherent fashion; the impression we get from the data is that what the analysis identifies is, above all, the text type; genres may share text types (homilies may contain narrative sequences), but in different proportions, so that narrative markers only surface as significant in purely narrative texts like the "scripture cluster"; in other genres, narrative characteristics may be swamped out by exposition.

5.6 POS-tag trigrams of Old English texts

Although in its broad outlines, the trigrams of the centre appear to make sense in terms of genre and text type (the quantifiers, the adjectives), going back into the data to find examples in the texts of the trigrams marked as significant in the correspondence analysis proved surprisingly hard, and the examples themselves (table 3.7) did not intuitively feel as in any way typical of the texts. The reason may well be that many trigram sequences containing quantifiers and adjectives are shared with other texts, so that the strings containing quantifiers and adjectives that emerge as significant in setting these texts apart are not necessarily very frequent in the data in an absolute sense. In spite of the fact that we know that the principle underlying the process is sound (i.e. repeated chi-squaring of groups of cells in a matrix), it has the "feel" of a black box because it is difficult to interpret the results. For that reason, we will finish this paper with a section comparing POS-tag trigrams in absolute terms, as a companion piece to the lexical 4-gramming of section 4, but without the sampling constraints required by the correspondence analysis. The decision to restrict the discussion in this paper to trigrams rather than 4-grams is based on the fact that the results of 4-grams are sufficiently finegrained to indulge in *fish-forking* (looking whether features already marked out as special in the lexical 4-gram tables survived the swamping inherent in POS-tag n-gramming), when what we are more interested in is getting an idea of the material that the black box of the correspondence analysis is using. What follows takes as its input the entire text of the four texts under discussion in this section (from YCOE).

The first point these trigrams bring home is just how much more rigid the internal structure of the PPs and NPs (DPs) is compared to clausal word orders; verbs move around, but determiners, adjectives and nouns inside an NP by and large do not, even if the internal structure of NPs in OE is still less rigid than in PDE. Postmodifications of nouns in the form of relative clauses will also follow the noun-head (unless they are extraposed), so that in a string like (8a), there is just one slot where each word can go:

(8) a. String: D^A ADJ^A N^A þe PRO^N
  b. Instance: +t+at^D^A +ace^ADJ^A lif^N^A +te^C he^PRO^N
  c. *þæt æce lif þe he to gesceapen wæs*
    'the eternal life that he had been created for' (ÆLS [Christmas] 56 48)

Although PPs allow stranding of the P in certain syntactic environments (as in (8)), intact PPs vastly outnumber stranded Ps, so that PPs, too, make it into the top twenty. This means that many trigrams in table 3.8, which shows the results for Gregory's *Dialogues* and Ælfric's *Lives of Saints*, represent fragments of PPs and DPs; in tables 3.8 and 3.9, strings that contain at least two elements as a fragment of such a PP or DP are indicated with shading; strings in the top-twenty of Gregory's *Dialogues* that do not occur in the top-fifty of the *Lives of Saints*, and vice versa, are marked with an asterisk; the same goes for table 3.9.

Tab. 3.8: POS-tag trigrams in narratives: Gregory's *Dialogues* and Ælfric's *Lives of Saints*[10]

rank	Gregory's *Dialogues* (C)	freq	Ælfric's *Lives of Saints*	freq
1	P D^D N^D	1,207	P D^D N^D	927
2	PUSM ÞÆT-C PRO^N	987	N^D PUSF CONJ	790
3	*PUSF CONJ ADV^T	530	D^D ADJ^D N^D	667
4	*D^G ADJ^G N^G	465	P D^D ADJ^D	655
5	D^D ADJ^D N^D	418	PUSF CONJ PRO^N	652
6	PUSF CONJ PRO^N	414	P ADJ^D N^D	626
7	D^N ADJ^N N^N	407	ADJ^D N^D PUSF	538
8	P D^D ADJ^D	395	*PUSF ADV^T VBDI	502
9	N^D PUSF CONJ	323	*PUSF CONJ VBDI	495
10	D^D N^D PUSM	317	D^N ADJ^N N^N	409
11	P POS N^D	307	ADJ^D N^D PUSM	396
12	*PUSM ÞÆT-C D^N	297	D^A ADJ^A N^A	391
13	*PUSF CONJ ADV	279	P POS N^D	356
14	*VBDI PUSM ÞÆT-C	272	N^A PUSF CONJ	354

---

[10] One of our anonymous reviewers suggests using standardized frequencies for these tables. We did the calculations, but the results did not add anything meaningful to the table. Absolute frequencies provide a clearer picture of the distributional nature of our data (i.e. the relationship between frequency and rank in the frequency table).

rank	Gregory's *Dialogues* (C)	freq	Ælfric's *Lives of Saints*	freq
15	P ADJ^D N^D	261	*PUSF CONJ D^N	336
16	PUSM P PRO^N	259	*FW FW FW	315
17	*PUSM ÞE-C PRO^N	258	*PUSM ÞÆT-C PRO^N	297
18	*N^G PUSF CONJ	256	*PUSF CONJ VBD	291
19	D^A ADJ^A N^A	251	*P N^D PUSF	277
20	*P D^A N^A	247	*ADV^T VBDI D^N	268

Another feature of table 3.8 is that Gregory's *Dialogues* has the string PUSM ÞE-C PRO^N in position 17, where Ælfric's *Lives of Saints* has PUSM ÞÆT-C PRO^N. Close inspection of the texts shows that the most likely cause of the appearance of this relative clause type at such a high position is due to different editorial practices: the editor of Gregory's *Dialogues* appears to have marked *þe*-relatives (but not *se þe*-relatives) with commas, indiscriminate of whether the clause is restrictive or non-restrictive, which pushes up the numbers of the PUSM ÞE-C PRO^N combination, where the editor of the *Lives of Saints* appears only to have marked non-restrictive *þe*-relatives with a comma. The vast majority of *þe*-relatives in OE are restrictive (van Kemenade 1987), so a difference in editorial practice here is likely to have an effect.[11] In the *Lives of Saints* the corresponding tag PUSM would be missing, and the trigram would include the element that precedes *þe*, most likely the head noun of the NP containing the relative clause. As this N would have a different tag depending on the case, this would fragment the trigram into four or five different trigrams, with lower frequencies for each.

A more substantial difference between the two texts in table 3.8 in terms of nominal postmodification is the high incidence of nouns postmodified by genitive nouns (D^G ADJ^G N^G in position 4), whereas genitive postmodification has not made it into the top twenty of the *Lives of Saints*. Many genitive postmodifications include typical restrictive phrases pinpointing a newly introduced protagonist (i.e. they are of the type *a priest of that same monastery*), which are to be expected in any narrative text. What is different in

---

11 We saw similar punctuation effects when POS-tag 4-gramming (not reported in this paper), where the results alerted us to differences in editorial practices skewing the numbers for reason clauses: unlike the Purpose Clause *to þon þæt*, the *for þan þe* of Reason Clauses is printed as two words: *for+þan þe*. The effect is that [PUSM *for+þan þe* {X}] is fragmented into several different 4-grams according to what appears in slot X, which can be any number of things: subjects (pronouns versus proper nouns versus other nouns, all in the nominative) or experiencers (pronouns versus proper nouns versus other nouns, all in the dative) of the type *him ofhreow* in (6).

Gregory's *Dialogues* is the appearance of head nouns that are nominalizations of verbs, and hence have genitive postmodifications to encode an argument "inherited" from that verb (since nominalizations, being nouns, cannot govern arguments in the accusative); see *teolung* 'labour' from *tilian* 'strive, labour', where the genitive DP *godcundra beboda* 'the divine commandments' is the "inherited" argument, as in (9):

(9) a. String: D^D N^D ADJ^G N^G:

b. Instance: to^P +t+are^D^D teolunge^N^D godcundra^ADJ^G beboda^N^G

c. to þære teolunge godcundra beboda

ac	þa nearonessa	his agenre costunge	hine gedydon	þy geornfulran
but	the distress	of-his own temptatation	him made	the more-eager
to	**þære teolunge**	**godcundra beboda.**		
to	the labour	of-divine commandments		

'But the distress caused by his own temptation made him all the more eager to follow the divine commandments' (GD [2] 4.26.18)

Lat.: *Hunc cum iuventutis suae tempora acri certamine carnis incentiva fatigarent, ipsae suae tentationis angustiae ad* **orationis studium** *solertiorem feciunt*

This postmodification appears to derive from the Latin original, so that the difference between the two texts could be due to register (translated versus original prose). This observation is based on a sample; nominalizations are not marked as such in the corpus, so that we cannot easily identify how many of the 465 occurrences of this string contain nominalizations, and how many of these reflect the Latin *Vorlage*. Table 3.9 shows the results for Ælfric's and Wulfstan's homilies.

Tab. 3.9: POS-tag trigrams in homilies: Ælfric's *Catholic Homilies I* and Wulfstan's *Homilies*

rank	Ælfric's *Catholic Homilies* I	freq	Wulfstan's *Homilies*	freq
1	P D^D N^D	1,049	FW FW FW	259
2	P ADJ^D N^D	783	P ADJ^D N^D	135
3	PUSF CONJ PRO^N	568	PUSM P PRO^N	114

rank	Ælfric's *Catholic Homilies* I	freq	Wulfstan's *Homilies*	freq
4	*P D^I ÞE-C	533	PUSF CONJ P	107
5	*D^D ADJ^D N^D	499	PUSF CONJ D^N	104
6	*D^N ADJ^N N^N	498	PUSF CONJ PRO^N	101
7	*PUSM P D^I	477	P D^D N^D	98
8	P D^D ADJ^D	472	*N^N CONJ N^N	96
9	N^D PUSF CONJ	457	N^D PUSF CONJ	88
10	FW FW FW	421	*PUSM FW FW	80
11	P POS N	406	*FW FW PUSM	67
12	*D^A ADJ^A N^A	378	*ADJ^N N^N PUSM	66
13	*PUSF D^N N^N	363	*FW PUSM FW	65
14	P POS N^D	344	P NR^G N	63
15	*D^I ÞE-C PRO^N	331	*PUSF CONJ ADV	62
16	*ADJ^D N^D PUSM	328	*PUSF CONJ ADV^T	62
17	PUSM CONJ P	325	*P D^A N^A	61
18	ADJ^D N^D PUSF	324	P N PUSF	61
19	*N^D PUSM CONJ	321	P Q^D N^D	61
20	P NR_G^N	280	*D^A N^A ÞE-C	57

The high number of FW tags (for Foreign Word) shows the impact of Latin quotations, often used by both authors as text-structuring devices. The impact of the *for þan þe* clauses in Ælfric, already noted in the lexical 4-grams in section 4.2, is clear, with P D^I ÞE-C in position 4, and related trigram fragments PUSM P D^I and D^I ÞE-C PRO^N in positions 7 and 15, respectively. A straightforward comparison of this feature in Wulfstan's text is not possible because of a coding difference: as in Gregory's *Dialogues* and Ælfric's *Lives of Saints*, the complex conjunction has been coded as a two-word rather than a three-word string (*for+þan^P þe^C, for+þam^P þe^C*), following the practice of the editions. A quick concordance of the POS files gives us 495 occurrences of *for þan þe/for þon þe* in Ælfric, versus 20 *for+þan þe, for+þam þe* occurrences in Wulfstan. Using the UCREL log-likelihood wizard,[12] which takes into account the difference in size between the texts, we get a log-likelihood (LL) of 130.04, well above the LL of 3.84 that indicates a significance at the $p<0.05$ level.

As in table 3.8, strings that contain at least two elements as fragments of a PP or DP are again indicated with shading in table 3.9. Of particular interest in Ælfric

---

[12] Created by Paul Rayson (http://corpora.lancs.ac.uk/clmtp/2-stat.php).

is the high ranking of D^N ADJ^N N^N in position 6; these are subject DPs containing adjectival premodification; this string does not appear in the top-fifty of Wulfstan's *Homilies*. For subjects to contain adjectival premodification is remarkable, as subjects overwhelmingly encode given information, i.e. refer to referents that have already been introduced into the discourse. Subjects can of course be new if they are extraposed in presentational *there*-constructions or "late subject" constructions, and premodified nominatives can also be part of a subject complement; but an in-depth investigation of Ælfric's text shows that the high position of these nominatives in the top-twenty is not due to high frequencies of either of those constructions. The process of checking his use of these nominative premodifiers saw us stumble upon a use of non-restrictive adjectives that appears to be peculiar to Ælfric.

Adjectival premodifiers can be either restrictive or non-restrictive; when restrictive, they serve to identify an individual entity (*the blue plate* as opposed to *the red plate*) or subset of a group (*the blue plates* = only the blue plates, not any others); when non-restrictive, they serve to embellish rather than to identify. This identifying function is specifically called for when an entity is first introduced, similar to the function of restrictive postmodifiers. Ælfric's argumentative style of comparison-and-contrast utilizes many purposeful pairings of the physical versus the spiritual, the immortal versus the mortal, the visible versus the invisible, etc., which require the liberal use of restrictive prenominal adjectives, and these will certainly add to the high numbers of nominative premodifiers. However, his use of non-restrictive adjectives in NPs, such as *se æðela cempa Stephanus* 'the noble champion Stephen' (ÆCHomI, 3:205.195.631), *se swicola Herodes* 'the treacherous Herod' (throughout ÆCHomI, 5), *þæt soðe Leoht Crist* 'the true light, Christ' (ÆCHomI, 9:257.250.1797), *ða heardheortan Iudei* 'the hard-hearted Jews' (ÆCHomI, 15:306.180. 2904), *Se miltsienda Drihten* 'The merciful Lord' (ÆCHomI, 24:377.193.4780), represents epithets that are purposefully used after homilies where the noble behaviour of Stephen, the treachery of Herod, the shining light of Christ, the hardhearted behaviour of the Jews, and the mercy of God are the central topics. A concordance of prenominal nominative adjectives shows that this is not part of Wulfstan's argumentative toolkit: Wulfstan's prenominal nominative adjectives mainly collocate with the devil, who is labelled *wicked, hostile, evil*, and, in the homilies about Antichrist, *human* and *visible*, in addition to other well-known collocations like *the Holy Ghost, the holy church, the famous king*, and *the evil spirits*.

What is particularly striking in Wulfstan's *Homilies*, in contrast, is his use of coordinating conjunctions (CONJ) to connect PPs or DPs; the string N^N CONJ N^N appears in position 8. High frequencies of *and* coordinating phrases rather than clauses is a feature that distinguishes didactic works in PDE (Biber et al. 1999: 81) as well as in earlier English (Culpeper and Kytö 2010: 183). This is apparently a remarkably stable feature of this genre – in which case its absence from Ælfric's top-fifty may be another sign that Ælfric's style is very much his own. An example from Wulfstan is given in (10):

(10) *Ealle þa þry   naman befehþ   an   godcund miht,   &*
     All   the three names comprise one   divine   power   and

   *is untodæled an   ece   Godd, **waldend & wyrhta** ealra gesceafta*
   is undivided one eternal God, ruler   and creator   of-all creation

   'All the three names comprise one divine power and is undivided, one eternal God, ruler and creator of all creation'
   (Whom 7, 31)

6 Conclusions

This study has undertaken a number of data-driven explorations: lexical tri-gramming, POS-tag n-gramming, and feeding the latter into correspondence analyses to visualize textual or stylistic differences. Our hope that we would find morphosyntactic features clustering in a meaningful way was justified. Even features that are predictable in a "Fish fork" sort of way – the typical fore-grounding in narratives by way of *þa*-V2 clauses, for instance – reveal the influence of genre in terms of text types: histories, homilies and saints' lives can all be expected to contain narrative passages, but it is only in Bible translations that narrative characteristics are not swamped by features of exposition (adjectives, coordinating conjunctions, quantifiers) or histories (postmodification). The morphosyntactic structures found are driven mostly by text type, but text type is itself a reflection of genre – very much in line with Ariel's (2007) argument that attested linguistic features seem to be primarily dependent upon the communicative goals of speech participants produced in a certain text domain (genre or register), rather than directly linked to a set of conventions, a "grammar", which may have emerged for that domain over the years.

There were also surprising findings where POS tags signalled potential salient characteristics of genre, register, text type, and even, be it ever so dimly, of author. We have briefly discussed two: the use of nominalizations in Gregory's *Dialogues* that we traced to the Latin original, and which could hence be regarded as a register marker; and Ælfric's use of non-restrictive prenominal adjectives as a strategy for making an argumentative point, which could be an instance of his own individual voice as an author. For an author whose voice is much more difficult to analyze than Wulfstan's, and is more likely to be stylistic than pragmatic (it is hard to see, for instance, what pragmatic devices, parallel to those found for Wulfstan in Green [1995], could be tabulated for Ælfric), such discoveries are important, particularly as our ideas of what late Old English syntax looks like are to a fair extent based upon his works. The investigations reported on in this study have identified other interesting outliers, which may in time help to construct a detailed morphosyntactic analysis of his style.

A final point to make is that quantitative work of this type requires interpretation; the results do not speak for themselves but need to be made sense of, and checked. There is a lot of scope for small differences in the tagging of the corpus, or in punctuation preferences of the editions on which the corpus is based, providing what later turn out to be false leads. The explorations carried out in the course of writing the paper produced many such false leads, most of which we have left undiscussed.

References

Agresti, Alan. 2002. *Categorical data analysis*, 2nd edn. Hoboken, NJ: Wiley.
Ariel, Mira. 2007. A grammar in every register? The case of definite descriptions. In Nancy Hedberg & Ron Zacharski (eds.), *The grammar–pragmatics interface: Essays in honor of Jeanette K. Gundel*, 265–292. Amsterdam & Philadelphia: John Benjamins.
Asher, Nicholas & Alex Lascarides. 2003. *Logics of conversation*. New York: Cambridge University Press.
Asher, Nicholas & Laure Vieu. 2005. Subordinating and coordinating discourse relations. *Lingua* 115 (4). 591–610.
Baayen, R. Harald. 2008. *Analyzing linguistic data: A practical introduction to statistics using R*. Cambridge: Cambridge University Press.
Baayen, R. Harald, Hans van Halteren & Fiona Tweedie. 1996. Outside the cave of shadows: Using syntactic annotation to enhance authorship attribution. *Literary and Linguistic Computing* 11 (3). 121–132.
Bécue-Bertaut, Mónica, Belchin Kostov, Annie Morin & Guilhem Naro. 2014. Rhetorical strategy in forensic speeches: Multidimensional statistics-based methodology. *Journal of Classification* 31 (1). 85–106.
Beh, Eric J. & Rosaria Lombardo. 2014. *Correspondence analysis: Theory, practice and new strategies*. Chichester: Wiley.
Bendixen, Michael T. 1996. A practical guide to the use of correspondence analysis in marketing research. *Marketing Research On-Line* 1 (1). 16–36.

Bergen, Linda van. 2003. *Pronouns and word order in Old English, with particular reference to the indefinite pronoun man*. London: Routledge.
Bethurum, Dorothy. 1957. *The homilies of Wulfstan*. Oxford: Clarendon Press.
Biber, Douglas, Susan Conrad & Viviana Cortes. 2004. If you look at …: Lexical bundles in university teaching and textbooks. *Applied linguistics* 25 (3). 371–405.
Biber, Douglas & Edward Finegan. 1989. Drift and the evolution of English style: A history of three genres. *Language* 65 (3). 487–517.
Biber, Douglas & Edward Finegan. 1997. Diachronic relations among speech-based and written registers in English. In Terttu Nevalainen & Leena Kahlas-Tarkka (eds.), *To explain the present: Studies in the changing English language in honour of Matti Rissanen*, 253–275. Helsinki: Société néophilologique.
Biber, Douglas, Stig Johansson, Geoffrey Leech, Susan Conrad & Edward Finegan. 1999. *Longman grammar of spoken and written English*. London: Longman.
Brinton, Laurel J. 1996. *Pragmatic markers in English: Grammaticalization and discourse functions*. Berlin: Mouton de Gruyter.
Burrows, John F. 1987. *Computation into criticism: A study of Jane Austen's novels and an experiment in method*. Oxford: Clarendon Press.
Chafe, Wallace. 1984. How people use adverbial clauses. In Claudia Brugman & Monica Macauly (eds.), *Proceedings of the tenth annual meeting of the Berkeley Linguistic Society: General session and parasession on subordination*, 437–449. Berkeley, CA: Berkeley Linguistics Society.
Corona, Gabriella. 2008. Ælfric's (un)changing style: Continuity of patterns from the *Catholic Homilies* to the *Lives of Saints*. *Journal of English and Germanic Philology* 107 (2), 169–189.
Cristofaro, Sonia. 2003. *Subordination*. Oxford: Oxford University Press.
Culpeper, Jonathan & Merja Kytö. 2010. *Early Modern English dialogues: Spoken interaction as writing*. Cambridge: Cambridge University Press.
Erman, Britt & Beatrice Warren. 2000. The idiom principle and the open choice principle. *Text* 20 (1). 29–62.
Ernestus, Mirjam, Margot van Mulken & R. Harald Baayen. 2006. Ridders en heiligen in tijd en ruimte: Moderne stylometrische technieken toegepast op Oud-Franse teksten [Knights and saints in time and space: Modern stylometric techniques applied to Old French texts]. *Taal & Tongval* 58. 70–83.
Fish, Stanley E. 1980. *Is there a text in this class? The authority of interpretive communities*. Cambridge, MA: Harvard University Press.
Forsyth, Richard S. 1995. *Stylistic structures: a computational approach to text classification*. Nottingham: University of Nottingham, PhD dissertation.
Givón, Talmy. 1990. *Syntax: A functional-typological introduction*, vol. 2. Amsterdam & Philadelphia: John Benjamins.
Glynn, Dylan. 2014. Correspondence analysis: Exploring data and identifying patterns. In Dylan Glynn & Justyna A. Robinson (eds.), *Corpus methods for semantics: Quantitative studies in polysemy and synonymy*, 443–485. Amsterdam: John Benjamins.
Green, Eugene. 1995. On syntactic and pragmatic features of speech acts in Wulfstan's Homilies. In Irmengard Rauch & Gerald F. Carr (eds.), *Insights in Germanic linguistics I: Methodology in transition*, 109–126. Berlin: Mouton de Gruyter.
Greenacre, Michael J. 1984. *Theory and application of correspondence analysis*. London: Academic Press.
Greenacre, Michael J. 2010. *Biplots in practice*. Madrid: BBVA Foundation.

Greenacre, Michael J. 2017. *Correspondence analysis in practice*, 3rd edn. London: Chapman & Hall.
Gries, Stefan Th., John Newman & Cyrus Shaoul. 2011. N-grams and the clustering of registers. *ELR Journal* 5 (1). http://ejournals.org.uk/ELR/article/2011/1 (Accessed 12 August 2017).
Healey, Antonette di Paolo & Richard L. Venezky. 1985 [1980]. *A microfiche concordance to Old English*. Toronto: Pontifical Institute of Mediaeval Studies.
Hooper, Joan B. & Sandra A. Thompson. 1973. On the applicability of root transformations. *Linguistic Inquiry* 4. 465–497.
Hornik, Kurt, Achim Zeileis, Torsten Hothorn & Christian Buchta. 2007. RWeka: An R Interface to Weka. R package version 0.4-34. https://CRAN.R-project.org/ package=RWeka.
Huddleston, Rodney D. & Geoffrey K. Pullum. 2002. *The Cambridge grammar of the English language*. Cambridge & New York: Cambridge University Press.
Hurt, James R. 1972. *Ælfric*. New York: Twayne Publishers.
Jones, Charles. 1991. *Purpose clauses: Syntax, thematics, and semantics of English purpose constructions*. Dordrecht, Boston & London: Kluwer Academic.
Kemenade, Ans van. 1987. *Syntactic case and morphological case in the history of English*. Dordrecht: Foris.
Kemenade, Ans van & Bettelou Los. 2006. Discourse adverbs and clausal syntax in Old and Middle English. In Ans van Kemenade & Bettelou Los (eds.), *The handbook of the history of English*, 224–248. Oxford: Blackwell.
Koopman, Willem F. 2005. Transitional syntax: Postverbal pronouns and particles in Old English. *English Language and Linguistics* 9 (1). 47–62.
Kytö, Merja (ed.). 1993. *Manual to the diachronic part of the Helsinki corpus of English texts: Coding conventions and lists of source texts*. 2nd edn. Helsinki: University of Helsinki, English Department.
Los, Bettelou. 2005. *The rise of the to-Infinitive*. Oxford: Oxford University Press.
Lubbers, Thijs. 2017. Towards profiles of periodic style: Discourse organisation in Modern English instructional writing. Edinburgh University, PhD dissertation.
Mitchell, Bruce, Catherine Ball & Angus Cameron (eds.). 1975. Short titles of Old English texts. *Anglo-Saxon England* 4. 207–221.
Mitchell, Bruce, Catherine Ball & Angus Cameron (eds.). 1979. Addenda and corrigenda. *Anglo-Saxon England* 8. 331–333.
Nenadić, Oleg & Michael J. Greenacre. 2007. Correspondence analysis in R, with two- and three-dimensional graphics: the ca package. *Journal of Statistical Software* 20. http://ww.jstatsoft.org/v20/i03 (Accessed 10 October 2017).
Ohkado, Masayuki. 2004. Coordinate clauses in Old English with special reference to Ælfric's Catholic Homilies. *Folia Linguistica Historica* 25 (1–2). 155–176.
Pahta, Päivi & Irma Taavitsainen. 2011. An interdisciplinary approach to medical writing in Early Modern English. In Irma Taavitsainen & Päivi Pahta (eds.), *Medical writing in Early Modern English*, 1–8. Cambridge: Cambridge University Press. (doi:10.1017/CBO9780511921193.002).
Pintzuk, Susan. 1999. *Phrase structures in competition: Variation and change in Old English word order*. New York: Garland Publishing.
Pope, John C. (ed.). 1967–1968. *Homilies of Ælfric: A supplementary collection*, vols. I & II (Early English Text Society Original Series 259–260). London & New York: Oxford University Press for the Early English Text Society.
R Core Team. 2017. R: A language and environment for statistical computing. R foundation for statistical computing, Vienna, Austria. https://www.R-project.org.

Rissanen, Matti, Merja Kytö & Minna Palander-Collin. 1993. *Early English in the computer age: Explorations through the Helsinki corpus.* Berlin: Mouton de Gruyter.

Sato, Kiriko. 2012. Ælfric's linguistic and stylistic alterations in his adaptations from the Old English *Boethius. Neophilologus* 96. 631–640.

Skeat, Walter W. 1966 [1881–1900]. *Ælfric's Lives of Saints: Being a set of sermons on saints' days formerly observed by the English church* (Early English Text Society Original Series, nos. 76, 82, 94 & 114). London: N. Trübner for the Early English Text Society.

Stamou, Constantina. 2008. Stylochronometry: Stylistic development, sequence of composition, and relative dating. *Literary and Linguistic Computing* 23 (2). 181–199.

Steele, Felicia J. 2001. *Ælfric's* Catholic Homilies*: Discourse and the construction of authority.* Austin, TX: University of Texas at Austin, PhD dissertation.

Stewart, Larry L. 2006. Computational stylistics. In Keith Brown (ed.), *Encyclopedia of Language & Linguistics*, 2nd edn., 769–775. Amsterdam: Elsevier.

Stubbs, Michael. 2005. Conrad in the computer: Examples of quantitative stylistic methods. *Language and Literature* 14 (1). 5–24.

Taavitsainen, Irma & Päivi Pahta (eds.). 2011. *Medical writing in Early Modern English.* Cambridge: Cambridge University Press.

Taylor, Ann, Anthony Warner, Susan Pintzuk & Frank Beths. 2003. *The York-Toronto-Helsinki parsed corpus of Old English prose.* Electronic texts and manuals available from the Oxford Text Archive. http://www-users.york.ac.uk/~lang22/YCOE/YcoeHome.htm (Accessed 8 June 2017)

Tummers, Jose, Dirk Speelman & Dirk Geeraerts. 2012. Multiple correspondence analysis as heuristic tool to unveil confounding variables in corpus linguistics. In *Proceedings of the 11th International Conference on the Statistical Analysis of Textual Data*, 923–936. Liège: Presses Universitaires de Louvain.

Tummers, Jose, Dirk Speelman & Dirk Geeraerts. 2014. Spurious effects in variational corpus linguistics: Identification and implications of confounding. *International Journal of Corpus Linguistics* 19 (4). 478–504.

Tyrkkö, Jukka. 2013. Exploring part-of-speech profiles and authorship attribution in Early Modern medical texts. In Andreas H. Jucker, Daniela Landert, Annina Seiler & Nicole Studer-Joho (eds.), *Meaning in the history of English: Words and texts in context*, 185–210. Amsterdam: John Benjamins.

Wårvik, Brita. 1995. Peak-marking in Old English narrative. In Brita Wårvik, Sanna-Kaisa Tanskanen & Risto Hiltunen (eds.), *Organization in discourse: Proceedings from the Turku Conference (Anglicana Turkuensia, 14)*, 549–558. Turku: University of Turku.

Wood, Johanna L. 2009. Structures and expectations: A systematic analysis of Margaret Paston's formulaic and expressive language. *Journal of Historical Pragmatics* 10 (2). 187–214.

Yerkes, David. 1982. *Syntax and style in Old English: A comparison of the two versions of Wærferth's translation of Gregory's Dialogues.* Binghamton: Center for Medieval & Early Renaissance Studies.

Belén Méndez-Naya
The intensifier system of the *Ormulum* and the interplay of micro-level and macro-level contexts in linguistic change

Abstract: This study offers an analysis of the intensifier system of the Middle English *Ormulum*, and explores the role both micro-level (i.e. linguistic) and macro-level contexts (here language contact) play in its configuration and development. At the micro-level it is argued that the emergence of degree meanings is triggered by the reinterpretation of adverbs in specific linguistic contexts. At the macro-level, norsification is shown to be an important feature of Orm's intensifier system, both as regards the inventory of intensifiers itself, with the inclusion of some Norse-derived items, and as regards the frequency and distribution of particular intensifiers, since some native forms appear to be bolstered by their Scandinavian cognates.

1 Introduction

The present article provides a detailed study of the intensifier system of the *Ormulum*, and shows how the notion of context is key to its configuration and development.[1] *Context* is here understood both as linguistic context at the micro-level, that is, the text immediately surrounding the construction at issue, and more generally as macro-level context, including specific contexts of situation, like multilingual settings and language-contact areas. At the micro-level, I discuss how the emergence of new intensifying meanings and functions is triggered by the reinterpretation of certain adverbs as expressions of degree in very specific

---

[1] I wish to thank Sara Pons-Sanz for her valuable comments on an earlier version of this article, and particularly for discussion on Scandinavian influence. Thanks are also due to Elizabeth C. Traugott and an anonymous reviewer for their insightful comments, and to the editors of this volume for their helpful suggestions. This research is funded by the National Programme for Excellence in Scientific and Technical Research (grant FFI2017-86884-P) and the Regional Government of Galicia, Directorate General for Scientific and Technological Promotion (grants ED431D 2017/09 and ED431B 2017/12).

Belén Méndez-Naya, University of Santiago de Compostela, Department of English and German, Santiago de Compostela, Spain, belen.mendez@usc.es

https://doi.org/10.1515/9783110682564-004

linguistic contexts and provide relevant examples from Orm's work. The notion of *context*, now understood at the macro-level, is also central to the understanding of the intensifier system of the *Ormulum*, a text produced in the language-contact region of the Danelaw, and perhaps the first Middle English text to show heavy Scandinavian influence in its grammar and lexis. Norsification is a notable feature of Orm's intensifier system: on the one hand, as regards the inventory of intensifiers itself, since it includes some Norse-derived items, and, on the other hand, as regards their rate of occurrence and distribution, since the frequency of some native forms is bolstered by their Scandinavian cognates.

The article is organized as follows: section 2 is an introduction to the lexico-grammatical category of intensifiers, while section 3 provides some necessary background on the *Ormulum* itself. Section 4 describes the intensifier system in this text and shows Orm's innovativeness as compared to other contemporary sources. The relevance of context for Orm's intensifier system, both at the micro- and macro-level, is discussed in detail in section 5. Section 6 summarizes the main findings of the study.

2 Intensifiers and change

The term "intensifier" has been understood in different ways in the literature. In the present study it is restricted to adverbial elements (e.g. *completely* in *completely stupid*, but not the corresponding intensifying adjective *complete* in *a complete idiot*), which scale the quality expressed by the modified item upwards of an established norm (Huddleston and Pullum et al. 2002: 585).[2] Two types of intensifier can be distinguished: boosters, which indicate a high degree (*very cold*), and maximizers, which express the highest point on a scale (*absolutely brilliant*). Boosters are scalar modifiers and collocate with unbounded heads.[3] In the case of adjectives, these are conceptualized in terms of more or less, e.g. *very cold*, *very*

---

[2] These items are also known as "amplifiers" (see e.g. Quirk et al. 1985: 589). The label intensifier has also been used in an even broader way to include "any device [adjectives, adverbs, syntactic forms, repetitions] that scales a quality, whether up or down or somewhere between the two" (Bolinger 1972: 17). Note that the term has also been commonly employed for a totally different concept, as in König and Siemund (1999), for the precursors of the *self*-reflexives.

[3] The concept of boundedness has to do with the presence or absence of boundaries (Paradis 2001). Bounded adjectives are those which are "associated with a boundary which has to be reached for the property to be present" (Davidse and Breban 2019: 341), while unbounded adjectives are inherently located on a scale and do not involve a boundary.

tall. Maximizers, by contrast, combine with bounded heads, either expressing an extreme value (e.g. extreme adjectives, as in *absolutely brilliant*) or those conceptualized in terms of either/or (limit adjectives, e.g. *absolutely true*). Degree adverbs are generally harmonic with their head as regards boundedness (Paradis's "boundedness hypothesis", see e.g. Paradis 2008). Occasional mismatches between the configurations of modifier and head may, however, occur, as in *very true* or *completely good* (Traugott 2007). Intensifiers can also collocate with verbs (*absolutely adore*), prepositional phrases (*totally against divorce*), and noun phrases (*quite the opposite*).

The study of intensifiers has been a very popular object of research for over a century now from early twentieth century references (e.g. Stoffel 1901; Borst 1902) to recently published ones (e.g. Breban and Davidse 2016). Various approaches have been taken to the analysis of these items, ranging from studies of a traditional, philological nature, perspectives embracing grammaticalization and sociolinguistics, as well as corpus-based approximations. One of the aspects most frequently noted is this category's enormous capacity for renewal (Hopper and Traugott 2003: 122; Brinton and Arnovik 2006: 82),[4] which identifies intensifiers as one of the most prominent areas of contemporary grammatical change in English (Brinton and Arnovik 2006: 441). In an influential observation, Bolinger claims that intensifiers afford "a picture of fevered invention and competition that would be hard to come by elsewhere" (1972: 18); the key issue here is expressiveness, the loss of this through frequent use, and the regaining of it by means of new expressions.

Intensifiers evolve through a variety of different processes. Innovations sometimes derive from language contact and enter the language through borrowing of foreign items. A recent example of this is the intensifier (or intensifying prefix) *uber*, discussed in Hoffmann (2009: 297–299) and illustrated in (1). This new English intensifier originates in the German prefix *über-* 'over', e.g. *überglücklig* 'very happy' (Lenker 2008: 248; see OED s.v. *uber-* prefix 2, acc. to OED from *Übermensch*; see also *Urban dictionary* s.v. *uber*):

(1) *The Daily Mail "contrasted this to her ex, this **uber** rich Mick Jagger".* (COCA, 2013, SPOK)

---

4 The concept of renewal has been revised and refined in a recent article by Reinöhl and Himmelmann (2017). Here I use it in its more descriptive sense to refer to a different way of saying the same thing (as in Hopper and Traugott 2003: 122, a regular concomitant of grammaticalization, and not as a distinct process.

Yet, the most important process giving rise to new intensifiers is internal to the language itself. From a historical point of view, intensifiers are typically recruited in lexis, especially among manner adverbs. The abundant literature on intensification in English has identified a number of lexical sources for English degree adverbs (see Peters 1994), which are also relevant cross-linguistically. Among the most salient ones are the following: adverbs denoting a positive quality or emotion (e.g. *well worth*), astonishment (e.g. *wonderfully rich*), veracity (*very/really/truly happy*), a negative quality or emotion (*terribly sorry*), the idea of death (*dead(ly) serious*), strength (*strongly critical*), quantitative adverbs expressing absoluteness or abundance (*completely absurd*), spatial notions (*downright good*), and taboo words (*fucking crazy*). Over time these adverbs lose at least part of their lexical content while taking on a more abstract and relational meaning, that of degree. Some scholars recognize here a process of delexicalization (or loss of this lexical meaning, e.g. Partington 1993; Lorenz 2002). However, elsewhere I have preferred to see this as a process of grammaticalization (Méndez-Naya 2003), in that semantic bleaching is accompanied by the acquisition of a new more abstract meaning, a "purely scalar function, i.e. with no semantic load other than that of grading" (Lorenz 1999: 97), one which is more centred on the speaker (i.e. subjectification, Traugott 1982). This change in meaning is concomitant with a number of structural cues, such as changes in scope or in position (e.g. fixation in premodifier position) and the loss of characteristics of the adverbial class (e.g. the ability to be marked for the comparative, etc. indicating decategorialization, Hopper 1991: 22). In some cases, the original lexical meaning of intensifiers is reflected in their distribution, particularly in their favoured collocations and in their semantic prosody (thus illustrating another characteristic of grammaticalization, persistence, Hopper 1991: 22). A clear example of this is *terribly*, an originally negatively connoted adverb, which even today is more commonly found with negative (e.g. *terribly sorry*) than with positive adjectival heads (*terribly good*) (Lorenz 2002: 144–145). Besides, some degree adverbs experience an extension in the types of collocates they can cooccur with (e.g. verbs, adjectives, adverbs, prepositional phrases), thus illustrating host-class expansion (Himmelmann 2004).

Old and new intensifiers compete for space (layering, Hopper 1991: 22) and this competition "allows, even encourages, the recession or loss of older forms" (Hopper and Traugott 2003: 124; see also Hundt 2014: 5 on the demise of constructions). Consistent with a pattern of loss, receding intensifiers show "distributional fragmentation" (Leech et al. 2009: 81): older degree adverbs retreat to certain kinds of discourse (e.g. *full* survives in poetry, see Bolinger 1972: 22) or to specific collocations (*precious few*, but no longer *precious hot*, see Bolinger 1972: 18). Occasionally old intensifiers are "recycled" (Ito and Tagliamonte 2003), as in the case of *well*, which was common in Old English, survived in fixed collocations (e.g. *well aware*), and is now one of the main intensifiers of teenager language in the British Isles (e.g. *well wicked*, see Paradis 2000; Palacios and Núñez-Pertejo 2012, among others).

Competition is particularly intense in transitional periods like Middle English, with its radical morphosyntactic changes. In the Middle English period, alongside the favourite *full*, we find the outgoing *swiþe*, the newcomer *right* and, at the very end of the period, the first instances of *very*. Unrivalled until the late twentieth century, *very* is now being displaced by *really* at a different pace across the different age groups and varieties of English (see Ito and Tagliamonte 2003; Tagliamonte 2008; D'Arcy 2015, among others). The waves of renewal among the most salient intensifiers in the history of English are represented in table 4.1. Here the most frequent items in each period are represented in capital letters. In the table Modern English spellings are used for convenience.

Tab. 4.1: Top intensifiers in the history of English

OE	ME	ModE	PDE	(late 20th c., 21st c.)
SWIÞE	FULL	VERY	VERY	REALLY
full	swiþe	full	really	very
well	well	right		
	right			
	very			

3 The *Ormulum*

The *Ormulum* is an early Middle English poem containing paraphrases of the Gospel readings used in the mass, together with their exegesis in homiletic form. The text was written by Orm, an Augustinian monk bearing a Scandinavian name.[5] The material that has come down to us contains 32 homilies in some 20,000 verse lines (Pons-Sanz 2015: 552), far from the original plan, which aimed at covering

---

5 Whereas there are many instances of Scandinavian influence in the text, it cannot be determined beyond doubt that the author was in fact Scandinavian. As noted by Page (1971: 192), a Norse name is itself not sufficient proof of Scandinavian ancestry.

the 242 Gospel texts read throughout the church calendar (as is clear from the author's *Dedication*). The text is preserved in a single autograph manuscript (Oxford, Bodleian Library, MS Junius 1) which was probably intended as a workshop draft (Burchfield 1956: 57). The manuscript has been dated to the late twelfth century (c. 1180) and located in Southwest Lincolnshire (Parkes 1983), within the focal area of Scandinavian influence (Samuels 1985: 269). Due to its early date of composition and its Lincolnshire provenance, the *Ormulum* is one of the crucial texts to document the linguistic changes taking place in the transition from Old to Middle English, and an essential source of evidence for the language in the Danelaw area.[6]

Its linguistic interest contrasts with its questionable literary quality: many have commented on its cumbersome style, full of repetitions and otiose words (Bennett and Smithers 1968: 174; Bennett 1986: 32; Denison 1981: 44), even though some scholars have also recently pointed out its "literary merits", which link it to the Old English verse homiletic tradition (McMullen 2014: 259).

One of the most widely discussed aspects of the *Ormulum* is its idiosyncratic phonetic spelling, which serves as evidence for phonological developments under way in the early Middle English period (see e.g. Anderson and Britton 1999). A further commonly noted aspect is Scandinavian influence: the *Ormulum* has been regarded as "the first Middle English text to show heavy norsification" (Miller 2012: 115), with over two hundred Scandinavian borrowings (Durkin 2014: 182–183; see Brate 1885), alongside a number of loanwords from other sources such as French and Low German. Also remarkable is the fact that much of Orm's vocabulary is not documented in any earlier sources, and thus the text provides many first attestations for OED and MED entries (Denison 1981:41).

Despite its early date of composition, the *Ormulum* displays a very advanced morphological system, with virtually no traces of grammatical gender and adjectival inflection, the complete *th*-paradigm of the third-person plural personal pronoun, and the almost total regularization of the plural inflection of nouns to *-es* (see e.g. Bennett and Smithers 1968: 362–363). These grammatical features have been associated with Old Norse (Miller 2012: 128–129, 133), acting either as a catalyst for ongoing developments (e.g. inflectional loss) or as a source for new forms (e.g. the pronouns *they/their/them*).[7] Alongside these morphological

---

[6] For a bibliography of the *Ormulum* see http://www.orrmulum.net/orrmulum_site.html. See also Pons-Sanz (2015) for a list of linguistic studies based on this text.

[7] Third person plural pronouns in *th-* (*they, them, their*) have traditionally been considered to be borrowings from Old Norse. Recent research by Cole (2018), however, convincingly shows that they can be traced back to the Old English set of demonstratives via reanalysis.

innovations, Orm's linguistic system also illustrates a number of important syntactic developments, such as the introduction of new conjunctions (e.g. *as if* OED s.v. *as* adv. and conj. P1 a; *þohh* 'though', Blake 1992: 12), the use of pleonastic *þat* with conjunctions (e.g. *ʒif þatt* 'if', Rissanen 1999: 303), phrasal verbs (Denison 1981), phrasal genitives (e.g. *þurrh þe Laferrd Cristess dæþ* 'through the Lord Christ's death', Miller 2012: 135), as well as changes in word order, with the establishment of SVO (Trips 2003). Interestingly, some of these syntactic features have also been linked to Scandinavian influence (Miller 2012: 134–145).[8]

As seen above, degree adverbs are, by definition, prone to innovation and replacement, expressivity lying at the very core of intensification. We now turn to the analysis of the intensifier system in the *Ormulum*. In the remainder of the study I will address the following questions: (i) whether the *Ormulum* is as linguistically advanced in terms of its intensifier system as has been shown to be in other areas of grammar; (ii) which mechanisms play a role in the make-up of the system, both internal (e.g. grammaticalization), and contact-induced (e.g. Norse influence), this leading us to consider the importance of context both at the micro-level of the text and co-text, and at a broader macro-level involving language contact in what was once a bilingual setting.

4 Intensifiers in the *Ormulum*

4.1 The inventory

The present study of the *Ormulum* is based on data drawn from *The Penn-Helsinki Parsed Corpus of Middle English* (PPCME2), which contains a lengthy extract from this work (totalling 82,970 words; the complete text has c. 110,000 words). I have followed a bottom-up method, reading the text in order to identify the intensifiers and subsequently collating my results with the list of degree adverbs provided by Fettig (1934: 11) for the whole text. I subsequently ran concordances using WordSmith Tools 6.0 (Scott 2012) in order to analyze the intensifiers identified during the bottom-up procedure. 604 tokens of adverbs of degree were recorded in the PPCME2 extract, modifying both adjectives and adverbs (that is, in degree

---

[8] While it is clear that Old Norse has influenced English on different levels, there are no grounds to regard English as a Scandinavian language (as claimed by Emonds and Faarlund 2014). See Bech and Walkden (2015) for a critique of this claim.

modifier function), and verbal heads (degree adjunct function).[9] The inventory and distribution of intensifiers in the *Ormulum* is set out in figure 4.1:[10]

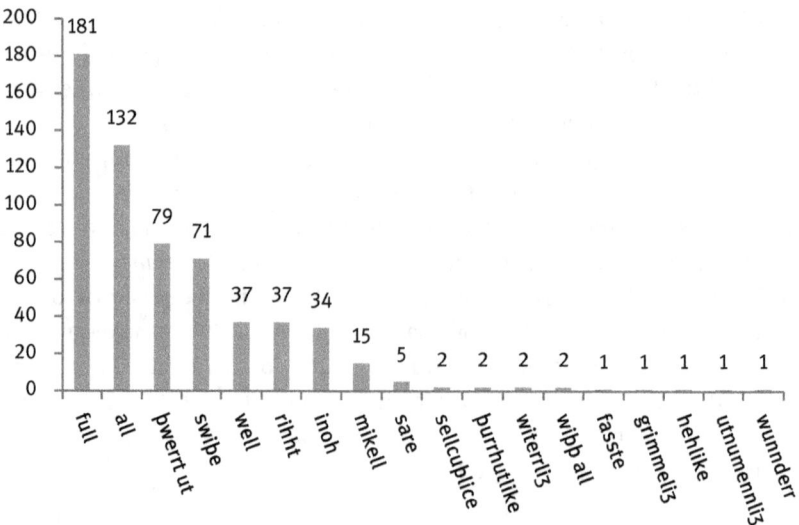

Fig. 4.1: Inventory and distribution of intensifiers in the PPCME2 sample of the *Ormulum* (raw numbers)

As can be seen in figure 4.1, 18 different intensifiers were recorded in the text. The inventory contains all the adverbs listed by Fettig (1934: 11) plus four additions: *fasste*, *sare*, *witerrliʒ*, and *wiþþ all*.[11] Seven out of these 18 present a high token frequency, with over 30 occurrences; these are, in order of decreasing frequency, *full*, *all*, *þwerrt ut*, *swiþe*, *well*, *rihht*, and *inoh*. The list contains boosters, which convey a high degree on the scale, such as *full*, *swiþe*, and *inoh*,[12] along with maximizers, which indicate the upper extreme of a scale, such as *all* and *þwerrt ut*.

---

9 Functions of degree adverbs, according to Huddleston and Pullum et al. (2002: 583, 720).
10 In figure 4.1, table 4.2 and whenever the *Ormulum* is referred to, the spellings of the relevant intensifiers are those which are recorded in this text. Elsewhere I will use modern spellings, with the exception of *swiþe*, for which <þ> will be kept.
11 Note that my figures are not directly comparable with Fettig's, since he uses the complete text of the *Ormulum*.
12 The primary meaning of *inoh* (PDE *enough*) in Middle English was 'very, very much, extremely' (MED s.v. *inough* adv. a). See also OED s.v. *enough* adj. (and n.) and adv. B.2.c.

We also find items wavering between the two interpretations, such as *rihht* (see Méndez-Naya 2007).

The degree adverbs occurring in the *Ormulum* go back to well attested source domains (see section 2 above). Thus, we find adverbs denoting positive evaluation (*well*), adverbs expressing fullness, absoluteness or abundance (*all, full, inoh* 'abundantly'), and adverbs indicating extreme dimensions (*hehlike* 'highly', *mikell* 'greatly'). Also present are the ideas of astonishment (*sellcuþlike* 'strangely', *wunnderr* 'wonderfully'), veracity (*witerrliʒ* 'plainly, evidently, truly'), and strength (*swiþe* 'strongly', *fasste* 'firmly', *grimmeliʒ* 'fiercely, terribly', *sare* 'sorely'). Finally, the inventory contains some intensifiers originating in spatial notions, like *rihht* 'right',[13] *þurrhutlike* 'throughout', *þwerrt ut* 'throughout', *utnumennliʒ* 'extraordinary' (lit. 'out-taken-ly'), and *wiþþ all* 'thoroughly'.

As noted in section 3, the *Ormulum* is linguistically very innovative from both lexical and grammatical viewpoints. Intensifiers straddle lexis and grammar, so the question to be addressed now is whether the intensifier system in the text can be regarded as innovative in itself and as compared to contemporary twelfth-century works as represented in the Helsinki Corpus (HC) and reported on in Fettig (1934).

4.2 Time-depth

The first step here was to establish the time-depth of the degree adverbs identified in the *Ormulum* material, as summarized in table 4.2, with information from the relevant literature and the standard historical dictionaries. As can be seen, eight of the intensifiers attested in the *Ormulum* were already in use as such in the Old English period, while the other ten seem to be Middle English innovations. So, some of Orm's additions to the paradigm are adverbs which were extant in Old English, but which developed a new degree reading in the Middle English period, as with *fasste*,[14] *grimmeliʒ*, and *rihht*. On the other hand, we also find new

---

13 The original meaning of *right* has to do with direction or position 'straight', and from there it develops a moral sense 'good, correct', i.e. positive evaluation, cf. Peters (1993: 129). Another extension of the spatial sense is 'precisely, exactly'; this latter sense is a likely source for the intensifying meaning (Méndez-Naya 2007).

14 The DOE entry for *fæste* suggests that this adverb could have had some maximizer readings in the *Paris Psalter* (DOE s.v. *fæste* 5 "in Paris Psalter, *perhaps* used more generally as an intensive: entirely, quite" [emphasis added]) with verbs such as *toweorpan* 'destroy' and *gefyllan* 'fill'. I thank Elizabeth C. Traugott for this observation. However, since this reading seems to be restricted to this particular text in Old English, I have regarded the degree reading as a possible Middle English innovation.

formations which are first recorded in Middle English, such as *sellcuþlike*,[15] *þurrh-utlike*, *þwerrt ut*, *utnumennliʒ*, *witerrliʒ*, and *wiþþalle*, both with schematic, degree senses alongside their more lexical meanings. Interestingly, for seven of these adverbs the OED and the MED do not record examples of these new forms or new senses prior to the *Ormulum* (see table 4.2).

Tab. 4.2: Intensifiers in the *Ormulum* (time-depth)

Old English	Middle English	
	Adverbs with new degree senses	New formations
all	fasste (Orm: MED s.v. faste adv. 7, 9)	sellcuþlike
full	grimmeliʒ	þurrhutlike (Orm: MED s.v. thurhutlice adv. c)
hehlike	mikell (Orm: MED s.v. muchel adv. 1.a, 2.a)	þwerrt ut (Orm: MED s.v. thwertout adv. a, b)
inoh	rihht (Orm: MED s.v. right(e adv. 2)	utnumennliʒ (Orm: MED s.v. utnumenli adv.)
sare		
swiþe		witerrliʒ
well		wiþþ alle (Orm: MED s.v. withal adv. 1.a)
wunnderr		

Grimmeliʒ, discussed below in section 5.1, is not identified as a degree adverb in any of the dictionaries, even though it does appear on Fettig's list of degree adverbs in the *Ormulum* (1934: 11). In the case of *sellcuþlike* and *witerrliʒ*, the dictionaries identify a specific degree sense, but do not cite the *Ormulum* as the source text in which this meaning is first recorded (see MED s.v. *selcouthli* b; s.v. *witterlī* (adv.) 2.c). The earliest example of the former with a degree reading quoted in the MED is dated c. 1275 (Layamon's *Brut*). However, example (2) below, in which *sellcuþlike* modifies the adjective *cweme* 'pleasing', clearly shows that the adverb was indeed used as an intensifier in the *Ormulum*.

---

15 The adjective *seldcuþ* 'strange' is attested in Old English (BTS s.v. *seldcuþ* I), but its corresponding adverb is not recorded until Middle English (see OED s.v. *selcouthly* adv.).

(2) *Forr nære ʒho nohht Drihhtin Godd* || *Swa* **sellcuplike cweme**, || *ʒiff þatt ʒho nohht ne wære full* || *Off soþfasst lufess mahhte* ; (CMORM, I, 88.779)

'because she would not be so wonderfully pleasing to God if she were not full of the power of true love.'

According to the MED, the adverb *witerrliʒ* has a degree sense 'completely, fully, utterly' (s.v. *witterlī* adv. 2c), the first example dated a1375. In Orm it is generally used with its more lexical meaning 'plainly, evidently; truly' (s.v. *witterlī* adv. 2a, b), as in (3) below, but the material also provides two interesting instances in which it is liable to be interpreted as an intensifier, see (4). In these, *witerrliʒ* collocates with the quasi-synonymous adjective *soþ*, 'evidently/truly true', thus inviting a degree reading: 'completely true'.

(3) *& wisstenn* **witerrliʒ** *þærþurrh* || *þatt swillc new king wass awwnedd* || *þatt wass soþ Godd & soþ mann ec*, (CMORM, I, 118.1028)

'and through this they truly knew that a new king appeared who was true God and true man also.'

(4) *& tatt wass* **witerrlike soþ** || *þatt Godess enngell seʒʒde*. (CMORM, I, 24.302)

'that was evidently/truly true, what God's angel said.'

Interestingly, a similar case of cooccurrence of synonymous forms is found in the early uses of the intensifier *par excellence* in Modern English, *very*, which originally meant 'true, truly' as well. As Breban and Davidse show (2016: 12, 18), the first recorded examples of *very* as a noun and adjective intensifier occur with the nouns *truth* and *sooth* (e.g. *a verray sooth*, OED c. 1386, Chaucer) and with the adjective *true* (e.g. *a very trewe evidence*, OED ?a 1450). Such cases qualify as what Lorenz calls "feature copying intensifiers", which achieve "their intensifying effect by copying a substantial part of the adjective denotation" (Lorenz 1999: 120, 2002: 148). The collocations here are clearly emphatic.

4.3 Frequent intensifiers

As shown in figure 4.1 above, the list of the most frequent intensifiers in the *Ormulum* contains the "usual suspects" for Middle English: *swiþe*, *full*, *well*, and *right*, which were in competition in the period (see Fettig 1934: 44–46). A further three intensifiers show a remarkably high token frequency in Orm, unparalleled in other late twelfth-century texts (see Fettig 1934: 10–12): these are *all*, *inoh*, and *þwerrt ut* as illustrated in (5) to (7).

(5) *Forrþi þatt teȝȝre dede iss **all** || **Unngod & all unnclene*** (CMORM, II, 265.2600)
 'because their deed is completely sinful and impure.'

(6) *Annd hire meȝe Elysabæþ || Wass **gladd inoh** & bliþe || Off hire dere child Johan* (CMORM, I, 109.931)
 'and her relative Elizabeth was very glad and happy for her dear child John.'

(7) *Wiþþutenn þatt tatt he wass wiss || **All þweorrt ut clene off sinne**.* (CMORM, I, 108.928)
 'except that he was certainly all completely clean of sin.'

In the PPCME2 *Ormulum* material *all* most typically intensifies adjectival and adverbial heads (114 examples.), as seen in (5), but may also occur with verbs (18 examples, *forwerpen* 16, and *forsen* 2, both of them meaning 'abandon'), as in (8) below.

(8) *& fele þede modiliȝ || Wiþþstodenn, & wiþþseȝȝdenn,|| & **all forrwurrpenn** heffness lihht ||* (CMORM, II, 267.2605–6)
 'and many people proudly avoid and oppose and completely reject the heavenly light.'

All shows a clear preference for negative heads. We find both formally and semantically negative items (e.g. *unclene* 'impure'), alongside others which are formally negative but semantically positive (e.g. *unskaþefull* 'harmless, innocent', *unwemmed* 'without imperfection'). Its most frequent adverbial collocates are the maximizers *full* (9 examples)[16] and *þwerrt ut* (this latter combination appears in 37 examples and seems to be a strong collocation, with an MI score over 5),[17] see (7). In these sequences, *all* appears to be clearly redundant. According to Fettig

---

16 Buchstaller and Traugott contend that one of the earliest contexts in which the degree modifier function of the adverb *all* occurred in Old English was in connection with *full*, originally a maximizer (2006: 352). The corpus examples in which *all* and the adverb *full* co-occur modify bounded adjectives (*openn* 'evident, overt', *soþ* 'true', *witerr* 'evident'). The meaning of *full* here is then likely to be 'completely'.
17 According to Clear (1993: 279), a MI score above 6 is considered high.

(1934: 64), *all* is especially frequent in poetry,[18] which suggests that it might have been used as a metrical filler. Its occurrence in tautological expressions such as *all full (open)* and *all þweorrt ut (clene)* in the *Ormulum*, which follows a "regular perfectly strict fifteen-syllable meter" (McMullen 2014: 259), seems to lend some support to the view that metrical issues could be in part responsible for the high incidence of *all* in the text, although this does not tell the whole story, as will be discussed in section 5.2 below.

Metrical considerations may also explain the high frequency of *inoh*, which seems to be particularly favoured in poetic works (Fettig 1934: 126). In the material, *inoh* typically postmodifies adjectives and adverbs (30 out of 34 examples), see (6), its semantic prosody being markedly positive, with the adjective *god* and the adverb *well* as its most common collocates.

Þwerrt ut is third in frequency in the *Ormulum* after *full* and *all*, but is almost wholly restricted to this text in the Middle English records.[19] It is a very versatile intensifier: It occurs with adjectives and adverbs, and, like other maximizers, is also found as a negator reinforcer (Fettig 1934: 173; Méndez-Naya 2014: 256). As mentioned above, it strongly collocates with *all*. Its semantic prosody is also quite remarkable, since it typically cooccurs with negative verbs (especially those meaning 'renounce, reject, abandon', e.g. *forwerpen*), but with positively connoted adjectives (e.g. *clene* 'pure'), as discussed in Méndez-Naya (2014: 258–259). Noteworthy is the fact that occurrences of *þwerrt ut* very often cluster together (30 of the 79 recorded examples occur in clusters), as can be seen in (9), which shows three tokens of the intensifier. *Þwerrt ut* also features prominently in lexical bundles which are repeated several times along the text, such as, *all þweorrt ut forwerppen* and *þatt þweorrt ut nohhte ne leȝheþþ*, which each occur six times in the corpus. These repetitions and parallel structures, so characteristic of Orm's style, would probably have made the learning and the recitation of the text easier.

(9) *Þe feorþe mahht iss hæfedd mahht* || *& haliȝ mahht wiþþ alle,*|| *Þatt tu beo* **þwerrt ut milde**, *& meoc,*||*& soffte,& stille, & liþe,*|| *&* **þwerrt ut clene** *off grimmcunndleȝȝc*|| *&* **þwerrt ut clene** *off braþþe*. (CMORM, I, 162.1340)

---

18 The other two texts corresponding to Fettig's 1100–1250 period which show a relatively frequent use of *all* are Layamon's *Brut* (Layamon B), a poetic work, and the *Ancrene Riwle*, a prose text (1934: 10–12).
19 The adverb is also attested once in the *Trinity Homilies*: (i) *Þat mannisse þe ne understart ne bisecheð god, is* **puertut forlore** *soule and lichame*. (c1200 Trin. Coll. Hom. 123; OED s.v. *thwert-out* adv.) 'The people who do not understand or pray to God are completely lost, both body and soul'.

'the fourth characteristic is a major and very sacred virtue, that you are completely merciful and compassionate, and kind, and meek, and gentle, completely free of cruelty, and completely free of rage.'

I will now focus on the central intensifiers over the Middle English period, *swiþe*, *full*, *well*, and *right*, comparing Orm to contemporary texts as represented in the HC material for the subperiod M1 (1150–1250). Figure 4.2 shows data drawn from the whole Middle English section of the HC (from Méndez-Naya 2004; Méndez-Naya and Pahta 2010: 197), and for the PPCME2 sample of the *Ormulum*. Frequencies have been normalized to 10,000 words.

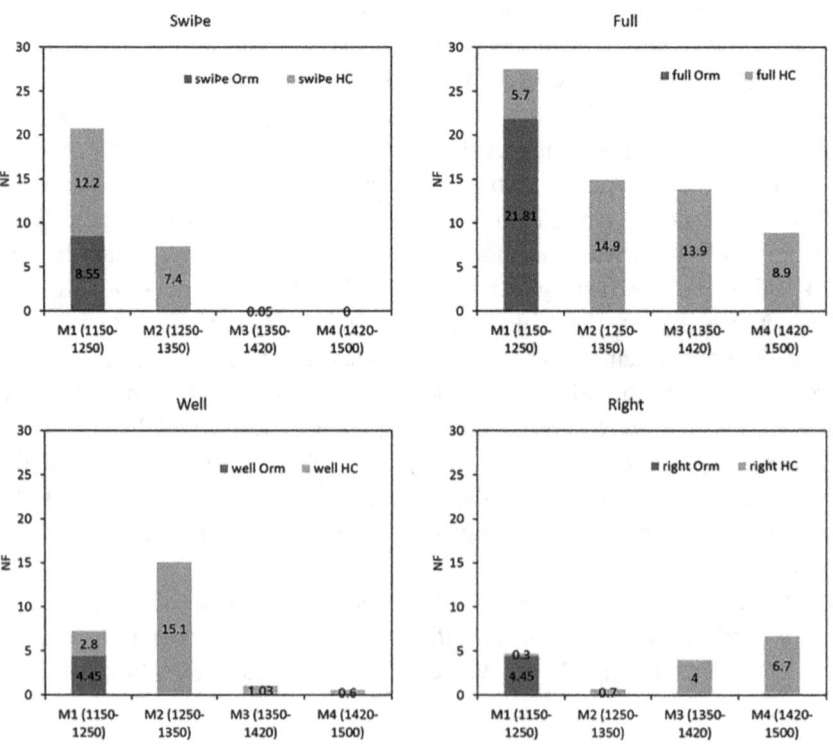

Fig. 4.2: Major Middle English intensifiers. General data from the HC; *Ormulum* data from PPCME2 (NF per 10,000 words)

Two observations immediately stand out from the data. First: *right*, which only attains any noticeable presence in the HC data in M3 (1350–1420),[20] is exceptionally frequent in the *Ormulum* (see Fettig 1934: 8, 149).[21,22] Second, the shift from *swiþe* to *full* as the dominant intensifier in Middle English, dated in the HC material to M2 (1250–1350) has already taken place in Orm.[23] In fact, the token frequency of *full* is extremely high in this text, almost quadrupling the general HC data for M1 (1150–1250).

According to Fettig (1934: 93) the expansion of *full* takes place first in the North and North East Midlands, and only later in other dialectal areas (see also Peters 1993: 134), but he dates it in the mid-thirteenth century. Clearly, then, the *Ormulum* (ca. 1180) is quite advanced in this respect. *Well* also shows a much higher frequency in the *Ormulum* than in other contemporary texts. We might note that all three adverbs, *rihht*, *full*, and *well*, are monosyllabic. Interestingly, the relatively high frequency of *full*, *eall*, and *well* in Old English poetry has been related to the fact that they involve monosyllables (Peltola 1971: 656).[24] Rhythmic issues may well have played a role in the *Ormulum*, since monosyllabic adverbs may have been useful for completing metrical lines (see also above for the high frequency of *all* in the text). For a further factor possibly influencing the prevalence of *full* in the *Ormulum*, see section 5.2.

The dominance of *full* in Orm's intensifier system is not only indicated by its high token frequency, but also by its wide range of collocates. It has often been observed that while well-established intensifiers collocate widely, incoming and receding intensifiers show a more restricted distribution across heads (Partington 1993: 183; Ito and Tagliamonte 2003: 268; Méndez-Naya and Pahta 2010: 199). This is exactly what we find in the *Ormulum* material, as illustrated in figure 4.3, which shows the distribution of *swiþe*, *full*, and *right* across heads. This figure only contains data on adjectives, since adjective modification is the most widely spread function of intensifiers (Bäcklund 1973: 279). Adjectives have been classified according to the semantic taxonomy proposed by Dixon (2004: 3–5).[25] *Full*,

---

20 See also Fettig (1934: 24).
21 Note that Fettig (1934) mentions only two other texts of the period in which *right* occurs, albeit infrequently, the *Ancrene Riwle* (one example) and Layamon's *Brut* (B; with two instances).
22 The HC material for M1 (1150–1250) contains three instances of the intensifier *right*, all of them from the *Ormulum*.
23 See also Fettig (1934: 13–14).
24 The marked peak of *well* in the HC, subperiod M2 can be partly explained by the fact that 13 out of the 17 texts in the subperiod are written in verse.
25 The adjectival classes identified in Dixon (2004) are: dimension ('big', 'small', 'short', 'wide', 'deep'); age ('new', 'young', 'old'); value ('good', 'bad', 'lovely', etc.); colour ('black', 'white',

the new favourite in the *Ormulum*, collocates with eight different adjective classes, *swiþe* is found with six, and the newcomer *right* with only two. In coherence with the evaluative function of intensifiers, the semantic class which is most commonly intensified is value (e.g. 'good', 'bad'), followed by human propensity (e.g. 'happy', 'kind'), adjective types that can be regarded as subjective (see Méndez-Naya 2008: 44). These two semantic classes seem to be the gateway through which new intensifiers are introduced, as seen in the data for *right*. Value also tends to become the stronghold of receding intensifiers (see Méndez-Naya and Pahta 2010: 205 for *right* in EMEMT).

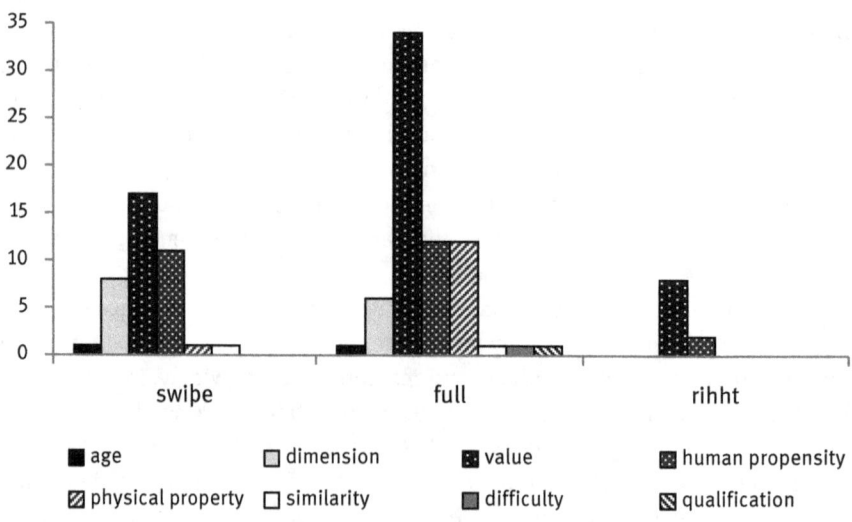

Fig. 4.3: *Swiþe, full, rihht* in the PPCME2 sample of the *Ormulum*. Width of collocation with adjectival heads (raw numbers)

As far as their mode of construal is concerned, most adjectival heads are unbounded (e.g. *cweme* 'pleasing', *god* 'good', *litel* 'little'), which indicates that *full* is a booster in the *Ormulum*, but some bounded adjectives are also found (e.g. *witerr*

---

etc.); physical property ('hard', 'soft', 'heavy', 'wet', 'well', 'sick', 'tired'); human propensity ('jealous', 'happy', 'kind'); speed ('fast', 'quick', 'slow'); difficulty ('easy', 'difficult', 'hard'); similarity ('like', 'unlike', 'similar', 'different'); qualification ('definite', 'true', 'probable', 'likely', 'common'); quantification ('all', 'many', 'some', 'few'); position ('high', 'low', 'near'); cardinal numbers and 'first', 'last'.

'clear, evident', *openn* 'evident, overt', especially in connection with the maximizer *all*, in yet another lexical bundle *all full openn bisne/takenn/spæche*), as in (10a, b). As can be seen, the parallel structures in (10) occur very close together in context (see the clustering of occurrences of *þwerrt ut* commented on above).

(10) a. *Þærþurrh wass uss bitacnedd wel* || *Wiþþ **all full openn** bisne,*
(CMORM, I, 227.1884)
b. *Þatt uss bitacneþþ witerrliȝ* || *Þurrh **all full openn** bisne,*
(CMORM, I, 228.1889)
c. *Þatt uss bitacneþþ opennliȝ* || *Þurrh **all full witerr** bisne,*
(CMORM, I, 228.1890)
'thereby was well shown to us with a quite clear example.'
'that clearly/openly shows us through a quite clear example.'

As seen in section 2, one of the core features of the category of degree adverbs is the capacity for renewal, triggered by their loss of expressiveness through frequent use. If *swiþe* was frequent but receding in Orm (see extension across semantic types), and *full* was the most common intensifier in terms of token frequency and the most widely spread item across semantic types, we might hypothesize that the intensifying force of these two adverbs was diminishing. The *Ormulum* provides interesting cases of recursion or cooccurrence which lend some support to this hypothesis.[26] Let us consider examples (11) to (13).

(11) *& þurrh þa seffne innseȝȝless wass* || ***Rihht swiþe** wel bitacnedd* || *þatt sefennfald godleȝȝc þatt Crist* || *Uss dide þurrh hiss come*; (CMORM, DED.L257.54)
'and by the seventh seal it was very (lit. 'very very') well illustrated the sevenfold benefit that Christ granted us with his advent.'

(12) *& tatt he **rihht full** herrsumm wass* (CMORM, I, 206.1679)
'that he was very (lit. 'very very') obedient.'

(13) *& beon **well swiþe** sare offdredd,* || *þatt all hiss gode dede* || *Ne mune himm nohht beon god inoh* || *To berrȝhenn himm fra pine.* (CMORM, I, 275.2250)
'and is very much (lit. very very sorely') afraid that all his good deeds will not be good enough to save him from the torments.'

---

26 On the cooccurrence of intensifiers, see Méndez-Naya (2017).

Note that these examples generally involve a very frequent item (*swiþe* and *full*) preceded by a more recent intensifier to its left, typically *rihht*, the newcomer, as in (11) and (12). Example (13) is particularly interesting in that it shows a third layer of intensification, with the adverb *sare* 'sorely' (*well swiþe sare offdredd*), whose degree reading in the *Ormulum* seems to be contextual. This will be discussed in section 5, which explores the relevance of context (both narrow and broad) for the intensifier system.

5 Context and change: Relevance for the intensifier system in the *Ormulum*

5.1 Context-induced changes

The importance of context for grammaticalization processes has long been recognized in the literature: grammatical meanings emerge in context. The role of context in grammaticalization has been studied in detail especially by Heine (2002), Diewald (2002), and Diewald and Smirnova (2012). At first, the new meaning arises as an inference, while the source meaning is still in the background (Heine's 2002 "bridging contexts"; Diewald's 2002 "untypical" and "critical contexts"), then the item spreads to contexts which are somewhat in conflict with properties of the source meaning, where the new meaning "provides the only possible interpretation" (Heine 2002: 85; "switch contexts"). Finally, the new sense becomes the inherent or usual meaning of the item in question and no longer needs the support of the context (Heine's 2002 "conventionalization" stage; Diewald's 2002 "isolating contexts"). While Heine (2002) focuses on pragmatic and semantic changes, Diewald (2002) contends that the different contexts are associated with different semantic and structural features. Once the item is grammaticalized, it becomes part of a "(relatively) closed paradigm"; Diewald and Smirnova (2012: 128) refer to this final stage as "paradigmatic integration".[27]

As mentioned in section 2, I consider the development of intensifiers to be a clear example of grammaticalization. Diachronically, a common pathway for the development of degree adverbs involves manner adverbs of various types which are reinterpreted in context so that a new degree inference is brought to the fore.

---

[27] According to Diewald and Smirnova (2012: 125–127), critical and isolating contexts are found in both grammaticalization and lexicalization. Paradigmatic integration is just found in the former process.

Méndez-Naya (2003) discusses one such path concerning the intensifier *par excellence* in the Old English period, namely *swiþe*. As seen above, a common source of intensifiers across languages is the meaning 'strength', sometimes verging on a sense of 'severely, violently strong'. *Swiþe* belongs to this group: it was originally a manner adverb derived from the adjective *swiþ* 'strong' by means of the derivative suffix -*e*, i.e. 'strongly'. In Old English, however, its degree meaning 'very' is already conventionalized, and therefore the primary use of the adverb is that of intensifier. The intermediate developmental stages can nevertheless be reconstructed by considering the effects of layering as illustrated in the different patterns in which the item occurs in Old English texts.

The degree reading of *swiþe* is likely to have started as an inference when the adverb occurred in connection with verbs harmonic with its original lexical meaning, e.g. *feohtan* 'fight' or *derian* 'injure': i.e. 'fight strongly', 'injure severely' > 'fight very much, injure greatly' (bridging contexts). We know this inference has become prominent by the time *swiþe* spreads to non-harmonic verbs, e.g. *blissian* 'rejoice' or *wundrian* 'admire', in which *swiþe* is clearly bleached (switch contexts). When *swiþe* combines with an adjective or adverb, its most common function in Old English, its original lexical sense is completely lost (conventionalization). Consider examples (14a) to (14d) in this respect. Key in the development of *swiþe* into a degree modifier is its occurrence with participles, as in (14e).

(14) a. & **feaht swyðe** ongean, oððæt he feol ofslagen,& his folc samod, mid swurdes ecge. (HC, QO3_XX_OLDT_AELFOLD QO3_XX_OLDT_AELFOLD)
'and he fought strongly/very much, until he was killed, together with his people, by sword's edge.'

b. ic **wundrige swyþe**, þæt æfre mihte be swilcum were & swa mycclum biscope beon undercropen seo deofollice scinnys þurh þa olehtinga þara preosta. (HC, QO2/4_NN_BIL_GDC)
'I wonder greatly at that, that the devilish spectre could have entered surreptitiously in such a man and such a great bishop through the adulation of the priests.'

c. and hi **swyðe wundrodon** þæs halgan weres geearnunga þæt þæt fyr ne mihte þa moldan forbærnan. (HC, QO3_NN_BIL_AELIVES26)
'and they wondered greatly at the holy man's merits, that the fire could not burn the dust.'

d. Ne beo þu to oferspræce, ac hlyst ælces monnes worda **swiðe georne**: (HC, QO3/4_IS_PHILO_DICTS)
'Don't be too talkative, but listen to the words of each person very earnestly.'

e. *ða wearð he on his mode **swiðe gedrefed**.* (HC, QO4_NN_HIST_CHRONE2)
'then he became very troubled in his mind.'

The semantic bleaching and pragmatic enrichment which it undergoes has structural correlates in terms of syntactic function (manner adjunct > degree adjunct > degree modifier) and word order: as a manner adjunct, *swiþe* enjoyed some freedom of position, it could follow or precede the verb, as illustrated in (14a, b vs. 14c); it typically precedes participles (14e), and when it modifies adjectives and adverbs, it is virtually restricted to premodifier position (14d). Table 4.3, based on Méndez-Naya (2003), summarizes the development of *swiþe*.

Tab. 4.3: Development of *swiþe* based on Méndez-Naya (2003)

manner adjunct >	degree adjunct >	degree modifier
Lexical meaning 'strongly, violently'	Grammatical meaning 'very much'	Grammatical meaning 'very'
+ harmonic verbs e.g. (14a)	+ non-harmonic verbs e.g. (14b, c)	+ adjectives and adverbs e.g. (14d)
mobility	mobility	preceding head
	degree adjunct + pples. e.g. (14e) typically preceding head	
BRIDGING CONTEXT	SWITCH CONTEXT	CONVENTIONALIZATION

As should be expected, in Orm the degree meaning of *swiþe* 'very' is fully conventionalized but interestingly, the *Ormulum* material provides support for this developmental pathway through evidence from semantically similar adverbs: *fasste, grimmeliʒ,* and *sare*. As we shall see, these adverbs illustrate in the *Ormulum* an incipient stage in the development, where the degree interpretation is still very much context-dependent.

Grimmeliʒ and *fasste* were both recorded once in the corpus with a clear degree nuance; *sare* occurs five times in the material, and in all these cases an intensifying nuance can be discerned. In examples (15) and (16) the degree reading emerges as an inference with harmonic verbs ('sin severely' > 'sin greatly'; 'weep sorely' > 'weep very much'; 'be severely afraid' > 'be very much afraid'). In (17) and (18) the adverbs modify participles, paving the way to their use as intensifiers of adjectives and adverbs. Note that in (18) *sare*, which modifies the participle *offdredd*, occurs in premodifying position. As can be seen, in (16) to (18) the newly recruited intensifiers co-occur with two well-established ones, *swiþe* and *full* (see Méndez-Naya 2017).

(15) *Forr baþe* **gilltenn grimmeliʒ** (CMORM, I, 155.1279)
'for both sins severely/dreadfully.' > 'greatly'

(16) *& wisste þatt mann munnde þa* || *Forr hemm full* **sare wepenn**, (CMORM, I, 281.23)
'and knew that one should weep for them very sorely.' > 'very much'

(17) *& tatt teʒʒ wærenn forr þatt lihht,* || *& forr þatt enngless sihhþte,* || **Forrdredde** *swiþe* **fasste** *anan*, (CMORM, I, 130.1107)
'and that they were at once very much afraid of the light and the vision of the angel.'

(18) *Forr þe birrþ beon full* **sare offdredd** || *Off helless grimme pine*, (CMORM, I, 276.2261)
'because it befits you to be very much afraid of the grim sufferings of hell.'

As would be expected according to the pathway described above, both *grimly* and *sore* come to collocate with adjectives at a later stage. (19), (20), and (21) below are MED examples of these adverbs functioning as adjective modifiers. *Fast*, by contrast, does not seem to have proceeded any further than the situation described for the *Ormulum* (i.e. occurrence with harmonic verbs and participles, see OED s.v. *fast* adv. 1.d). In fact, this is suggested in the MED entry for *fast*: "[t]he meaning of *faste* is largely contextual. In many passages *faste* can be read as a modal adverb (i.e. with a specific meaning), as an adverb of degree, or as a mere intensive." This is not unusual, as grammaticalization does not necessarily reach completion, but can be "arrested before it is fully 'implemented'" (Hopper and Traugott 2003: 131).

It is also likely that with *grimly* the degree meaning never went far beyond the switch context stage. The MED examples in which it modifies an adjective are found in sequences where the original lexical meaning 'severely' is still somewhat present in the background, as in (19) in the vicinity of the noun *wound* (*woundys grymly wyde*).[28]

---

28 In fact, whereas the MED provides a specific degree sense 'sorely, severely, **greatly**, dangerously' (MED s.v. *grimlī* adv. 3.a), the OED only gives the meanings 'dreadfully, frightfully, shock-

(19) a1500 (?c1400) EToulouse (Cmb Ff.2.38) 126: *Ther was takyn thre c and fyfty Of grete lordys..Wyth woundys **grymly wyde**.* (MED s.v. *grimli* adv. 3.a)

'350 great lords were taken there, with sorely/severely/very large wounds.'

Sore, by contrast, has a longer history and reaches a more advanced developmental stage as an intensifier. In the late Middle English period (fourteenth and fifteenth centuries) it collocates with adjectives harmonic with its original lexical meaning, as in *sore syk* in example (20). Additionally, it can also occur with non-harmonic heads, such as the adjective *delicate* 'voluptuous' in (21) and the adverb *well* in (22), which indicates that the degree reading has attained conventionalization (MED s.v. *sore* adv. 9b; OED s.v. *sore* adv. 11). Also relevant in this respect are examples such as (23) in which *sore* modifies a prepositional phrase. This extension in the type of collocates of *sore* clearly indicates host-class expansion, one of the key features of grammaticalization processes (Himmelmann 2004). *Sore* continues to be found with adjectives and adverbs in the Modern English period (see OED s.v. *sore* adv. 11; MED s.v. *sore* adv. 9.b, c), but is nowadays mainly restricted to dialects.[29] Interestingly, its cognate *sehr* has become over time one of the central intensifiers in German.[30]

(20) c1325 (c1300) Glo.Chron.A (Clg A.11) 3385 *Þe king lay þo **sore syk**.* (MED s.v. *sore* adv. 9b)

'The king lay then sorely/very sick.'

(21) (a1393) Gower *CA* (Frf 3) 6.960 *If that thou understode What is to ben delicious, Thou woldest noght be curious Upon the lust of thin astat To ben to **sore delicat**,* (MED s.v. *sore* adv. 9.b)

'If you understood what is to be guilty of delicacy, you would not be intent on the desire of your soul to be very voluptuous,'

---

ingly, terribly' s.v. 2). In some of the examples provided in the OED, however, the context invites a degree nuance: (ii) 1240 *Ureisun* in *Cott. Hom.* 187 *Mine sunnen habbeþ **grimliche iwreþed** me.* 'my sins have injured me greatly'; (iii) 1460 *Lybeaus Disc.* 1632 *Whan they togydere mette, Ayder yn other scheld hytte, Strokes **grimly greete**.* 'when they met, they hit each other's shields with terribly/very great strokes'.

29 The last OED example is from Eliot's *The Mill on the Floss* (1860). See also EDD (s.v. *sore* adj., adv., and sb. 11).

30 The first example of *sehr* with degree meaning provided in Grimm's dictionary dates back to Luther's Bible (1545) (DWB s.v. *sehr* adv. 2).

(22) 1474 CAXTON tr. *Game & Playe of Chesse* (1883) III. vii. 141 *The kynge denys had a broder whom he louyd **sore well**.* (OED s.v. *sore* adv. 11)

'King Denis had a brother whom he loved very dearly.'

(23) a1500 (a1460) *Towneley Pl.* (Hnt HM 1) 16/255 *Bot it gos **sore agans my will**,* (MED s.v. *sore* adv. 9.c)

'But it goes very much against my will.'

5.2 The wider context: Language contact

Let us now focus on the wider context, more specifically on the *Ormulum* as a text illustrating linguistic practices in the Danelaw and on the role of language contact for the intensifier system.

The prevailing linguistic situation in the area of the Danelaw in the Middle English period has been and still is a matter of heated debate. As Dance (2012: 1727–1728) puts it, when we talk about the Anglo-Norse contact situation we are actually subsuming under that label "a long period of contacts in diverse local settings". This contact situation encompasses typical processes of borrowing of Old Norse material by speakers of Old English (especially lexical borrowing) and the transfer into English of "Norse-derived elements,[31] including more fundamental components of the lexicon (basic vocabulary and function words) and morphosyntactic features" by speakers of Old Norse who shifted to English. Dance (2013: 43) calls this process "imposition". Since it could well be the case that Orm was of Scandinavian ancestry (his name is certainly Scandinavian), the Scandinavian features in his linguistic system might be attributed in the main to the second type of process.[32] Yet, we must be tentative here, because, as noted by Miller (2012: 99), the degree to which an English expression is derived from Old Norse is not easy to ascertain.[33]

---

31 Following Dance (2012: 1728), I adopt here the term "Norse-derived word", which refers not only to loanwords, but also loanshifts (both semantic loans and loan translations).

32 There is some evidence that Norse was spoken in the Danelaw in the eleventh century (see Parsons 2001), but whether the heavy Scandinavian nature of the language in the *Ormulum* can still be put down to the existence of a bilingual culture at the end of the twelfth century is uncertain.

33 See in this connection the recently launched Gersum Project <www.gersum.org>, one of whose aims is to provide evidence to identify and categorize Norse-derived words.

In the inventory of intensifiers in the *Ormulum* we find three items which have been identified by some scholars as possible cases of Scandinavian influence. These are *þwerrt ut*, *rihht*, and *witerrliȝ*.

As seen above, *þwerrt ut* is one of Orm's favourite intensifiers while being virtually unattested in other texts. According to Fettig (1934: 172), the adverb is a Scandinavian loanword. The form *þwerrt* is clearly Scandinavian (see OED s.v. *thwart* adv., prep., and adj.; MED s.v. *twert*).[34] The combination of ON *þvert* and ON *út*, however, is not recorded either in standard dictionaries of Old Icelandic, such as Cleasby and Vigfusson (1874), Zoëga (1910), and the *Dictionary of Old Norse Prose*, or in corpora of Old and Modern Icelandic.[35] This suggests that, rather than having been borrowed from Old Norse, it might be a case of relexification of English *þurhut* (an adverb which already had a degree reading in Old English, Méndez-Naya 2014: 250–257) using Norse material. In fact, this is suggested in the etymology provided in the MED (s.v. *thwert-ŏut* adv.): "From *thwart* adv. & *ŏut(e* adv., perh. by analogy with *thurgh-ŏut(e* adv."

The existence of forms of this type suggests that some kind of accommodation between the two languages is taking place (see Miller 2012: 98, 101). Curiously enough, Orm never employs the native form *þurhut*, while he does use its derivative *þurrhutlike*, as in (24).

(24) *& wisste wel to soþe ,‖ Þatt all Drihhtiness bodeword ‖ & all Goddspelless lare ‖ Iss filledd **þurrhutlike** wel, ‖ ȝiff þatt soþ lufe iss filledd;* (CMORM, I, 181.1498)

'and he knew well for truth that all the Lord's commandments and all the teaching of the Gospels are completely well fulfilled if the true love is fulfilled.'

Scandinavian influence has often been adduced in the case of the intensifier *right*, one of the favourite Middle English boosters, on the basis of the existence of a similar intensifier in Nordic languages (cf. Swedish *rätt*; see Stoffel 1901: 36).

---

34 Conclusive evidence comes from phonology (loss of /x/, cf. PGmc *þwerxwa-* and OE *þweorh*) and morphology (suffix -*t*, originally an adjectival ending, is used in Old Norse to form adverbs) (Sara Pons-Sanz, p.c.). Therefore, *þwerrt ut* would qualify as a Type A Norse-derived word in Dance's (2013) typology, that is words which present morphological or phonological features "indicating that a given word has followed a distinctively Scandinavian rather than Old English line of descent from Proto-Germanic" (2013: 45), irrespective of the fact that the meaning seems to have been derived from Old English.

35 Thanks are due to Thórhallur Eythórsson (Háskóli Íslands) for his help with corpora of Icelandic.

This hypothesis might be seen to find some support in both the dialectal and chronological distribution of the item in Middle English, two of the criteria proposed in the literature to identify Scandinavian borrowings (Dance 2011: 92). The intensifier *right* was always used more frequently in the North than in more southerly areas and the earliest examples of this adverb in degree modifier function indeed occur in the heavily norsified *Ormulum*. In order to confirm or disconfirm a possible case of Scandinavian influence here, I considered evidence from Old Norse dictionaries (Fritzner 1867; Cleasby and Vigfusson 1874; and Zoëga 1910) and corpora (*Old Norwegian Corpus* and the *Icelandic Parsed Historical Corpus*).[36] The only dictionary that provides a degree meaning is Fritzner (1867) (s.v. *rétt* adv. 3): "tilfulde, til Fuldkommenhed, just, netop" ('fully, to perfection, accurately, precisely'). However, the examples therein, along with corpora examples, suggest that in Scandinavian the meaning 'accurately, precisely' was the most salient one (in fact, it is the only one provided for *rétt* in the other two dictionaries). This was also a prominent meaning of English *right* (see Méndez-Naya 2006). It might have been the case that the degree sense of the Scandinavian adverb, rather than being the source of the degree reading of English *right*, actually represents a parallel development, which is also replicated later in other Germanic languages such as German (e.g. *recht gut*, see DWB s.v. *recht* 7b, earliest quoted example from 1548). In fact, taking the dictionary and corpora evidence for Scandinavian languages, and the evidence for English (Méndez-Naya 2006, 2007), we could hypothesize a developmental path from 'straight' > 'precisely, exactly' > 'completely' > 'very'.

In Orm, *rihht* seems to be used mostly as a maximizer, since it usually combines with bounded heads such as *wod* 'mad', illustrated in (25). It also very commonly occurs with negative adverbs (26), as other maximizers do (cf. *þwerrt ut* above).

(25) *Loc nu ʒiff þatt tu narr* **rihht wod** *|| & all wittess bidæledd, || þatt willt forrlesenn þin Drihhtin || & all þe blisse off heoffne,* (CMORM, I, 161.1333)

'Consider now, if you were not completely mad and deprived of all your wits, that you will abandon your Lord and all the bliss of heaven.'

(26) *tu þe sellf narrt* **rihht nohht** *wurrþ || Wiþþutenn Godess hellþe,* (CMORM, I, 173.1428)

'you yourself are absolutely not worth without God's help.'

---

[36] I would like to thank Valentine Pakis (DOE Project, Toronto) and Kristin Bech (University of Oslo) for their help with dictionaries and corpora respectively.

Finally, the third intensifier mentioned in the literature as Norse-derived is Orm's *witerrliȝ*, which has been classified by Bennet and Smithers (1968: 364) as a loanword from Old Norse (see also OED s.v. *witterly* adv.; MED *witterli* adv.), even though in recent studies Pons-Sanz (2013, and p.c.) is somewhat more cautious.[37] The dictionaries consulted for Scandinavian mostly give the meaning 'wisely' for the adverb *vitrliga*. In Zoega's dictionary (s.v. *vísliga* 1) the meaning 'for certain' is also provided, but there is no mention of a possible degree reading. For English only the MED provides a degree sense for the adverb (MED *witterli* adv. 2.c 'completely, fully; also, utterly'). As discussed above, *witerrliȝ* in Orm would qualify as a "feature copying intensifier" (Lorenz 1999: 120, 2002: 148) when used in connection with quasi-synonymous adjectives (e.g. *soþ*). It is likely that in the *Ormulum* material this degree reading does not go beyond an inference arising in context (bridging context).

The three adverbs discussed so far seem to illustrate a likely case of hybridization (*þwerrt ut*, a new formation with Scandinavian material on analogy of a native word, and therefore with a native meaning), a parallel development in English and Scandinavian (*rihht*), and a plausible loanword (*witerrliȝ*). I turn now to other possible cases of Scandinavian influence with regard to the intensifier system which have not, to my knowledge, been discussed in the literature thus far. This concerns the use of *full* and *all* in Orm.

As seen in section 3, *full* is by far the prevailing intensifier in the *Ormulum*, with a high token frequency (almost 22/10,000 words) compared to contemporary texts, and a very wide collocational profile. The adverb *all* comes second and also shows a notably higher incidence in this text than in other works from the same period (see Fettig 1934: 10–12). In section 4, I suggested that metrical factors could have favoured the selection of these two monosyllabic intensifiers. However, metre alone cannot be said to account for the extremely high frequency of these items in the *Ormulum* as compared to contemporary texts. In my view, Scandinavian influence might play a significant role here: Old Norse makes frequent use of the intensifying prefixes/combining forms *full-* (see e.g. Cleasby and Vigfusson s.v. *full-*; Fritzner s.v. *full-*; Bayldon 1870: 89; Cleasby and Vigfusson 1874: xxvii), and *al-/all-* (Bayldon 1870: 83; Rask 1843: 145). These forms seem to be very productive, judging from the number of different types reflected in dictionary entries, among them *fullglaðr* 'full glad', *full-langt* 'full long', *full-gamall* 'full old', and *alheill* 'all hale', *allgóðr* 'very good'. These booster prefixes also existed in Old English (see

---

[37] According to Pons-Sanz (2013: 465, 502, and p.c.) the morphological and dialectal evidence for regarding this as a Type A Norse-derived form is not fully conclusive.

Ingersoll 1978: 120–121; Lenker 2008; Buchstaller and Traugott 2006: 353),[38] alongside the adverbs *full* and *all*. What seems to have happened here is that two native forms were reinforced by the existence of cognate patterns in Old Norse in a norsified text such as the *Ormulum*.[39] Scandinavian influence would also account for the fact that *full* increases in frequency earlier in the area of the Danelaw than in the other dialectal areas[40] (see Fettig 1934: 93, who dates it to the mid-thirteenth century; see also Peters 1993: 134). Pressure from Norse could perhaps also explain the marked increase in frequency of the intensifier *all* in Middle English observed by Buchstaller and Traugott (2006: 354).[41]

6 Concluding remarks

This study has dealt with the system of intensifying adverbs in the *Ormulum* (ca. 1180), and has discussed how micro-level (i.e. linguistic) and macro-level contexts (in this case language-contact situation) are central for its configuration.

Despite the early date of its composition, the *Ormulum* has been shown to be very innovative, in terms of both its lexis and its grammatical system, and this innovativeness also applies to its inventory of intensifiers. More than half the degree adverbs recorded in it represent Middle English incorporations to the inventory, and, remarkably, the *Ormulum* is the source of the first attestations for these in the MED and the OED. Moreover, Orm anticipates some important changes to come in the intensifier system, such as the shift from *swiþe* to *full* as the dominant Middle English intensifier, which will be generalized in the mid-thirteenth century, and the introduction of the intensifying use of *right*, which will only reach a notable incidence in other Middle English texts from the mid-fourteenth century onwards. The replacement of *swiþe* by *full* is clearly motivated by its loss of expressivity through frequent use, since this had been the prevailing degree adverb from the Old English period. The evidence discussed here lends support to this

---

38 Lenker (2008: 251) identifies ten different types for *eall-* and twelve different types for the booster prefix *ful-*.
39 This would qualify as influence of Type C in Dance's (2013) typology (Sara Pons-Sanz, p.c.).
40 This Northern distribution seems to hold also in later periods, see EDD (s.v. *full* adj., adv. sb² and v¹. 10, 13).
41 In fact, Buchstaller and Traugott (2006: 354, fn 13) refer to a reviewer's comment here: "An anonymous reviewer suggested that there may have been influence from Old Norse, in which there was a very productive prefix, *al-*, that could be attached to both bounded and unbounded participles, adjectives and adverbs."

view, with examples in which *swiþe* and *full*, which are very common and therefore no longer that emphatic in the *Ormulum*, are reinforced by the newcomer *right*. I have also suggested that the unexpected high frequency of some intensifiers used by Orm (e.g. *full*, *all*, *well*, *rihht*) may be partly attributable to their monosyllabic nature, which renders them especially useful as metrical fillers.

The different lexical sources for intensifiers identified in the relevant literature are well represented in the *Ormulum* material, but special attention has been paid here to adverbs denoting 'strength'. The developmental path suggested for Old English *swiþe* in Méndez-Naya (2003) is replicated by other synonymous adverbs in Orm, thus helping to illustrate the intermediate stages of the 'strength' pathway from manner adverb 'strongly, severely' to degree modifier 'very'. The reinterpretation of manner as degree is triggered by the occurrence of these 'strength' adverbs with harmonic verbs and participles in contexts where a new degree reading emerges as an inference (bridging contexts). So, this is another example of the key importance of the immediate linguistic context for grammaticalization. However, in this study I have also drawn attention to the macro-level context: the *Ormulum* is a text produced in the Danelaw, by a speaker of likely Scandinavian ancestry, perhaps a descendant of those Norse speakers who had switched to English "bringing some basic nuts-and-bolts Norse vocabulary with them" (Dance 2013: 43). Old Norse influence, which permeates the text in its lexis and grammar, also features prominently in Orm's intensifier system in various ways, ranging from the borrowing (*witerrliʒ*) and hybridization of forms (*þwerrt ut*), to the reinforcement of native intensifiers (*full*, *all*) by means of cognate Norse patterns.

References

Anderson, John & Derek Britton. 1999. The orthography and phonology of the *Ormulum*. *English Language and Linguistics* 3 (2). 299–334.
Bäcklund, Ulf. 1973. *The collocation of adverbs of degree in English*. Uppsala: Almqvist & Wiksell.
Bayldon, George. 1870. *An elementary grammar of the Old Norse or Icelandic language*. Edinburgh: Williams & Norgate.
Bech, Kristin & George Walkden. 2015. English is (still) a West Germanic language. *Nordic Journal of Linguistics* 39 (1). 65–100.
Bennett, Jack A. W. & Douglas Grey. 1986. *Middle English literature (1100–1400)*. Oxford: Clarendon Press.
Bennett, Jack A. W. & Gavin V. Smithers. 1968. *Early Middle English verse and prose*. Oxford: Clarendon Press.
Blake, Norman. 1992. Introduction. In Norman Blake (ed.), *The Cambridge history of the English language*. Vol. II: *1066–1476*, 1–22. Cambridge: Cambridge University Press.
Bolinger, Dwight. 1972. *Degree words*. The Hague & Paris: Mouton De Gruyter.

Borst, Eugen. 1902. *Die Gradadverbien im Englischen*. Heidelberg: Winter.
Brate, Erik. 1885. Nordische Lehnwörter im *Ormulum*. *Beiträge zur Geschichte der deutschen Sprache und Literatur* 10. 1–80 & 580–586.
Breban, Tine & Kristin Davidse. 2016. The history of *very*: The directionality of functional shift and (inter)subjectification. *English Language and Linguistics* 20 (2). 221–249.
Brinton, Laurel J. & Leslie K. Arnovik. 2006. *The English language: A linguistic history*. Oxford: Oxford University Press.
Buchstaller, Isabelle & Elizabeth Closs Traugott. 2006. *The lady was al demonyak*: Historical aspects of adverb *all*. *English Language and Linguistics* 10 (2). 345–370.
Burchfield, Robert W. 1987. Ormulum. In Joseph R. Strayer (ed.), *Dictionary of the Middle Ages*. Vol. 9, 280. New York: Charles Scribner's Sons.
Clear, Jeremy. 1993. From Firth principles – computational tools for the study of collocation. In Mona Baker, Gill Francis & Elena Tognini-Bonelli (eds.), *Text and technology: In honour of John Sinclair*, 271–292. Amsterdam & Philadelphia: John Benjamins.
Cleasby, Richard & Gudbrand Vigfusson. 1874. *An Icelandic-English dictionary*. http://www.ling.upenn.edu/~kurisuto/germanic/oi_cleasbyvigfusson_about.html.
Cole, Marcelle. 2018. A native origin for Present-day English *they, their, them*. *Diachronica* 35 (2). 165–209.
Dance, Richard. 2012. English in contact: Norse. In Alexander Bergs & Laurel J. Brinton (eds.), *English historical linguistics: An International handbook*, Vol. 2: 1724–1737. Berlin & New York: Mouton De Gruyter.
Dance, Richard. 2013. "Tor for to telle": Words derived from Old Norse in *Sir Gawain and the Green Knight*. In Judith A. Jefferson & Ad Putter (eds., with the assistance of Amanda Hopkins), *Multilingualism in Medieval Britain (c. 1066–1520)*, 41–58. Turnhout: Brepols.
D'Arcy, Alexandra. 2015. Stability, stasis and change. The longue dureé of intensification. *Diachronica* 32 (4). 449–493.
Davidse, Kristin & Tine Breban. 2019. A cognitive-functional approach to the order of adjectives in the English noun phrase. *Linguistics* 57 (2), 327–371.
Denison, David. 1981. *Aspects of the history of English group-verbs: With particular attention to the syntax of the Ormulum*. University of Oxford, PhD dissertation.
Diewald, Gabriele. 2002. A model for relevant types of contexts in grammaticalization. In Ilse Wischer & Gabriele Diewald (eds.), *New reflections on grammaticalization*, 103–120. Amsterdam & Philadelphia: John Benjamins.
Diewald, Gabriele & Elena Smirnova. 2012. Paradigmatic integration. In Kristin Davidse, Tine Breban, Lieselotte Brems & Tanja Mortelmans (eds.), *Grammaticalization and language change: New reflections*, 111–134. Amsterdam & Philadelphia: John Benjamins.
Dixon, Robert M. W. 2004. Adjective classes in typological perspective. In Robert M. W. Dixon & Alexandra Y. Aikhenvald (eds.), *Adjective classes: A cross-linguistic typology*, 1–49. Oxford: Oxford University Press.
DOE = Cameron, Angus, Ashley Crandell Amos, Antonette diPaolo Healey et al. 2018. *Dictionary of Old English: A to I online*. Toronto: Dictionary of Old English Project.
Durkin, Philip. 2014. *Borrowed words: A history of loanwords in English*. Oxford: Oxford University Press.
DWB = *Deutsches Wörterbuch von Jacob und Wilhelm Grimm*. 16 vols. in 32 serial vols. 1854–1961. Quellenverzeichnis Leipzig 1971.
EDD = Wright, Joseph. 1896–1921. *English dialect dictionary*. London: Henry Frowde.

Emonds, Joseph E. & Jan Terje Faarlund. 2014. *English: The language of the Vikings*. Olomouc: Palacky University.

Fettig, Adolf. 1934. *Die Gradadverbien im Mittelenglischen*. Heidelberg: Winter.

Fritzner, Johan. 1867. *Ordbog over det gamle norske sprog*. Kristiania: Feilberg & Landmark.

Himmelmann, Nikolaus P. 2004. Lexicalization and grammaticalization: Opposite or orthogonal? In Walter Bisang, Nikolaus P. Himmelmann & Björn Wiemer (eds.), *What makes grammaticalization – A look from its components and its fringes*, 21–44. Berlin: Mouton de Gruyter.

Heine, Bernd. 2002. On the role of context in grammaticalization. In Ilse Wischer & Gabriele Diewald (eds.), *New reflections on grammaticalization*, 83–102. Amsterdam & Philadelphia: John Benjamins.

Hoffmann, Sebastian. 2009. Lexical change. In Jonathan Culpeper, Francis Katamba, Paul Kerswill, Ruth Wodak & Tony McEnery (eds.), *English language. Description, variation and context*, 286–300. London: Palgrave Macmillan.

Hopper, Paul J. 1991. On some principles of grammaticalization. In Elizabeth Closs Traugott & Bernd Heine (eds.), *Approaches to grammaticalization*, Vol. I, 17–35. Amsterdam & Philadelphia: John Benjamins.

Hopper, Paul J. & Elizabeth Closs Traugott. 2003. *Grammaticalization*. 2nd edn. Cambridge: Cambridge University Press.

Huddleston, Rodney & Geoffrey Pullum et al. 2002. *The Cambridge grammar of the English language*. Cambridge: Cambridge University Press.

Hundt, Marianne. 2014. The demise of the *being to V* construction. *Transactions of the Philological Society* 112 (2). 167–187.

Ingersoll, Sheila M. 1978. *Intensive and restrictive modification in Old English*. Heidelberg: Winter.

Ito, Rika & Sali Tagliamonte. 2003. *Well weird, right dodgy, very strange, really cool*: Layering and recycling in English intensifiers. *Language in Society* 32. 257–279.

König, Ekkehard & Peter Siemund. 1999. Intensifiers as sources and targets of semantic change. In Peter Koch & Andreas Blank (eds.), *Historical semantics and cognition*, 237–257. Berlin: Mouton De Gruyter.

Leech, Geoffrey, Marianne Hundt, Christian Mair & Nicholas Smith. 2009. *Change in contemporary English. A grammatical study*. Cambridge: Cambridge University Press.

Lenker, Ursula. 2008. Booster prefixes in Old English – an alternative view of the roots of ME *forsooth*. *English Language and Linguistics* 12 (2). 245–265.

Lorenz, Gunter. 1999. *Adjective intensification – Learners versus native speakers: A corpus study of argumentative writing*. Amsterdam & Atlanta: Rodopi.

Lorenz, Gunter. 2002. *Really worthwhile* or *not really significant*? A corpus-based approach to the lexicalization and grammaticalization of intensifiers in Modern English. In Ilse Wischer & Gabriele Diewald (eds.), *New reflections on grammaticalization*, 143–161. Amsterdam & Philadelphia: John Benjamins.

McMullen, A. Joseph. 2014. *Forr þeʒʒre sawle need*: The *Ormulum*, vernacular theology and a tradition of translation in Early England. *English Studies* 95. 256–277.

MED = Kurath, Hans et al. 1952–2001. *Middle English Dictionary*. Ann Arbor: University of Michigan Press. http://ets.umdl.mich.edu/m/med/

Méndez-Naya, Belén. 2003. On intensifiers and grammaticalization: The case of *swiþe*. *English Studies* 84 (4). 372–391.

Méndez-Naya, Belén. 2004. *Full good, right good, well good?* On the competition of intensifiers in the Middle English period. Paper presented at 13 ICEHL, Vienna, August 2004.

Méndez-Naya, Belén. 2006. Adjunct, modifier, discourse marker: On the various functions of *right* in the history of English. *Folia Linguistica Historica* 27. 141–169.

Méndez-Naya, Belén. 2007. *He nas nat right fat*: On the origin and development of the intensifier *right*. In Gabriella Mazzon (ed.), *Studies in Middle English forms and meanings*, 191–207. Bern: Peter Lang.

Méndez-Naya, Belén. 2008. "The which is most and right harde to answere": Intensifying *right* and *most* in earlier English. In Richard Dury, Maurizio Gotti & Marina Dossena (eds.), *English Historical Linguistics 2006*. Vol. II: *Lexical and semantic change*, 31–51. Amsterdam & Philadelphia: John Benjamins.

Méndez-Naya, Belén. 2014. Out of the spatial domain: 'Out'-intensifiers in the history of English. *Folia Linguistica Historica* 35. 241–274.

Méndez-Naya, Belén. 2017. Iteration and co-occurrence of intensifiers in earlier English. *English Text Construction* 10 (2). 249–273.

Méndez-Naya, Belén & Päivi Pahta. 2010. Intensifiers in competition: The picture from early English medical writing. In Irma Taavitsainen & Päivi Pahta (eds.), *Early Modern English medical texts: Corpus description and studies*, 193–215. Amsterdam: John Benjamins.

Miller, D. Gary. 2012. *External influences on English: from its beginnings to the Renaissance*. Oxford: Oxford University Press.

OED = Oxford English Dictionary Online. http://www.oed.com/

Page, Raymond I. 1971. How long did the Scandinavian language survive in England? The epigraphical evidence. In Peter Clemoes & Kathleen Hughes (eds.), *England before the Conquest*, 165–181. Cambridge: Cambridge University Press.

Palacios, Ignacio & Paloma Núñez-Pertejo. 2012. He's absolutely massive. It's a super day. Madonna, she is a wicked singer. Youth language and intensification: A corpus-based study. *Text & Talk. An Interdisciplinary Journal of Language, Discourse & Communication Studies* 32 (6). 773–796.

Paradis, Carita. 2000. *It's well weird*. Degree modifiers of adjectives revisited: The nineties. In John Kirk (ed.), *Corpora galore: Analysis and techniques in describing English*, 147–160. Amsterdam & Atlanta: Rodopi.

Paradis, Carita. 2001. Adjectives and boundedness. *Cognitive Linguistics* 12 (1), 47–65.

Paradis, Carita. 2008. Configurations, construals and change: Expressions of degree. *English Language and Linguistics* 12 (2). 317–343.

Parkes, Malcolm B. 1983. On the presumed date and possible origin of the manuscript of the 'Ormulum'. In Eric G. Stanley & Douglas Gray (eds.), *Five hundred years of words and sound: A festschrift for Eric Dobson*, 115–127. Cambridge D. S. Brewer.

Parsons, David N. 2001. How long did the Scandinavian language survive in England? Again. In James Graham-Campbell, Richard A. Hall, Judith Jesch & David Parsons (eds.), *Vikings and the Danelaw*, 299–312. Oxford: Oxbow.

Partington, Alan. 1993. Corpus evidence of language change: The case of the intensifier. In Mona Baker, Gill Francis & Elena Tognini-Bonelli (eds.), *Text and technology. In honour of John Sinclair*, 177–192. Amsterdam & Philadelphia: John Benjamins.

Peltola, Niilo. 1971. Observations on intensification in Old English poetry. *Neuphilologische Mitteilungen* 72. 649–690.

Peters, Hans. 1993. *Die englischen Gradadverbien der Kategorie* booster. Tübingen: Narr.

Peters, Hans. 1994. Degree adverbs in Early Modern English. In Dieter Kastovsky (ed.), *Studies in Early Modern English*, 269–288. Berlin: Mouton De Gruyter.

Pons-Sanz, Sara. 2013. *The lexical effects of Anglo-Scandinavian linguistic contact on Old English*. Turnhout: Brepols.

Pons-Sanz, Sara. 2015. Norse-derived terms in Orm's lexico-semantic field of EMOTION. *Journal of English and Germanic Philology* 114 (4). 552–586.

PPCME2 = Kroch, Anthony & Ann Taylor. 2000. *The Penn-Helsinki parsed corpus of Middle English* (PPCME2). Department of Linguistics, University of Pennsylvania. CD-ROM, second edition, release 4. http://www.ling.upenn.edu/ppche/ppche-release-2016/PPCME2-RELEASE-4.

Quirk, Randolph, Sydney Greenbaum, Geoffrey Leech & Jan Svartvik. 1985. *A comprehensive grammar of the English language*. London: Longman.

Rask, Erasmus. 1843. *A grammar of the Icelandic or Old Norse tongue*. [English translation by George Webbe Dasent]. London. William Pickering.

Reinöhl, Uta & Nikolaus P. Himmelmann. 2017. Renewal: A figure of speech or a process sui generis. *Language* 93 (2). 381–413.

Rissanen, Matti. 1999. Syntax. In Roger Lass (ed.), *The Cambridge history of the English language*. Vol. III: *1476–1776*, 187–331. Cambridge: Cambridge University Press.

Samuels, Michael L. 1985. The great Scandinavian Belt. In Roger Eaton, Olga Fischer, Willem F. Koopman & Frederike van der Leek (eds.), *Papers from the 4th International Conference on English Historical Linguistics, Amsterdam, April 10–13, 1985*, 269–281. Amsterdam & Philadelphia: John Benjamins.

Scott, Mike. 2012. *WordSmith tools version 6*. Stroud: Lexical Analysis Software.

Stoffel, Cornelis. 1901. *Intensives and downtoners*. Heidelberg: Winter.

Tagliamonte, Sali. 2008. So different and pretty cool! Recycling intensifiers in Toronto, Canada. *English Language and Linguistics* 12 (2). 361–394.

Traugott, Elizabeth C. 1982. From propositional to textual and expressive meanings: Some semantic-pragmatic aspects of grammaticalization. In Winfred P. Lehmann & Yakov Malkiel (eds.), *Perspectives on historical linguistics*, 245–271. Amsterdam & Philadelphia: John Benjamins.

Traugott, Elizabeth C. 2007. The concepts of constructional mismatch and type-shifting from the perspective of grammaticalization. *Cognitive Linguistics* 18 (4). 523–557.

Trips, Carola. 2003. Stylistic fronting in the *Ormulum* – Scandinavian syntactic phenomena in Early English texts. *Tromsø University Working Papers on Language and Linguistics* 31 (2). 457–472.

Zoëga, G. T. 1910. *A concise dictionary of Old Icelandic*. http://www.ling.upenn.edu/ ~kurisuto/germanic/oi_zoega_about.html.

Lynn Anthonissen
Constructional change across the lifespan
The nominative and infinitive in early modern writers

> Man erforschte zwar eifrigst die *sprachen*, aber viel zu wenig *den sprechenden menschen*.
> Osthoff and Brugmann (1878: III)

Abstract: This paper presents one of the first attempts at exploring whether constructional change of syntactic constructions is possible within the adult lifespan of individual speakers. It does so by zooming in on diachronic changes in passives of the type *He is said to be a thief*, a construction known as the nominative and infinitive (NCI). Two main usage types are discerned: the evidential NCI (*He is said to be a sinner*) and the modalized NCI (*He may be said to be a sinner*). Exploring the writings of four early modern authors, the study demonstrates that the proportions of these usage types shift during the lifetimes of all investigated authors, with informants showing linear trends that persist into old age. The general increase in evidential uses is argued to reflect the construction's growing emancipation from the passive construction and its increasing specialization into a reportative evidential marker.

1 Introduction: Individual trajectories in language change

This contribution investigates change in individuals and takes initial steps to clarify whether constructional change of syntactic constructions is possible within the adult lifespan of an individual. The expanding use of the *Nominativus cum Infinitivo* construction (NCI) in Early Modern English will serve as a case study. NCI patterns, i.e. passives of the type *He is believed to be a thief*, emerged in Late Middle English, but only really gained ground in Early Modern English. The present study zooms in on diachronic changes in the NCI's constructional semantics during this period and contrasts early modern writers' individual

---

Lynn Anthonissen, University of Antwerp & LMU Munich, Linguistics Department, 2000 Antwerpen, Belgium, lynn.anthonissen@uantwerpen.be

https://doi.org/10.1515/9783110682564-005

trajectories in the use of the NCI. In what follows, I will clarify the main theoretical assumptions underlying this study.

Grounded in usage-based and constructionist approaches to language which hold that linguistic knowledge is shaped and reshaped by experience (e.g. Goldberg 1995; Croft 2001; Bybee 2010), the present analysis takes as its starting point the idea that no two speakers have the same mental grammar. While the existence of individual differences in language use has been attested extensively in corpus-linguistic research (e.g. Coniam 2004; Barlow 2013; Schmid and Mantlik 2015) and even forms the backbone of research and applications in related fields (e.g. stylometrics and authorship attribution, forensic linguistics), an increasing body of research now indicates that this holds true not only for language use, but also for L1 acquisition of core grammatical constructions (Chipere 2001, 2003; Dąbrowska and Street 2006; Street and Dąbrowska 2010, 2014). Street and Dąbrowska (2010), for instance, demonstrate that native speakers may differ substantially in their attainment of constructions that are generally considered part of the core grammar of a language (e.g. passives and quantifiers), thus challenging the widely-held belief that children converge on the same grammar despite substantial variation in language input (e.g. Crain and Thornton 1998). Language development has also been shown to exhibit effects of education (Mills and Hemsley 1976; Street and Dąbrowska 2010, 2014) and socioeconomic status in general (Ginsborg 2006; Pakulak and Neville 2010). Given these facts, it is only natural that usage-based linguistics has long moved past the idea that linguistic theory must be "concerned with the ideal speaker-hearer, in a completely homogeneous speech-community, who knows its language perfectly" (Chomsky 1965: 3). Yet, the bulk of work is still concerned with the average speaker-hearer, which, though closer to psychological reality, nevertheless entails decontextualization because individual differences are obscured. While making generalizations about language use is a valid and important objective in itself, we must be aware that significant interspeaker differences exist, which, as I will argue in the following paragraph, has important consequences for usage-based models of language, and language change in particular.

Linguists (of various persuasions) have usually treated grammatical change as happening at the level of speech communities to a shared system of communicative conventions succinctly referred to as "the language" of that community. However, these changes ultimately represent the cumulative effect of recurrent changes across a substantial set of individual language users whose innovative language use reflects adjustments in the mental representation of their linguistic knowledge. In other words, conventionalization ("language change" rather than "innovation") takes place when several such individual grammars are aligned during interaction. While this is often implicitly or explicitly acknowledged (e.g. Fischer 2010: 182; Traugott and Trousdale 2013: 46; Baxter and Croft 2016; Noël 2016), few studies of grammatical change have operationalized the notion of the "linguistic individual" (see Johnstone 1996). Admittedly, there is a large body of research within (historical) sociolinguistics that deals with interspeaker variation, social networks and the role of individual speakers in ongoing change (see Bergs 2005; Nevalainen, Raumolin-Brunberg, and Mannila 2011; Raumolin-Brunberg and Nurmi 2011; Nevalainen 2015, to name a few). However, for practical reasons, these studies are often limited to changes associated with high frequency elements, such as phonological change in PDE real-time and apparent-time studies (e.g. Sankoff and Blondeau 2007 and references therein), and lexical or morphological change in older stages of the language (typical examples for the early modern period include pronominal variation (*thou/you*) and variation in third-person singular verbal suffixes (*-th/-s*) (Raumolin-Brunberg 2005)). Intragenerational changes relating to syntactic constructions (which are less likely to be socially indexed, see Labov 2001: 28–29) mostly stay out of the picture.

In keeping with the usage-based constructionist research programme, the individual dimension is not only valuable for a social analysis of change, but also and perhaps especially, given the emphasis on its being a "psychologically plausible, generative theory of human language" (Hoffmann and Trousdale 2013: 3), for a cognitive analysis of change. Analogy, for instance, a domain-general cognitive process (see Gentner, Holyoak, and Kokinov 2001; Itkonen 2005) that is recognized as one of the major mechanisms of language change (see De Smet and Fischer 2017 for an overview), strongly invites an individualist perspective, as it operates essentially at the micro-level of the individual mind: while the process itself may be largely subliminal, it is individuals who perceive similarities between linguistic elements, by virtue of which they can abstract over concrete instances and align novel utterances with existing schemas. The same arguably holds for such usage-based notions as entrenchment, chunking and categorization. Given the natural connection between cognitive processes and the individual mind, it is surprising that usage-based corpus linguists in general, and diachronic construction grammarians in particular, have largely refrained from integrating the cognitive dimension into their studies (see also remarks along those lines in Noël 2016 and Hilpert 2018). If we are serious about the cognitive commitment, research on language (change) as an abstract structure must be complemented by research on variation and change in the linguistic individual. As pointed out by Schmid and Mantlik (2015) and De Smet (2016), variation in language use reflects differences in how language is cognitively represented. Therefore, "any patterns or tendencies found in this variation may reveal something about the organization of mental representation" (De Smet 2016: 251), and, I would add, possibly also about the extent to which the adult mind can adapt to ongoing linguistic change.

Related to the focus on individuals are theoretical and methodological considerations of lifespan change. If we assume that individual mental grammars change, and if we find ways to attest and chart such changes, this could shed new light on the highly polarized debate on language change, emanating from two conflicting views on the fundamental nature of language acquisition and language change. Broadly speaking, research embedded in the generative tradition assumes the existence of a Universal Grammar, an initial state of the grammar, that is hard-wired in the brain and "passes through a series of states in early childhood, reaching a relatively stable steady state that undergoes little subsequent change, apart from the lexicon" (Chomsky 1995: 14). Proponents of this view typically consider children as the primary instigators of change (e.g. Lightfoot 1979; Clark and Roberts 1993; Henry 1997). Conversely, usage-based/constructionist approaches attribute a central role to language use in both the acquisition process and in language change. Children are argued to construct their linguistic knowledge from the input and learn grammatical "rules" by generalizing over item-specific instances (Tomasello 2003), or lack thereof (see statistical preemption, e.g. Boyd and Goldberg 2011), rather than analyzing that input in terms of predefined, innate categories. Linguistic change is considered to originate in speaker interaction (in line with sociolinguistic findings), which implies that it is not solely or primarily initiated by children (see Aitchison 2001: 37–52; Bybee 2010: 105–119; Traugott and Trousdale 2013: 21), in part because they do not actively participate in the social networks that propagate changes through a population.[1] It follows that speakers may adopt novel constructions both in childhood and later in life, a view that is strongly opposed to the idea discussed earlier that a person's grammar is fixed by the time they become adults. The present article aims to add to this discussion, investigating the extent to which lifespan changes affecting syntactic constructions are possible. Longitudinal studies of this kind are still few and far between, for obvious reasons: the scarcity of resources that are suitable for the study of syntactic change combined with the individual lifespan approach has long prevented researchers from undertaking

---

1 Bybee (2010), referring to a study by Slobin (1997), furthermore argues that children might not have developed the skills to advance complex changes such as the development of epistemic meanings in grammaticalization: "The type of inferencing that is necessary for semantic change to proceed in grammaticalization is something that children learn later in development" (Bybee 2010: 116).

such studies (notable exceptions include Raumolin-Brunberg 2009; Petré and Van de Velde 2014, 2018). However, the recent creation of large-scale longitudinal author corpora such as the EMMA corpus (Petré et al. 2019), which will be discussed more elaborately in section 3, makes such an enterprise more feasible.

The paper is structured as follows: section 2 presents an overview of the NCI construction's history, focusing on language-external and -internal factors in the propagation of the NCI. While section 2.1 and 2.2 concentrate on the NCI's initial spread, section 2.3 elaborates on the NCI's construction-specific semantics as another potential factor in its rise and introduces the key notions on which the corpus study is based. In section 3, I discuss the design and results of the corpus study, presenting evidence of constructional change in all investigated authors. Section 4 concludes with a number of implications and avenues for further research.

2 The NCI in the history of English

Our insights into the origins and spread of the NCI have been established in a piecemeal fashion ensuing from a general interest in the history of accusative and infinitive patterns (ACIs). Accordingly, early accounts have treated NCI patterns on a par with their active counterparts (e.g. Zeitlin 1908; Bock 1931; Warner 1982; Fischer 1989, 1992, 1994). While the term "ACI" has been used to refer to the various patterns illustrated in (1), that is, NP+(*to-*)INF complementation patterns after verbs of perception (1a), causative verbs (1b), persuade verbs (1c) and *verba cogitandi et declarandi* (1d),[2] the term "NCI" is typically used in a more restricted sense, indicating the passive of the type presented in (1d) only.

(1) Accusative and infinitive
 a. *They **saw** him enter the building.*
 b. *A stranger **made** him open the door.*
 c. *The judge **ordered** him to be released from prison.*
 d. *They **believed/declared** him to be involved in the crime.*

---

2 Early accounts differ in how they categorize ACI verbs. In particular the class of persuade-type verbs has often been singled out as being structurally different from the other ACI verbs (cf. Fischer 1989: 174–204).

The sentences in (2) illustrate the various classes of NCI matrix verbs, often shortened to "PCU verbs" for perception[3] (2a), cognition (2b) and utterance verbs (2c) (see Givón 2001: 153).

(2) Nominative and infinitive
   a. *A stranger was **seen** to enter the building about the time the crime was committed.*
   b. *He was **believed** to be involved in the crime.*
   c. *The victim is **said** to have suffered severe injuries.*

While the ACI patterns illustrated in (1a)-(1c) are unmistakably native to the English language, the NCI (2) and its active variant (1d), sometimes referred to as "Latin-type ACI" (e.g. Fischer 1994), are often considered to be borrowings, as they first started to appear in Latin-influenced writings in the late fourteenth century (Warner 1982). However, the role of Latin in the construction's spread has been a matter of debate. More importantly still, the early accounts have failed to address that the NCI, from its first appearance, is far more frequent than one would expect on the basis of the general distribution of actives and passives.

In what follows, I will discuss the main scenarios for the spread of the Latin-type ACI/NCI as offered by Warner (1982), Fischer (1989, 1992, 1994), Los (2005, 2009) and Noël (2001, 2008). The various approaches appear in a more or less chronological fashion, which reflects the shift from a more externally motivated explanation for the spread of the ACI/NCI that hinges on Latin as external prestige model (section 2.1), to a more internally motivated one, involving language-internal structural factors (section 2.1), discourse-pragmatic factors (section 2.2) and construction-specific semantics (section 2.3) at work. It is the discourse-pragmatic factors that most convincingly explain the incipient spread of the NCI and its establishment into the English grammar, yet the extremely skewed distribution in favour of the NCI today was possibly also advanced by an increase in its use as an evidential marker. This hypothesis is presented in section 2.3, which furthermore delineates the key concepts that my own investigation (section 3) will build on. In the remainder of this section I will use the term "ACI" to refer to the Latin-type ACI (1d) only, unless otherwise stated.

---

3 Perception verbs are followed by a *to*-infinitive in the passive (like the *verba cogitandi and declarandi*). However, they are treated as a separate class in the active because of their different structural behaviour (bare-infinitival complement) and history (ACIs with perception verb already appeared in Old English).

2.1 Contact-induced grammaticalization

Like most early work, Warner (1982) does not differentiate between the ACI and NCI construction, capturing both under the [NP *to* VP] pattern, which may surface in various ways. Ascribing a central role to Latin as an external prestige model, Warner sets out to demonstrate how the ACI/NCI construction spread in Late Middle English by means of minimal alterations. In the early stages, the construction remains most acceptable in Latin-inspired texts. In addition to the Latin-relatedness of the text, Warner discusses a number of grammatical parameters that govern the acceptability of the newly introduced infinitival complementation pattern ([NP *to* VP]), which according to him could not be straightforwardly adopted unless there was some kind of modification of an existing analogous structure to facilitate accommodation of the Latin target construction. Two of these contextual parameters seem to be particularly corroborated by his data, one involving the high incidence of *be* as the non-finite verb and another involving NP-fronting. Often these two contexts are combined.

Warner argues that the prevalence of *be*-infinitives in the ACI hinges upon it being a minimal alteration of an already existing complementation pattern of verbs of thinking and knowing, namely [NP PRED] (e.g. *They consider [her a great scientist]*; see also Bock 1931: 243; Denison 1993: 184; D'Hoedt 2017: 254–255). Extension of this predicative pattern to [NP *to be* PRED], which is considered only a minor change, facilitated the acceptance of the ACI (*... her to be a great scientist*). Warner furthermore observes that early instances of the ACI particularly occurred in the context of NP-fronting, as in relative clauses (3a) or in the passive (hence NCI), e.g. (3b).

(3) a. *whom thei knewen to be prince of the paleis*
    (Esth 9.4 LV, Warner 1982: 142)

   b. *the zodiak in hevene is ymagyned to ben a superfice*
    (Chaucer Astr I.21.36, Warner 1982: 146)

The data show that ACIs with fronted noun phrases (which include NCIs) are not only more common, but also "less restricted in occurrence outside Latin translation" (Warner 1982: 136). This may be explained by the lower syntactic saliency when noun phrase and complement are separated by the main verb, which would make the use of the new syntactic expression less noticeable. Yet, it is unclear how this fits exactly into the story of minimal alterations, as the changes involve fairly complex operations, and, as Warner (1982: 156) himself acknowledges, particularly the passive version "is without a convincing and satisfactory surface analogy".[4] Moreover, given that the preference for moved noun phrases (with passives, i.e. NCIs, in particular) persists to date, Warner (1982: 155) admits that "it is difficult to see how such long term stability in variation can have been maintained with parameters which are merely a consequence of the 'least noticeable' changes which happened to be available in lME syntax". He concludes that these parameters must be "somehow natural" (Warner 1982: 155), implying that they are structural rather than mechanisms of change, but leaves this issue to further research.

Assuming that Latin influence could not have been the only factor at play, Fischer (1989, 1994) argues that the structural preferences Warner observed can in fact be interpreted as relating to a single language-internal change, namely the change from OV to VO. She explains that speakers would only use the construction if the noun phrase preceding the infinitive "can *only* or fairly easily be interpreted as a subject", thereby avoiding misinterpretation of the syntactic status of the nominal element which would previously be understood as the object of the infinitive (Fischer 1989: 211). One strategy to reduce the syntactic ambiguity of the pre-infinitival noun phrase is NP-fronting (see Warner's second parameter). Even though the fronted noun phrase could still be ambiguous, Fischer argues this posed less of a problem to speakers because they were used to the versatility of the clause-initial position, which could host both objects and subjects (Fischer 1989: 211). Since this hypothesis is only briefly touched upon, it remains rather speculative. A more detailed explanation is offered for the prevalence of *be* and other intransitive verbs (including passive infinitives) in the new construction, which are conceived of as another disambiguating strategy (see Warner's first parameter). In a series of studies, Fischer elaborates on the role of the passive infinitive in this process (Fischer 1992, 1994; Fischer et al. 2000). In brief, the passive infinitive was introduced in infinitival complements in order to avoid awkward object infinitives (active infinitives preceded by the object of that infinitive, e.g. [4]) when word order changed from OV to VO.

(4) he sette   scole   7   on þære   he let   cnihtas   læran
    he set-up   school   and   in it   he let   boys-ACC.PL.   teach-INF.
    'He set up a school in which he had boys taught'
    (*Bede* 3(O)14.208.8, Fischer et al. 2000: 226)

---

[4] Warner (1982: 156) adds that the prevalence of the NCI "may be more deeply motivated", possibly connected with "the changing status of English objects", but does not go into detail. As Dreschler's (2015: ch. 3) study demonstrates, there were other types of passives (the prepositional passive, e.g. *he was laughed at*, and the recipient passive, e.g. *he was given a book*) that came into use around this time and which could have served as analogous models for the NCI.

As the use of passive infinitives became current with causative verbs (such as *let*), other verb classes started to appear with passive infinitives. A key development was the analogical extension of the passive infinitive to (causative) persuade-type verbs because it introduced the ACI pattern with this verb class, that is, persuade-type verbs followed by a nominal element and a *to*-infinitive could innovatively be interpreted as two-place ACI patterns (e.g. *[order] [him to be released]*), whereas before only a three-place object control interpretation (e.g. *[order] [him] [to go]*) was possible (see Fischer 1992: 64–69, 1994: 98–103).[5] These new usage patterns of native ACIs, which innovatively combine a *to*-infinitive (rather than a bare infinitive) and a two-place ACI interpretation, facilitated the introduction of the Latin-type ACI. Fischer concludes: "The influence from Latin was present all along, but only became effective when the syntactic structures of English had been altered in such a way that Latin AcI's resembled the new native AcI's" (Fischer et al. 2000: 246).

2.2 The discourse-linking function of the NCI

While both Warner and Fischer noticed the relatively high incidence of passive ACIs, i.e. NCIs, in the early stages, it was not until more recently that this remarkable fact was connected to the changing mapping of syntax and information structure in the history of English (see Los 2005, 2009; Dreschler 2015). One of the first to elaborate on the information-structural function of the NCI was Mair (1990), who suggested that the discourse-linking function of the passive is one of the primary reasons for the predominance of NCIs over ACIs in Present-day English. The following example may illustrate how information-structural conditions motivate the speaker or writer's use of the NCI (as compared to ACI and both active and passive structures with *that*-clauses, see [6]).

(5) *Thanks to the ubiquitous television set, the best known Canadians in Britain are, quite possibly, Bernard Braden, Hughie Green and Robert McKenzie. Others more talented – Jon Vickers, Lynn Seymour, Mordecai Richler, Sir William Butlin, John Hemming, Oscar Petersen, Garfield Weston, Paul Anka, Glenn Ford, Yvonne de Carlo, Raymond Burr, Donald Sutherland and Christopher*

---

5 Los (2005: 239–252) refines this scenario by demonstrating that the persuade-type group of verbs in fact conflates two different groups of verbs, verbs of persuading and urging on the one hand, and verbs of commanding and permitting on the other. It is the latter group that innovatively started to appear in a configuration with a *to*-infinitive *and* a two-place/ACI (instead of a three-place/object control) interpretation.

> *Plummer – are probably seldom identified as Canadians.* **Many of them** *are generally assumed* **to be Americans**, *which raises the whole question of Canada's continuous struggle to maintain a separate identity from her giant neighbour.*
> (W.11.4d.9, Mair 1990: 180, emphasis in the original)

Mair argues that there are good reasons that the writer opted for the NCI even though other options would have been equally felicitous in strictly grammatical terms (see [6]). The subject of the NCI (*many of them*) meronymically relates to the names introduced in the preceding sentence, thereby complying with the natural tendency to present given before new information. The other options, presented in (6a)–(6c), fail to establish such a link with the preceding discourse, and, as such, are less suitable in terms of "textual cohesion" (Mair 1990: 181).

(6) a. *People generally assume many of them to be Americans.*
b. *People generally assume that many of them are Americans.*
c. *It is generally assumed that many of them are Americans.*
(Mair 1990: 180–181)

Building on Mair's suggestions about the discourse-structuring potential of the NCI, Los (2005, 2009) proposes that information structure was also key to the introduction and spread of the NCI in Late Middle English and Early Modern English (for a similar view, see Dreschler 2015). More specifically, she argues that the discourse-linking function of the passive, which crucially hinges on its ability to create unmarked themes, catered for the increased need for subject-topics after word order changes established SVO as the default sentence pattern. Before English developed from a V2 to a strict SVO language, speakers had various ways to satisfy the given-before-new requirement in discourse organization: the clause-initial position could be filled with given subjects, objects and adverbials alike to provide an unmarked link to the preceding sentence. The finite verb thereby served to mark the boundary between given and new information (Hinterhölzl and Petrova 2010: 319). With the decline of V2 and the fixing of SVO word order, the different word order options became restricted: clause-initial objects and adverbials became marked and only the subject remained as an unmarked discourse linker (see also Los and Dreschler 2012). This led to a situation in which information status was increasingly tied to syntactic function, with objects being associated with new information, and subjects with given information (Los and van Kemenade 2012). When given objects could no longer be used as unmarked topics, passivization presented itself as a convenient means to obtain a similar effect: a given object could be turned into an unmarked subject to sit in its preferred clause-initial linking position. This explains the sharp rise of the NCI in the aftermath of the loss of V2 (as documented by Dreschler [2015: 370] in the Penn-Helsinki Parsed Corpus of Early Modern English), and the overall increase of passives in Early Modern English (Seoane 2000, 2006).

2.3 Construction-specific semantics and pragmatics

By shifting the focus to the discourse-structuring function of the NCI, which it inherits from the higher-order passive construction, accounts by Los (2005, 2009) and Dreschler (2015) have elegantly demonstrated how grammar may be shaped by communicative needs. However, while their accounts go a long way towards explaining the rise of the NCI in Early Modern English, which secured the construction's survival in the English grammar, the information-rearranging function of the NCI by itself can only partly account for the remarkable distribution of ACIs and NCIs in Present-day English. Today the passive NCI makes up 70–74% of all ACI/NCI instances (Mair 1990; Noël 1998, 2001), an increase of roughly 30% compared with the early modern aggregate (see Dreschler 2015: 370, table 6.24). Regular passives, by contrast, merely account for 11% of Present-day English active and passive sentences combined (Francis and Kučera 1982: 554).[6] This difference suggests that there must be another factor in addition to the discourse-structuring function (which is shared among passives of all types) that helps explain why the NCI caught on so spectacularly. This factor may be found in the semantic-pragmatic meaning conveyed by the construction, which has been largely glossed over by the accounts presented in sections 2.1 and 2.2, but has been discussed at length by Noël (most notably, Noël 2001, 2008).

Much of the theoretical discussion in Noël's work is concerned with the NCI's potential to mark evidentiality, which is hypothesized to have played a role in the NCI's increase in certain Late Modern English genres (Noël 2008).[7] This

---

6 It should be noted that this is probably a fairly conservative count, seeing that Francis and Kučera (1982) do not seem to have factored in transitivity in this comparison (intransitive verbs should have been excluded from the comparison since they do not qualify for passivization).
7 In earlier work (e.g. Noël 2001), Noël viewed the evidential NCI as a grammaticalized auxiliary-like construction that developed out of the regular passive NCI source construction. This grammaticalization account was rejected in a later paper which suggested instead that the evidential use was most likely borrowed directly from Latin, but that it may have played a role in the increase of the NCI in certain genres in the Late Modern English period (Noël 2008). Note that the English NCI does not qualify as an evidential proper in Aikhenvald's (2004) terminology (i.e. as

hypothesis is worth investigating, as it complements the picture established in sections 2.1 and 2.2, and would imply that around the time the NCI had already significantly expanded as a result of the increased need for subject-topics, speakers started to exploit the NCI's potential as an evidential strategy, which in turn may have given the NCI additional impetus and could have led to an overall semantic shift. In the remainder of this section, I comment on and expand Noël's semantic classification of the NCI, which will serve as a basis to verify this hypothesis in section 3.

Noël (2008) discerns three separate constructions. The first, illustrated in (7a), is merely the realization of a passive construction, instantiating a "spatiotemporally locatable utterance act"; the other two, the "evidential NCI" (7b) and the "descriptive NCI" (7c), serve to qualify the proposition at hand (Noël 2008: 317).

(7) a. *In this book authorities **are said to** be limited also by the kinds of reasons on which they may or may not rely in making decisions* [...] (ANH 148)

b. *BRAVO, a new on-screen booking system* [...], *has entered its launch phase. It **is said to** offer independent hotels the kind of exposure which hotels in big groups can derive from international booking systems* [...] (AOC 456)

c. [...] *in every poem there are striking effects of word order which, on the one hand, may **be said to** have been contrived, or willed by the poet* [...] (J7P 44)
(Noël 2008: 317, emphasis in the original)

The descriptive NCI is said to "link up a description with a descriptum" (Noël 2008: 319), whereas the evidential NCI signals that there is evidence for the speaker's claim. The latter may sometimes have the pragmatic effect of "shed[ding] responsibility for the truthfulness of this information" (Noël 2008: 318). Noël argues the three constructions differ in semantics, not in formal composition, and therefore cannot be objectively distinguished from each other (Noël 2008: 317–321).

I would like to argue instead that the different semantic interpretations Noël observes do arise from formal differences. Descriptive NCIs are marked as modalized utterances; they locate the underlying proposition in the space of possibilities, i.e. refer to possible worlds rather than real events. This may be illustrated by (7c), where leaving out the modal verb *may* would trigger an evidential interpretation. Likewise, adding a modal like *can* or *may* in (7b) precludes an

---

an obligatory grammatical category), but rather is an evidentiality strategy. The use of "evidential" and "evidential marker" will be used as a shorthand for "evidentiality strategy".

evidential reading. Because evidential markers have wide scope, i.e. they semantically scope over propositions, they cannot themselves be within the scope of modal markers (see Boye 2012). Incidentally, modal markers in the NCI often seem to function as hedging devices: what an utterance like (7c) does is not fully captured by the definition of linking up a description (*be contrived or willed by the poet*) with a descriptum (*striking effects of word order*). Rather it seems the speaker wants to present an assertion (i.e. that the striking word order effects are contrived by the author) in a tentative manner.

This pragmatic effect is related to what I believe constitutes the core function of the NCI construction, that is, the speaker's epistemic qualification of a proposition p, e.g. *that black cats are a symbol of misfortune* in (8), which predicates something about the subject of the NCI. More specifically, the NCI provides the speaker with a means to express that there is an epistemological basis for p, either (a) by referring to the existence of an external source for the information contained in the proposition, without the speaker having to explicitly name that source (evidential use), or (b) by specifying the degree to which the assertion is compatible with her current knowledge (modalized, i.e. descriptive, use).[8] One could furthermore argue that the evidential NCI is essentially reportative in nature, even though the underlying basis for the evidence, as specified by the PCU verb, may be sensory (e.g. *see*) or cognitive (e.g. *believe*) rather than discourse-related (e.g. *say*). As Bednarek (2006: 643) puts it: "What the writer says is that his/her knowledge is in fact based on what a third party has either expressed linguistically (HEARSAY) or mentally (MINDSAY)", whereby mindsay or "quoted mental experience" concerns utterances marked "as having been thought/felt/experienced by a 'Senser'".

(8) a. *Black cats are said to be a symbol of misfortune.*
     '[that black cats are a symbol of misfortune]$_p$ [is said]$_{\text{epist. qual.}}$.'[9]
     b. *Black cats may be said to be a symbol of misfortune.*
     '[that black cats are a symbol of misfortune]$_p$ [may be said]$_{\text{epist. qual.}}$.'

---

8 The notions of evidentiality and modality are conceptually distinct, but closely related. The theoretical debate about the exact relation of the two, e.g. whether one category is subsumed by the other, falls outside the scope of this article (see Wiemer 2018 for a recent overview).
9 This paraphrase is inspired by Seuren and Haman (2009), who argue that the subjects of NCIs and other subject-to-subject raising constructions resemble clauses and characterize the NCI's function as evidential predication (qualification).

By specifying how the speaker knows (8a) or assesses (8b) *p*, both the evidential and modalized use serve to justify the utterance. If a speaker plainly asserted that black cats are a symbol of misfortune, it would create a binding commitment to the truth of the proposition, which the speaker may not want to make. The NCI allows the speaker to modify that commitment, hence the incidental pragmatic effects of hedging and shedding responsibility that have been observed in the literature.

The distinction between regular passives and evidential NCIs, which implies a difference in evidentiality, is hard to maintain. The difference Noël proposes seems to emerge from a difference in the perceived genericity of the statement and specificity of the source, brought about by contextual elements, rather than an actual difference in terms of evidentiality (see Seuren and Hamans [2009: 154] for a similar criticism). Compare the following sentences.

(9) a. *Black cats are said to be a symbol of misfortune.*
b. *Black cats are said by some to be a symbol of misfortune.*
c. *At that time black cats were said to be a symbol of misfortune.*
d. *In this book black cats are said to be a symbol of misfortune.*
'[that black cats are a symbol of misfortune]$_p$ [is said (by some/at that time/in this book)]$_{\text{epist. qual.}}$'

In (9), the NCI encodes the source the speaker has for a particular assertion (i.e. that black cats are a symbol of misfortune), irrespective of whether the utterance act is spatiotemporally locatable. Optional agent phrases and adverbials either specify the source or serve to demarcate the subspace of the reference world in which the assertion holds true, i.e. they modify the basic constructional frame that encodes evidentiality. Theoretically, one could order evidential statements on a cline of genericity, but the presence or absence of additional detail does not affect their status as evidential markers. This may be compared to the German reportative evidential *sollen*, which may or may not be combined with specific referral to the source (see *SportBild* in the following example).

(10) *Auch der FC Barcelona soll laut SportBild abgelehnt haben.*[10]
'According to SportBild, FC Barcelona has declined as well.'

---

10 The example was taken from *https://www.tz.de/sport/fc-bayern/fc-bayern-berater-bot-bvb-star-ousmane-demb-l-beim-fcb-an-lehnte-ab-8465881.html* (accessed 25 September 2017). Vanderbiesen (2015: 25) notes: "Reportives use the reference to the existence of a source only as a means to an end, namely the justification of a proposition, therefore they will often omit overt reference to this source."

In sum, all non-modalized NCIs carry evidential potential by virtue of the lexical content of the PCU matrix verb (e.g. *said*). If the utterance is modalized, the focus lies on the speaker's evaluation of the statement along the dimensions of necessity and possibility. While the distinction between modalized and evidential NCIs is warranted on both semantic and formal grounds, they share the underlying function of epistemic justification. This is why I will speak of different usage types (reflecting constructional polysemy) rather than different constructions. As Coleman and De Clerck (2011) convincingly demonstrate for the double object construction, (polysemous) constructions may undergo semasiological shifts such as specialization. A significant increase in evidential uses of the NCI, which according to Noël (2008) could be responsible for the general increase of the NCI pattern in certain Late Modern English genres, would be indicative of such a constructional change. However, Noël himself refrains from undertaking any quantitative study operationalizing his classification, which could have shed some more light on the development of the NCI through time.[11] In what follows, I will present the results of such a diachronic analysis that combines the semantic motivations for using the NCI with the speaker-central perspective outlined in section 1.

3 The NCI in seventeenth-century authors

3.1 Data and methodology

In order to investigate constructional changes in the NCI at the level of the individual mind, the present study draws on data from the EMMA corpus (*Early Modern Multiloquent Authors*), which has recently been published online (Petré et al. 2019). The EMMA corpus is a large-scale specialized corpus that comprises the writings of a selection of 50 individuals across five generations of seventeenth-century authors. The body of texts, amounting to c. 90 million words, was mainly collected from the EEBO and ECCO databases following an extensive author selection (and for ECCO data, an OCR correction) process.[12] The set of criteria to be

---

[11] Detailed diachronic semantic analyses do exist for specific NCIs, most notably for *be supposed to*, which has developed into a marker of deontic modality (Ziegeler 2003; Visconti 2004; Berkenfield 2006; Moore 2007; Noël and van der Auwera 2009; Disney 2016). This construction will not be discussed separately here.

[12] *Early English Books Online* (EEBO) and *Eighteenth Century Collection Online* (ECCO) contain scans and transcriptions of most of the works printed in the UK between 1470–1800. Texts from our selection of authors that were not transcribed manually but whose electronic version was

fulfilled by the prospective authors included, among other things, a long career with sufficient material across career stages (amounting to a minimum of 500,000 words per author), a demonstrable link with London, and social, political and stylistic connections within and across generations. EMMA comes with a rich metadata database and a corpus query and annotation tool (CosyCat).[13]

In this section, I will report on the findings of a qualitative and quantitative corpus analysis of four first-generation EMMA authors whose aggregate corpus size amounts to nearly 10 million words (see table 5.1).[14] The corpus was queried by means of regular expressions consisting of a finite or non-finite form of the verb *to be* followed by a participle of a PCU verb[15] (within a six-word-window) and by *to* (within a three-word-window of the participle). After manual inspection for false positives, the dataset contains 3,437 instances.

Tab. 5.1: Sample of first-generation EMMA authors, attestations of NCIs

Author	Corpus size	Attestations
Thomas Fuller (1608–1661), *Church of England clergyman, historian*	2,648,691	733
John Milton (1608–1674), *Poet, polemicist*	729,651	144
John Owen (1616–1683), *Nonconformist church leader*	4,349,249	2,236
Roger L'Estrange (1616–1704), *Licenser of the Press, pamphleteer*	2,014,874	324
Total	**9,742,465**	**3,437**

---

automatically generated by means of OCR (optical character recognition) and therefore prone to errors have been manually corrected at the University of Antwerp by the Mind-Bending Grammars research team and a number of students, interns and volunteers.

13 https://github.com/emanjavacas/cosycat

14 The results presented here are preliminary results of a larger ongoing project that examines the NCI in a sample of EMMA authors from five generations (30 authors). The choice of these authors was based on the authors' profiles to ensure comparability across generations with respect to distribution of narrative versus non-narrative authors. At the time of writing this article, the compilation process for other generations was not yet complete, hence the focus on first-generation authors.

15 The list contains 113 verbs and is based on the PCU verbs listed by Noël (2008: 328), Mair (1990: 237–238), Los (2005: 254) and Postal (1974: 297–317). Main spelling variants were accounted for.

For each instance, it was verified which of the three NCI types (as proposed by Noël, see section 2.3) is instantiated.[16] I started from Noël's classification, but used terms that better reflect the formal differences between the usage types. The "descriptive NCI" was replaced by the formal characterization "modalized NCI" (MOD), "evidential NCI" (EVID) remained the same, and "explicit evidential" (EVID.EXP) rather than "regular passive of an ACI" was used to refer to those instances in which either the source or type of evidence is explicitly indicated (e.g. by an agent phrase) or in which the action expressed by the PCU verb is located in space and/or time by means of adverbials. The use of EVID and EVID.EXP moreover reflects my argumentation in section 2.3 that the perceived difference between these types does not concern their evidential function. Apart from constructional semantics, the relevant sentences were annotated for a number of formal and semantic variables, including, if applicable, subject animacy, subject definiteness, subject form, clause type, lemma PCU verbs, lemma *to*-infinitive, type *to*-infinitive, tense, negation, modality, agent phrase and adverbials. In the remainder of the paper, these additional parameters will only be returned to if they are relevant for the discussion at hand.

Bearing in mind the general increase in frequency of the NCI in the early modern period, the main purpose of this diachronic investigation is to verify whether constructional change is also attested during the lifetimes of individual speakers. In particular, I will look at variation and change in the distribution of semantic-pragmatic usage types across different stages in adult life. More generally, though, as this corpus study provides the first quantitative account of these three construction types, the findings may also advance their theoretical description. A possible correlation with verb semantics is most relevant in this respect and will be addressed in section 3.2.1 before zooming in on the dynamics of these usage types in individual lifetimes in section 3.2.2.

---

[16] For the most frequently used PCU verb *say*, the results were extrapolated if there were more than 100 attestations with *say* per author. This was the case for Owen (1,259/2,236) and Fuller (352/733). For Owen, 10% of the attestations of *say* were annotated for semantic usage type, for Fuller 50%.

3.2 Results and discussion

3.2.1 The relationship between verbs and constructions

In constructionist approaches to argument structure, it is assumed that the verb elaborates the meaning of the construction (Goldberg 1995). Typically, the verbs code the meaning of the construction lexically (such as *give* in the ditransitive construction or *push* in the caused-motion construction), but this need not be the case, e.g. *sneeze* in *she sneezed the napkin off the table*. In the latter example, the verb designates how the motion is brought about, but the idea of motion itself is encoded by the construction. Similarly, the various PCU verbs in the evidential NCI may serve to accentuate the type or quality of the evidence the speaker has for her statement (e.g. hearsay, mindsay). In modalized NCIs, it is arguably the modal verbs that present the main means of elaboration (by positioning the description of the subject within the dimensions of possibility and necessity). In light of these observations, it seems likely that the PCU verb may bear a different relation to the construction depending on usage type; in particular, the question arises if and to which extent the various PCU verbs correlate with particular usage types.

In this study 92 different PCU verbs are attested in the NCI, with counts for the individual authors ranging between 37 and 70 in line with the overall size of the corpora. Examples (11)–(14) may serve to illustrate some of the patterns found.

(11) *He **is reported not to have suffered** any woman to come in his sight; not because he was a hater of their sex, but because he was to deale with dangerous adversaries, he would warily cut off all occasions of suspition; [...]*
(EMMA A40646 Fuller, 1651)

(12) *In the mean while a blazing Star, 7 Mornings together, about the end of April, **was ſeen to ſtream** terribly, not only over England, but other parts of the World; [...]*
(EMMA A50902 Milton, 1670)

(13) *And yet such monsters **are** all the Saints of God **supposed to be**, who, if their Father once give them the least Assurance of the Continuance of his Love, they presently resolve to doe him all the dishonour, despite, and mischeife they can: [...]*
(EMMA A53688 Owen, 1654)

(14) *No child unborn **can be thought to be** Guilty of an actual crime, such as killing the King, or subverting the Government of a Nation; and consequently no Child*

unborn **can be said to be** Innocent of those actual crimes, as not being the proper subject of actual Guilt or Innocence.
(EMMA A47831 L'Estrange, 1680)

To gauge the relationship between verb semantics and constructional semantics, I carried out a correspondence analysis for each author. Figures 5.1 and 5.2 illustrate the results for Owen, the most prolific author in the sample, whose data account for two thirds of the attested NCIs and also exhibit the greatest variety of PCU verbs.[17]

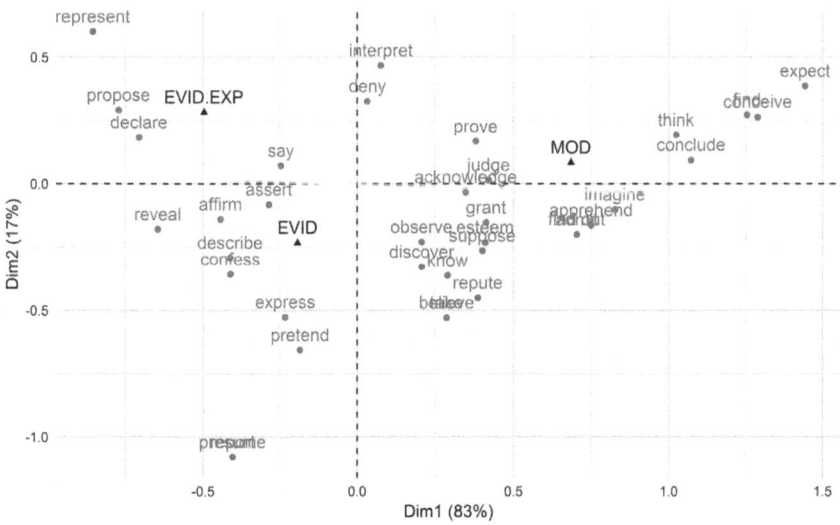

Fig. 5.1: Symmetric biplot of John Owen's dataset

Correspondence analysis (CA) is a statistical method that returns factor scores (principle coordinates) for row and column frequencies (in this case verb semantics and constructional usage types) in a contingency table. These coordinates are used to represent the association between row and column variables in a two-dimensional space. There are two types of CA: symmetric and asymmetric biplots. Symmetric biplots represent row-to-row and column-to-column distances in a common space. This entails that PCU verbs (rows) with a similar distributional profile for their usage types (columns) will be found close to each other; usage

---

[17] Note that I only included verbs that were attested at least 5 times.

type profiles (columns) that are similar will also be found closer to each other. However, whereas row-to-row distances and column-to-column distances reflect χ2-distances between the row profiles and column profiles, respectively, symmetric biplots only give a general idea of row-to-column or column-to-row distances and therefore cannot be used to interpret the association between rows and columns (i.e. between PCU verbs and usage types) directly (Bendixen 2003; Levshina 2015). The latter can be achieved by means of an asymmetric biplot, which is essentially the same plot except that it plots column profiles in row space. The acuteness of the angle between the column arrow and the row points reflects the degree of association between the two.

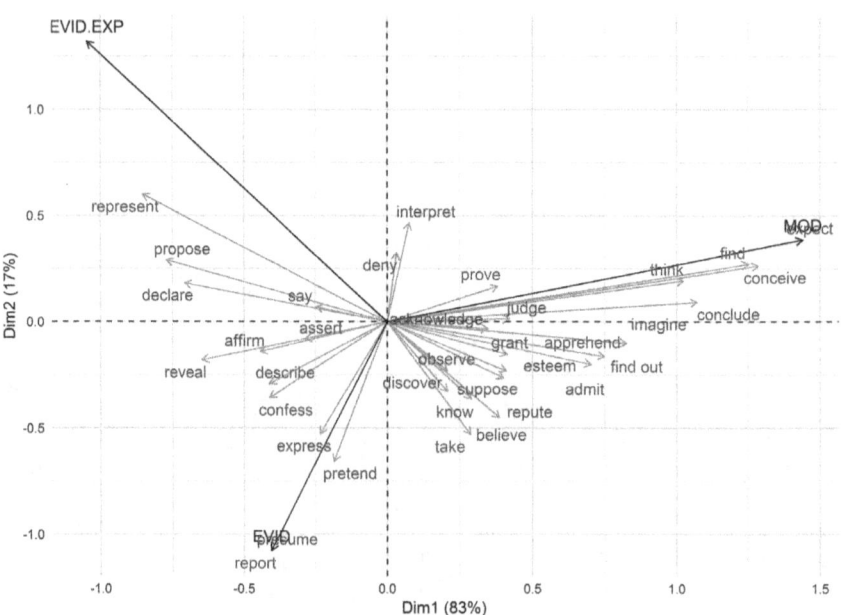

Fig. 5.2: Asymmetric biplot of John Owen's dataset

Figures 5.1 and 5.2 demonstrate that many verbs tend to be more strongly associated with one of the usage types. Utterance verbs (*say, assert, affirm, report, declare, confess, express, propose*) are typically found towards the left of the vertical axis, that is, in evidential uses (whether explicit or not) such as (11). Verbs with a higher incidence of explicit evidential uses (*declare, propose, deny, represent*) seem to be lexically associated with a clearly identifiable agent. This is corroborated by the fact that they are also more commonly used in ACIs (i.e. in actives, which specify the agent) than in NCIs (e.g. *declare/deny* in Noël and Colleman's [2010] study on collexemes of the ACI/NCI). The same holds for perception verbs (like *see* and *hear*), e.g. (12), which are too infrequent in Owen's data and are therefore not plotted. However, data from the other authors indicate a strong association between perception verbs and evidential or explicit evidential uses. A group of verbs towards the outer right (*think, find, conceive, expect, conclude*), primarily cognition verbs, is strongly associated with the modalized use (e.g. 14), and their being situated in close proximity of each other underlines how similar their distributional profiles are. Another group of cognition verbs (including *know, suppose, believe, esteem, acknowledge, judge*) does not show a particular preference for the evidential or modalized use, being commonly attested in both construction types. Overall, utterance and perception verbs tend to express evidentiality, which ties in with their semantics, and the cognition verbs are split into two groups, one exhibiting a strong preference for the modalized NCI, another showing no preference for either function.

The results also bear directly upon theoretical discussion concerning the constructional status of the three NCI constructions proposed by Noël (see section 2.3). Seeing that 83% of the variance is explained by the first dimension (modalized vs. evidential/explicit evidential), the graphs support the view presented in section 2.3 that there are basically two rather than three main constructional usage types (this finding is replicated for the other authors in the sample). Further support comes from the observation that verbs commonly found in explicit evidentials are lexically (rather than constructionally) associated with an explicit agent. The category of evidentials being situated nearest to the intersection of the dimensions (i.e. the average profile) furthermore demonstrates that evidentiality is the prototypical meaning associated with the NCI.

3.2.2 Variation and change across the lifespan

This section examines the distribution of the semantic-pragmatic usage types across different stages in the authors' lives. An overview of these distributions can be found in figure 5.3, which shows the proportion of modalized and evidential uses per age group. Explicit evidentials are, in line with the findings outlined in the previous section, subsumed under the category of evidentials.[18]

---

18 The category "other" contains (i) indeterminate examples where the distinction between evidential and modalized use is blurred due to the interaction of the NCI with other constructions

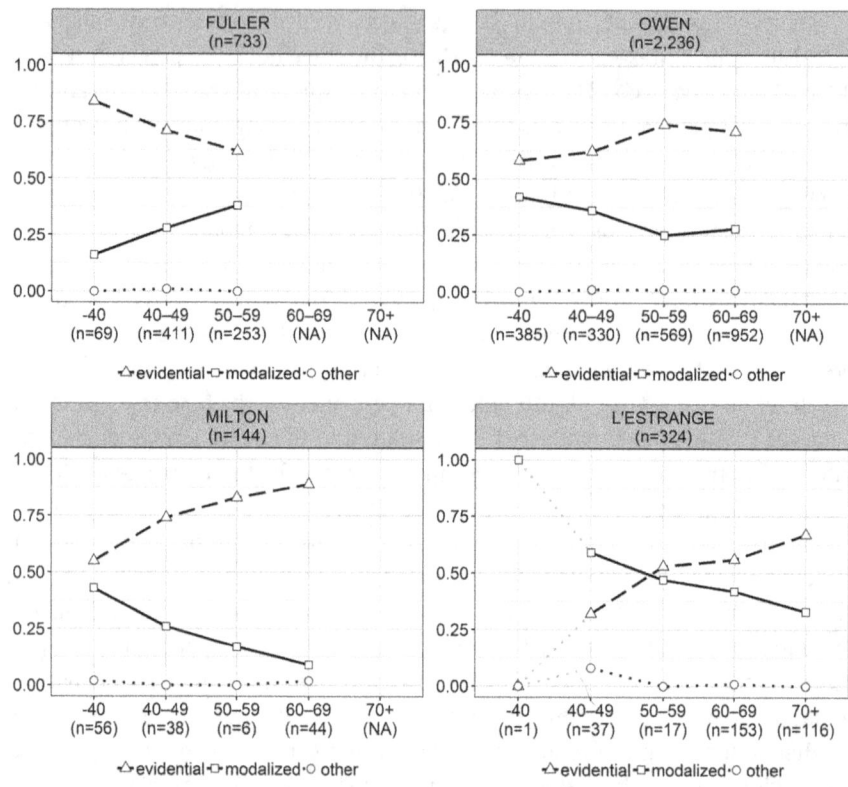

Fig. 5.3: Proportion of modalized/evidential uses across the lifespan[19]

All authors exhibit significant change in their use of the NCI construction over time: in each case, the proportional distribution of evidential and modalized uses shifts within a single lifetime.[20] Importantly, the trends are linear and persist well

---

(e.g. conditionals) and (ii) deontic or ambiguous uses of *be supposed to* and *be expected to* (cf. fn. 12).
19 For L'Estrange, the lines between age –40 and 40–49 are backgrounded because the NCI is attested only once in the first period.
20 In order to measure the ordinal association between age and usage type, I calculated Kendall's rank correlation coefficient (the category 'other' was excluded). The modalized use was ranked 0 and the evidential use 1, which means that a positive correlation between age and the evidential use will result in positive z-scores and tau coefficients (τ) and a positive correlation between age and the modalized use in negative z-scores and tau coefficients (i.e. a negative correlation between age and the evidential use). The results show a statistically significant

into old age, which provides tentative evidence for the broader claim that constructional changes affecting syntactic constructions are not restricted to childhood and adolescence, but may continue throughout the lifespan. One could also argue that the cross-individual trend towards more evidential uses with age (with the exception of Fuller, but see below) is not a constructional change, but a stylistic one. This raises the pertinent question of why this would be the case. Why would speakers adopt a preference for the evidential NCI over time, if not on the grounds that the NCI specializes into a reportative evidential? Although the possibility of cross-individual stylistic change cannot be excluded, a number of observations seem to support the latter view that the shift may indicate constructional change. First, the change is not restricted to a single genre, but is found in religious, narrative as well as political writings (as represented by Fuller/Owen, Milton and L'Estrange, respectively).[21] Second, the rise in the proportion of evidential uses as compared to modalized ones is accompanied by an increase in the normalized frequency of the evidential NCI (in all four writers), whereas the normalized frequency of the modalized NCI drops (in all writers except Fuller, but see below). In other words, one subset of meanings – attribution of p to a (usually) unspecified information source – gains in strength of representation, while the other meaning – the speaker's evaluation of p – fades, not only proportionally, but also in absolute terms. This frequency effect attests to a semasiological shift that may arguably signal the NCI's specialization into a (dedicated) reportative marker and as such its growing emancipation from the passive construction. Data from Present-day English furthermore show that several PCU verbs (e.g. *say*,

---

correlation between age and usage type for each of the authors (Fuller: $z = -3.67$, $p < 0.001$, $\tau = -0.13$; Milton: $z = 3.82$, $p < 0.001$, $\tau = 0.300$; Owen: $z = 4.81$, $p < 0.001$, $\tau = 0.094$, L'Estrange: $z = 3.24$, $p = 0.001$, $\tau = 0.17$). Milton, Owen, and L'Estrange's data exhibit a positive correlation between the author's age and the frequency of evidential uses; Fuller a negative correlation (cf. the discussion).

21 Note, however, that genre may well affect how often a construction is used in the sense that certain topics and styles may induce or obviate the need for a construction like the NCI (which has as its main function the justification of the utterance at hand). In this small sample of authors, it is the religious writers (Fuller and Owen) who use the NCI more frequently (cf. the number of instances per million words for Fuller [277] and Owen [514] versus Milton [197] and L'Estrange [160]), but more pertinent still is the individual variation. Follow-up studies with more authors will be better suited to assess the extent to which genre effects may explain individual variation. For the case presented here, we may conclude that genre differences might explain at least some of the variation found in frequency of usage, but not the construction's semasiological shift which is attested across individuals and genres.

rumour, repute) only occur in the NCI, but not in the ACI,[22] and that the former is subject to fewer restrictions regarding the use of infinitives other than *be* and *have* (including passive and perfect infinitives; see Noël 2001: 257–259; Mair 1990: 176), which attests to the view that the NCI is not merely a passive.

Nahkola and Saanilahti's (2004) findings provide an interesting perspective on the observations presented here. In a panel study pertaining to various phonological and morphological changes in Finnish, they suggest that the possibility of lifespan changes relates to the categoricalness with which variants are acquired:

> If a speaker, as a child, "learns" a feature with little or no variation in it, no major changes are likely to take place during the speaker's lifetime. [...] If, however, a speaker adopts a feature as a variable one, [...] it is possible that the balance of the variants will shift during the speaker's lifetime. (Nahkola and Saanilahti 2004: 75)

The latter applies to the NCI construction as well. All authors had presumably acquired the NCI with its two variant uses by the time they were adults. For Milton, Owen and L'Estrange, the difference between modalized and evidential uses does not exceed 20% in their earliest writings, that is, their use of the NCI is highly variable. However, the evidential use slowly gains ground and prevails towards the end of their lives. Fuller deviates from this shared pattern in two ways. First, his use of the NCI is more categorical in the beginning than at the end of his career, whereas the other authors show a high degree of variation. Second, as the proportion of modalized uses expands significantly over time, Fuller once more counteracts what appears to be a communal trend.

However, a closer look at Fuller's distribution of semantic-pragmatic usage types reveals that figure 5.3 [FULLER] conflates two different developments. When treated separately, the data show that the nature of the trend varies with the PCU verb used in the NCI construction (see figure 5.4 below).[23]

A consistent finding across all authors is that *say* is by far the most frequently attested PCU verb, accounting for 50% of all instances across the board (1,730/3,437). Separating the verb *say* from all the other attested verbs alters the

---

[22] This has not necessarily always been the case, in particular for *repute*. For the authors under investigation, there is one instance of the ACI with *repute*, none with *say* and *rumour*. In the EMMA corpus as a whole, there are 3 instances of the ACI with *say*, 17 with *repute* and none with *rumour*, e.g. *I hope by this time, the Way he takes to prove George Fox what he wickedly ſayes him to be, is evidently detected of Inſufficiency* [...] (William Penn, 1672), *They repute the Papiſts to be Hereticks* (Richard Baxter, 1657).

[23] There is a statistically significant correlation between age and usage type for *say* ($z = -5.08$, $p < 0.001$, $\tau = -0.26$), but not for the other verbs ($z = -0.16$, $p = 0.87$, $\tau = -0.01$). These calculations are based on the Kendall correlation statistic (cf. fn. 20).

picture of Fuller's diachronic development drastically, indicating that there is a strong negative linear trend in his evidential use of the NCI with *say* against the backdrop of stable usage of the NCI with other PCU verbs. By contrast, in Milton, Owen and L'Estrange's writings, the diachronic upward trend of evidential uses is found for both *say* and the group of other verbs when treated separately, indicating that the evidential NCI is entrenched as a schema with *say* as the prototypical reportative verb. Interestingly, Fuller's use of PCU verbs excluding *say* is already relatively categorical in his early career and remains so throughout his lifetime, with the proportions of roughly 75% to 25% for evidential/modalized uses mirroring the endpoint of the developments in the other authors. Fuller appears to have developed an idiosyncratic use of the *say*-NCI, increasingly favouring its modalized use, which can be used as an argumentative device (cf. the discussion of [7c] in section 2.3 and L'Estrange's argumentation in [14]). In fact, 85% of Fuller's modalized uses with *say* are of the type *may be said to V*, as in the following example.

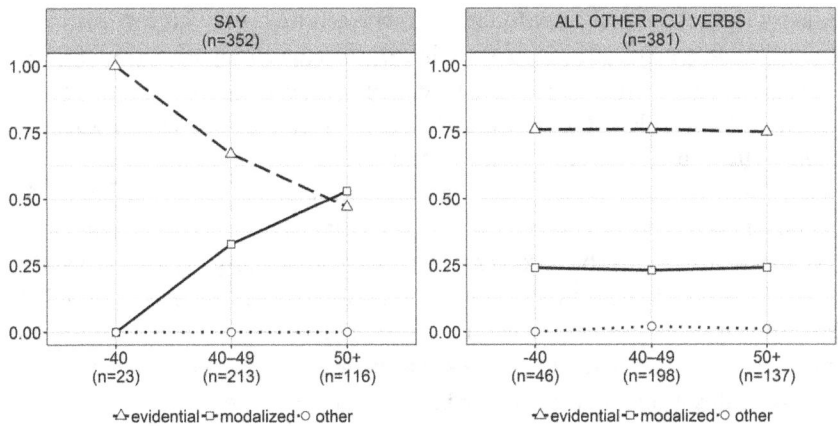

Fig. 5.4: Proportion of modalized/evidential uses for *say* and all other PCU verbs (Fuller)

(15) *THe World is a volumne of Gods works, which all good people ought studiously to peruse. Three sorts of men are too blame herein. First such as observe nothing at all; seeing, but neither marking nor minding the daily accidents that happen, with Gallio the secure deputie of Achaia, They care for none of these things. Secondly, Such as observe nothing observable.* **These may be said to weed the world**; *[...] Lastly, Such who make good observations, but no applications.* (EMMA 99862561 Fuller, 1649)

In (15), the NCI serves not to provide evidence of shared responsibility for the statement that people who observe nothing observable weed the world. Rather, while such modalized utterances (especially with *may* and *can*) may appear to characterize or describe the proposition as a possibility, the speaker is here using this device to present his attitudes or views in a tentative manner.

4 Conclusion

This paper has investigated change in individuals and has taken initial steps to clarify whether constructional change of syntactic constructions is possible within the adult lifespan of an individual. Having drawn attention to the idiosyncrasy of linguistic knowledge, I introduced the expanding use of the NCI in Early Modern English as a suitable case study to verify whether constructional change can also be modelled at the level of the individual.

NCI patterns emerged in Late Middle English, but only really gained ground in Early Modern English. Key to the NCI's burst in frequency during this period were information-structural demands that arose in the aftermath of the loss of V2. Gradually evolving into a strict SVO language, English lost its versatile clause-initial position which served to establish a connection with the preceding discourse and could host given discourse referents in various constituent forms (subjects, objects, adverbials). With only subjects remaining as unmarked discourse linkers, a need emerged for strategies that could turn non-agentive discourse referents into subject-topics. The passive, which promotes given patients to topic position, is such an "information-rearranging device" (Seoane 2000: 24). Unsurprisingly, its use increased in the early modern period and so did that of the NCI, which inherited the passive's discourse-structuring potential.

While this is an important factor in explaining why the NCI in many cases is favoured over its active counterpart (ACI), I have argued that the information-structuring function of the NCI can only partly explain the skewed distribution of NCIs and ACIs today. As Givón (1984: 44) notes, "one may view syntax as a communicative compromise, a compromise between the need to code propositional-semantic information and the need to code – simultaneously and by the same structure – discourse pragmatic function". Concerning the propositional-semantic contribution of the construction, the NCI appears to outstrip the ACI in functionality as well. In its non-modalized form the NCI signifies that there is an external source of evidence for the speaker's claim, without her having to point out the exact source of that evidence (the agent typically remains unexpressed). As such, the NCI seems predisposed to evolve into a dedicated reportative marker (much like German *sollen*). It is, however, still poorly understood how this particular usage type developed in Early Modern English, when the NCI in general was shown to expand, and how possible changes in the evidential NCI might have affected the other established usage type, that is, the modalized NCI (which may also serve to justify the utterance, but does not resort to an external, and therefore perhaps more objective, epistemological source). The present study has attempted not only to shed light on these specific issues, but also more generally on the scope and limits of constructional change in the linguistic individual.

The main outcome of the corpus study is that the proportional distribution of evidential and modalized NCIs shifts throughout the lifetimes of the informants. Milton, Owen and L'Estrange exhibit a considerable degree of variation in their use of the NCI in early writings which becomes more categorical in favour of the evidential use towards the end of their careers, modalized uses becoming the minority pattern. I have argued that the cross-individual propagation of the evidential use and decline of the modalized use reflect the NCI's increasing entrenchment as a reportative evidential and its growing emancipation from the passive construction. The semasiological shift that happens during the lifetime of the individuals is one of specialization (semantic narrowing) towards the evidential use. Regarding Fuller, two separate trends need to be discerned: while his use of the NCI (all verbs except *say*) is already fairly categorical at the beginning of his career and remains stable over time (with a strong predominance of the evidential NCI), his use of the *say*-NCI specializes towards the hedging function of the modalized NCI.

In more general terms, the present study has highlighted the importance of research on individual variation and change. The variation attested in this study, in particular Fuller's idiosyncratic development, which deviates from the trends observed in the other authors, indicates that language change, like synchronic grammatical competence, is an abstraction that may describe collective behaviour, but says little about individual cognition. Not only did the empirical analysis show that language usage may vary considerably during the individuals' lifetimes, it also revealed non-random patterns in that individuals exhibited linear trends of semasiological change in the NCI construction. These findings provide tentative evidence for the broader claim that constructional changes affecting syntactic constructions are possible after adolescence. While it is clear that more empirical studies need to be conducted to further substantiate this claim and extend the scope of this contribution (e.g. to assess the interaction between individuals and the speech community within and across generations), I hope the results presented here may encourage others to follow suit.

Acknowledgements

The research reported on in this paper is part of the project *Mind-Bending Grammars*, which is funded by the ERC Horizon 2020 programme (Project ID 639008; www.uantwerpen.be/mind-bending-grammars/), and is hosted at the University of Antwerp. Both institutions are hereby gratefully acknowledged. I would also like to thank Peter Petré, Tanja Mortelmans, the editors and two anonymous reviewers for their helpful suggestions and detailed comments on an earlier version of this paper.

References

Aikhenvald, Alexandra Y. 2004. *Evidentiality*. Oxford: Oxford University Press.
Aitchison, Jean. 2001. *Language change: Progress or decay?* 3rd edn. Cambridge: Cambridge University Press.
Barlow, Michael. 2013. Individual differences and usage-based grammar. *International Journal of Corpus Linguistics* 18 (4). 443–478.
Baxter, Gareth & William Croft. 2016. Modeling language change across the lifespan: Individual trajectories in community change. *Language Variation and Change* 28. 129–173.
Bednarek, Monika. 2006. Epistemological positioning and evidentiality in English news discourse: A text-driven approach. *Text & Talk* 26 (6). 635–660.
Bendixen, Mike. 2003. A practical guide to the use of correspondence analysis in marketing research. *Marketing Bulletin* 14. 1–15.
Bergs, Alexander. 2005. Social networks and historical sociolinguistics. *Studies in morphosyntactic variation in the Paston Letters (1421–1503)*. Berlin: De Gruyter Mouton.
Berkenfield, Catie. 2006. Pragmatic motivations for the development of evidential and modal meaning in the construction "be supposed to [X]". *Journal of Historical Pragmatics* 7 (1). 39–71.
Bock, Hellmut. 1931. Studien zum präpositionalen Infinitiv und Akkusativ mit dem *to*-Infinitiv. *Anglia* 55. 114–249.
Boyd, Jeremy K. & Adele E. Goldberg. 2011. Learning what *not* to say: The role of statistical preemption and categorization in *a*-adjective production. *Language* 87 (1). 55–83.
Boye, Kasper. 2012. *Epistemic meaning: A cross-linguistic and cognitive study*. Berlin: De Gruyter Mouton.
Bybee, Joan. 2010. *Language, usage and cognition*. Cambridge: Cambridge University Press.
Chipere, Ngoni. 2001. Native speaker variations in syntactic competence: Implications for first language teaching. *Language Awareness* 10. 107–124.
Chipere, Ngoni. 2003. *Understanding complex sentences: Native speaker variation in syntactic competence*. New York: Palgrave Macmillan.
Chomsky, Noam. 1965. *Aspects of the theory of syntax*. Cambridge, MA: MIT Press.
Chomsky, Noam. 1995. *The Minimalist Program*. Cambridge, MA: MIT Press.

Clark, Robin & Ian Roberts. 1993. A computational model of language learning and language change. *Linguistic Inquiry* 24. 229–345.

Colleman, Timothy & Bernard De Clerck. 2011. Constructional semantics on the move: The semantic specialization in the English double object construction. *Cognitive Linguistics* 22 (1). 183–209.

Coniam, David. 2004. Concordancing oneself: Constructing individual textual profiles. *International Journal of Corpus Linguistics* 9 (2). 271–298.

Crain, Stephan & Rosalind Thornton. 1998. *Investigations in Universal Grammar: A guide to experiments on the acquisition of syntax and semantics*. Cambridge, MA: MIT Press.

Croft, William. 2001. *Radical construction grammar: Syntactic theory in typological perspective*. Oxford: Oxford University Press.

D'hoedt, Frauke. 2017. *Language change in constructional networks: The development of the English secondary predicate construction*. Leuven: KU Leuven, PhD dissertation.

Dąbrowska, Ewa & James Street. 2006. Individual differences in language attainment: Comprehension of passive sentences by native and non-native English speakers. *Language Sciences* 28 (6). 604–615.

Denison, David. 1993. *English historical syntax: Verbal constructions*. London: Longman.

De Smet, Hendrik. 2016. The roots of *ruthless*: Individual variation as a window on mental representation. *International Journal of Corpus Linguistics* 21 (2). 250–271.

De Smet, Hendrik & Olga Fischer. 2017. The role of analogy in language change: Supporting constructions. In Marianne Hundt, Sandra Mollin & Simone E. Pfenninger (eds.), *The changing English language: Psycholinguistic perspectives*, 215–239. Cambridge: Cambridge University Press.

Disney, Steve. 2016. Another visit to BE *supposed to* from a diachronic constructionist perspective. *English Studies* 97 (8). 892–916.

Dreschler, Gea. 2015. *Passives and the loss of verb second: A study of syntactic and information-structural factors*. Utrecht: LOT.

Fischer, Olga. 1989. The origin and spread of the accusative and infinitive construction in English. *Folia Linguistica Historica* 8 (1/2). 143–217.

Fischer, Olga. 1992. Syntactic change and borrowing: The case of the accusative-and-infinitive construction in English. In Marinel Gerritsen & Dieter Stein (eds.), *Internal and external factors in syntactic change*, 17–89. Berlin: De Gruyter Mouton.

Fischer, Olga. 1994. The fortunes of the Latin-type accusative and infinitive construction in Dutch and English compared. In Toril Swan, Endre Mørck & Olaf Jansen Westvik (eds.), *Language change and language structure: Older Germanic languages in a comparative perspective*, 91–133. Berlin: De Gruyter Mouton.

Fischer, Olga. 2010. An analogical approach to grammaticalization. In Katerina Stathi, Elke Gehweiler & Ekkehard König (eds.), *Grammaticalization: Current views and issues*, 181–218. Amsterdam: John Benjamins.

Fischer, Olga, Ans van Kemenade, Willem Koopman & Wim van der Wurff. 2000. *The syntax of early English*. Cambridge: Cambridge University Press.

Francis, W. Nelson & Henry Kučera. 1982. *Frequency analysis of English usage: Lexicon and grammar*. Boston: Houghton Mifflin.

Gentner, Dedre, Keith J. Holyoak & Boicho N. Kokinov (eds.). 2001. *The analogical mind: Perspectives from cognitive science*. Cambridge, MA: MIT.

Ginsborg, Jane. 2006. The effects of socio-economic status on children's language acquisition and use. In Judy Clegg & Jane Ginsborg (eds.), *Language and social disadvantage: Theory into practice*, 9–27. Chichester: Wiley.

Givón, Talmy. 1984. *Syntax: A functional-typological introduction*, vol. 1. Amsterdam: John Benjamins.

Givón, Talmy. 2001. *Syntax: An introduction*, vol. 1. Amsterdam: John Benjamins.

Goldberg, Adele E. 1995. Constructions: A construction grammar approach to argument structure. Chicago: The University of Chicago Press.

Henry, Alison. 1997. Viewing change in progress: The loss of verb-second in Hiberno-English imperatives. In Ans van Kemenade & Nigel Vincent (eds.), *Parameters of morphosyntactic change*, 273–296. Cambridge: Cambridge University Press.

Hilpert, Martin. 2018. Three open questions in diachronic construction grammar. In Evie Coussé, Peter Andersson & Joel Olofsson (eds.), *Grammaticalization meets construction grammar*, 21–39. Amsterdam: John Benjamins.

Hinterhölzl, Roland & Svetlana Petrova. 2010. From V1 to V2 in West Germanic. *Lingua* 120. 315–328.

Hoffmann, Thomas & Graeme Trousdale. 2013. Construction grammar: Introduction. In Thomas Hoffmann & Graeme Trousdale, *The Oxford handbook of construction grammar*, 1–12. Oxford: Oxford University Press.

Itkonen, Esa. 2005. *Analogy as structure and process: Approaches in linguistic, cognitive psychology and philosophy of science*. Amsterdam: John Benjamins.

Johnstone, Barbara. 1996. *The linguistic individual: Self-expression in language and linguistics*. Oxford: Oxford University Press.

Labov, William. 2001. *Principles of linguistic change*, vol. 2. *Social factors*. Oxford: Blackwell.

Levshina, Natalia. 2015. *How to do linguistics with R: Data exploration and statistical analysis*. Amsterdam: John Benjamins.

Lightfoot, David. 1979. *Principles of diachronic syntax*. Cambridge: Cambridge University Press.

Los, Bettelou. 2005. *The rise of the to-infinitive*. Oxford: Oxford University Press.

Los, Bettelou. 2009. The consequences of the loss of verb-second in English: Information structure and syntax in interaction. *English Language and Linguistics* 13 (1). 97–125.

Los, Bettelou & Gea Dreschler. 2012. The loss of local anchoring: From adverbial local anchors to permissive subjects. In Terttu Nevalainen & Elizabeth Closs Traugott (eds.), *The Oxford handbook of the history of English*, 859–871. Oxford: Oxford University Press.

Los, Bettelou & Ans van Kemenade. 2012. Information structure and syntax in the history of English. In Alexander Bergs & Laurel L. Brinton (eds.), *English historical linguistics: An international handbook*, vol. 2: 1475–1490. Berlin: De Gruyter Mouton.

Mair, Christian. 1990. *Infinitival complement clauses in English*. Cambridge: Cambridge University Press.

Mills, John A. & Gordon D. Hemsley. 1976. The effect of level of education on judgments of grammatical acceptability. *Language and Speech* 19 (4). 324–342.

Moore, Colette. 2007. The spread of grammaticalized forms: The case of *be+supposed to*. *Journal of English Linguistics* 35 (2). 117–131.

Nahkola, Kari & Marja Saanilahti. 2004. Mapping language changes in real time: A panel study on Finnish. *Language Variation and Change* 16. 75–92.

Nevalainen, Terttu, Helena Raumolin-Brunberg & Heikki Mannila. 2011. The diffusion of language change in real time: Progressive and conservative individuals and the time depth of change. *Language Variation and Change* 23. 1–43.

Nevalainen, Terttu. 2015. Age-related variation and language change in Early Modern English. In Annette Gerstenberg & Anja Voeste (eds.), *Language development: The lifespan perspective*, 129–146. Amsterdam: John Benjamins.

Noël, Dirk. 1998. Infinitival copular complement clauses in English: Explaining the predominance of passive matrix verbs. *Linguistics* 36 (6). 1045–1063.

Noël, Dirk. 2001. The passive matrices of English infinitival complement clauses: Evidentials on the road to auxiliarihood. *Studies in Language* 25 (2). 255–296.

Noël, Dirk. 2008. The nominative and infinitive in Late Modern English: A diachronic constructionist approach. *Journal of English Linguistics* 36 (4). 314–340.

Noël, Dirk. 2016. For a radically usage-based diachronic construction grammar. *Belgian Journal of Linguistics* 30. 39–53.

Noël, Dirk & Timothy Colleman. 2010. *Believe*-type raising-to-object and raising-to-subject verbs in English and Dutch: A contrastive investigation in diachronic construction grammar. *International Journal of Corpus Linguistics* 15 (2). 157–182.

Noël, Dirk & Johan van der Auwera. 2009. Revisiting *be supposed to* from a diachronic constructionist perspective. *English Studies* 90 (5). 559–623.

Osthoff, Hermann & Karl Brugmann. 1878. *Morphologische Untersuchungen auf dem Gebiete der indogermanischen Sprachen*, vol. 1. Leipzig: Hirzel.

Pakulak, Eric & Helen J. Neville. 2010. Proficiency differences in syntactic processing of monolingual native speakers indexed by event-related potentials. *Journal of Cognitive Neuroscience* 22 (12). 2728–2744.

Petré, Peter, Lynn Anthonissen, Sara Budts, Enrique Manjavacas, Emma-Louise Silva, William Standing & Odile A. O. Strik. 2019. Early Modern Multiloquent Authors (EMMA): Designing a large-scale corpus of individuals' languages. *ICAME Journal* 43. 83–122.

Petré, Peter & Freek Van de Velde. 2014. Tracing real-life agents' individual progress in ongoing grammaticalization. In Luc Steels & Remi van Trijp (eds.), *Proceedings of 'How grammaticalization processes create grammar' (Evolang-X workshop), Vienna, Austria, 14 April 2014*. (http://emergent-languages.org/wp-content/papercite-data/pdf/proceedings.pdf; accessed 15 August 2017).

Petré, Peter & Freek Van de Velde. 2018. The real-time dynamics of individual and community in grammaticalization. *Language* 94(4). 867–901.

Postal, Paul M. 1974. *On raising: One rule of English grammar and its theoretical implications*. Cambridge, MA: MIT Press.

Raumolin-Brunberg, Helena. 2005. Language change in adulthood: Historical letters as evidence. *European Journal of English Studies* 9 (1). 37–51.

Raumolin-Brunberg, Helena. 2009. Lifespan changes in the language of three early modern gentlemen. In Arja Nurmi, Minna Nevala & Minna Palander-Collin (eds.), *The language of daily life in England (1400–1800)*, 165–196. Amsterdam: John Benjamins.

Raumolin-Brunberg, Helena & Arja Nurmi. 2011. Grammaticalization and language change in the individual. In Heiko Narrog & Bernd Heine (eds.), *The Oxford handbook of grammaticalization*, 251–262. Oxford: Oxford University Press.

Sankoff, Gillian & Hélène Blondeau. 2007. Language change across the lifespan: /r/ in Montreal French. *Language* 83 (3). 560–588.

Schmid, Hans-Jörg & Annette Mantlik. 2015. Entrenchment in historical corpora? Reconstructing dead authors' minds from their usage profiles. *Anglia* 133 (4). 583–623.

Seoane, Elena. 2000. The passive as an information-rearranging device in Early Modern English. *Studia Neophilologica* 72. 24–33.

Seoane, Elena. 2006. Information structure and word order change: The passive as an information-rearranging strategy in the history of English. In Ans van Kemenade & Bettelou Los (eds.), *The handbook of the history of English*, 360–391. Oxford: Blackwell.

Seuren, Pieter A. M. & Camiel Hamans. 2009. Semantic conditioning of syntactic rules: Evidentiality and auxiliation in English and Dutch. *Folia Linguistica* 43 (1). 153–169.

Slobin, Dan. 1997. The origins of grammaticizable notions: Beyond the individual mind. In Dan Slobin (ed.), *The cross-linguistic study of language acquisition: Expanding the contexts*, vol. V: 1–39. Mahwah, NJ: Lawrence Erlbaum.

Street, James & Ewa Dąbrowska. 2010. More individual differences in language attainment: How much do adult native speakers of English know about passives and quantifiers? *Lingua* 120 (8). 2080–2094.

Street, James & Ewa Dąbrowska. 2014. Lexically specific knowledge and individual differences in adult native speakers' processing of the English passive. *Applied Psycholinguistics* 35 (1). 97–118.

Traugott, Elizabeth Closs & Graeme Trousdale. 2013. *Constructionalization and constructional changes*. Oxford: Oxford University Press.

Tomasello, Michael. 2003. *Constructing a language: A usage-based theory of language acquisition*. Cambridge, MA: Harvard University Press.

Vanderbiesen, Jeroen. 2015. The grounding functions of German reportives and quotatives. *Papers of the Linguistics Society of Belgium* 9. 16–39.

Visconti, Jacqueline. 2004. Conditionals and subjectification: Implictions for a theory of semantic change. In Olga Fischer, Muriel Norde and Harry Perridon (eds.), *Up and down the cline: The nature of grammaticalization*, 169–192. Amsterdam: John Benjamins.

Warner, Anthony R. 1982. *Complementation in Middle English and the methodology of historical syntax: A study of the Wyclifite sermons*. London: Croom Helm.

Wiemer, Björn. 2018. Evidentials and epistemic modality. In Alexandra Y. Aikhenvald (ed.), *The Oxford handbook of evidentiality*, 85–109. Oxford: Oxford University Press.

Ziegeler, Debra. 2003. On the generic origins of modality in English. In David Hart (ed.), *English modality in context: Diachronic perspectives*, 33–69. Bern: Lang.

Zeitlin, Jacob. 1908. *The accusative with infinitive and some kindred constructions in English*. Columbia University, PhD dissertation.

Ruth Möhlig-Falke
Contextualizing dual-form adverbs in the *Old Bailey Corpus*
An assessment of semantic, pragmatic, and sociolinguistic factors

Abstract: This article is concerned with the so-called *dual-form adverbs* of English, which are a group of adverbs that may occur both with and without the adverbial suffix *-ly* in similar syntactic environments. Based on data taken from the *Old Bailey Corpus* 2.0 for the period between c. 1730–1910, this study explores the impact of micro- and macro-context on variable adverb marking with the aim of identifying factors that explain why these adverbs have resisted the general trend towards -LY-marking for so long, with some of them still appearing with variable adverb marking up to today. The main reasons for this variability are identified to be the semantic-pragmatic orientation of individual adverbs to different entities in the clause, the general fuzziness of the category boundary between adjective and adverb, and the adverbs' highly context-sensitive interpretation. Sociolinguistic aspects, mentioned as possible additional factors in the literature on variable adverb marking, are identified as only secondarily responsible.

1 Introduction

> Adjectives are sometimes employed as Adverbs, improperly, and not agreeably to the Genius of the English Language. As, "extreme elaborate;" *Dryden, Essay on Dram. Poet.* "marvellous graceful;" *Clarendon, Life p. 18.* "extreme unwilling;" "extreme subject:" *Swift, Tale of a Tub, and Battle of Books* [...] (Lowth 1762: 125-126, note 8; emphasis in the original)

Bishop Robert Lowth, author of one of the most influential grammars of the English language in the late 18th and 19th century, here comments in a footnote on the allegedly "improper" use of adverbs that are not marked by the suffix -LY – a usage that he finds even in renowned authors who are considered to be the main authorities in defining "the best" English, setting the norms for others to follow

---

Ruth Möhlig-Falke, Heidelberg University, English Department, 69117 Heidelberg, Germany, ruth.moehlig@as.uni-heidelberg.de

https://doi.org/10.1515/9783110682564-006

(Tieken-Boon van Ostade 2010, 2014).¹ This quote quite nicely illustrates how actual language use collided with normative attitudes to the English language, at a time when the norms for what was developing into Standard English were being codified and spread throughout the English speech community. It also illustrates a problem that still exists in English: the existence of adverbs that *should* appear with a -LY-suffix by rule, but which do not do so in some contexts and uses. Thus, typical learners' grammars and usage guides of English tell us that adverbs are "regularly" or "correctly" marked by a LY-suffix in English.²

Of course, if we look more closely into this issue, there are many adverbs that never appear with a -LY-suffix (e.g. *fast, down, very*), some adverbs have different meanings with and without the -LY-suffix (e.g. *hard* vs. *hardly, near* vs. *nearly, even* vs. *evenly*),³ and furthermore, -LY may also be used as an adjective-forming suffix (e.g. *bodily, costly, courtly, daily, friendly, manly, motherly, yearly*). This is so because the English suffix -LY was grammaticalized as an adverbial marker rather late in the history of English. This process started in Late Middle English and has continued well into the Late Modern English period and may still be ongoing today (e.g. Baayen 1994; Nevalainen 1994a; Baayen and Renouf 1996; Swan 1997: 187–189; Pounder 2001; Killie 1998, 2000, 2015; see also section 3).

Using data from from the *Old Bailey Corpus* 2.0 (OBC), this paper will concentrate on variation in adverb marking in the field of the so-called *dual-form adverbs* between c. 1730 and 1910, i.e. in the period when the norms for Standard English,

---

1 I thank Kristin Bech and Kristin Killie for their comments on earlier versions of this paper. I am grateful to Kristin Bech for her detailed editorial comments and to Kristin Killie for many helpful suggestions, from which the discussion in this paper has greatly benefitted. Thanks are also due to Magnus Huber for his assistance with background information on the OBC data.
2 See, for instance Jane Straus's *Blue Book for Grammar and Punctuation* (¹¹2010): rule 1 on adverbs, for instance, says: "Many adverbs end in *-ly*, but many do not. Generally, if a word can have *-ly* added to its adjective form, place it there to form an adverb"; Rule 6 on degrees of adverbs states: "There are also three degrees of adverbs. In formal usage, do not drop the *-ly* from an adverb when using the comparative form." (See http://www.grammarbook.com/grammar/adjAdv.asp) This is only one, maybe rather typical example of how the topic of adverbs and -LY-marking is treated in modern prescriptive grammars and usage guides. A more descriptive account is, for instance, found in the corpus-based *Longman Grammar of Spoken and Written English* by Biber et al. (1999: 539–541), who note that some adverbs may appear both with and without a -LY-suffix in conversation, but more rarely in British English than in American English, and seldom in written registers.
3 In these adverb pairs, the zero-form is used as a verb-modifying adjunct of manner from which the -LY-form is derived, having a disjunctive or sentence-adverbial function. The -LY-form in these pairs has a more subjective and abstract meaning than the zero-form, because it expresses the speaker's evaluation of the State of Affairs (Swan 1997, see also Nevalainen 1994a: 253, Ungerer 1988: 34).

and amongst them those for adverb-marking, came to be codified and established throughout the speech community. The term of *dual-form adverbs* was introduced by Donner (1991) and taken up, for instance, by Nevalainen (1994a, 1994b, 1997) and Opdahl (2000). It is applied to variation in adverb form, where the formal alternation between a -LY-form and a zero-form may occur in similar or identical syntactic contexts without apparent differences in lexical meaning (such as exists for *hard* vs *hardly*) or syntactic function,[4] e.g.

(1) a. *The next afternoon couldn't <u>come</u> **quick** enough.* (BNC, *Where there's life*, 1991)
 b. *The end of the season could not <u>come</u> **quickly** enough for Atkinson.* (BNC, *Today*, 1992)

(2) a. *He supplied shops with the best quality wood which he <u>bought</u> **cheap** from sawmills* [...] (BNC, *Where there's life*, 1991)
 b. *He lived in Notting Hill Gate, in a house he'd <u>bought</u> **cheaply** in the late fifties, which he now seldom left* [...] (BNC, *Imajica*, 1992)

Two semantic domains of adverbs have been identified in the literature, where zero-forms tend to appear as an alternative to -LY-forms:

Degree adverbs (subjuncts, modifying an adverbial, adjectival, participial or verbal head, and having an intensifying or downtoning function), e.g.

(3) *All I want is some friends, but as soon as I get some **real** <u>good friends</u> they go off and leave me.* (BNC, A74 1213)

(4) *Now a pressmaster <u>dare</u> **scarce** <u>carry</u> an impressed man through the streets* [...] (BNC, BNB 181)

Manner adverbs (adjuncts, modifying a verbal head and adding information about the nature or circumstances of the verbal event), e.g.

(5) *'<u>Drive</u> **slow**, Max, <u>drive</u> **slow**,' she urged, anxious that none of her friends walking to the meeting should fail to notice her in the darkness.* (BNC, FRJ, 1562)

(6) *If I <u>walk</u> **quick** I don't feel too cold.* (BNC, A74 2472)

---

4 It has been observed that the zero-form sometimes has a more concrete reference than the -LY-form, which has an additional abstract or figurative meaning (e.g. *direct(ly), high(ly)*; Jespersen 1942: 38; Opdahl 1989: 245; cf. Donner 1991: 4; Nevalainen 1994a: 251; Killie 2015: 208).

(7) He fired again as the wounded bull turned and began galloping clumsily towards the safety of the trees, but this second shot <u>went</u> **wide**. (BNC, FU8 1328)
(8) But old assumptions <u>run</u> **deep** and die hard. (BNC, ADP 329)
(9) I mean if I <u>sold</u> it **cheap** [...] (BNC, KCL 1704)

The main issues with regard to dual-form adverbs are the questions of why these adverbs may appear both with a zero- and a -LY-form in similar syntactic contexts, and whether the two formal variants express differences in meaning and/or use, or whether they are in free variation, i.e. unconstrained by any syntactic, semantic or pragmatic factors. Previous investigations have shown that the problem is a complex one, because several different factors seem to play a role in the choice of one over the other formal variant.

The suffixless variant in such adverb pairs has traditionally been explained as a non-standard variant which reflects regional or national, social or stylistic variation (Opdahl 2000). The spread of the suffix -LY as *the* adverbial marker in English is closely tied to the standardization process of English and particularly to its codification phase, beginning in the middle of the 18th century and reaching its peak in the mid-19th century, when numerous grammars, spelling books and usage guides for the English language were published and spread through society, setting the norms of "correct" English usage (Görlach 1998, 1999a, 1999b). Pounder (2001: 336–338) states that although the early grammars of English on the whole show a more or less neutral stance towards the question of adverb formation, some of them, such as illustrated by the initial comment by Lowth (1762), occasionally include examples of 'false' adverb use for readers or even explicitly state that 'adjectives' (i.e. suffixless forms) should not be used in adverbial function. Even though individual grammars may have had a limited circulation, the overlap between these grammars in many issues, and particularly in the issue of adverb formation, is very large, which had a cumulative effect on the general preference for -LY-forms (Pounder 2001: 338; Killie 2005). Especially in the 19th century, knowledge of correct grammar in speech as well as in writing was an indicator of education and general understanding (correct and clear language being considered to reflect the ability to think clearly and logically; Pounder 2001: 338), presumably adding to the social stigmatization of suffixless adverbs that may be seen from the 20th century onwards (Pounder 2001: 342–344).[5] Thus,

---

5 See also Finegan (1998: 369, 396) on American English, who quotes Webster and Leonard's (1932) *Current English Usage. National Council of Teachers of English Monograph* who condemn the use of zero-form, or "flat adverbs", and judge it "illiterate".

Pounder notes that zero-form adverbs are much more common in the 18th and 19th centuries than they are today, especially in informal writings, and it is only from the 20th century on that zero-form uses appear to be socially stigmatized (Pounder 2001: 342–344).

In Present-day English, the suffixless variants of dual-form adverbs are, for instance, reported to be found more often in American English than in British English,[6] less educated people tend to use them more often than educated ones, men do so more often than women, and they are generally disfavoured in formal style (e.g. Biber et al. 1999: 539–541; Opdahl 2000: 160–162; Kortmann and Szmrecsanyi 2004: 1193).[7] Further, some suffixless adverbs are found more often in the speech of the older generation (Opdahl 2000). However, as Tagliamonte and Ito (2002: 256) emphasize in their investigation of York English, the social variables of education, gender, and age have a quantitative rather than a qualitative effect on constraining the use of a suffixless form. It follows from this that the main motivation behind using a zero-form adverb seems to be semantic and pragmatic and closely dependent on the context of use.

The present study will investigate the micro-contextual semantic-pragmatic factors playing a role for the choice of a zero-form adverb as against a -LY-adverb in 18th- and 19th-century English by analyzing the usage patterns of fourteen selected dual-form adverbs. In a second step, the study will also look into the macro-contextual factors that may be linked to the social variables of social class, degree of education, and gender. The analysis shows that the group of dual-form adverbs is extremely heterogeneous at closer inspection and displays various types of semantic-pragmatic orientation,[8] these being crucial for the choice of adverb form.

---

6 Variable adverb use may thus have been influenced to different degrees by the development, codification, and manifestation of a British English as against an American English standard between c. 1700–1900, American English being reported to be more liberal than British English in allowing suffixless forms (Rice 1927; Pooley 1933). It has even been claimed that American English is on the way of dropping the -LY-suffix from adverb formation for adverbs of manner altogether (Ross 1984), a claim which does not seem to have proven true so far.
7 Zero-form adverbs occur in a wide range of regional and national, non- or semi-standard varieties of English (see e.g. Chambers 2004; Kortmann and Szmrecsanyi 2004). Chambers (2004) counts their occurrence among the "vernacular universals", i.e. linguistic features that tend to occur more or less universally in the vernacular varieties of English world-wide.
8 The term *orientation* refers to the semantic and pragmatic relationship between the item in question (here, an adverb) and the item which it modifies, or on which it gives additional information. An adverb's orientation arises from its interpretation in its semantic and pragmatic context (Killie 1994: 47, 52–53; Valera 1998; see also section 4.1).

Section 2 describes the nature of the data used for this investigation and the methodological steps of analysis, after which section 3 will provide an overview of the diachronic development of adverbial -LY-marking. Section 4 will discuss the results from the investigation of OBC data. Section 5 will provide some concluding remarks.

2 Data and method

For this investigation, the *Old Bailey Corpus* 2.0 (OBC) Online was used as a data source. The OBC is based on the *Proceedings of the Old Bailey*, London's central criminal court, and comprises trial records from c. 1720 to 1913. Almost 85% of these trial records consist of transcripts of spoken language (Huber 2007: section 3.1).

The OBC offers a good database for an investigation of the diachronic development of dual-form adverbs in the Late Modern English period for several reasons. Firstly, it records non-literary, 'written-as-spoken' language from the 18th and 19th centuries, i.e. those centuries that are particularly interesting for the investigation of linguistic phenomena having to do with the establishment of grammatical norms in English. Even though the reliability of the scribal records is not always beyond all doubt (Huber 2007: section 3.2), this is as near as one may hope to get to the vernacular speech of a fairly wide selection of speakers. Secondly, the OBC 2.0 is a rather large corpus, consisting of 24.4 million spoken words in total.[9] The size of the corpus is important in so far as variation in adverb form is a feature that may be expected to be or to become rare in this period and chances are better to find relevant instances in a large corpus of several million words. Thirdly, the OBC Online provides easy access to the linguistic, or discourse contexts of the investigated utterances. Checking the overall discourse context was frequently necessary in the analysis, where the interpretation was ambiguous between adjectival or adverbial use. Finally, the OBC adds sociobiographical information on a large number of speakers (though not on all of them, by far), so that it is possible to evaluate the impact of sociolinguistic factors on variable adverb use at least to some degree (see section 4.3 for further details).

---

9 See the OBC 2.0 statistics sheet, available under http://fedora.clarin-d.uni-saarland.de/oldbailey/documentation.html.

Tab. 6.1: Numbers of occurrences for the individual search items as adverbs and predicative adjectives (numbers in brackets refer to normalized frequencies per 1,000,000 words; N24,443,588)

Search items	number of occurrences
cheap / cheaply	243 (9.94)
clean / cleanly	396 (16.2)
deep / deeply	453 (18.53)
easy / easily	756 (30.93)
flat / flatly	106 (4.34)
high / highly	903 (36.94)
loud / loudly	346 (14.16)
nice / nicely	66 (2. 7)
quick / quickly	770 (31.5)
rash / rashly	14 (0.57)
scarce / scarcely	324 (13.26)
sharp / sharply	224 (9.16)
slow / sowly	181 (7.4)
wide / widely	534 (21.85)
Total	**5,316 (217.48)**

The analysis took a lexical approach in that all instances occurring with fourteen selected adjective/adverb pairs were collected. The selection of adjective/adverb pairs was based on previous discussions of dual-form adverbs, focusing on core items (Beckmann 1880; Jespersen 1942: §22.94, 1949: §1.55; Poutsma 1926: 623–625; Quirk et al. 1985: §§7.7–7.9; Opdahl 2000; Nevalainen 1994a, 1997; Tagliamonte and Ito 2002). Both adverbial and predicative adjectival uses were included, yielding 5,316 instances in total, which are very unevenly spread across the different search items (see table 6.1 above).

Including predicative adjectival uses of the selected search items was necessary, as there is a grey area between zero-form adverbial and some adjectival uses, such as in depictive and resultative constructions (see section 4.2), such as in (10) and (11):[10]

---

[10] Patterns like those found in examples (10) and (11) are overtly similar to adverbial patterns, where the adverb is in post-verbal position. However, in (10), the focus is not on a modification of the verbal event, but on the emotional condition of either *John* (the subject) or *Mary* (the

(10) *John left <u>Mary</u> **sad*** (depictive construction, see Geuder 2004: 131)
(11) *Willy watered <u>the plants</u> **flat*** (resultative construction, example from Goldberg and Jackendoff 2004: 538)

Attributive adjectival uses, where the adjective is part of a noun phrase, were, however, excluded. Also included are instances where the search item is part of an adjective phrase, including participles that are used as adjectives, as in *(to be) <u>clean</u> shaven*, which may display ambiguous contexts in that the adjective/adverb (here *clean*) is semantically oriented towards a state resulting from a verbal event. Instances like these are also often ambiguous for having phrasal or already lexicalized compound status (see Giegerich 2012: 349–350; Payne et al. 2010: 59–60).

The OBC comprises the years 1720 to 1913 – as 1913 is the last year included in the *Proceedings of the Old Bailey*, on which the OBC is based – and the total number of occurrences of search items, as listed in table 6.1 above, refers to this time span. However, in the further discussion of results, the first decade, 1720–1729, will be excluded, because only five of the fourteen search items appeared in this decade (*deep/deeply* with 1 occ., *easy/easily* with 8 occ., *high/highly* with 1 occ., *quick/quickly* with 20 occ., *wide/widely* with 3 occ.). The investigation detailed in sections 4.2 and 4.3 thus covers the period 1730–1913.

The data obtained from the OBC for the fourteen search items were in a first step contextually analyzed for (a) the grammatical status of the search item as either a proper adjective, a zero-form adverb or a -LY-adverb, and (b) its semantic-pragmatic orientation to other elements in the clause. Especially in distinguishing between zero-form adverbial and adjectival uses, such an analysis cannot be done mechanically. Frequently, clear formal markers for a possible interpretation as either an adjective or a zero-form adverb are lacking so that only the reading of the overall co(n)text in which the utterance was made helps to decide on an interpretation. The results of this analysis will be discussed in section 4.2. This analysis shows that cases where the variability in adverb form is more or less free and unrestrained from any semantic and pragmatic factors is very limited. The potential impact of sociolinguistic factors on variation in adverb form was accordingly investigated only for a further selection of adverbs, discussed in section 4.3.

---

object; see Geuder 2004: 131–132). In (11), *flat* denotes a state resulting from Willy's watering of the plants.

3 The suffix -LY in diachronic perspective

The coexistence of -LY-suffixed and suffixless adverbs has its historical roots in early English. Adverbial -LY originates in the Old English derivational suffix -līc, by which adjectives like *frēondlīc* 'friendly' and *cynelīc* 'kingly, royal' could be formed from nouns (OED, s.v. -*ly* suffix[1,2]). These -*līc*-adjectives could be marked as adverbs by adding the regular Old English adverbial suffix -*e* [e]. -*Līce* seems to have become productive as an adverbial suffix on simple adjectival bases from late Old English on (Pounder 2001: 307; Nevalainen 1997: 155–157). This means that there were two types of adverb formation available already from the late Old English period on, one with a suffix -*e*, and the other with a suffix -*līce*, as can be seen in the following two Old English quotes from the *Dictionary of Old English Corpus* (DOEC):

(12) *Scearplice se drenc hæleþ nædran bite.* 'This drink <u>effectually</u> heals a snake bite' (DOEC, *Medicina de quadrupedibus*, 0065 (3.15)')
(13) *Sume swiðe **scearpe** and swiðe **swotele** lociað.* 'Some see very <u>sharply</u> and very <u>clearly</u>' (DOEC, *Soliloquies* 1, 0402 (45.14))

Where both of these adverb formations from the same adjective are recorded, however, they seem to display differences in meaning, as can be seen in (12) and (13). Due to the general phonological trend towards losing vowels in final unstressed position, the adverbial suffix -*e* was lost in pronunciation in the late Middle English period (Nevalainen 1997: 155). This provided the English language with two formally identical but functionally different suffixes -LY (one adverbial, and the other adjectival), alongside simple adjective-adverb pairs without any overt formal marking. The grammaticalization of -LY consisted in a specialization of the suffix to adverbial function (Nevalainen 1997: 148).[11] Nevalainen (1997) shows that alternation between suffixless adverb forms and -LY-forms was much more frequent in Middle English both in terms of types and tokens, and that this alternation decreased in the course of the Early Modern English period, when -LY

---

[11] Killie (2015) describes the grammaticalization of -LY in the light of the concept of secondary grammaticalization, referring to an already grammatical element developing an additional grammatical function, as the initial grammaticalization of -LY was as an adjectival suffix. However, as an initial problem lies in defining what exactly "grammatical" and "more grammatical" mean, she proposes to leave the terminological distinction between primary and secondary grammaticalization and rather sub-classify grammaticalization processes on semantic-pragmatic grounds instead.

became specialized to adverbial function. Donner (1991) shows that adverbial -LY first became productive with the class of manner adverbs, from which it spread to other functions (Killie 2015: 204–207). The spread of adverbial -LY thus began long before the effects of codification and spreading of prescriptive grammatical norms could be felt. The grammaticalization of adverbial -LY was, however, never fully completed. Adverbial -LY has never become fully obligatory in English (Croft 2003: 259), which is why Nevalainen (1997: 146) calls the adjective-adverb boundary a "weakly codified area of [English] grammar".

We may assume that -LY gradually took over as a marker of adverbial function because it was the morpho-phonologically stronger variant by which the category boundary between adjectives and adverbs could be marked more explicitly and more transparently. But it is also clear that the two formal variants coexisted for a very long time in the history of English, thus providing speakers of English with a certain choice between them, depending on context and use.

There has been some discussion in the literature about whether adverbial -LY is an inflectional rather than a derivational suffix (e.g. Bybee 1985; Nevalainen 1994b, 1997; Zwicky 1995; Payne et al. 2010; Plag 2003; Giegerich 2012; Pittner 2015; Killie 2015), which would mean that adverbs do not form a distinct lexical category in English (such as do NOUNS vs. VERBS), but a grammatical one (comparable to SINGULAR vs. PLURAL). Evaluating the pros and cons of each analysis would go beyond the scope of this paper,[12] and the investigation of dual-form adverbs in the present context does not seem to require a firm decision on this point. Regardless of whether they are considered to be two lexical or two grammatical categories, ADJECTIVE and ADVERB were formally distinguished already in Old English (by the suffix -e) and the speakers of Middle, Early, and Late Modern English seem to have seen a certain need to restore the formal differentiation between them by -LY, as -e was receding. However, the two categories of ADJECTIVE and ADVERB are prototypically structured and have fuzzy boundaries (see also Rauh 2015: 42), with a significant area of overlap between them, as will be further outlined in section 4.2.[13]

---

[12] For a comprehensive overview on the debate, see Killie (2015: 208). Pittner (2015) also discusses the different arguments put forward for both positions, i.e. whether -LY is an inflectional or a derivational marker. She comes to the conclusion that -LY, although traditionally assumed to be a derivational marker, largely has properties that align it with inflectional markers, such as the fact that it "does not occur word-internally, is determined by the syntactic environment, encodes only grammatical information, and exhibits great generality" (Pittner 2015: 153).

[13] Aikhenvald (2015) describes the class of adverbs as "elusive" and notes that "the concept of 'adverb' is perhaps the most problematic of all word classes" (Aikhenvald 2015: 97).

Adverbial -LY presumably developed several semantically overlapping functions during its grammaticalization as an adverbial marker, which were – and still are – layered (Croft 2003: 262) and which have given rise to the partly confusing situation of adverbial marking in present-day English.

4 Dual-form adverbs in the OBC

The following section will present the results of the analysis of fourteen selected dual-form adverbs in the *Old Bailey Corpus* 2.0. First, the general diachronic trends found for these adverbs will be presented (section 4.1). The focus will then be placed on the role of scope and orientation as semantic and pragmatic concepts, and the relevance of syntactic constructions such as depictive and resultative uses (section 4.2). Finally, the relevance of sociolinguistic factors like social class and education (roughly deducible from a speaker's profession) and gender (speaker's sex) for the variation between suffixless and -LY-suffixed adverbs will be assessed (section 4.3).

4.1 Diachronic developments visible in the data

Considering the fact that adverbial -LY gradually expanded its range of application from Late Middle English to the present day, and that the standardization and codification of English beginning in the second half of the 18th century and further developing in the 19th century (see e.g. Tieken-Boon van Ostade 2008; Beal 2010) has played a major role in this, it might be expected that -LY-forms would become more frequent than zero-forms in the course of the investigated period between c. 1730 and 1910. Further, in light of the prescriptive attitudes going along with the spread of Standard English, typically favouring the marking of adverbs by -LY (e.g. Lowth 1762), sociolinguistic factors may be expected to become relevant for variable adverb marking in the course of the 19th century, when the notion of Standard English as the "correct" and appropriate form in formal language use manifested itself in the minds of speakers (e.g. Görlach 1999a: 10–25; Hickey 2010).

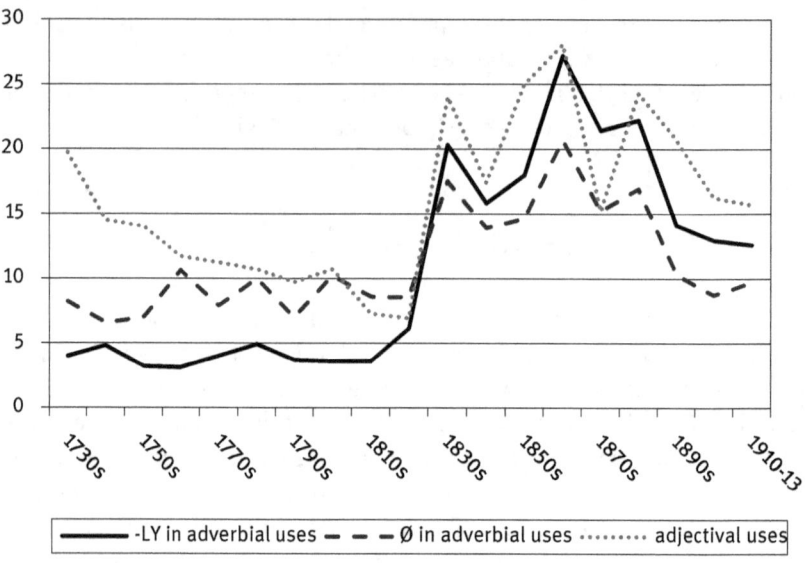

Fig. 6.1: Chronological distribution of adverbial and adjectival uses for the investigated items in the OBC (frequencies normalized by 100,000 words)[14]

Figure 6.1 illustrates the diachronic development of the investigated items between 1730 and 1913. It is quite striking that from roughly 1830 onwards, the search items occur much more frequently in both adverbial as well as in adjectival uses, rising until the 1860s and then dropping down again to some extent.[15] On the whole, adverbial -LY-forms keep constant and lower in frequency than zero-forms until c. 1820, when they begin to increase, reaching a peak in the 1860s and then decreasing again. From the 1830s on the frequency levels of -LY-forms remain above adverbial zero-forms more or less constantly. However, zero-forms also increase around 1830. They follow the fluctuations of -LY-forms in rises and falls between c. 1830 and 1913, but remain below them in after c. 1830,

---

14 All figures present the data decade for decade rather than in thirty-year periods, as is often done in the literature. This is a conscious choice to highlight the great variability of dual-form adverb usage in the investigated data.

15 The rather dramatic rise in occurrence of both adverbial and adjectival uses of the search items in the OBC data after c. 1830 may have to do with the strategies of record keeping followed by the court scribes, making their records more detailed and more faithful to the descriptions of persons, states and events as stated by the witnesses. As a hypothesis, this needs to be further investigated.

Contextualizing dual-form adverbs in the *Old Bailey Corpus* — **169**

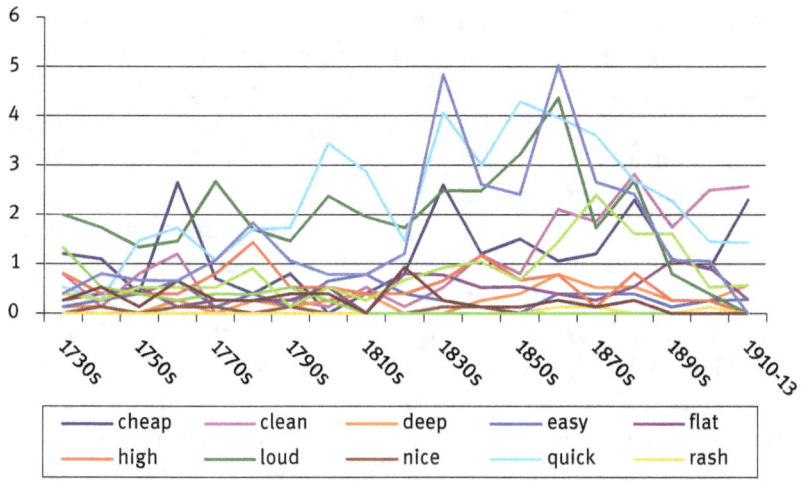

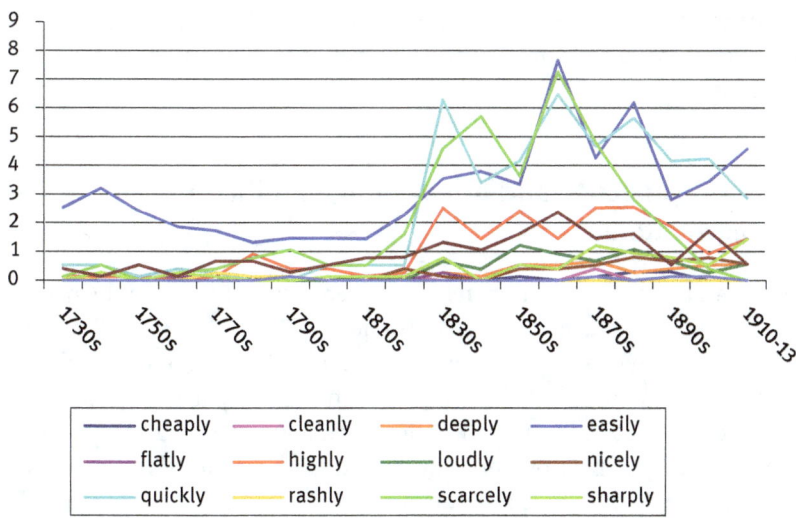

Fig. 6.2: Adverbial zero-forms (top) and -LY-forms (bottom) found in the OBC between 1730 and 1913

though not significantly. Zero-forms remain in use until the end of the investigated period. This picture only partly meets the expectation stated before that there should be a general and constant rise in the frequency of -LY-forms as a consequence of the spread of Standard English. Instead, there seems to be a certain area of adverb usage that resists the adoption of -LY until the early 20th century, which requires further explanation.

Focusing only on the adverbial uses and disregarding adjectival ones, figure 6.2 above illustrates how great the range of individual frequencies of occurrence is for the fourteen search items, both concerning the total number of occurrences – which ranges from 26.59 (650 occ.) adverbial uses in total for *quick/ly* down to 0.33 (8 occ.) for *rash/ly* – as well as the diachronic development in the ratio of -LY- and zero-forms. Some adverbs seem to favour zero-forms until the end of the investigated period (such as *cheap, clean, deep, flat, loud,* and *wide*), while others favour -LY-forms right from the beginning of the investigated period (such as *easily*), or they develop a preference for -LY-forms over time (e.g. *scarcely* after c. 1800, *quickly* and *slowly* from c. 1830 on). On the whole, however, the picture is far from clear. Frequency counts alone do not suffice to explain what is going on, but more details as to the syntactic, semantic and pragmatic properties of these items have to be considered.

4.2 The role of scope and orientation, modification and foregrounding

Scope is originally a syntactic term referring to an adverb's area of influence that depends on its position in the clause (Killie 1994: 43). Several authors (e.g. Jackendoff 1972; Swan 1990; Swan and Breivik 1990; Ungerer 1988) have widenend the notion of scope to include semantic and pragmatic aspects (for an overview, see Killie 2000: chapter 5). Following Killie (1994: 47; 2000), however, I will in the following speak of scope only with respect to syntactic scope and use the term *orientation* for the semantic and pragmatic aspects instead. An adverb's orientation is the reference relation between the adverb and the item which it modifies, or on which it gives additional information. It arises from the interpretation of the adverb within its semantic and pragmatic context (Killie 1994: 47, 52–53; see also Valera 1998; Killie 2000). Adverbs may show event orientation (e.g. *John opened the door **slowly***), participant orientation towards either the subject- or the object-participant (e.g. *The skirt flapped **wetly*** vs. *She bought the house **cheap***), or speaker orientation, as in ***Luckily**, she did not fall off his bicycle*, where the adverb expresses how the speaker thinks or feels about the State of Affairs (see Himmelmann and Schultze-Bernd 2005; Ernst 2009). Adverbs may further be oriented towards an adverbial phrase denoting a temporal or local reference point (e.g. *They were **scarcely** five minutes gone, I came **close** to the house*), which I will call reference-point oriented. Finally, adverbs may also be oriented towards adjectives or participles (e.g. *He is a **highly** respected person, She appeared to be **cleanly** dressed*), which I will call state-oriented in the following.

The main semantic function of adverbs that underlies the concept of orientation is that of *modification*: adverbs semantically modify verbs, adjectives, adverbials or whole sentences, but not nouns. The modification of nouns, either attributively as part of a noun phrase or predicatively as subject or object complement, is the functional domain of adjectives (Quirk et al. 1985: §§7.2–7.4; Huddleston & Pullum 2002: 562; Swan 1997: 183). A crucial pragmatic function that underlies the concept of orientation is that of *foregrounding*, i.e. directing the focus of attention and giving special salience to either the nature of the verbal event or a property of one of the participants in the State of Affairs.

Being a semantic and pragmatic concept, the interpretation of an adverb's orientation may vary in different contexts of use and several of the investigated dual-form adverbs show different orientations. Such differences in orientation may play a role in the occurrence of an adverb with or without the -LY-suffix, particularly with the group of adverbs that may show participant orientation to either the subject participant or an object participant. Like adverbs, adjectives also have an orientation, typically to a nominal or pronominal participant in the clause, either to the subject or the object (e.g. *The metal is **flat**, He hammered the metal **flat***). It is here, where adjectives and adverbs have areas of overlap and where the category boundaries between ADJECTIVE and ADVERB are fuzzy.[16]

Patterns of the type *He hammered the metal **flat*** are also known as resultative constructions, where *flat* is an adjective that functions as a secondary predicate oriented towards the object participant (*the metal*), referring to a state that results from the verbal event of hammering (see e.g. Boas 2003, 2005; Goldberg and Jackendoff 2004). A related type of construction is found in sentences like *John left Mary **sad***, called a depictive construction, where the adjective *sad* as a secondary predicate is oriented towards either the subject participant (*John*) or the object participant (*Mary*) (Geuder 2000, 2004; Himmelmann and Schultze-Berndt 2005). Geuder (2004: 135–136) notes that there is an overlap between depictives

---

[16] Quirk et al. (1985: §7.8) note that it may sometimes be contested whether a zero-form adverb is actually an adverb rather than an adjective. Because of the indeterminacy in grammatical interpretation that is exhibited by participant-oriented adverbial and adjectival adjuncts cross-linguistically, Himmelmann and Schultze-Berndt (2005) speak of *participant-oriented adjuncts* as a category-neutral term.

and manner adverbs in syntax, as both invariably occur in postverbal position in English, i.e. depictive adjectives as well as manner adverbs are VP-adjuncts. A certain indeterminacy in interpretation arises particularly with adjectives that are "derived from stative predicates of individuals like *sad, angry*, etc." (Geuder 2004: 141; see also Killie 2000).

Geuder (2004) distinguishes three types of adjuncts which are closely related: manner adverbs, transparent adverbs and depictive adjectives. While pure manner adverbs are event-oriented, focussing on the nature of the verbal event and giving additional information about it (such as in *John read the paper **slowly*** → *John read the paper in a slow manner*), transparent adverbs and depictive adjectives are participant-oriented. However, with transparent adverbs there is a causal or motivational link between the verbal event denoted by the main predicate and the condition denoted by the participant-oriented adjunct, while with depictives there is only a relation of "mere temporal overlap" between the two (Himmelmann and Schultze-Berndt 2005: 8–9), as illustrated in (14) and (15) below.

(14) *John **angrily** left the room* (transparent adverb)

(15) *John left the room **angry*** (depictive adjective)

Both resultative and depictive adjective constructions are formally similar to constructions of the type *John bought the carrots cheap* with an object-participant orientation, i.e. all three have the form [NP$_{subject}$ V NP$_{object}$ ADJ$_{unct}$]. Whether the adjunct is a resultative or depictive adjective, or whether it is a participant-oriented adverb depends on the micro- and macro-context of concrete utterances, and on the semantic and pragmatic interpretation of the relationship between the adjunct and the other elements in the clause. This may also occasionally give rise to insecurity as to the semantic-pragmatic orientation and the grammatical status of the adjunct, and whether a -LY suffix should be added or not. See the following examples:

(16) *John bought the carrots **quickly*** = event-oriented manner adverb, -LY-marked

(17) *John bought the carrots **quick*** = ?event-oriented manner adverb, or ?subject-oriented transparent adverb, unmarked by -LY

(18) *John bought the carrots **cheap*** = object-oriented transparent adverb, unmarked by -LY

(19) *John bought the carrots **fresh*** = object-oriented depictive adjective

While example (16) illustrates a fairly clear case of event-oriented interpretation of the adverb, with *quickly* modifying the transfer event of buying, example (17)

exhibits an ambivalent semantic-pragmatic interpretation of the relationship between *quick* and the other elements in the clause. *Quick* may, on the one hand, be event-oriented towards the transfer event of buying; on the other hand, a subject orientation may also be present in that *John* <u>was</u> *quick* in buying the carrots.

In example (18), *cheap* is in a direct causal relation with the verbal event of *buying*, thus falling into Geuder's (2004) category of transparent adverbs.[17] *Cheapness* is not an inherent property of carrots, but it is a momentary condition directly linked with the concrete transfer event of buying that is referred to and the subjective evaluation given to it by *John*, the customer. It might, for instance, be that the next customer considers the carrots to be expensive; i.e. there is a situationally context-dependent pragmatic relation between *cheap*, the carrots, the concrete transfer event, and *John* the concrete customer.[18] In example (19), for comparison, *fresh* is a more objective property of the carrots, and hence one that is less situationally context-dependent, and there is merely a temporal relationship between the verbal transfer event of buying and the fact that the carrots are still fresh at that time.

The interpretation of adjuncts as either adjective or adverb is thus occasionally highly context-sensitive, depending on the micro-context and the semantic relationship between the elements as well as on the macro-context of the speech situation. Some of the dual-form adverbs discussed in the following, such as *cheap*, *clean*, *deep*, *high* or *wide*, are frequently found in such highly context-sensitive uses and thus fall into the grey area between an interpretation as manner adverb, transparent adverb, or depictive adjective.

Additionally, in their adverbial uses most of these items show several orientations, depending on context, and there is frequently a correlation between type of orientation and zero- or -LY-form. Table 6.2 lists the types of adverbial orientation found with the fourteen investigated search items in the OBC 2.0 and how they are distributed between zero- and -LY-forms (numbers in brackets refer to percentages of the total of zero- or -LY-forms for each search item).

---

[17] Kristin Killie (p.c.) points out that the term *transparent adverb* is usually used with reference to adverbs denoting states of mind only. However, following Geuder's definition of transparent adverbs, the term can be extended to other types of adverbs as well which are causally or motivationally related with the verbal event.

[18] Killie (1994: 63) notes that utterances like *John bought the carrots* **cheaply** (in contrast to *John bought the carrots* **cheap**) are used but frowned upon occasionally in present-day English. This further illustrates the indeterminacy in the interpretation of the adverb's orientation. While *cheap(ly)* is participant-oriented in both cases, the -LY-form seems to be more closely associated with an event-oriented interpretation. This could explain why *John bought the carrots* **cheaply** is felt to be wrong by some speakers.

Tab. 6.2: Distribution of different types of orientation over adverbial zero- and -LY-forms found in the OBC between 1730 and 1913 (numbers in brackets are normalized by 1,000,000 words, N24,443,588)

Orientation	event		participant		reference point		state	
Adverb	zero	-LY	zero	-LY	zero	-LY	zero	-LY
cheap / cheaply	12 (0.49)	4 (0.16)	148 (6.05)	2 (0.08)	–	–	–	–
clean / cleanly	7 (0.29)	–	31 (1.27)	–	24 (0.98)	–	81 (3.31)	4 (0.16)
deep / deeply	17 (0.7)	11 (0.45)	–	–	3 (0.12)	3 (0.12)	15 (0.61)	14 (0.57)
easy / easily	43 (1.76)	311 (12.72)	–	–	–	–	3 (0.12)	117 (4.79)
flat / flatly	5 (0.2)	3 (0.12)	–	–	58 (2.37)	–	2 (0.08)	2 (0.08)
high / highly	8 (0.33)	11 (0.45)	10 (0.41)	–	55 (2.25)	–	8 (0.33)	128 (5.24)
loud / loudly	267 (10.92)	47 (1.92)	–	–	–	–	9 (0.37)	1 (0.04)
nice / nicely	3 (0.12)	20 (0.82)	–	–	–	–	2 (0.08)	15 (0.61)
quick / quickly	315 (12.89)	292 (11.95)	–	–	–	5 (0.2)	5 (0.2)	40 (1.64)
rash / rashly	3 (0.12)	5 (0.2)	–	–	–	–	–	–
scarce / scarcely	18 (0.74)	177 (7.24)	9 (0.37)	62 (2.54)	–	–	4 (0.16)	37 (1.51)
sharp / sharply	75 (3.07)	48 (1.96)	–	–	2 (0.08)	–	38 (1.55)	4 (0.16)
slow / sowly	38 (1.55)	127 (5.2)	–	–	–	–	–	–
wide / widely	2 (0.08)	1 (0.04)	–	–	2 (0.08)	–	232 (9.49)	3 (0.12)
Total	813 (33.26)	1.037 (42.42)	198 (8.1)	64 (2.62)	144 (5.89)	8 (0.33)	399 (16.32)	365 (14.93)

The table shows that -LY-forms predominate in event-oriented contexts, whereas they are almost absent from participant-oriented contexts, rare in reference-point oriented ones and in almost equal shares with zero-forms in state-oriented contexts. Adverbs that are predominantly event-oriented are: *easi(ly)*, *loud(ly)*, *nice(ly)*, *quick(ly)*, *rash(ly)* (although for the latter, with only eight adverbial and fourteen total instances, this is difficult to assess), *sharp(ly)*, and *slow(ly)*. They are rather typical adverbs of manner that focus on the nature of the verbal event. Zero-form *nice* is on the whole much less frequent than *nicely* (only 1.25%, i.e. 5 of 40 adverbial instances), an overwhelming 87.5% of all instances of *nice(ly)* (35 of 40 adverbial instances) found in the data showing the -LY-form. The zero-form first appears in 1791, in the following example, which is clearly event-oriented:

(20) *I told him he <u>dried them</u> very **nice*** (OBC, t17911207-9, 1791)

In contrast, *quick(ly)* shows a diachronic development from a preference of the zero-form until c. 1830, after which the LY form takes over and begins to dominate. Similarly, *slowly* outnumbers *slow* in frequencies after c. 1830 and *easily* begins to outnumber *easy* already from c. 1810 onwards. Thus, *quick(ly)*, *slow(ly)*, and *easi(ly)* follow the general trajectory for adverbs illustrated in figure 6.1 above.

It should be noted that *easily* is very often found in modal constructions with *can*, *could*, *may* or *might*, e.g.

(21) [...] *but that she stole such a Piece, which <u>might</u> very **easily** <u>be</u>*, [...] (OBC, t17261012-41, 1726)

(22) *I <u>could</u> as **easily** <u>have done it</u> as I could have put out my hand.* (OBC, t18070114-32, 1807)

Easily is here not just a manner adverb with event or state orientation, but rather a stance marker, i.e. the speaker expresses his or her subjective point of view on the State of Affairs (see Biber et al. 1999: §10.3.1.4). In such instances, the adverb also seems to have speaker orientation.

Scarce(ly) shows a similar, though maybe more dramatic, diachronic development as *quick(ly)* in that the zero-form clearly dominates in the earlier decades, until c. 1780, after which zero-forms disappear entirely from the data and -LY-forms take over. In contrast to *quick(ly)*, however, *scarce(ly)* is no manner adverb but rather an adverb of degree with participant orientation by which the speaker expresses a subjective evaluation of, for instance, a time-span, as in examples (23) and (24). This seems to develop into a stance adverbial with speaker orientation, i.e. the speaker subjectively evaluates his/her degree of knowledge over the whole State of Affairs, as in example (25):

(23) *I seldom saw her in the Market **scarce** <u>a month</u> together* [...] (OBC, t17470909-21, 1747)

(24) *I was not there **scarcely** <u>a minute</u>* [...] (OBC, t18500408-802, 1850)

(25) [...] <u>*I can*</u> ***scarcely*** <u>*say how late he sat up*</u> [...] (OBC, t18430227-461, 1843)

The findings for speaker-oriented *easily* and *scarcely* align with previous observations that -LY-forms tend to mark more subjective evaluations of a State of Affairs from Early Modern English on (e.g. Nevalainen 1997; Swan 1997).

Of the clearly event-oriented adverbs, *loud(ly)* and *sharp(ly)* are the only ones for which the zero-form more or less strongly persists until the end of the investigated period. *Loudly* appears for the first time in the data in 1787:

(26) [...] *he <u>was calling</u> **loudly** for White* (OBC, t17870523-39, 1787)

It is only from c. 1830 that *loudly* appears somewhat more frequently, but in contrast to the other event-oriented adverbs, its occurrence is generally much less frequent than that of zero-form *loud* until the 1880s, after which both appear equally rarely in the corpus. *Loud(ly)* is predominantly used with a small number of verbs: *speak, cry (out), call (out), shout, say, talk, sound, hear*, i.e. utterance verbs and verbs of audio perception. These eight verbs make up 81.5% (265 of N325) of all adverbial uses of *loud(ly)* in the corpus, and the persistence of zero-form *loud* may be due to these fairly strong collocational restrictions (see Boas 2003: 168–173, 2005: 456–457). The other 18.5% of adverbial uses (60 of N325) are shared among 28 other verbs.

Sharply appears in 1740 for the first time, but it remains in competition with *sharp* in similar syntactic and semantic-pragmatic contexts until c. 1910, see examples (27) and (28):

(27) [...] *I saw her <u>walk up</u> **sharply** to Johnson Street* [...] (OBC, t18360815-1871, 1836)

(28) [...] *we <u>walked away</u> as **sharp** as we could to the Bank* [...] (OBC, t19020407-331, 1902)

The adverbs with a more or less clear participant orientation are *cheap(ly)*, partly *clean* and *high*, and *scarce(ly)*. On the whole, the zero-form dominates in participant-oriented usage (see table 6.2 above). The adverbial zero-form *cheap* is not only most frequent, but it is also found fairly robustly until the end of the investigated period. It tends to collocate with a very limited number of verbs, particularly *buy X cheap*, *sell X cheap*, *have X cheap*, and *get X cheap*, i.e. verbal expressions of possession and transfer, which together amount to 75% of all instances (i.e. 120 of N160). The zero-form adverb *cheap* typically shows orientation towards the object participant, but for instance in a mediopassive construction (e.g. Hundt 2007: 7–9), it may show orientation towards the subject participant, see example (29):

(29) *I was informed there were goods selling **cheaper** than they could be made* [...] (OBC, t17670909-75, 1767)

Event-oriented *cheap* occurs in the data in 1762 for the first time but remains rare throughout the investigated period (only 7.5% of all attested adverbial zero-forms for *cheap*) and then for instance in combination with a comparative that generally privileges the zero-form, e.g. example (30):

(30) [...] *when you <u>could have lain</u> **cheaper** in your quarters* (OBC, t17600910-39, 1760)

Cheaply occurs as late as 1853 for the first time in the corpus, and then with event orientation:

(31) *Do not you know that these gentlemen* [...] <u>do business</u> **more cheaply** *than you?* (OBC: t18530228-374, 1853)

It is not until 1871 that *cheaply* appears with a participant orientation, e.g.

(32) [...] *he said he <u>had bought them</u>* [i.e. books] *from a gentleman rather **cheaply*** [...] (OBC, t18710109-107, 1871)

The occurrence of *cheaply* with participant orientation, even though rare, is nevertheless interesting, as it seems to indicate that -LY-forms are beginning to intrude into a rather typical zero-form domain in the later decades of the 19th century.

Zero-adverb *high* is partly participant-oriented (12.2% of zero-form uses) and partly event-oriented (11% of zero-form uses, see example 33), whereas *highly* is never participant-oriented but either state- or event-oriented (see example 34):

(33) *and they are sure <u>not to value it</u> too **high*** (OBC, t18820109-203, 1882)

(34) *and his ministry <u>was</u> very **highly** <u>valued</u> there* (OBC, t18430130-594, 1843)

Additionally, *highly* as a degree adverb shows a more subjective meaning (see Quirk et al. 1985: §§8.5–8.9), being an expression of the speaker's subjective evaluation of degree of X, e.g.

(35) *yet on the other hand, it <u>would be</u> **highly** <u>dangerous</u> to the public* [...] (OBC; t17870115-1, 1787)

(36) *I <u>thought</u> **highly** of her* [...] (OBC, t18430821-2362, 1843)

The -LY-form seems to gain ground from the 1830s onwards, especially in such contexts where *highly* expresses a subjective evaluation of degree.

Zero-adverbs that show state orientation rather frequently are, for instance, *clean, deep, high, sharp,* and *wide*, e.g.

(37) *Were the edges of the wound **clean** <u>cut</u>?* (OBC, t18601217-94, 1860)

(38) *there was a **deep** <u>punctured</u> wound* (OBC, t18710227-227, 1871)

(39) *he came out with another basket loaded with coals, but not so **high** <u>piled</u>* (OBC, t17870418-80, 1787)

(40) *I observed his tail was **sharp** <u>cock'd</u>* (OBC, t17551204-31, 1755)

(41) *I endeavour'd to shove the door **wide** <u>open</u>* (OBC, t17661022-4, 1766)

These patterns are often ambiguous between a phrasal and a lexicalized interpretation. Several of the combinations of a zero adverb plus (participial) adjective develop into lexicalized compounds that can also be used as compound adjectives modifying a noun phrase, such as *high-spirited, nice-sized, sharp-pointed, clean-cut*, see for instance

(42) *It is practically impossible for one man to harness and put in line a large team of **high-spirited** <u>dogs</u>.* (OED s.v. *high-spirited*; 1929 *Boys' Life* Feb. 19/3)

(43) *"You've a **nice-sized** <u>room</u> here," observed Eve.* (OED s.v. *nice-sized*; 1879 *Littell's Living Age* 20 Dec. 734)

(44) *Dame Pluche, repulsing them on either side with her **sharp-pointed** <u>elbows</u>.* (OED s.v. *sharp-pointed*; 1890 S. L. Gwynne *Musset's Comedies* 123)

(45) Rocks [...] cut through so as to expose **clean-cut** <u>surfaces</u>. (OED s.v. clean-cut; 1878 T. H. HUXLEY *Physiogr.* [ed. 2] 23)

It may be that -LY-forms come to be used to specifically mark the phrasal status of such combinations between state-oriented adverb and participial adjective, but this is difficult to assess on the basis of the data, see e.g.[19]

(46) *the upper part <u>was</u> **cleanly** <u>cut</u>, but the lower part was torn* [...] (OBC, t18720226-256, 1872)

(47) *servants came out of the publick-house, with baskets of coals loaded;* **highly** <u>piled</u> *with coals* (OBC, t17870523-21, 1787)

The combination *wide open* seems to keep its phrasal status, but it has to be noted that it makes up 87.9% (204 of N232) of all state-oriented adverbial uses of *wide*, being a fixed collocation and as such presumably more resistant to change. The phrase *(to be) wide awake* is converted into a nominal compound denoting a type of hat fashionable in the 18th and 19th century. There are 21 occurrences of this compound in the data for *wide* between c. 1860 and 1880, e.g.

(48) *after leaving the house, I gave Hunter his hat; he put a white* **wide-awake** *which he had on, into it, and put it on his head* (OBC; t18620106-193, 1862)

Adverbs with a reference-point orientation are *clean, flat*, and *high* (not *highly*), and rarely *wide*. Zero-forms tend to predominate in reference-point oriented contexts especially with spatial reference points, e.g.

(49) *He then stagger'd like a drunken man, <u>fell</u> **flat** <u>upon his back</u>, and never spoke another word* (OBC, t17531024-58, 1753)

(50) *[...] he said he had a friend <u>living up</u> **higher** <u>in the street</u>* [...] (OBC, t17921031-4, 1792)

(51) *a pane of glass in the window <u>was cut</u> **clean** <u>out</u>* (OBC, t18800803-427, 1880)

---

19 The OBC data do not show a clear picture as to a syntactic-functional distribution such as that the zero-form is preferred as a modifier for adverbs and adjectives, while the -LY-form is preferred with verbs and participles, which has been noted in the literature (Nevalainen 1994a: 245–246; see also Jespersen 1946: 371, Poutsma 1926: 634–635).

(52) *I measured it – the window was* **wide** *up and I could see you.* (OBC, t18720708-547, 1872)

Reference points (particularly spatial ones) and participants are non-eventive and hence non-dynamic, and they are conceptually bounded – i.e. they have 'nouny' properties rather than 'verby' ones. It seems as if zero-forms persisted better here than in clearly event-oriented, dynamic and durative/temporally unbounded contexts. Such uses are less prototypical of the category of adverb (Swan 1997: 183) and closer to that of adjective.

The same group of zero-form adverbs that appears with reference-point orientation also appears in adjectival depictive and resultative constructions in the OBC data: *clean* (8.8% of all its adjectival uses; see examples 53 and 55), *flat* (36% of all its adjectival uses, see example 56), *high* (12.2% of all its adjectival uses, see example 54), and *wide* (4.1% of all its adjectival uses since 1730, see example 57):

(53) *Did the linen come* **clean** *to you or dirty?* (OBC, t17621020-13, 1762)
 → **depictive**

(54) *[...] and heard him ask a Man if he had seen any Body run that Way, for a Person (says he) has been robbed a little* **higher** *[up the street]?* (OBC, t17390502-5, 1739) → **depictive**

(55) *[...] but a cat has since licked it* **clean**. (OBC, t18380226-874, 1838)
 → **resultative**

(56) *The silver mug was squeezed quite* **flat** *then [...]* (OBC, t17570526-5, 1757)
 → **resultative**

(57) *I did not mean to do it; I fired* **wide**; *I never intended to hurt my husband* (OBC, t19070910-22, 1907) → **resultative**

The line between an adjectival interpretation, where there is just a temporal overlap between the predicate event and the state denoted by the adjunct, and an adverbial one, where there is also a causal link between the two (Geuder 2004; Himmelmann and Schultze-Berndt 2005; see also section 4.2), may occasionally be thin in such combinations. This might explain why adverbs in reference-point oriented contexts tend to preserve the zero-form.

A look at the issue of orientation and the semantics of the adverb shows that there are very few contexts in which an adverbial zero-form and a -LY-form are in free variation, but very often there is a distributional difference between the two formal variants that seems to depend on differences in orientation. The influence of the sociolinguistic factors of profession (social class, degree of education) and speaker's sex (gender) will therefore in the following be assessed only for those adverbs where some assumedly free variation persists throughout the whole investigated period.

4.3 Evidence for sociolinguistic variation as an effect of standardization?

The OBC also includes sociobiographical speaker information on speaker's gender, age, occupation and social class (see http://www.uni-giessen.de/oldbaileycorpus/index.html). The notations for occupations follow the *Historical International Standard Classification of Occupations* (HISCO), and the classifications of social classes follow HISCLASS, a social-class scheme based on HISCO, which consists of nine social classes derived from information about historical occupations.[20] In this classification, classes 1 (e.g. judges, lawyers, medical doctors, teachers, interpreters), 2 (e.g. managers, legislative officials), and 3 (e.g. government executive officials, stenographers, bookkeepers) refer to people with a higher social status and educational background as well as those who presumably used more formal and written language in their every-day dealings. Classes 4 and 5 comprise, for instance, salespersons, clerks, technical workers, working proprietors, policemen and detectives, while classes 6–9 comprise, for instance, foremen, house-keepers, skilled craftsmen, farmers, seamen and various kinds of lower skilled and unskilled labourers, i.e. people who normally did not have much formal education in the 18th and 19th centuries and who needed lesser formal or written language as part of their occupation, or even none at all.

As noted in the introduction (section 1), the zero form of dual-form adverbs has developed into a stylistically and socially marked feature in contemporary English. The social and stylistic dimension in the use of the English dual-form adverbs is, historically speaking, a very recent phenomenon which only developed in the course of the 19th and 20th century. It is commonly thought to be linked with the standardization process that English underwent during the late 18th and 19th century, which is the period when English grammar was codified in numerous widely influential grammar books. The grammar books of Joseph Priestley (1761), Robert Lowth (1762), John Ash (1793), Lindley Murray (1795) and others

---

[20] See http://historyofwork.iisg.nl/major.php; for the HISCO system see http://historyofwork.iisg.nl/ and for HISCLASS see http://historyofwork.iisg.nl/list_pub.php?categories=hisclass (last accessed July 2019).

codified and thus formed the linguistic norms of English speakers for generations (e.g. Finegan 1998; Görlach 1998). -LY-suffixation of adverbs was explicitly favoured in these books, because it made the language less ambiguous, more transparent, and more logical if the category change from adjective to adverb was accompanied by an overt change in formal marking (Pounder 2001, see also Killie 2015: 209).

On the basis of the OBC data alone, the relevance of style for the use of a zero- or -LY-form cannot be assessed, as all data are transcripts of spoken language of a more or less formal nature produced by speakers who were participants in a court trial, either as court official, defendant, victim or witness. For the assessment of style, a comparison would be needed, such as with a corpus that includes written texts belonging to different genres and text types (e.g. CLMET, COHA). However, this has to be reserved for future investigations. What remains is the possibility to investigate the impact of the sociolinguistic factors of occupation, indicative of social class and degree of education, and gender. The evaluation of these factors for the distribution and development of dual-form adverbs is, however, impaired by the fact that not all data sets obtained from the OBC actually include the necessary sociobiographical information for such an analysis. Many speakers are anonymous, or their sex is known but not their social class and profession.

In the following, sociolinguistic findings will be presented for the adverbial uses of *quick/ly*, *rash/ly*, *sharp/ly* and *slow/ly*, because with these sets the two formal variants seem to be in more or less free variation in event-oriented contexts throughout the whole investigated period (see table 6.2 above). For *sharp/ly*, only the 123 adverbial instances that have been classified as event-oriented will be considered (i.e. 73.6% of N167), as the other 44 instances (i.e. 26.4% of N167) with different orientations would presumably distort the picture.

Figure 6.3 below shows the diachronic development of -LY-forms as against zero-forms for the social variable of gender (numbers for speakers whose sex is unknown are left out).[21] First of all, it is quite striking that the data for the four dual-form adverbs considered show a higher number of female speakers using them at all, namely 56.7% female as against 43.2% male speakers for the whole time-span (i.e. 555 vs. 423 occ., N978). This is noteworthy, as only 15.9% of words uttered in the whole OBC 2.0 are by female speakers, as against 84% by male

---

21 The OBC 2.0 Manual (http://fedora.clarin-d.uni-saarland.de/oldbailey/downloads/OBC_2.0_Manual%202016-07-13.pdf) notes that speaker's gender is known for 97% of all speakers in the whole corpus, i.e. about 3% are unknown (see OBC 2.0 Manual, page 7). This corresponds quite well with the data found for the investigated dual-form adverbs, where on average about 2% of the speakers are unknown.

speakers, and 2.9% by unknown speakers (see OBC 2.0 Manual, page 7, and statistics sheet).[22] Taking a look at the overall uses of -LY-forms as against zero-forms, female speakers show a clear preference with 63.4% -LY-forms over 36.6% zero-forms (i.e. 352 vs. 203, N555). Male speakers on the whole show a more balanced picture, with 53.9% LY-forms and 46.1% zero-forms (i.e. 228 vs. 195, N423).

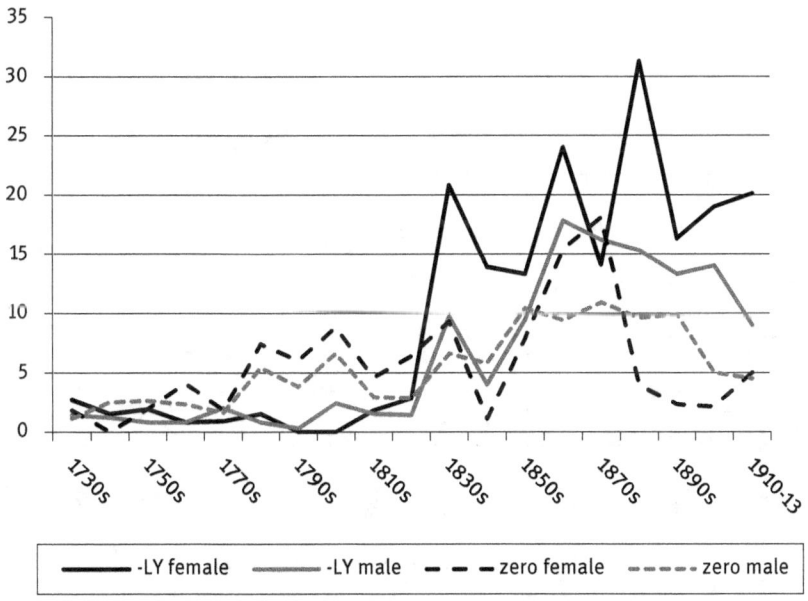

Fig. 6.3: Distribution of -LY-forms and zero-forms across female and male speakers

As noted before, there is a general rise in the occurrence of the investigated adverb lexemes in the data from c. 1830 onwards (see figure 6.1 above), which is also reflected in figure 6.3. The diachronic distribution shows that female speakers begin to prefer -LY-forms over zero-forms from c. 1810 onwards and especially after the 1870s, when the use of zero-forms by female speakers drops sharply. Male speakers also prefer -LY- over zero-forms after c. 1850, but the drop of zero-

---

[22] Both available under http://fedora.clarin-d.uni-saarland.de/oldbailey/documentation.html. The OBC 2.0 statistics page lists 83,258 different speakers of which 15,461 are female (i.e. 18.6%) and 67,797 (i.e. 81.4%) are male (http://www.uni-giessen.de/oldbaileycorpus/stats.html, last accessed June 2018).

forms is less sharp than with female speakers. All this may be taken as support for the claim made by Opdahl (2000) for 20th-century English that women use fewer zero-forms than men, possibly because they are more norm-oriented in conforming to prestige forms (Labov 2001: 261–293), but it should also be kept in mind that the raw numbers of occurrences are generally low (see table 6.2), so that it is difficult to form generalizations.

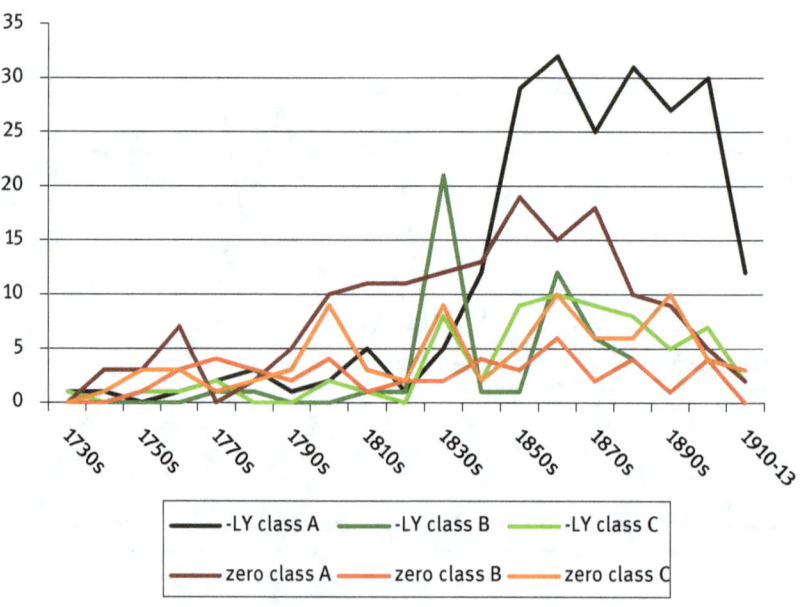

Fig. 6.4: Distribution of -LY-forms and zero-forms across different social/occupational classes (A: 1–3, B: 4–5, C: 6–9)

Figure 6.4 shows the distribution of -LY- as against zero-forms for social classes. OBC classes 1 to 3 are merged in A, 4 and 5 are merged in B, and 6 to 9 are merged in C. Speakers of class A (OBC classes 1–3) generally use the investigated four adverbs most (see also Macaulay 1995) – with 60.6% (385 of N635) – followed by speakers of class C (OBC classes 6–9) with 23.6% (150 of N635), and speakers of class B (OBC classes 4–5) with 15.8% (100 of N635).[23] The steep rise in the

---

23 The OBC 2.0 statistics page (available under http://fedora.clarin-d.uni-saarland.de/oldbailey/documentation. html) lists occupational classes by proceeding and by decade but merges

preference of -LY-forms with speakers of class A is seen from c. 1840 onwards. Interestingly, speakers of class B and C show relatively equal proportions of -LY- and zero-forms throughout. This might point to a beginning influence of social factors, such as higher social class and a higher degree of education, on the spread of -LY-forms from the middle of the 19th century onwards.

It nevertheless seems that the influence of the sociolinguistic variables of social class/educational background (occupation) and gender (sex) on the spread of -LY on the one hand and the retention of zero-forms on the other was rather limited in comparison with syntactic, semantic and pragmatic factors in the 18th and 19th centuries. It may additionally be that scribal interpolation plays a role especially in the earlier decades, so that the linguistic patterns that are observable in the OBC data are sociolinguistically less heterogeneous than we might hope (see also Huber 2007: section 2.2). Pounder (2001), who analyzes literary texts of the 19th and 20th centuries, finds that the zero-form variants of dual-form adverbs become socially marked only in the literature of the 20th century. There is some indication in the OBC data that this preference for -LY-forms was being prepared for from the middle of the 19th century onwards in more educated speech where the semantics and pragmatics of the adverbs allowed an option. Further research including more kinds of data will have to be conducted to assess this.

5 Conclusion

Throughout the investigated period, -LY-forms spread fairly systematically in particular syntactic, semantic and pragmatic contexts, while other contexts are largely reserved for zero-forms. Occasionally, the influence of fixed collocations between particular verbs and adverbs for the retention of a zero-form (as with *loud* or *wide*) must also be considered a relevant factor. The spread of adverbial -LY may presumably be linked to the diffusion of grammar-related knowledge through the population, i.e. it may be seen in the context of the ongoing standardization of the English language and the spread and distribution of normative attitudes in grammars, usage guides, and through teaching. -LY is the variant that is favoured in this language-social context. This might also explain why there is a tendency in the data for women to use more -LY forms, especially from

---

classes 1–5 and 6–13. According to the OBC 2.0 statistics sheet, the words uttered by speakers of classes 1–5 in the whole OBC 2.0 amount to 43.8%, and those uttered by speakers of classes 6–13 to 20.2%. For 36% of the words the speaker's social class is unknown.

the late 19th century on. However, -LY does not spread to any possible domain of usage, but it widens its range of application only in certain domains that seem to be more prototypical for the category of adverb, such as the marking of event-oriented manner adverbs in dynamic contexts (e.g. *they were calling **loudly***), subjective speaker-oriented stance adverbs (e.g. *might **easily** be seen*, ***highly** respectable*, ***scarcely** know*), but less at the borders to the category of ADJECTIVE, i.e. in the realm of reference-point adverbs (e.g. *he lives **higher** in the street*), and participant-oriented transparent adverbs (e.g. *I bought them **cheap***).

The impact of the sociolinguistic variables of occupation (social class and education) and speaker's sex (gender) was assessed only for a limited selection of four adverbs that appeared in event-oriented contexts, as these were the only ones where the alternation of the two adverbial variants could be considered to be relatively unconstrained by semantic and pragmatic factors, i.e. in free variation. Although a certain tendency could be found that female speakers use -LY-forms more frequently than zero-forms, and more so than male speakers, the question remains whether any general conclusions should be drawn from the limited data set available. The results for occupation (social class and education) showed that it is especially the upper social classes who begin to favour -LY-forms in the second half of the 19th century. The next step might be a multivariate analysis including other linguistic data from different textual genres, which would have to clearly distinguish between the different types of semantic-pragmatic orientation in addition to the social variables.

Taking a diachronic perspective on the issue of variation in adverb form in English is necessary in order to understand why a certain amount of free variation between -LY- and zero-forms exists with some adverbs and in some contexts in contemporary English: -LY has never made it full scale in becoming *the* adverb marker in English, i.e. its grammaticalization stopped half-way, partly because of non-typical adverb functions, because of the high degree of conventionalization of suffixless forms especially among the more frequent adverbs (Payne et al. 2010), because of semantic and pragmatic ambiguities in interpretation, and because of the general fuzziness of the category boundary between ADJECTIVE and ADVERB in terms of orientation. A clearer impact of social factors may potentially become visible only after 1900 (see Pounder 2001). More research is needed in 20th- and 21st-century language material and also on the grammaticalization of -LY in the Late Modern English period (1700–2000) in corpora including different genres and text types to further assess this issue.

References

Ash, John. 1793. *Grammatical institutes: or, an easy introduction to Dr. Lowth's English grammar, designed for the use of schools, And to lead Young Gentlemen and Ladies into the Knowledge of the first Principles of the English Language. By John Ash, with an appendix, containing, I. The Declension of irregular and defective Verbs. II. The Application of the Grammatical Institutes. III. Some useful Observations on the Ellipsis*. 4th edn., revised and corrected by the author. London: printed for E. and C. Dilly in the Poultry.

Aikhenvald, Alexandra Y. 2015. *The art of grammar. A practical guide*. Oxford: Oxford University Press.

Baayen, Harald. 1994. Derivational productivity and text typology. *Journal for Quantitative Linguistics* 1. 16–34.

Baayen Harald & Antoinette Renouf. 1996. Chronicling the times. Productive lexical innovations in an English newspaper. *Language* 72. 69–96.

Beal, Joan C. 2010. Prescriptivism and the suppression of variation. In Raymond Hickey (ed.), *Eighteenth-century English. Ideology and change*, 21–37. Cambridge: Cambridge University Press.

Deckmann, E. 1880. Über die doppelformigen englischen Adjektiv-Adverbien. *Archiv für das Studium der neueren Sprachen und Literaturen* 64. 25–70.

Biber, Douglas, Stig Johansson & Geoffrey Leech. 1999. *Longman grammar of spoken and written English*. Harlow: Pearson Education Ltd.

BNC = *British National Corpus* (http://www.natcorp.ox.ac.uk/; last accessed January 2018)

Boas, Hans C. 2003. *A constructional approach to resultatives*. Stanford, CA: CSLI Publications.

Boas, Hans C. 2005. Determining the productivity of resultatives: A reply to Goldberg and Jackendoff. *Language* 81. 448–464.

Bybee, Joan. 1985. *Morphology: A study of the relation between meaning and form*. Amsterdam: John Benjamins.

Chambers, Jack. 2004. Dynamic typology and vernacular universals. In Bernd Kortmann, ed. *Dialectology meets typology*, 127–145. Berlin: Mouton de Gruyter.

CLMET = *Corpus of Late Modern English Texts* (URL: https://perswww.kuleuven.be/~u0044428/; last accessed January 2018)

COHA = *Corpus of Historical American English* (http://corpus.byu.edu/coha/; last accessed January 2018)

Croft, William. 2003. *Typology and universals*. Cambridge: Cambridge University Press.

DOEC = *Dictionary of Old English Corpus in Electronic Form, TEI-P5 conformant version, 2009 Release*. 2009. Compiled by diPaolo Healey, Antonette, Joan Holland, David McDougall, Ian McDougall & Xin Xiang. Toronto: DOE Project, University of Toronto. (http://www.doe.utoronto.ca; last accessed January 2018)

Donner, Morton. 1991. Adverb form in Middle English. *English Studies* 72. 1–11.

Ernst, Thomas. 2009. Speaker-oriented adverbs. *Natural Language & Linguistic Theory* 27 (3). 497–544.

Finegan, Edward. 1998. English grammar and usage. In Suzanne Romaine(ed.), *The Cambridge history of the English language*, vol. 1: *1776–1997*, 536–588 Cambridge: Cambridge University Press.

Geuder, Wilhelm. 2000. *Oriented adverbs. Issues in the lexical semantics of event adverbs*. Dissertation Universität Tübingen. University of Tübingen Online Publication System.

Geuder, Wilhelm. 2004. Depictives and transparent adverbs. In Jennifer Austin, Stefan Engelberg & Gisa Rauh (eds.), 2004. *Adverbials. The interplay between meaning, context, and syntactic structure*, 131–166. Amsterdam: John Benjamins.

Giegerich, Heinz. 2012. The morphology of *-ly* and the categorial status of 'adverbs' in English. *English Language and Linguistics* 16 (3). 341–359.

Görlach, Manfred. 1998. *An annotated bibliography of nineteenth-century grammars of English*. Amsterdam: John Benjamins.

Görlach, Manfred. 1999a. *English in nineteenth-century England. An introduction*. Cambridge: Cambridge University Press.

Görlach, Manfred. 1999b. Social class and linguistic correctness in 19th-century England. In Manfred Görlach (ed.), *Aspects of the history of English*, 162–178. Heidelberg: Winter.

Goldberg, Adele & Ray Jackendoff. 2004. The English resultative as a family of constructions. *Language* 80. 532–568.

Hickey, Raymond. 2010. Attitudes and concerns in eighteenth-century English. In Raymond Hickey (ed.), *Eighteenth-century English. Ideology and change*, 1–20. Cambridge: Cambridge University Press.

Himmelmann, Nikolaus & Eva Schultze-Berndt. 2005. Issues in the syntax and semantics of participant-oriented adjuncts: An introduction. In Nikolaus Himmelmann & Eva Schultze-Berndt (eds.), *Secondary predication and adverbial modification*, 1–67. New York: Oxford University Press.

Huddleston, Rodney & Geoffrey K. Pullum. 2002. *The Cambridge grammar of the English language*. Cambridge: Cambridge University Press.

Huber, Magnus. 2007. The Old Bailey Proceedings, 1674-1834. Evaluating and annotating a corpus of 18th- and 19th-century spoken English. In Anneli Meurman-Solin & Arja Nurmi (eds.), *Annotating variation and change*. (*Studies in variation, contact and change in English/Varieng* 1). University of Helsinki. (URL: http://www.helsinki.fi/ varieng/series/volumes/01/huber/#section2.2)

Hundt, Marianne. 2007. *English mediopassive constructions. A cognitive, corpus-based study of their origin, spread, and current status*. Amsterdam: Rodopi.

Jackendoff, Ray. 1972. *Semantic interpretation in Generative Grammar*. Cambridge, MA: MIT Press.

Jespersen, Otto. 1942. *A Modern English grammar on historical principles*, Part VI: *Morphology*. London: Allen & Unwin.

Jespersen, Otto. 1946. *Essentials of English grammar*. 6th edn. London: Allen & Unwin.

Jespersen, Otto. 1949. *A Modern English grammar on historical principles*, Part VII: *Syntax*. London: Allen & Unwin.

Killie, Kristin. 1994. The orientation of manner adverbs: A synchronic and diachronic study. *Nordlyd* 21. 42–77.

Killie, Kristin. 1998. The spread of *-ly* to present participles. In Jacek Fisiak & Marcin Krygier (eds.), *Advances in English historical linguistics*, 119–134. Berlin: Mouton de Gruyter.

Killie, Kristin. 2000. *Stative adverbs in English: A study of adverbial productivity and orientation*. Doctoral dissertation, University of Tromsø. [https://munin.uit.no/handle/10037/292]

Killie, Kristin. 2005. On the role of prescriptivism in the spread of the English adverbial *-ly* suffix. In Gulbrand Alhaug, Endre Mørck & Aud-Kirsti Pedersen (eds.), *Mot rikare mål å trå. Festskrift til Tove Bull*, 68–79. Oslo: Novus.

Killie, Kristin. 2015. Secondary grammaticalization and the English adverbial *-ly* suffix. *Language Sciences* 47. 199–214.

Kortmann, Bernd & Benedikt Szmrecsanyi. 2004. Global synopsis: morphological and syntactic variation in English. In Bernd Kortmann & Edgar W. Schneider (eds.), *A Handbook of varieties of English. A multimedia reference tool.* Vol. 2: *Morphology and syntax*, 1142–1202. Berlin: de Gruyter.

Labov, William. 2001. *Principles of linguistic change.* Vol. 2: *Social factors.* Malden, MA: Blackwell.

Lowth, Robert. 1762. *A short introduction to English grammar. With critical notes.* London: A. Millar, R. & J. Dodsley.

Macaulay, Ronald K. S. 1995. The adverbs of authority. *English World-Wide* 16. 37–60.

Murray, Lindley. 1795. *English grammar: Adapted to the different classes of learners. With an appendix, containing rules and observations for promoting perspicuity in speaking and writing.* York: printed and sold by Wilson, Spence, and Mawman.

Nevalainen, Terttu. 1994a. Aspects of adverbial change in Early Modern English. In Dieter Kastovsky (ed.), *Studies in Early Modern English*, 243–259. Berlin: Mouton de Gruyter.

Nevalainen, Terttu. 1994b. Diachronic issues in English adverb derivation. In Udo Fries, Gunnel Tottie & Peter Schneider (eds.), *Creating and using English language corpora: Papers from the fourteenth International Conference on English Language and Computerized Corpora, Zürich 1993*, 139–147. Amsterdam: Rodopi.

Nevalainen, Terttu. 1997. The process of adverb derivation in Late Middle and Early Modern English. In Matti Rissanen, Merja Kytö & Kirsi Heikkonen (eds.), *Grammaticalization at work: Studies of long-term developments in English*, 145–189. Berlin: Mouton de Gruyter.

OBC = *Old Bailey Corpus* (http://www.uni-giessen.de/oldbaileycorpus/index.html; last accessed January 2018)

OBC 2.0 Manual (http://fedora.clarin-d.uni-saarland.de/oldbailey/downloads/OBC_2.0_Manual%202016-07-13.pdf)

OED = *Oxford English Dictionary Online* (www.oed.com; last accessed January 2018)

Opdahl, Lise. 1989. Did they purchase it 'direct' or 'directly'? On direct and directly as verb modifiers in present-day British and American English. In Leiv Egil Breivik, Arnoldus Hille & Stig Johansson (eds.), *Essays on English language in honour of Bertil Sundby*, 245–257. Oslo: Novus.

Opdahl, Lise 2000. *LY or zero suffix? A study in variation of dual-form adverbs in present-day English.* 2 volumes. Frankfurt/Main: Peter Lang.

Payne, John, Rodney Huddleston & Geoffrey K. Pullum. 2010. The distribution and category status of adjectives and adverbs. *Word Structure* 3. 31–81.

Peters, Hans. 1994. Degree adverbs in Early Modern English. In Dieter Kastovsky (ed.), *Studies in Early Modern English*, 269–288. Berlin: Mouton de Gruyter.

Pittner, Karin. 2015. Between inflection and derivation: Adverbial suffixes in English and German. In Karin Pittner, Daniela Elsner & Fabian Barteld (eds.), *Adverbs. Functional and diachronic aspects*, 133–156. Amsterdam: John Benjamins.

Plag, Ingo. 2003. *Word-formation in English.* Cambridge: Cambridge University Press.

Pooley, Robert C. 1933. Real and sure as adverbs. *American Speech* February. 60–62.

Pounder, Amanda. 2001. Adverb-marking in German and English: System and standardization. *Diachronica* 18. 301–358.

Poutsma, Hendrik. 1904–1926. *A grammar of Late Modern English.* II, II. Groningen: Noordhoff.

Priestley, Joseph. 1761. *The rudiments of English grammar: Adapted to the use of schools. With observations on style.* London: printed for R. Griffiths, in the Strand.

Quirk, Randolph, Sidney Greenbaum, Geoffrey Leech & Jan Svartvik. 1985. *A comprehensive grammar of the English language.* London: Longman.

Rauh, Gisa. 2015. Adverbs as a linguistic category(?). In Karin Pittner, Daniela Elsner & Fabian Barteld (eds.), *Adverbs. Functional and diachronic aspects*, 19–46. Amsterdam: John Benjamins.

Ross, Claudia. 1984. Adverbial change: Implications for a theory of lexical change. In David Testen, Venna Mirshra & Joseph Drogo (eds.), *Chicago Linguistics Society. Papers from the parasession on lexical semantics*, 243–249. Chicago: Chicago University Press.

Rice, Wallace. 1927. Go slow – proceed slowly. *American Speech* September. 489–491.

Straus, Jane. 2010. *Blue book for grammar and punctuation*. 11th edn. Indianapolis, IN: Wiley.

Swan, Toril. 1990. Subject-oriented adverbs in 20th-century English. *Nordlyd: Tromsø University Working Papers in Language and Linguistics* 16. 14–58.

Swan, Toril. 1997. From manner to subject modification: Adverbialization in English. *Nordic Journal of Linguistics* 20. 179–195.

Swan, Toril & Leiv Egil Breivik. 1997. Subject-oriented adverbs in a diachronic and contrastive perspective. In Raymond Hickey & Stanislaw Puppel (eds.), *Festschrift for Jacek Fisiak*, 395–421. Berlin: Mouton de Gruyter.

Tagliamonte, Sali & Rika Ito. 2002. Think *really different*: Continuity and specialization in the English dual form adverbs. *Journal of Sociolinguistics* 6. 236–266.

Tieken-Boon van Ostade, Ingrid. 2008. *Grammars, grammarians and grammar-writing in eighteenth-century England*. Berlin: Mouton de Gruyter.

Tieken-Boon van Ostade, Ingrid. 2010. Lowth as an icon of prescriptivism. In Raymond Hickey (ed.), *Eighteenth-century English. Ideology and change*, 89–105. Cambridge: Cambridge University Press.

Tieken-Boon van Ostade, Ingrid. 2014. Eighteenth-century English normative grammars and their readers. In Gijsbert Rutten, Rik Vosters & Wim Vandenbussche (eds.), *Norms and usage in language history, 1600–1900. A sociolinguistic and comparative perspective*, 129–150. Amsterdam: John Benjamins.

Ungerer, Friedrich. 1988. *Syntax der englischen Adverbialien*. Tübingen: Niemeyer.

Valera, Salvador. 1998. On subject-orientation in English *-ly* adverbs. *English Language and Linguistics* 2. 263–282.

Webster's dictionary of English usage. 1989. Springfield, MA: Merriam-Webster.

Zwicky, Arnold M. 1995. Why English adverbial *-ly* is not inflectional. In Barbara Need (ed.), *Papers from the 31st Regional Meeting of the Chicago Linguistic Society*. Vol. I: *The Main Session*, 523–535. Chicago, IL: Chicago Linguistic Society.

Dagmar Haumann and Kristin Killie
Bridging contexts in the reanalysis of *naturally* as a sentence adverb: A corpus study

Abstract: This paper argues that the delimitation of bridging contexts (Heine 2002) for the reanalysis of narrow-scope *naturally* as a sentence adverb feeds on the interplay of a number of syntactic factors. The overarching factor is the presence of a full left periphery as instantiated in matrix clauses and certain types of subordinate clauses, notably those that have independent illocutionary force (Haegeman 2002, 2012). The relative scope of *naturally* vis-à-vis other sentence elements, such as sentential negation or other adverbs, is an additional structural determinant for the bridging contexts for *naturally*. In addition to syntactic factors, the reanalysis of *naturally* is subject to lexical, pragmatic and contextual constraints.

1 Introduction: The aims of this study

The contributions in the present volume are concerned with contexts in grammatical change.[1] Context may, of course, be defined in many different ways and may involve factors from various domains, including both linguistic and extralinguistic ones. This article is concerned with the concept of "bridging context" in syntactic reanalysis (also referred to as "critical context", see Diewald 2002). A bridging context is a context in which the old and the new analysis are both possible (Evans and Wilkins 1998: 5; Heine 2002: 84; see section 2.4 for a closer discussion of the concept). A large number of studies have demonstrated that bridging contexts involve factors from various domains (see e.g. Traugott 2012). This study is concerned with the bridging contexts of the adverb *naturally*, discussing factors of various sorts which may have allowed or promoted the reanalysis of

---

[1] We thank the anonymous reviewers and the volume editors for valuable feedback.

Dagmar Haumann, University of Bergen, Department of Foreign Languages, Bergen, Norway, dagmar.haumann@uib.no
Kristin Killie, UiT The Arctic University of Norway, Department of Education, Tromsø, Norway, kristin.killie@uit.no

https://doi.org/10.1515/9783110682564-007

narrow-scope *naturally* into a sentence adverb. Our focus is on copular *be* sentences (see section 2.3 for the reasons behind this selection).[2]

We argue that the reanalysis of narrow-scope *naturally* into a sentence adverb depends on the interplay of a number of factors, but that syntax is fundamental as it determines the contexts in which a reanalysis is possible: evidential *naturally* can only be licensed in clauses that project a ForceP specified for assertive illocutionary force, viz. in matrix declaratives and certain types of subordinate clauses. In such clauses, a reanalysis is most likely to occur if *naturally* occurs between a finite form of the copula *be* and the predicative complement, e.g. AP or DP, with no other elements intervening between the two. However, a reanalysis does not automatically occur if the syntactic conditions are met; the reanalysis is also subject to lexical, pragmatic and contextual constraints.

The paper is organized as follows: section 2 provides some more background to the paper, discussing some important concepts, principles, assumptions and hypotheses. The section also contains a description of our corpus and method. Then, in section 3, we discuss the bridging contexts of *naturally* in copular *be* sentences, before we sum up the main points in section 4.

2 Background

2.1 Sentence adverbs

Sentence adverbs (SAs) such as those in (1)–(4) are customarily defined as taking scope over the entire sentence, providing a speaker perspective on the proposition:

(1) **Frankly/briefly**, I do not like him at all.
(2) **Surprisingly/unfortunately**, I want my husband to behave.
(3) a. She has **evidently/obviously** lost the contest.
     b. She will **definitely/probably** lose the contest.
(4) **Wisely/carefully**, she answered the question.

---

[2] The paper represents the first step in a larger project which aims to shed light on the reanalysis of English narrow-scope *-ly* adverbs into wide-scope sentence adverbs.

Swan, in her 1988 study of the development of the SAs in (1)–(4), essentially adopts Bellert's (1977) taxonomy. Thus, *frankly/briefly* in (1) are classified as pragmatic adverbs (i.e. speech act adverbs or illocutionary adverbs), which either refer to the content of the proposition and the speaker's honesty in expressing it, as expressed by *frankly*, or the form of the utterance, as expressed by *briefly* (see Bellert 1977: 349–350; Swan 1988: 66–77). Adverbs like *surprisingly/unfortunately* in (2) are classified as evaluative adverbs which express the speaker's evaluation of the fact expressed by the sentence (see Bellert 1977: 342–343; Swan 1988: 30–40). Modal adverbs (3) are concerned with the speaker's subjective perception of the truth of the proposition (see Bellert 1977: 343–347; Swan 1988: 41–56). They are either evidential, such as *evidently/obviously* (3a), and relate to the evidence the speaker has for her assertion, or they are epistemic, such as *definitely/ probably* (3b), and express degrees of the speaker's certitude about the proposition being true (see section 2.2 for discussion). While the adverbs in (1)–(3) come together as speaker-oriented adverbs expressing the speaker's perspective on the proposition (see Jackendoff 1972: 56–58; Bellert 1977: 342–350), *wisely/carefully* in (4), which are referred to as subject disjuncts or subject-oriented adverbs, make up a class of their own in that they express the speaker's judgment about both the subject and the action under consideration (see Jackendoff 1972: 90; Quirk and Greenbaum 1986: 245; Swan 1988: 57–66). In providing a speaker perspective on the proposition, the SAs in (1)–(4) function at the discourse or "interpersonal" level (Halliday 1985) and can thus be described as subjective elements (Swan 1988; Traugott 1989; Fischer 2007; Swan and Breivik 2011).

Before turning to the categorization of sentence adverb *naturally* (section 2.2), some comments on the set of sentence adverbs referred to as modal adverbs (3) are in order. One of the longstanding debates in modality research concerns the question whether evidentiality, as expressed by e.g. adverbs like *evidently/obviously* (3a), and epistemicity, as expressed by e.g. adverbs like *definitely/probably* (3b), represent two discrete categories (see de Haan 2001; Diewald and Smirnova 2011) or mark the extremes of one scalar category (see Aijmer 1996; Traugott 1997; see Simon-Vandenbergen and Aijmer 2007: 24–39 for a detailed discussion). For the purpose of our paper, we subscribe to the former view. According to de Haan (2001: 203), evidentiality and epistemicity represent "entirely different cognitive areas," which must be distinguished both semantically and syntactically. Semantically, evidential adverbs differ from epistemic expressions in that they state "the existence of a source of evidence for some information" (Aikhenvald 2003: 1, see also section 2.2), whereas epistemic adverbs express the "the degree of certitude of the truth value, expressed in terms of possibility or necessity" (Ernst 2001: 73). Syntactically, evidential adverbs differ from epistemic adverbs in that the former may take scope over the latter, but not vice versa (see among others Cinque 1999: 33, 135; Haumann 2007: 370–376):

(5) a. ***Obviously**, Kate has **probably** forgotten her appointment.*
    b. ***Probably**, Kate has **obviously** forgotten her appointment.*

Also, evidential adverbs, but not epistemic adverbs, may take scope over subject-oriented adverbs (6), and subject-oriented adverbs may take scope over epistemic adverbs, but not over evidential adverbs (7):

(6) a. *Kate would **obviously** have **carefully** planned the event.*
    b. **She would **possibly** have **carefully** avoided all contact with her family.*
(7) a. *She will **carefully** have **possibly** avoided all contact with her family.*
    b. **Kate would **carefully** have **obviously** planned the event.*

2.2 The categorization of sentence adverb *naturally*

The categorization of sentence adverb *naturally* is somewhat controversial. Swan (1988: 33) classifies it as an evaluative adverb, but admits that the classification is not straightforward. She hypothesizes that "there may well be a scale between MA [modal adverbs] and EA [evaluative adverbs], rather than totally separated classes, with adverbs like *naturally* and *predictably* being somewhere in the middle" (1988: 49).[3]

Swan (1988) essentially follows Bellert (1977: 342–434) in assuming that evaluative adverbs are predicates over facts (factive predicates), i.e. true propositions, whereas modal adverbs are predicates over "the truth of the proposition […] not the fact, event, or state of affairs denoted by the sentence in question" (Bellert 1977: 343). By analyzing *naturally* as an evaluative adverb, Swan (1988: 45–53) indirectly classifies *naturally* as a factive predicate. However, as argued by Bellert (1977: 345), factive predicates are semantically incompatible with *if … then*-clauses, which express hypothetical or counterfactual propositions, as the speaker would simultaneously assert and non-assert the truth of the proposition. Thus, evaluative adverbs are barred from occurring within the scope of *if … then*-clauses, as shown in (8a) and (9a). Conversely, as the contrasts in acceptability between (8a, b) and (9a, b) show, both evidential adverbs and epistemic adverbs

---

[3] Note that Swan does not distinguish between evidential and epistemic adverbs, but subsumes them under modal adverbs (see also Ernst 2009).

are compatible with hypothetical or counterfactual propositions (examples adapted from Bellert 1977: 345):

(8) *If John had not been sick,*
   a. *he would *fortunately/*surprisingly/*luckily have done it.*
   b. *he would probably/certainly/evidently have done it.*
(9) *If John were sane,*
   a. *he would *fortunately/*surprisingly/*luckily accept the offer.*
   b. *he would probably/certainly/evidently accept the offer.*

Swan (1988: 49) conjectures that the ban on evaluative adverbs in hypothetical or counterfactual contexts may not be absolute and that *naturally* alongside *predictably* may be acceptable in the contexts under consideration; therefore, she favors the aforementioned scale between modal adverbs and evaluative adverbs, which would allow for *naturally* to be a not purely evaluative adverb.

Rather than assuming, as Swan (1988) does, that *naturally* is an evaluative adverb with a somewhat irregular (i.e. modal) distribution, we take the distribution of *naturally* to determine the interpretation of the adverb (Cinque 1999, 2004; Alexiadou 1997; Haumann 2007). The distribution of individual adverb classes is also vital with respect to the delimitation of possible bridging contexts. Given that *naturally*, in fact, is compatible with counterfactual propositions (10), the sentence adverb *naturally* should be classified as an evidential and not as an evaluative adverb:

(10) a. *If Lord George had concocted this little scheme, he would **naturally** be ignorant of the true event of the robbery* [...] (ECF2, 1873)
    b. *If he was acquainted with Smith's work he would **naturally** have assumed that the French Academy knew it too, and that the point of the competition was to fill in the details of Smith's proof.* (BNC, B7N)

This view seems to be congruent with the analysis of this adverb offered by Chafe (1986) and Simon-Vandenbergen and Aijmer (2007: ch. 8). They place sentence adverb *naturally* among their subset of "expectation adverbs", which belongs within the larger class of "certainty adverbs". While certainty adverbs "express the speaker's judgement regarding the truth of the proposition" (Simon-Vandenbergen and Aijmer 2007: 27), the class of expectation adverbs:

> [...] express[es] certainty together with 'according to/in conformity with expectations'. It includes: *of course, naturally, inevitably, necessarily*. What they share is the expression of commitment to the truth of the proposition, based on the fact that the state of affairs referred

to in that proposition is to be expected, follows from other states of affairs or from what we know about the world. (Simon-Vandenbergen and Aijmer 2007: 172)

Simon-Vandenbergen and Aijmer's certainty adverbs belong within their larger category of epistemic adverbs (Simon-Vandenbergen and Aijmer 2007: 298). Within Swan's system, this would presumably place them in the group of modal adverbs.

According to Chafe (1986: chapter 3.2), adverbs like *naturally, of course, inevitably* and *necessarily* are evidential in nature as they express that the content of the statement is to be expected on the basis of what is supposed to be known. Chafe's analysis of sentence adverb *naturally* is very close to Simon-Vandenbergen and Aijmer's (2007) analysis of expectation adverbs in general and sentence adverb *naturally* in particular.

We agree with Chafe (1986) and Simon-Vandenbergen and Aijmer (2007) about the basic meaning and function of sentence adverb *naturally*. We therefore categorize the adverb as an evidential adverb (using the well-established term rather than the more recent one introduced by Simon-Vandenbergen and Aijmer 2007). Evidential elements are concerned with sources of information, which Aikhenvald (2004: 63–64) presents as follows:

I. VISUAL: covers information acquired through seeing.
II. NON-VISUAL SENSORY: covers information acquired through hearing, and is typically extended to smell and taste, and sometimes also to touch.
III. INFERENCE: based on visible or tangible evidence, or result.
IV. ASSUMPTION: based on evidence other than visible results: this may include logical reasoning, assumption, or simply general knowledge.
V. HEARSAY: for reported information with no reference to those it was reported by.
VI. QUOTATIVE: for reported information with an overt reference to the quoted source.

Naturally combines the properties of inferred and assumed evidentials, as the information at hand is either inferred from visible or tangible results, or is based on general knowledge or reasoning.

Thus, what is categorized as natural is not a fact, as with evaluative adverbs, but an inference or a conclusion. In other words, *naturally* does not mean 'it is natural that', but 'it is natural to conclude that', or, in the words of Simon-Vandenbergen and Aijmer (2007: 236), "it follows from the nature of things that this should be so". The evidence which lies at the base of inferences and assumptions may be of various types, such as direct physical evidence, general knowledge, or the speaker's experience with similar situations (see Aikhenvald 2004). In section 3.3 we argue that the concept of 'general knowledge' is important in the reanalysis of *naturally* into a SA.

2.3 Hypotheses about the development of sentence adverbs (in general) and of *naturally* in particular

As is well known, English has a large number of *-ly* adverbs which have both narrow-scope uses (adjuncts, word modifiers) and wide-scope uses (sentence adverbs). Swan (1988: 524–539) claims that the latter have developed out of the former through a mechanism referred to as "SA shifts":

> [...] the mechanism of SA shifts can be seen as including the presence of word-modifiers (such as intensifiers or manner adverbs) and a speaker comment concept (historically often in the form of an adjectival phrase like *It is Adj that* ...). These blend in the adverbial form which become [sic] SA (or rather, the adverb usually becomes polysemous and functions both as SA and non-SA). (Swan 1988: 531–532)

The key process in the development of sentence adverbs must have been reanalysis: adverbs which were intended as modifying a head or a phrase were taken to modify the whole clause or proposition. Nevalainen's (1994: 243) concept of "functional-semantic shifts" of *-ly* adverbs seems to be congruent with a reanalysis scenario, and so does Ramat and Ricca's (1994: 310) proposal that sentence adverbs in *-ly* can be understood as "extensions which keep the Manner semantics relatively stable and extend the modifier function to syntactic units other than the Verb Phrase" (see Killie 2015 for an overview and discussion).

Given the subjective nature of SA, it is uncontroversial that the category has developed through the process(es) of "subjectification" (see e.g. Traugott 1989; Swan 1997; Fischer 2007; Swan and Breivik 2011). Subjectification has been defined as the process "whereby meanings become increasingly based in the speaker's subjective belief state/attitude toward the proposition, in other words, towards what the speaker is talking about" (Traugott 1995: 31, see also Traugott 1982, 1989, 1990). It involves the development of propositional elements (in our case adjuncts and/or modifiers) into expressive ones, i.e. the relevant elements come to have a function at the interpersonal or discourse level (see section 2.1).

Naturally is given separate treatment in Swan (1988). She argues that this adverb has gone through an "abstraction evolution": "from the adverb meaning, essentially, 'by nature', it eventually comes to mean 'of course' or 'understandably'" (Swan 1988: 402). Swan illustrates the development of *naturally* through six examples (her examples 4.102–4.107), which are given in (11)–(16) below:

(11) (4.102) *But should it be proved that woman is **naturally** weaker than man* (V127 = Wollstonecraft, *Vindications of the Rights of Woman*)

(12) (4.103) *that strange effects, are **naturally** taken for miracles by weaker heads* (PE150 = Robbins, R., *Sir Thomas Browne's Pseudoxia Epidemice or Enquiries into Very Many Received Tenets and Commonly Presum Truths*)

(13) (4.104) *The grief which we **naturally** feel at the death of* [...] (SJ61 = Taylor, J., *Samuel Johnson: Sermons on Different Subjects Left for Publication by John Taylor*)

(14) (4.105) *Thus, a man who intends keeping pointers **naturally** tries to get as good dogs as he can* (D34 = Darwin, *On the Origin of Species*)

(15) (4.106) *Gerard Douw began to fear, **naturally** enough, that the poor girl* [...] (F97 = Le Fanu, J. S., *The Watcher*)

(16) (4.107) *All these combined, not **unnaturally** induced me to* [...] (F132 = Le Fanu, *The Watcher*)

Swan links the examples above to the proposed abstraction evolution, or "abstraction process", in the following manner:

> In 4.102 (18th century) the post-verbal adverb clearly means 'by nature' (i.e. a non-SA) [...] However, in the 17th century 4.103 *naturally* is ambiguous between SA and non-SA readings. 4.103–4.104 and 4.105 may represent steps in the abstraction process of the adverb; in 4.103 and 4.104 *naturally* is ambiguous, while in 4.105 it is clear that the adverb may only refer to the state of affair being understandable, not that there is something inherent in a man which inclines him in a certain way. In 4.106, too, *naturally* is a true SA; here it is postposed, and set off with commas for the sake of (parenthetical) emphasis. Finally, 4.107 shows a negated adverb with SA function ('it was not unexpected that ...'). (Swan 1988: 404)

While Swan's examples of, and comments on, the evolution of *naturally* are interesting, her study goes back to the time before digital corpora, when every corpus example had to be extracted manually. Her material is limited to 26 tokens and is not comprehensive enough to serve as a basis for a close study of the bridging contexts of *naturally*. Our study aims to shed more light on the development of this adverb by providing a large number of tokens.

According to Swan (1988: 525–533), some sentence adverbs have developed out of adverbs modifying a VP, others out of adverbs modifying an XP, i.e. AP, PP or DP. A third group has both VP-modifying and XP-modifying uses and hence may have a dual origin. As shown in (17) and (18), *naturally* belongs to this latter group:

(17) *I want my husband to behave **naturally**.*
(18) *When it comes to physical strength, women are **naturally** weak.*

While *naturally* in (17) has the meaning 'in a natural manner', *naturally* in (18) means 'by nature'. Simon-Vandenbergen and Aijmer (2007: 185) hypothesize that sentence adverb *naturally* is most likely to have developed out of narrow-scope uses where the meaning is 'by nature'. Their rationale is that "[i]f something is said to be the case 'by nature' then by subjectification the speaker can present it as 'to be expected'" (Simon-Vandenbergen and Aijmer 2007: 185). According to Simon-Vandenbergen and Aijmer (2007: 185), "[t]here are instances in the corpus which show that the two meanings are actually very close". They give the following two examples from ICE-GB (their examples 140 and 141):

(19) *With his interest in unusual sounds and instruments he **naturally** followed developments in music technology* (ICE-GB:S2B-023/16)

(20) *The first question that **naturally** rises out of this confusion is what was actually meant by the classical terminology of Pict and why it had had such staying power.* (ICE-GB:W1A-009/97)

In their discussion of the example in (19), Simon-Vandenbergen and Aijmer (2007) argue that "[t]he reference to his specific interest presents the fact that he followed developments in music technology as resulting 'by nature' from that interest. At the same time the speaker sees this fact as 'expected' on the basis of his interest". They argue that a similar interpretation can occur with the sentence in (20). Although we agree with Simon-Vandenbergen and Aijmer (2007) that the 'by nature' meaning represents a promising source meaning for the development of *naturally* as SA, we do not agree that *naturally* in (19) and (20) may have this meaning. A 'by nature' interpretation seems to be blocked here, presumably because the predicates of these sentences – *naturally follow* and *naturally rise* – describe temporal stages of their subjects, i.e. are "stage-level predicates" (see Carlson 1977). The 'by nature' meaning appears to be linked to "individual-level predicates", i.e. predicates which are true throughout the existence of an individual (Carlson 1977). Such predicates presumably often involve copular *be*, as in *She was naturally beautiful/clever*. Copular *be* sentences therefore represent the focus of this study.

2.4 The concept of bridging context

As we have seen, the reanalysis of *naturally* into a sentence adverb has been termed variously as "SA shifts" and "abstraction evolution/process" (Swan 1988), "functional-semantic shifts" (Nevalainen 1994), "extensions" (Ramat and Ricca

1994), and "subjectification" (Swan 1997; Simon-Vandenbergen and Aijmer 2007). Some of these terms focus on the syntactic and others on the semantico-pragmatic aspects of the process. However, regardless of what we choose to call the process, there is one aspect that needs to be addressed: the fact that the relevant change must have taken place in specific contexts, so-called bridging contexts.

As mentioned in section 1, a bridging context is a context in which both the older and the newer meanings of a linguistic item represent possible interpretations. According to Heine (2002: 84–85), bridging contexts have the following properties:

a. They trigger an inferential mechanism to the effect that, rather than the source meaning, there is another meaning, the target meaning, that offers a more plausible interpretation of the utterance concerned.
b. While the target meaning is the most likely to be inferred, it is still cancellable (see Grice 1967), that is, an interpretation of the source meaning cannot be ruled out.
c. A given linguistic form may be associated with a number of different bridging contexts.
d. Bridging contexts may, but need not, give rise to conventional grammatical meanings.

As pointed out in (a.), the new meaning arises due to context-induced inferences (also referred to as "conversational" or "pragmatic" inferences, see Traugott 2012). As mentioned in section 2.2, it will be argued that the concept of "general knowledge" is crucial for the inferencing processes that gave rise to the sentence adverb meaning of *naturally*. The exact role of the relevant inferences is explained in section 3.3.

Point (b.) is crucial. As pointed out by Kuteva (2001), bridging contexts are characterized by a mismatch between speaker intention and hearer interpretation. Ambiguity is the very essence of bridging contexts and is what allows grammatical change to take place.

With respect to point (c.), there may well be a number of possible bridging contexts for *naturally*, but as mentioned in sections 1 and 2.3 and further explained in section 2.5, we will argue that a reanalysis of *naturally* is most likely to occur when it is positioned between a finite form of copular *be* and the predicative complement, e.g. AP or DP, with no other elements intervening between the two. This, then, is the context in which the kind of contextual inferences referred to above most frequently arise.

As pointed out in (d.), the relevant conversational inferences may become "conventionalized" or "semanticized", i.e. they may become a part of the semantic meaning of the linguistic form (Hopper and Traugott 2003: 71; Heine 2002: 85;

Traugott 2010, 2012). Kuteva (2001: 150) refers to this process as "context-absorption". Well-known examples are *since* and *be going to*, where the causal meaning of the former and the temporal-modal meaning of the latter developed when specific conversational inferences became semanticized (see e.g. Traugott 2012). As we will see in section 3.3, something similar has happened to *naturally*.

There is, of course, no easy explanation as to why some inferences become semanticized and others not. It is, however, generally agreed that a certain level of frequency is required (Heine 2002: 84, Traugott 2012: 2). In the words of Evans and Wilkins (2000: 550), the new meaning "often comes into existence because a regularly occurring context supports an inference-driven contextual enrichment of A to B [...] this contextual sense may become lexicalized [i.e. semanticized, DH/KK] to the point where it need no longer be supported by a given context". As shown in section 2.6, the syntactic context under scrutiny here ($V_{be\_}XP$) occurs at a certain level of frequency, which opens up for the possibility that the inferences required to arrive at a sentence adverb reading of *naturally* may have arisen with some level of frequency as well.

2.5 Some assumptions concerning clause structure and adverb placement

For the purpose of our analysis, we take the copula to occupy the lowest verbal head position, V, within the lexical layer of the clause, as depicted in figure 7.1 below. The lexical layer of the clause, vP, is located below the base position of modal verbs or the infinitive marker (T) and the perfect auxiliary *have* Aux,[4] with the projection of sentential negation, NegP, intervening between the two.

The copula shares with non-lexical verbs the property of raising to T in finite clauses, as can be seen in sentences where *be* precedes negation (21a), cliticizes onto a pronominal subject (21b), and occurs in the head position of Foc(us)P in the complementizer layer of the clause, as can be seen in subject inversion structures such as interrogatives (22):

(21) a. *I see that your Lordship is naturally **not** very much inclined to quit your present occupation* (ECF2, 1826)
 b. *I am sure I am glad to hear it because as Arthur's mother **it**'s naturally pleasant to my feelings to have a better opinion of her* (ECF2, 1857)

---

4 As the copula is a stative verb, it does not normally combine with the progressive auxiliary.

(22) a. *Her mamma had never seemed to get much enjoyment out of life, and if Gwendolen had been at this moment disposed to feel pity she would have bestowed it on herself – for* was **she** *not naturally and rightfully the chief object of her mamma's anxiety too?* (ECF2, 1876)
b. *"And the night that Clarke left you, were* **you** *aware of his absence?"* (ECF2, 1832)

The paradigm of copula *be* contains a perfective participle, *been*, and the absolute, i.e. non-progressive, participle *being*. These two verbal elements raise to higher verbal head positions to have their features checked: the perfective participle *been* raises to the head position of PerfP, and the absolute participle *being* to the head position of Abs(olute)P. The infinitive form, *be* raises from V to v.

The topmost projections in figure 7.1 below, FinP, FocP and ForceP, constitute the left periphery of the clause and interface between "propositional content" and the "articulation of discourse" (see Rizzi 1997: 283).[5] FinP encodes the finiteness properties of the clause, FocP hosts quantificational operators and is targeted in inversion structures and ForceP encodes the illocutionary force of the sentence which, as we shall see, is not only vital for the interpretation of sentences (see Rizzi 1997, 2004: 3), but also for the licensing of speaker-oriented adverbs, such as evidential *naturally* (see section 3.1, see also Travis 1988: 290, 299).

Adapting an essentially Cinquean (1999) analysis, we take adverbs that are modifiers in verbal projections, i.e. traditional VP-adverbs and sentence adverbs, to be specifiers of designated functional projections in clause structure, all of which have their "specific semantic interpretation" (see Cinque 1999: 132). With respect to the distributional subset of *naturally* in copular *be* sentences, we assume that only two functional projections are involved (see figure 7.2 below): EvidP for evidential *naturally* and ByNatureP for individual level *naturally*, with EvidP being located above NegP and ByNatureP being located within the lexical layer of the clause, i.e. vP.[6]

---

[5] In addition to FinP, FocP and ForceP in figure 7.1, the Rizzian (1997, 2004, 3) left periphery contains positions for topicalized and otherwise fronted constituents.
[6] Note that figure 7.2, for reasons of space, builds on a slightly truncated version of figure 7.1 above, with the focus being on the relative positions of EvidP licensing evidential *naturally* and ByNatureP licensing for individual level *naturally*.

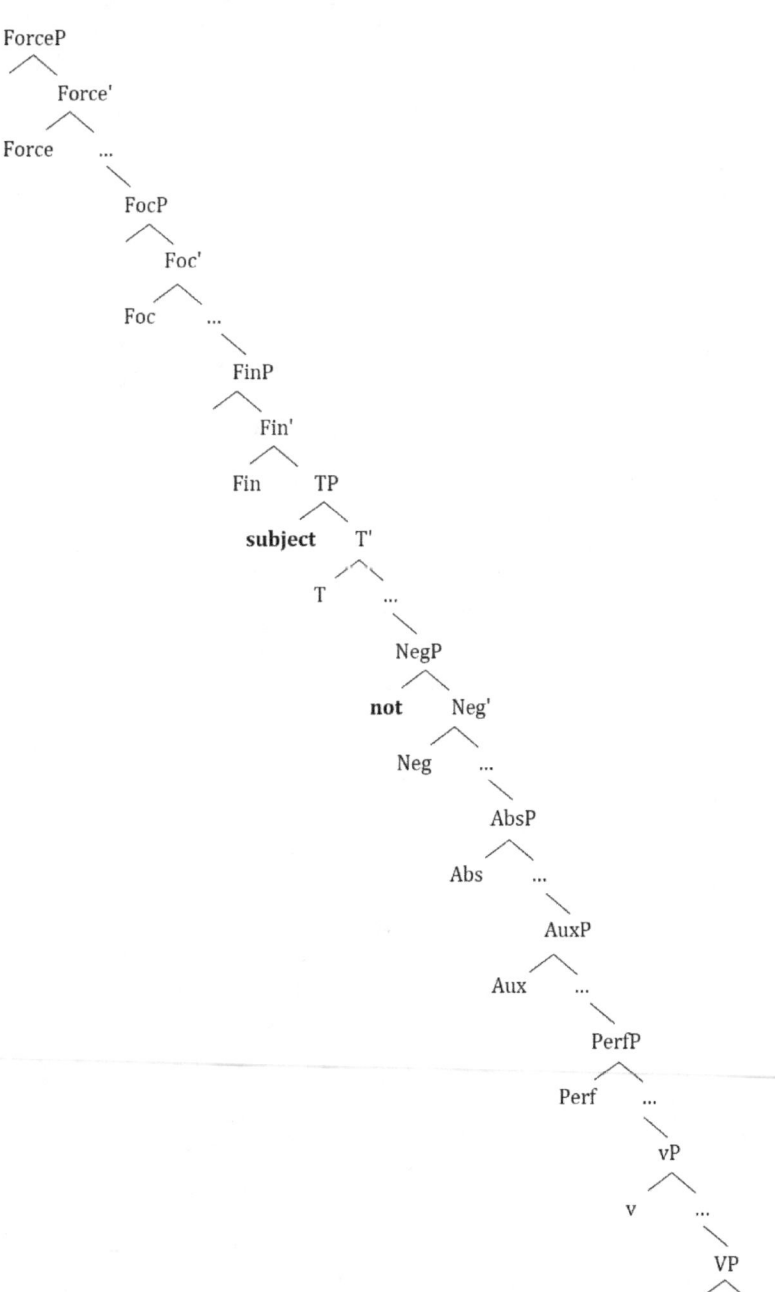

Fig. 7.1: The structure of the clause

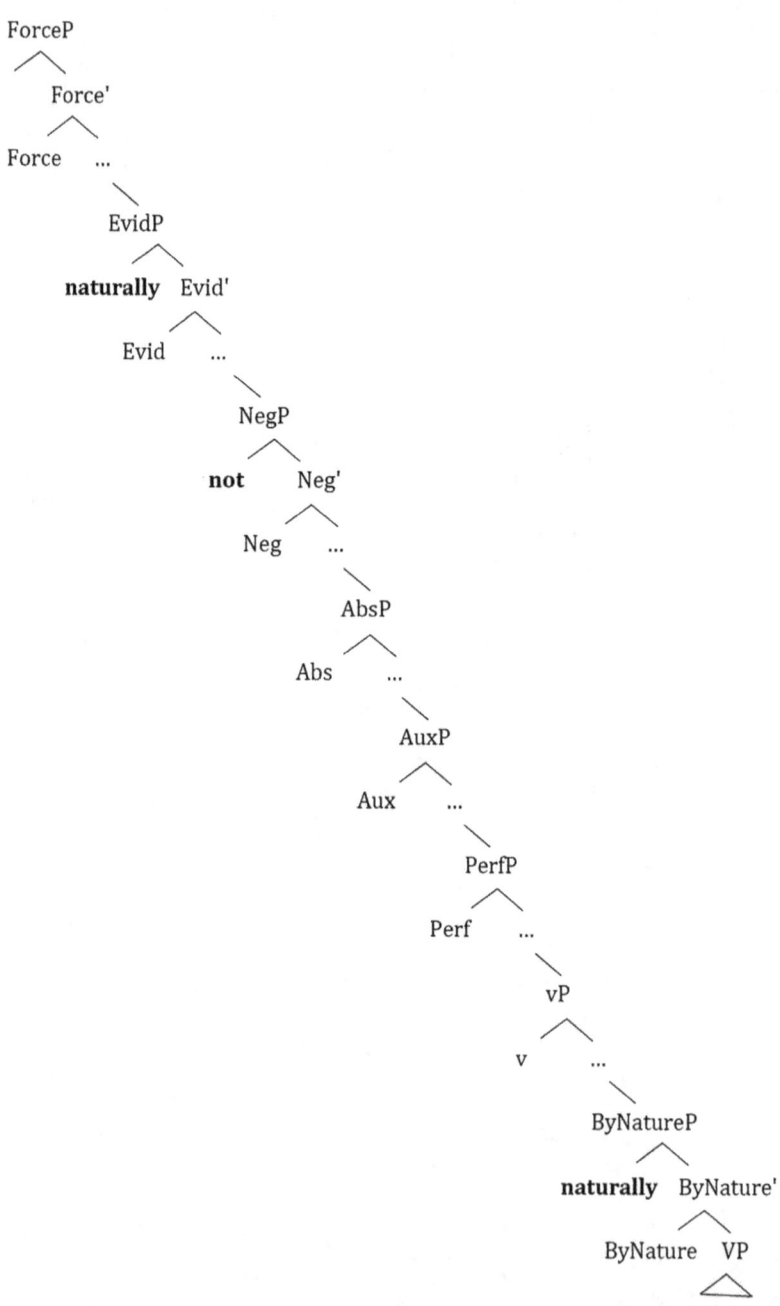

Fig. 7.2: The positions of EvidP and ByNatureP

2.6 Data and method

As bridging contexts must presumably occur with a certain frequency to have a lasting impact on the grammar, any empirically valid study of these contexts must be based on a large diachronic dataset. Our study is based on data from the *Early English Prose Fiction* corpus (EEPF), the *Eighteenth-Century Fiction* corpus (ECF) and the *Nineteenth-Century Fiction* corpus (NCF).

Tab. 7.1: The distribution of *naturally* in copular *be* sentences

distribution		corpus examples	tokens
_S	pre-subject	*Naturally, children are a nuisance; especially so if you live in a whirlpool.* (ECF2, 1897)	26
S_M	between subject and modal	*The offer of this sporting wager, which naturally would have been very gratifying to Mary, was lost upon her* (ECF2, 1858)0	2
S_V$_{be}$	between subject and *be*	*The Nonconformist himself naturally was less sober in his thoughts.* (ECF2, 1863)	32
M_AUX	between modal and auxiliary	*This would naturally have been flattering to Johnny had it not been that he was in truth absorbed by the story which he had heard.* (ECF2, 1867)	4
M_V$_{be}$	between modal and *be*	*Shop-girls, minor actresses, the inferior sort of governess, must naturally be on their guard; their insecurity was traditional;* (ECF2, 1897)	33
AUX_V$_{be}$	between auxiliary and *be*	*indeed, had she not naturally been of an opposite disposition, the displeasing manner in which her aunt's ill-temper was* (NCF1, 1800)	6
V$_{be}$_XP	between *be* and predicate	*They are naturally dull of wit, and slow of apprehension, and yet notwithstanding most perfect in all the art* (EEPF, 1613)	782
V_M	between raising verb and *to*-infinitive	*longer than it had rested on Lizzie, "both because your brother ought naturally to be the originator of any such scheme, and because I hoped to be ab* (ECF2, 1865)	1
V$_{be}$+XP_	following *be* and the predicate	*But then of course you and I are different, naturally.* (ECF2, 1882)	10
Total			**896**

These three corpora comprise roughly 57 million words of texts from the mid-fifteenth to the late nineteenth century. With a time window set to 1550–1899, these corpora were searched for *naturally* (incl. the spelling variants listed in the *Oxford English Dictionary* [OED]). From our overall corpus with 3,534 relevant occurrences of the adverb, we extracted all and only strings with *naturally* occurring in copular *be* sentences, 896 strings in total, which corresponds to 25.4% of the entire corpus. In a first step, all these occurrences were manually analyzed into the distributional classes in table 7.1 above.

In a second step, the strings were annotated for both (morpho)syntactic and semantic properties (see below) with the aim to determine the status of *naturally* as sentence adverb or narrow scope adverb. The diachronic trajectories of the sentence adverb *naturally* and its narrow scope counterpart are presented in figure 7.3:[7]

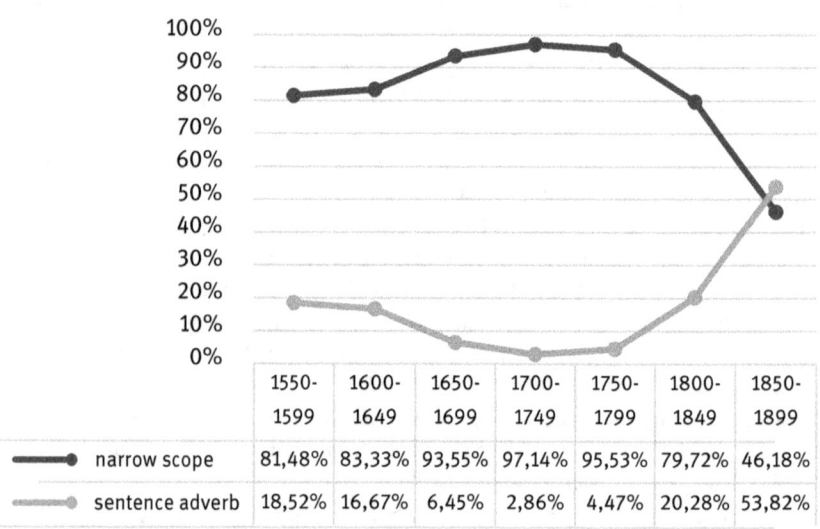

Fig. 7.3: The diachronic trajectory of *naturally* as sentence adverb and narrow scope adverb in copular *be* sentences (n = 896)

As figure 7.3 shows, the use of *naturally* as a sentence adverb did not become common until the first half of the nineteenth century, but when it started to

---

7 Of course, given that some uses may be interpreted as either narrow or wide-scope uses, the figures here are not necessarily exact. They represent a "conservative" estimate in the sense that uses which may be interpreted as narrow-scope readings have been categorized as such (since this is the original use of the adverb), while *sentence adverb* means "unambiguous uses of SA".

happen, the process was so massive that by 1850 the sentence adverb use was more common than the narrow-scope uses.[8] However, the bridging contexts, which are the focus of this paper, will have started to occur long before this.

Table 7.2 gives an overview of *naturally* as sentence adverb and narrow scope adverb across distributional classes, in copular *be* sentences:

Tab. 7.2: *Naturally* as sentence adverb and narrow scope adverb across distributional classes (n = 896)

distribution		sentence adverb	narrow scope
_S	pre-subject	23	3
S_M	between subject and modal	2	---
S_V$_{be}$	between subject and *be*	20	12
M_AUX	between modal and auxiliary	2	2
M_V$_{be}$	between modal and *be*	33	---
AUX_V$_{be}$	between auxiliary and *be*	6	---
V$_{be}$_XP	between *be* and predicate	128	654
V_M	between raising verb and *to*-infinitive	1	---
V$_{be}$+AP_	following *be* and the adjectival predicate	7	3

As argued in section 2.4, we have reason to believe that the distributional class V$_{be}$_XP is of particular interest in the reanalysis of narrow-scope *naturally* as a SA. In what follows, we therefore take a closer look at this class.

3 Preconditions for and impediments to reanalysis

This section zooms in on the factors that promote or block the reanalysis of narrow scope *naturally* in ByNatureP as evidential *naturally* in EvidP in copular *be* sentences, where *naturally* occurs between the copular and the predicative XP.

---

[8] According to Swan (2014), also sentence adverb *hopefully* shows a marked increase in frequency after 1850.

3.1 Illocutionary force

As we have seen in section 2, evidential adverbs express the (type of) evidence the speaker has for her assertion. Assertion is one of the instantiations of the illocutionary force of the sentence, and it is tied to declarative matrix clauses. The illocutionary force of the sentence is represented in ForceP (section 2.5). Since the presence of ForceP is contingent on the presence of a finite verb, evidential adverbs, by transitivity, are restricted to occurring in finite clauses (23). Thus, *naturally* in non-finite clauses (24) can only instantiate ByNatureP, which takes narrow scope over VP:

(23) a. *The poor Curate was **naturally** very much dismayed at the contemplated departure of his pupil.* (ECF2, 1849)

b. *Blank dismay was **naturally** my first sensation on making the discovery;* (ECF2, 1870)

c. *Peggotty was **naturally** in low spirits at leaving what had been her home so many years,* (ECF2, 1850)

(24) a. *His complexion seems [to have been **naturally** too fine for a man].* (ECF1, 1754)

b. *However, [being **naturally** a bold lively-spirited man], he entered into the humour of the thing, and sate down to the feast,* (NCF1, 1830)

c. *He seemed [to be **naturally** of an inquisitive disposition];* (ECF2, 1773)

Note that although illocutionary force is typically associated with matrix clauses which, by definition, are finite, as in (23), it is not restricted to them. As has been argued by Hooper and Thompson (1973), certain types of subordinate clauses (but not others) display matrix properties. Essentially, sentences that constitute assertions (e.g. complement clauses to non-factive predicates, concessive adverbial clauses and non-restrictive relative clauses) license matrix properties, whereas clauses that are presupposed, such as (e.g. complement clauses to factive predicates, temporal clauses, restrictive relative clauses) do not license main clause properties. Subordinate clauses, as has been argued by Haegeman (2012: 149–194, 257–286), building on Hooper and Thompson,[9] fall into two types: those that are subordinate in the traditional sense, and those that display matrix or root properties, such as having an independent illocutionary force. The two types of subordinate clauses differ structurally with respect to the presence vs. absence of

---

9 See also Haegeman (2002, 2006, 2010).

left peripheral functional projections, among others ForceP, which is crucial for the licensing of evidential adverbs; (25) is adapted from Haegeman 2002: 159, where Sub stands for 'subordinate clause'):

(25) a. Sub   Force   ...   Foc   ...   Fin (full left periphery)
    b. Sub   Fin (reduced left periphery)

Given that the licensing of evidential adverbs is contingent on the presence of an assertive ForceP, the presence of an assertive ForceP should also be a precondition for the reanalysis of narrow scope *naturally* as an evidential adverb. That is, narrow scope *naturally* should be amenable to reanalysis in all and only assertive ForcePs, unless reanalysis is blocked by independent factors, as discussed in section 3.2.

3.1.1 Complement clauses

As mentioned above, Haegeman (2012: 189, 257–259) argues that only a subset of finite complement clauses (*that*-clauses) is assertive and thus displays matrix properties. A case in point is clausal complements to non-factive verbs, such as *assume* and *see* (26). These have an assertive ForceP and, potentially, license evidential adverbs, i.e. they allow for the interpretation of *naturally* as an evidential adverb:[10]

(26) a. *The world **assumes** that being the favoured of Heaven you are **naturally** and necessarily a member of the Church.* (ECF2, 1870)

       b. *"[...] you will, therefore, **see** that I am **naturally** reluctant to tell you any thing about him, unless your honour will inform me of the why and the wherefore".* (ECF2, 1828)

Conversely, clausal complements to factive verbs, such as *be aware* and *observe* (27) presuppose "that the embedded clause expresses a true proposition" (Kiparsky and Kiparsky 1971: 348). They do not constitute assertions and thus

---

10 As has been pointed out by Kevin McCafferty (p.c.), the coordinate structure [naturally and necessarily] helps rule out the narrow scope reading of *naturally*. See Haumann (2007: 374–376) for (reversed orders of) speaker-oriented adverbs in coordinate structures.

cannot license evidential adverbs; hence the reanalysis of narrow scope *naturally* is precluded. The same goes for complement clauses to nouns (28):[11]

(27) a. *Philosophie to proue a generall Axiome by a particuler instaunce, whereas you **auerre** that wemen are **naturally** couetous, and know not the cause, your affection semeth to proceede rather of rancor then* (EEPF, 1584)

b. *it was easy to **observe**, (if it had not been his general character) that his temper is **naturally** haughty and violent; and I had seen enough of that untractable spirit in my brother,* (ECF1 1748)

(28) a. *[...] and Chowley, who had the **claim** upon him that he was **naturally** of a maritime build,* (ECF2, 1848)

b. *But the Barons added a Prouiso, that when they hadde wonne their wager, the Knight by no meanes should hurt his wife, and from that time forth shold giue ouer his false **opinion**, that women were not **naturally** giuen to the sutes and requests of amorous persones.* (EEPF, 1567)

3.1.2 Adverbial clauses

According to Haegeman (2012), adverbial clauses are of two kinds: central adverbial clauses and peripheral adverbial clauses. The former modify the event expressed by the matrix clause, whereas the latter relate to or structure the discourse context. Central adverbial clauses and peripheral adverbial clauses differ in both their external and internal structure. While central adverbial clauses are integrated into structure inside TP and are thus within the scope of sentential operators in the matrix, peripheral adverbial clauses occupy higher positions and thus escape the scope of operators in the matrix (see Haegeman 2012: 166–171 and elsewhere). As regards their internal structure, central adverbial clauses have a reduced left periphery, whereas peripheral adverbial clauses have a full left periphery and thus, among other properties, independent illocutionary force (see section 3.1).

Concessive clauses (29), rationale clauses (30) and result clauses (31) establish a relation between two propositions. They are peripheral clauses and as such

---

11 Note that the nominal expression containing the complement clause in (28a) is contained within a non-restrictive relative clause.

they have a full left periphery and can license evidential adverbs and thus provide a context for reanalysis:

(29) *My dear Mrs Pigeon,* **though** *a mother is* **naturally** *anxious for her son, nothing on earth would induce me to advise him to break such a tie as that!* (ECF2, 1863)

(30) *Glegg paused,* **for** *speaking with much energy for the good of others is* **naturally** *exhausting.* (ECF2, 1860)

(31) *Indeed her Penitence* **so** *nearly resembled that of Calista,* that *her Mind was* **naturally** *filled with the same kind of Meditations;* (ECF2, 1759)

Temporal adverbial clauses (32), event related reason clauses (33), conditional clauses expressing the condition for an event (34) are central adverbial clauses and have only a reduced left periphery. Crucially, since they do not have assertive illocutionary force, they cannot license evidential *naturally* and thus do not provide a context for reanalysis:[12,13]

(32) *The lawyer had thought to postpone further consideration of the whole matter* **till** *he and everybody else would be* **naturally** *in London ---, till November that might be, or, perhaps, even till after Christmas.* (ECF2, 1873)

(33) *Glumdalclitch was prevailed on to be of the Company, very much against her Inclination,* **for** *she was* **naturally** *tender-hearted:* (ECF1, 1726)

(34) *'I do not believe in a woman marrying a bad man in the hope of making him good.' 'Especially not* **when** *the woman is* **naturally** *inclined to evil herself. It will half kill him when he reads all this about me* (ECF2, 1876)

3.1.3 Relative clauses

According to Haegeman (2002), only non-restrictive relative clauses have a full left periphery and thus may display matrix properties. Restrictive relative clauses and free relative clauses have a reduced left periphery, which precludes matrix

---

12 Note that in (32), *naturally* is within the scope of non-finite *be*, which, as we shall see in section 3.2.1 is an independent factor impeding the reanalysis of narrow scope *naturally*.
13 Note that the event conditional in (34) is within the scope of negation. Also note that the collocation *naturally inclined* works against the sentence adverb reading (see section 3.2.3).

properties (see section 3.1). In other words, non-restrictive relative clauses (35) are similar to non-factive complement clauses and peripheral adverbial clauses in that their left periphery contains an assertive ForceP, which is vital for the licensing of evidential adverbs:

(35) a. *You must consider also that reputed relies, such as you have mentioned, are generally in the custody of religious bodies, who are **naturally** very jealous of attempts to prove them spurious* (ECF2, 1848)

b. *[...] she still continued to run away from me, not only with the speed of the current, but by the whole amount of her leeway, which was **naturally** great.* (ECF2, 1883)

The lack of an assertive ForceP in restrictive relative clauses prevents the licensing of evidential *naturally*. Thus, the occurrences of *naturally* in (36) must be instantiations of ByNatureP:

(36) a. *Loue maketh a man which is **naturally** adicted vnto vice to be indewed with vertue, to applie himself vnto all lawdable exercises* (EEPF, 1584)

b. *[...] that her brother should have found himself unable to discuss a subject that was **naturally** so very distasteful to him, and begged Mr. Gowran to come to her again the next morning.* (ECF2, 1873)

3.2 Factors impeding a reanalysis

So far, this section has focused on the presence of ForceP as the ultimate precondition for reanalysis. There are, however, a number of factors that undermine illocutionary force, i.e. factors that impede the reanalysis of narrow scope *naturally* even in contexts that would structurally sanction reanalysis (in both matrix and subordinate clauses).

3.2.1 Within the scope of non-finite *be*

Occurrences of *naturally* following non-finite *be*, as in (37) and (38), are not amenable to reanalysis. The clauses under consideration are finite matrix clauses (37) and finite subordinate clauses that have a full left periphery, such as non-factive complement clauses (38a) and concessives (38b), and therefore, in principle, should provide a context for reanalysis. Yet, *naturally* can only be interpreted as instantiating ByNatureP:

(37) a. *For all our days we have* **been naturally** *[PP of a most sedate turn of mind];* (NCF1, 1823)

b. *A modest woman must* **be naturally** *cold, reserved, and shy.* (ECF1, 1748)

(38) a. *I am inclined to* **think** *that her own disposition must be* **naturally** *bad, or she could not be guilty of such an enormity, at so early an age.* (NCF1, 1813)

b. *I must bear false witness, you see, out of self-defence,* **though** *I may be* **naturally** *a most reliable, truth-telling man.* (NCF2, 1862)

Recall from section 2.5 that ByNatureP is a functional projection in the lexical layer of the clause, vP. The perfective participle, *been*, as well as the infinitive *be* undergo raising to higher head positions. *Been* raises to the head of PerfP and *be* to the head of vP, which gives us the surface linear orders with non-finite *be* preceding *naturally*, as illustrated in (39a, b) for (37a) and (38a), respectively:[14]

(39) a. ... [PerfP **been** [vP ... [ByNatureP [*naturally*] [vP [t$_i$] [DP a rather shrewd girl]] ...]]] ...

b. ...   [vP **be** [ByNatureP [*naturally*] [vP [t$_i$] [AP bad]] ...]]] ...

The relative linear orders of non-finite *be* and *naturally* are indicative of *naturally* instantiating ByNatureP, which is clearly contained within the lexical layer of the clause and thus not amenable to reanalysis.

3.2.2 Cooccurrence with other sentence adverbs and the like

We have seen in section 2.1 above that sentence adverbs of different classes may cooccur. There are, however, restrictions on their cooccurrence (see Jackendoff 1972: 87–93): they cannot be adjacent, each class is restricted to one occurrence (unless adverbs are coordinated) and they must respect the relative linear order

---

14 As argued in section 2.5, the form *being* in the paradigm of the copula is the non-progressive, absolute participle which is restricted to occurring in non-finite clauses that do not have illocutionary force and thus cannot promote reanalysis (see section 3.1).

in (40), which reflects their respective scope properties (see among others Cinque 1999: 33, 135; Haumann 2007: 370–376):

(40) illocutionary > evaluative > evidential > subject-oriented > epistemic

In (41), *naturally* is outscoped by the epistemic adverb *indeed*. Since epistemic adverbs operate on unspecified truth values "expressed in terms of possibility or necessity" (Ernst 2001: 73), and since evidential adverbs are predicates of the truth value of the sentence, the latter cannot be in the scope of the former. Thus, *naturally* must represent the narrow scope variety, with the presence of *indeed* blocking the reanalysis of *naturally*:

(41) *Now that Part of his Head which Nature designed for the Reservoir of Drink, being very shallow, a small Quantity of Liquor overflowed it, and opened the Sluices of his Heart; so that all the Secrets there deposited run out. These Sluices were **indeed naturally** very ill secured.* (ECF2, 1749)

The set of adverb classes in (40) linearly precedes and takes scope over, among other elements, aspectual adverb(ial)s, such as *for the most part* (42), and sentential negation, as expressed by *not* or [$_{DP}$ *no country*] (43). Hence, an occurrence of *naturally* that follows aspectual adverbs and sentential negation must be an instantiation of ByNatureP:[15]

(42) *They are, **for the most part, naturally** cool, phlegmatic and crafty, and by a long habit of dissimulation, have gained an absolute dominion over the hasty passions of the heart;* (ECF2, 1751)

(43) a. *He is **not naturally** an ill-temper'd man; and in his person and air, and in his conversation too, when not under the torture of a gouty paroxysm, everybody distinguishes the gentleman born and educated.* (ECF1, 1748)

b. *Perhaps **no country** is **naturally** so well protected against our invader; nor has nature anywhere been so well assisted by the hand of man* (NCF1, 1826)

---

15 See Haegeman (1995: 106–107, 180–190; 2012: 39–42 and elsewhere) for a discussion of negative constituents inducing sentential negation.

3.2.3 Lexical and contextual constraints on reanalysis

Our corpus contains a number of cases in which a reanalysis should be possible structurally, but where it is blocked due to lexical or contextual constraints. For example, strong collocations, such as *naturally inclined* and *naturally disposed* in (44), may work against the reanalysis of *naturally* as an evidential adverb:

(44) a. *For (sayde he) beasts knowe their contraries, and flye them, but man is **naturally inclined** to searche and loue his enimie: the woman who for that she was created of a Ribbe* (EEPF, 1578)

b. *We are **naturally disposed** to love what gives us pleasure, and what more pleasing than a beautiful face--when we know no harm of the possessor at least?* (NCF2, 1867)

The coordinated matrix clause in (45), the adversative adverbial clause in (46) and the non-restrictive relative clause in (47) all allow for the reanalysis of *naturally* structurally, but the context dictates that *naturally* be interpreted as narrow-scope adverb, in ByNatureP. In (45), the narrow scope interpretation of both occurrences of *naturally* is triggered by the contrast reading of the two conjuncts. Similarly, in (46), the PP *by nature* in the matrix (a clear instantiation of ByNatureP) dictates the narrow scope reading of *naturally* in the subordinate clause. Finally, in (47), the narrow scope analysis of *naturally* is forced by the context, notably [$_{DP}$ his constitutional drowsiness]:

(45) *He is **naturally** light-hearted and hopeful; I am **naturally** the opposite.* (ECF2, 1891)

(46) *Some are, **by Nature**, industrious and ingenious, such as China and Holland, it is their Propensity, their Talent; while Others, like Ireland, are **naturally** lazy and listless, and therefore remain in well merited Indigence.* (ECF2, 1765)

(47) *The German, who was **naturally** of a phlegmatic habit, and never went to bed without a full dose of the creature, which added to his constitutional drowsiness* (ECF2, 1753)

3.3 Pragmatic and contextual factors promoting a reanalysis

The interpretation of *naturally* in a context which allows both narrow and wide-scoped readings must be supported by pragmatic and contextual factors. Thus, the narrow scope readings in (45)–(47) above result from inferential processes based on the linguistic context. The reanalysis of *naturally* as a sentence adverb also depends on inferential processes, but of a different kind. As with other evidentials that to a large extent are based on assumption, sentence adverb *naturally* typically implies that the information was not personally experienced but was inferred from indirect evidence, such as logical reasoning and general knowledge (see section 2.2). The concept of general knowledge has probably played an important role in the reanalysis of *naturally*, the reanalysis being frequently based on some sort of general knowledge or agreement about the topic under discussion. As explained above, there must also be a mismatch between speaker intention and hearer interpretation (see section 2.4), which arises because interlocutors possess a different set of experiences and world views (Kuteva 2001). In the case of *naturally*, we hypothesize that there must be an asymmetry between what the addressee knows and what the speaker thinks she knows in the sense that the addressee knows more than what the speaker assumes she does. As a result, the speaker offers information which is not needed about the nature of some person or phenomenon, breaking Grice's Maxim of Quantity. The addressee's response is to try to make sense of the speaker's superfluous information by interpreting the adverb at the interpersonal level, assuming that it means 'of course'/'as we both know' and hence refers to shared knowledge. What happens to the adverb during the reanalysis, from a pragmatic point of view, is consequently that it is shifted to a different level of discourse: to the speaker it expresses information at the "ideational" level, while to the addressee it functions at the discourse or interpersonal level (Halliday 1985). Some candidates for a reanalysis of this kind are given in (48)–(50):

(48) *Negroes are **naturally** faithful and affectionate, though on great provocation, their resentment is unbounded, and they will indulge their revenge, through to their own certain destruction* (ECF2, 1766)

(49) *"A little management is necessary in all families," she says. "The ladies are **naturally** a little jealous one of the other; but they are both of them not unkind to me in the main; and I have to bear no more than other women in my situation."* (ECF2, 1861)

(50) *Sensible men have been known to say that the straightener should in strict confidence be told of every physical ailment that is likely to bear upon the case; but people are **naturally** shy of doing this, for they do not like lowering themselves in the opinion of the straightener [...]* (ECF2, 1872)

The sentences in (48)–(50) may well be meant as informing the addressee about the genetic predispositions of the subject. Yet, given the right circumstances, an 'of course' interpretation may arise. Imagine that the addressee in (48) already "knows", perhaps thinks it is self-evident, that black slaves are faithful and grateful, as was apparently a stereotype at the time of American slavery. When the speaker in (48) utters his statement, the addressee assumes that *naturally* does not provide factual information but refers to their shared knowledge about the relevant state of affairs, taking the adverb to mean 'of course'/'as we both know'. A similar interpretation may arise in (49) on the basis of widely shared, stereotypical ideas of women as being more prone to jealousy than men. Finally, in (50), the reading that people 'of course' hesitate to tell strangers of their ailments because they do not wish to lose face does not seem far-fetched, as this seems to be wholly congruent with typical human feelings and behaviour.

The situations in (48)–(50) may all involve an asymmetry between the assumed and real knowledge of the addressee in the sense that the addressee knows more than what is assumed by the speaker. However, as pointed out by one reviewer, the opposite situation may also occur: the addressee may know *less* than the speaker assumes she does. In that case, one out of the following (two) scenarios may occur: (1) the addressee interprets the adverb as a narrow-scope adverb, and nothing happens, or (2) the addressee understands that the adverb was intended to mean 'as we both know', 'of course', but she does *not* know precisely what she is supposed to know. In such cases the addressee may or may not ask for clarification. Whatever she does, this type of situation is crucial in the transmittance of the newer sentence adverb reading of the adverb. However, it does not represent a bridging context as such contexts occur when the speaker intends the old meaning, while the addressee hears the new meaning (see section 2.4).

4 Conclusion

On the basis of a large scale empirical study of *naturally* in copular *be* sentences, we have argued that the reanalysis of narrow scope *naturally* as an evidential adverb depends on the interplay of a number of factors, with syntax determining the contexts in which a reanalysis is possible: evidential *naturally* can only be licensed in clauses that project a ForceP specified for assertive illocutionary force. This is the case in matrix declaratives and certain types of subordinate clauses. In clauses that project a ForceP, a reanalysis is most likely to occur if *naturally* occurs between the finite copula and the predicative complement. However, a reanalysis does not automatically occur in all contexts sanctioned by syntax, but is subject to lexical, pragmatic and contextual constraints. Thus, a study of bridging contexts in reanalysis must be based on a multifactorial analysis to provide a truthful picture of the phenomenon.

References

Aijmer, Karin. 1996. Swedish modal particles in a contrastive perspective. *Language Sciences* 18. 393–427.
Aikhenvald, Alexandra Y. 2003. Evidentiality in typological perspective. In Alexandra Aikhenvald & Robert M. W. Dixon (eds.), *Studies in evidentiality*, 1–31. Amsterdam: John Benjamins.
Aikhenvald, Alexandra Y. 2004. *Evidentiality*. Oxford: Oxford University Press.
Alexiadou, Artemis. 1997. *Adverb placement: A case study in antisymmetric syntax*. Amsterdam: John Benjamins.
Bellert, Irena. 1977. On semantic and distributional properties of sentential adverbs. *Linguistic Inquiry* 8 (2). 337–350.
BNC Davies, Mark. (2004–) *BYU-BNC*. (Based on the *British National Corpus* from Oxford University Press). (Available online at http://corpus.byu.edu/bnc/.)
Carlson, Greg. 1977. *Reference to Kinds in English*. Amherst, MA: University of Massachusetts, PhD dissertation.
Chafe, Wallace. 1986. Evidentiality in English conversation and academic writing. In Wallace Chafe & Joanna Nichols (eds.), *Evidentiality: The linguistic coding of epistemology*, 261–272. Norwood, NJ: Ablex.
Cinque, Guglielmo. 1999. *Adverbs and functional heads. A cross-linguistic perspective*. Oxford: Oxford University Press.
Cinque, Guglielmo. 2004. Issues in adverbial syntax. In Artemis Alexiadou (ed.), *Taking up the gauntlet. Adverbs across frameworks*. [Special Issue]. *Lingua* 114. 683–710.
De Haan, Ferdinand. 2001. The relation between modality and evidentiality. *Linguistische Berichte*, 9. 201–216.
Diewald, Gabriele. 2002. A model for relevant types of contexts in grammaticalization. In Ilse Wischer & Gabriele Diewald (eds.), *New reflections on grammaticalization. International symposium, Potsdam, 17–19 June, 1999*, 103–120. Amsterdam: John Benjamins.
Diewald, Gabriele & Elena Smirnova. 2011. German evidential constructions and their origins: A corpus-based analysis. In Tanja Mortelmans, Jesse Mortelmans & Walter De Mulder (eds.), *In the mood for mood*, 81–100. Amsterdam & New York: Editions Rodopi.
ECF *Eighteenth-Century Fiction*. 1996. Cambridge: Chadwyck-Healey.
EEPF *Early English Prose Fiction*. 1997. Cambridge: Chadwyck-Healey.
Ernst, Thomas. 2001. *The syntax of adjuncts*. Cambridge: Cambridge University Press.
Ernst, Thomas. 2009. Speaker-oriented adverbs. *Natural Language & Linguistic Theory* 27 (3). 497–544.
Evans, Nicholas & David Wilkins. 1998. *The knowing ear: An Australian test of universal claims about the semantic structure of sensory verbs and their extension into the domain of cognition*. Cologne: Institut für Sprachwissenschaft.

Evans, Nicholas & David Wilkins. 2000. In the mind's ear: The semantic extensions of perception verbs in Australian languages. *Language* 76. 546–592.
Fischer, Olga. 2007. *Morphosyntactic change: Functional and formal perspectives*. Oxford: Oxford University Press.
Grice, Herbert P. 1967. *Logic and conversation*. [The William James lectures]. Harvard University.
Halliday, Michael A. K. 1985. *An introduction to functional grammar*. London: Edward Arnold.
Haegeman, Liliane. 1995. *The syntax of negation*. Cambridge: Cambridge University Press.
Haegeman, Liliane. 2002. Anchoring to speaker, adverbial clauses and the structure of CP. *Georgetown University Working Papers in Theoretical Linguistics* 2. 117–180.
Haegeman, Liliane. 2006. Conditionals, factives and the left periphery. *Lingua* 116. 1651–1669.
Haegeman, Liliane. 2010. The internal syntax of adverbial clauses. *Lingua* 120. 628–648.
Haegeman, Liliane. 2012. *Adverbial clauses, main clause phenomena, and the composition of the left periphery*. Oxford: Oxford University Press.
Haumann, Dagmar. 2007. *Adverb licensing and clause structure in English*. Amsterdam: John Benjamins.
Heine, Bernd. 2002. On the role of context in grammaticalization. In Ilse Wischer & Gabriele Diewald (eds.), *New reflections on grammaticalization. International Symposium, Potsdam, 17–19 June, 1999*, 83–101. Amsterdam: John Benjamins.
Hooper, John & Sandra Thompson. 1973. On the applicability of root transformations. *Linguistic Inquiry* 4. 465–497.
Hopper, Paul J. & Elisabeth Closs Traugott. 2003. *Grammaticalization*. Cambridge: Cambridge University Press.
Jackendoff, Ray. 1972. *Semantic interpretation in generative grammar*. Cambridge, MA: MIT Press.
Killie, Kristin. 2015. Secondary grammaticalization and the English adverbial *-ly* suffix. *Language Sciences* 47(B). 199–214.
Kiparsky, Paul & Carol Kiparsky. 1971. Fact. In Leon A. Jakobovits & Danny D. Steinberg (eds.), *Semantics. An interdisciplinary reader*, 345–369. Cambridge: Cambridge University Press.
Kuteva, Tania. 2001. *Auxiliation: An enquiry into the nature of grammaticalization*. Oxford: Oxford University Press.
NCF *Nineteenth-Century Fiction*. 1999–2000. Cambridge: Chadwyck-Healey.
Nevalainen, Terttu. 1994. Aspects of adverbial change in Early Modern English. In Dieter Kastovsky (ed.), *Studies in Early Modern English*, 243–259. Berlin: Mouton de Gruyter.
OED *Oxford English Dictionary*. (http://www.oed.com/)
Quirk, Randolph & Sidney Greenbaum. 1986 *A University grammar of English*. London: Longman.
Ramat, Paolo & Davide Ricca. 1994. Prototypical adverbs: On the scalarity/radiality of the notion of ADVERB. *Rivista di Linguistica* 6. 289–326.
Rizzi, Luigi. 1997. The fine structure of the left periphery. In Liliane Haegeman (ed.). *Elements of grammar*, 281–337. Dordrecht: Kluwer.
Rizzi, Luigi. 2004. Locality and left periphery. In Adriana Belletti (ed.), *Structures and beyond. The cartography of syntactic structures*, vol. 3, 223–250. Oxford: Oxford University Press.
Simon-Vandenbergen, Anne-Marie & Karin Aijmer. 2007. *The semantic field of modal certainty: A corpus-based study of English adverbs*. Berlin: Mouton de Gruyter.
Swan, Toril. 1988. *Sentence adverbials in English: A synchronic and diachronic investigation*. Oslo: Novus.
Swan, Toril. 1997. From manner to subject modification: adverbialization in English. *Nordic Journal of Linguistics* 20. 179–195.

Swan, Toril. 2014. *Hopefully*: The evolution of a sentence adverbial. In Kari E. Haugland, Kevin McCafferty & Kristian A. Rusten (eds.), *'Ye whom the charms of grammar please': Studies in English Language History in Honour of Leiv Egil Breivik*, 99–116. Bern: Peter Lang.

Swan, Toril & Leiv Egil Breivik. 2011. English sentence adverbials in a discourse and cognitive perspective. *English Studies* 92(6). 679–692.

Traugott, Elisabeth Closs. 1982. From propositional to textual and expressive meanings: Some semantic-pragmatic aspects of grammaticalization. In Winfred P. Lehmann & Yakov Malkiel (eds.), *Perspectives on historical linguistics*, 245–271. Amsterdam: John Benjamins.

Traugott, Elisabeth Closs. 1989. On the rise of epistemic meanings in English: An example of subjectification in semantic change. *Language* 65 (1). 31–55.

Traugott, Elisabeth Closs. 1990. From less to more situated in language: The unidirectionality of semantic change. In Sylvia M. Adamson, Vivien A. Law, Nigel Vincent & Susan Wright (eds.), *Papers from the Fifth International Conference on English Historical Linguistics*, 497–517. Amsterdam: John Benjamins.

Traugott, Elisabeth Closs. 1995. Subjectification in grammaticalisation. In Dieter Stein & Susan Wright (eds.), *Subjectivity and subjectification*, 31–54. Cambridge: Cambridge University Press.

Traugott, Elisabeth Closs. 1997. Subjectification and the development of epistemic meaning: The case of *promise* and *threaten*. In Toril Swan & Olaf J. Westvik (eds.), *Modality in Germanic languages: Historical and comparative perspectives*, 185–210. Berlin: de Gruyter.

Traugott, Elisabeth Closs. 2010. (Inter)subjectivity and (inter)subjectification: A reappraisal. In Kristin Davidse, Lieven Vandelanotte & Hubert Cuyckens (eds.), *Subjectification, intersubjectification and grammaticalization*, 29–69. Berlin: Mouton de Gruyter.

Traugott, Elisabeth Closs. 2012. Pragmatics and language change. In Keith Allan & Kasia M. Jaszczolt (eds.), *Cambridge handbook of pragmatics*, 549–565. Cambridge University Press.

Travis, Lisa. 1988. The syntax of adverbs. *McGill Working Papers in Linguistics – Special Issue on Comparative Germanic Syntax*. 280–310.

Reijirou Shibasaki
From parataxis to amalgamation

The emergence of the sentence-final *is all* construction in the history of American English

Abstract: This study explores the emergence of the sentence-final *is all* construction in American English. The construction stems from an amalgamation of sequenced sentences (or clauses), i.e. SENTENCE/CLAUSE + (and/but) *that is all*, giving rise to a type of anacoluthon, i.e. CLAUSE *is all*. Results of the survey tell us that the sentence-final *is all* construction begins life in the early twentieth century and demonstrates an upward trend towards the present. Theoretically, the specifiable linear sequence of sentences or clauses in particular pragmatic conditions, i.e. co-text (Halliday 2004), provides partial evidence for a cline of clause integration in grammaticalization: parataxis > hypotaxis > subordination (Hopper and Traugott 2003). This newly-born construction originating in American English is introduced to other varieties of English in the same way as some other innovations, such as *be like* and *the bottom line is (that)*, have already been used worldwide.

1 Introduction

This study explores the emergence of the sentence-final *is all* construction in American English. The construction stems from an amalgamation of sequenced sentences/clauses (i.e. parataxis, a clausal complex chained by a coordinate conjunction), i.e. SENTENCE/CLAUSE + (and/but) *that is all*, giving rise to a type of anacoluthon, i.e. CLAUSE *is all*. The sentence-final *is all* has not come under close scrutiny either descriptively or theoretically, presumably due to the relatively small number of examples; however, Mencken (1948), Ando (1969, 2005), and Fujii (2006) quickly perceive such changes in American English as seen in the middle of the twentieth century (see sections 2.1 and 2.2). In this section, we will briefly examine the literary works by J. D. Salinger published in the 1950s and 1960s to see how the *is all* construction is used, while in later sections, we will

Reijirou Shibasaki, Meiji University, School of Interdisciplinary Mathematical Sciences, Tokyo, Japan, reijiro@meiji.ac.jp

https://doi.org/10.1515/9783110682564-008

use a variety of corpora to investigate more fully the development of this construction in the history of American English (see section 4).

Example (1) from *The Catcher in the Rye* by J.D. Salinger serves to illustrate the construction. Note that the term anacoluthon means an instance of anacoluthia: a "want of grammatical sequence; the passing from one construction to another before the former is completed", according to the *Oxford English Dictionary* (OED3 online).[1]

(1) "Anything. Anything descriptive. A room. Or a house. Or something you once lived in or something – you know. Just as long as it's descriptive as hell." He gave out a big yawn while he said that. Which is something that gives me a royal pain in the ass. I mean if somebody yawns right while they're asking you to do them a goddam favor. "Just don't do it too good, **is all**," he said. "That sonuvabitch Hartzell thinks you're a hot-shot in English, and he knows you're my roommate. So I mean don't stick all the commas and stuff in the right place." (1951 J. D. Salinger *The Catcher in the Rye*, 4, emphasis mine)

In (1), Holden Caulfield, the protagonist of the work, is sitting on the washbowl next to Ward Stradlater, his roommate, who has coaxed Holden into writing a composition for his English class. After a short interval of thinking about a theme for the composition, Holden says "What on?" and Stradlater answers quickly as in (1). In the same work, there is one more example of *is all*, which is part of Holden's utterance to his sister, Phoebe:

(2) "Here," old Phoebe said. She was trying to give me the dough, but she couldn't find my hand. "Where?" She put the dough in my hand. "Hey, I don't need all this," I said. "Just give me two bucks, **is all**. No kidding – Here." I tried to give it back to her, but she wouldn't take it. "You can take it all. You can pay me back. Bring it to the play." (1951 J. D. Salinger, *The Catcher in the Rye*, 23)

One can come across this expression, albeit sporadically, in other literary works in the early and middle of the twentieth century, and it continues to be used in the present, as shown in sections 2.1 and 4.2. Costello (1959) took note of young people's vernacular in *The Catcher in the Rye* shortly after the publication of the work, but even he made no mention of this sentence-final *is all*. Furthermore, no usage

---

[1] Such structural integration is sometimes called *apo koinou* or *apo-koinou* (Gr. ἀπὸ κοινοῦ 'in common'), which the OED defines as a construction that consists "of two clauses which have a word or phrase in common" (see Corminboeuf 2012: 215–216 for related terms).

guides have ever paid attention to the usage of *is all* as in (1) and (2), except Follett (1966) below. The brackets mean that the expression therein can be omitted.

(3)   a. *He has his facts wrong **is all** [that's the matter with him].*
      b. *She's gone to the hairdresser **is all** [that accounts for her absence].*

(Follett 1966: 56, emphasis mine)

Follett's account of this usage seems to be grammatically reasonable. Nevertheless, none of the literary works by Salinger I have checked, i.e. *The Catcher in the Rye* (1951), *Nine Stories* (1953), a collection of nine short stories, and *Raise High the Roof Beam, Carpenters* (1963), include such expressions as suggested in (3). On the other hand, the following set of variations is worth mentioning, because (4) can be considered as an amalgamated construction, i.e. anacoluthon, of two such adjacent clauses or sentences as in (5) and (6), respectively.

(4)   *"I know," he said quickly, and took his foot down from the window seat. He raised the window slightly and snapped his cigarette streetward. Then he turned, finished at the window. "Hey. Do me a favor. When this guy comes, will ya tell him I'll be ready in a coupla seconds? I just gotta shave **is all**. O.K.?" Ginnie nodded.* (J. D. Salinger 1953: *Just Before the War with the Eskimos* in *Nine Stories*)

(5)   *"It's still bleedin' like mad. Ya think I oughta put something on it? What's good to put on it? Mercurochrome any good?" "Iodine's better," Ginnie said. Then, feeling her answer was too civil under the circumstances, she added, "Mercurochrome's no good at all for that." "Why not? What's the matter with it?" "It just isn't any good for that stuff, **that's all**. Ya need iodine." He looked at Ginnie.* (J. D. Salinger 1953: *Just Before the War with the Eskimos* in *Nine Stories*)

(6)   *"Stop worryin' about it," Mrs. Snell ordered. "What good's it gonna do to worry about it? Either he tells her or he don't. **That's all**. What good's worryin' gonna do?"* (J. D. Salinger 1953: *Down at the Dinghy* in *Nine Stories*)

Both (4) and (5) are part of the conversation between a teenage girl, Ginnie, and her friend Selena's older brother Franklin; he is twenty-four years old according to Selena's utterance near the end of the story. In (6), Mrs. Snell is complaining to Sandra, the maid of the lady of the house, Boo Boo Tannenbaum, about her son's behaviour in the house. Follett (1998: 21) states that such sentences accompanied by *is all* as in (1), (2) and (4) are restricted to colloquial use; in fact, all of these examples are found only in the conversation part of each work. In contemporary English as well, the sentence-final use of *is all* can be attested in spoken genre as in (7):

(7) "*Look, I'm just saying I'm undecided,* **is all**." (NPR 2015: SPOK, COCA)

Therefore, one may argue that the *is all* construction has gradually developed out of two sequentially aligned clauses or sentences, presumably in informal and interpersonal contexts, representing patterns seen in the language over time. If this is true, this particular case supports a central assumption of Systemic Functional Grammar, i.e. the assumption that a lexical or grammatical item can be properly construed only in a given stretch of discourse (e.g. Halliday 2004: 271; Halliday and Matthiessen 2014); the co-textual use of adjacent clauses smoothes the way for amalgamation, creating a context-dependent meaning of *is all*.[2] Furthermore, the historical development of *is all* in sentence-final position acknowledges that the emergent nature of grammar can best be seen in spoken language (Hopper 2011; Hopper and Thompson 2008) in contrast with the traditional attitude towards written language that "has spread from ancient Greek practices of learning writing [...] to linguistics, and from there into a layman view on language" (Steffensen and Fill 2014: 16; but see section 4.2 for survey results contrary to this common belief). Reconsidering this theoretical and descriptive common ground, this study delves into the recent development of the sentence-final *is all* construction in American English and shows how the emergence of the construction contributes to a better understanding of language change.

This study is structured as follows. In section 2, I will briefly introduce the history of the sentence-final *is all* construction, referring to a few important descriptive works with respect to the construction; in section 3, I will indicate the corpora used for this study. In section 4, the survey results are given, which will then be analyzed from a theoretical standpoint.

---

[2] Halliday (2004: 271) attributes the origin of the term *co-text* to Catford (1965: 30–31).

2 A brief history of sentence-final *is all*

2.1 From sequential use to amalgamation: A language-internal factor of change

Thus far only a handful of works, including Follett (1966, 1998), have paid attention to sentence-final *is all*. Ando (1969: 135–173) investigates a variety of examples of teenage conversational styles in *The Catcher in the Rye*, which Costello (1959: 172) considers not just as a literary work but also as an example of teenage vernacular in the 1950s, saying the following: "As such, the book will be a significant historical linguistic record of a type of speech rarely made available in permanent form. Its linguistic importance will increase as the American speech it records becomes less current" (Costello 1959: 172). In contrast to Costello's (1959) forecast, the occurrence of this particular usage has been increasing, albeit slowly, mainly in the genre of fiction, but also, if less so, in the genre of conversation in American English (see section 4.2).

Ando's (1969) idea is as follows. The elements in focus in (2) are repeated as (8a):

(8) a. *Just give me two bucks,* **is all** (*The Catcher in the Rye*, 23)
 b. *Just give me two bucks,* **that is all**. (Ando 1969: 154–155)

What he suggests here is that the two adjacent clauses in (8b) are integrated into one sentence, deleting the demonstrative *that*, as realized in (8a). In addition, Ando (2005: 28) seems to follow Follett's (1998: 21) statement that the *is all* construction is used exclusively in colloquial language.

Ando's view on this particular change is worth reconsidering for the following reason. Phillipps (1978: 71) points out that William Makepeace Thackeray (1811–1863) listened carefully to the language of the youth of his days and reflected it in his works; a frequent part of one young character's utterances, *that's all*, as in (9), is an example of this. Note that the non-capitalized forms *that* and *wasn't* in (9a) might imply that the clauses form one sequential unit.

(9) a. *Wasn't Reynolds a clipper?* **that's all!** *and wasn't Rubens a brick?* (W. M. Thackeray 1855, *The Newcomes*, I Ch. 12; Phillipps 1978: 71)
 b. *Mr Smee, you are looking at my picture of "Boadishia",' says Gandish. Wouldn't he have caught it for his quantities at Grey Friars,* **that's all**? (W. M. Thackeray 1855, *The Newcomes*, I Ch. 17; Phillipps 1978: 71)

Phillipps (1978) explains that the young character Clive, Colonel Newcome's son, frequently uses *that's all* as in (9) in order to add "extra emphasis to his statements". Interestingly, he goes on to state that this expression is peculiar to "school boys and minors, and Clive does not use it when he becomes a man" (Phillipps 1978: 71). Presumably the young people's vernacular *that's all* at the end of a sentence at the time of Thackeray continues to be used over generations or diffuses into other areas, subsequently giving rise to an elliptical form as in (1) and (2), around the middle of the twentieth century and onwards in American English. Ando's synchronic view that *that's all* is reduced to *is all* deserves to be readdressed diachronically in a verifiable way (see figure 8.1 in section 2.3; see Fujii 2006: 222 for his similar observations on the impact of Irish English on American English; see sections 4.1 and 4.2 for the survey result for British English.[3])

2.2 Language contact issues: A language-external factor of change

Another scholar who studies the usage of the sentence-final *is all* is Fujii (2006), who probes into common speech in American English, not necessarily restricting the study to young people's language. His thorough survey covers a variety of American literary works in the twentieth century, and he assumes that the usages of the sentence-final *is all* and *that's all* as in (4) and (5) can be traced back to those in Irish English as in (10), probably due to the increase in language contact. The relevant part of (5) is repeated as (11), while one similar example is added in (12).

(10) *He is a great old schemer,* **that's what he is.** (Joyce 1910: 11; cited in Fujii 2006: 222)

(11) *"Why not? What's the matter with it?" "It just isn't any good for that stuff,* **that's all.** *Ya need iodine." He looked at Ginnie.* (J. D. Salinger 1953: *Just Before the War with the Eskimos* in *Nine Stories*)

(12) *"Awful. Awful. It's sad, actually,* **is what it is.** *Your father said last night–"* (J. D. Salinger 1953: *A Perfect Day for Bananafish*)

The earliest example of the sentence-final *is all* construction in American English is attested in 1907 (and much later in British English) according to the surveys in

---

3 Note in passing that only one example of *(and) that is all* is found in the spoken component of BYU-BNC, while the others are all found in the written component of the corpus (cf. Crystal 2017: 171–172 below).

section 4.1, while relevant constructions in Irish English as in (10) can be witnessed around the same time. I cannot assert definitely that Irish English facilitated the process of syntactic reduction from *that's all* to *is all*; however, constructions such as *that's all*, *that's what it is*, and *that's what I'm saying* can be considered to have developed in clusters as stance markers in clause- or sentence-final position. Joyce (1910: 10) states, for example, that the expression in bold type in (10) is often added "as a sort of clincher to give emphasis" in sentence-final position, which implies that such an anacoluthonic construction as in (8a) emerges from (8b) through repeated use over time; the same development can be observed in the emergence of the part in bold type in (12) (see Shibasaki 2017a for details).

Crystal (2017: 171–172) also touches on the sentence-final *is all*, considering it as a new idiomatic usage of *be* in colloquial North American English that serves a summative function of the preceding statements; he states that the usage is increasing although he takes care not to commit himself to specifying particular genres in which the summative *is all* shows a steady increase. This issue is addressed in section 4.2 (see Uppstad 2005 for another notion, namely "spoken language bias").

Crystal's (2017) interpretation of the sentence-final *is all* as a summative function is worth consideration, because such a function of *is all* may be related to its cognates German *all(e)* and Dutch *al*. In fact, Mencken (1948: 160, 175, 230, 233) assumes that the meaning of *all(e)* used by German immigrants residing in Pennsylvania may have had some impact on the usage of American English at that time, as in (13). Hook and Mathews (1958: 58) also give a similar example in (14), which they consider to be the result of language contact, i.e. the influence of Pennsylvania Dutch on the American English of those days. Another possible case of contact-induced change was also cited in (10) above, i.e. Irish English.

(13) The influence of Pennsylvania German on American English *The butter is all*. (lit. "The butter is exhausted") (Mencken 1948: 160)[4]

(14) The influence of Pennsylvania Dutch on American English *The sugar is all*. (lit. "The sugar is all gone") (Hook and Mathews 1958: 58)

What is most important for this study is the following example, which Mencken (1948: 148) assumes is derived by analogy with the usage of *is all* in (13) and (14)

---

4 As recorded in Mencken (1948: 160, 175, 230, 233), the same usage was attested in the following states: Indiana, Iowa, Kansas, Maryland, Michigan, Nebraska, Ohio, Virginia, West Virginia as well as Pennsylvania.

(see Fischer 2007; Bybee 2015: chapter 5). The structural change in the choice of grammatical subject from a noun phrase to a finite clause can be regarded as a case of "host class expansion" in the framework of Himmelmann (2004); but see figure 8.1 in section 2.3.

(15) *It's in a bad neighborhood, **is all**.* (C. F. Ransom, July 8, 1939; Mencken 1948: 148)

The clausal reduction of *that is all* to *is all* corresponds to what Lehmann (2008) exemplifies by analyzing focus constructions in languages such as Hittite and Latin; Lehmann (2008) pays attention to an erstwhile initial bi-clausal cleft construction which undergoes a reduction to a mono-clausal structure (see section 5.1 for a relevant discussion). Viewed from the perspective of textual cohesion i.e. co-text, the sequencing of two clauses can facilitate the advancing of integration, with one clause subordinate to the other (see figure 8.1).

2.3 Clauses or sentences that follow *is all*

So far, we have discussed the morpho-syntactic status of *that is all* or *that's all* with respect to the preceding clause or sentence and how their summative function emerges in reference to language contact issues. However, clauses or sentences that follow *that is all* or *that's all* seem to be as important as those preceding them, because they etch the shape of the summative function or meaning of *that is all* or *that's all* as discourse unfolds; this is likely to serve to gain a better comprehension of the emergence of the sentence-final *is all*.

Consider the following examples. Examples (16) and (17) illustrate the usage of *that's all* that means no more than what is stated in the preceding sentences; such an interpretation is evidenced by the following expression in each example (see section 3.1 for a list of corpora used for the current study).

(16) *we've got to wait, **that's all**. What could I do now?* (1921 *Play the Game*: FIC, COHA)
(17) *[…] for two weeks […] as a minister […] **That's all** […] nothing more […]* (1958 Play: *Hysterical Turtle*: FIC, COHA)

The next examples include *all*-relative clauses that emphasize the preceding utterances in a different way from (16) and (17).

(18) *I wanted you to have hold of me all the time.* ***That's all that mattered.*** (1924 *Plastic Age*: FIC, COHA)

(19) *It's the way to make money,* ***that's all that counts.*** (1937 *White Mule*: FIC, COHA)

(20) *Some women are more impetuous than some men.* ***That's all that means.*** (1943 *Lady In Lake*: FIC, COHA)

(21) *[...] with it, she has one chance in a thousand.* ***That's all I can promise you.*** (1968 *Testimony Two Men*: FIC, COHA)

Other expressions such as *that's all I'm saying, that's all I've got to say, that's all I heard, that's all I know about, that's all men talk about, that's all you've got*, etc. can be seen in the corpus. However, such an anacoluthonic type of *all*-relative clause is not frequently witnessed in the recent past; it seems that *that's all* has been formally reduced with the gradual loss of *that*, as in (22) and (23), and with its relative clause following *all*, resulting in the form of the sentence-final *is all* in (7), which is repeated as (24) below.

(22) Rubin:(Pause) *Fix yourself another drink, darling.*
Petra: *Get on with it,* ***is all I'm saying.*** (1990 *Lake No Bottom*: FIC, COHA)

(23) *The ways of Gates are devious and subtle, amigos. Just keep your eyes open,* ***is all I'm saying.*** (2003 *Pictures from an Expedition*: FIC, COHA)

(24) *"Look, I'm just saying I'm undecided,* ***is all.****"* (2015 NPR: SPOK, COCA)

Compared to the non-expanded usage *that's all*, the expanded *all*-relativization usage as in (18) through (21) is much more infrequent in COHA and even in CLMETEV (see section 3.1 for a list of the corpora used), while a little more frequent in the *Old Bailey Corpus*.[5] An explanation for this historical distribution might be that *that's all* or *that is all* was used first with relative clauses, and then the complex clause structure was gradually reduced, resulting in the formulaic *that's all* or *that is all*, and then a type of sentence-final pragmatic marker (Brinton and Kolbe-Hanna 2018; see Traugott 2008; Brinton 2017: 221–228 for related issues). Such a view appears to be a reasonable inference viewed from the

---

5 I used the *Old Bailey Corpus* while I was revising the current paper. Since I cannot fully include the survey result in this paper under tight time pressure, I will leave it for my future studies on related issues.

perspective of grammaticalization. Figure 8.1 may serve as a summary of the forthcoming discussion in section 4, based on the example in (15). S=sentence; SUB=subject.

parataxis:	It's in a bad neighborhood.	That is all
	[...] sentence 1	[*That's all*] sentence 2
Syntax:	preceding S	following S
Pragmatics:	theme	rheme
	⇩	⇩
amalgam:	It's in a bad neighborhood,	is all
	[clause SUB +	is all] sentence 1
Syntax:	clausal subject	predicate
Pragmatics:	theme	rheme

Fig. 8.1: Amalgamation of paratactic sentences

What figure 8.1 tells us about this change is that in the historical development of the sequential alignment, the theme-rheme relation is realized repetitively and discourse-driven. There is a reduction in structural scope from a paratactic construction to an amalgam construction, but the sequential relation from theme to rheme remains the same despite the structural reduction. Simply said, a lexical or grammatical element can be understood in light of the linguistic environment of an utterance, i.e. co-text (see section 5.1 for further details).[6]

However, we need to give due consideration to the fact that the *Old Bailey Corpus* is trial-oriented; therefore, it is no surprise that the majority of the examples show *all*-relative clauses by which witnesses, victims, or defendants attested in court, giving colour to their statements, presumably either marking important points in the treatment of a current topic or signaling the end of the topic.[7] In COHA, on the other hand, the largest portion of examples comes from fiction, and the relative frequency of *all*-relative clauses is accordingly not extremely high; examples from COLMOBAENG (*A Corpus of Late Modern British and American English Prose* 1732–1879) do not show such a tendency. Seen from another

---

6 In a similar way, Traugott (2003: 624) states that "[...] early in grammaticalization, lexemes grammaticalize only in certain highly specifiable morphosyntactic contexts, and under specifiable pragmatic conditions".
7 For example, Rissanen (1991) states that, while trial records reflect the oral mode of speech of those times, they are "not typical specimens of sixteenth-century spoken discourse" (Rissanen 1991: 330), although this still seems to be debatable.

standpoint (see section 4.2), it is possible that the degree of formulaicity in *that's all* or *that is all* is more advanced in American English than in British English.

2.4 Interim summary

In this section, we identified two factors that seem to have facilitated the degree of clausal integration: language-internal and language-external factors. The sequential use of one clause with *that's all* is reported in the middle of the nineteenth century in British English (9); it can be considered that through repeated use, two clauses gradually undergo syntactic integration. Such a local linguistic environment, which is called co-text in a synchronic context (Halliday 2004), turns out to have a stimulating effect on language change in a diachronic context. Notice that such sequential use can also be found in nineteenth-century American English (see section 4.1).

On the other hand, the summarizing function of the sentence-final *is all* has something to do with more than a mere syntactic integration of adjacent clauses, because the newly derived discourse-syntactic function of *is all* may be the result of contact with Pennsylvania German and Dutch as well as Irish English, as shown in (13) and (14). Particularly interesting is the anacoluthonic structure in (15), which can be thought to have emerged under the influence of Irish English (Joyce 1910; Fujii 2006) and is still underway (Crystal 2017). Judging from these observations, we cannot ignore the possibility that both language-internal and language-external factors have a bearing on the emergence of the sentence-final *is all* construction (see Bybee 2015: chapter 11 for relevant discussions).

3 Corpora and coding properties

3.1 Corpora

The following corpora are used for this study. Since I mainly analyze the rise of the sentence-final *is all* construction in the history of American English, I take full advantage of the corpora in (25a) through (25c). Furthermore, I use the two corpora of British English in (26a, b) in order to gain an understanding of the development of *is all* in sentence-final position in British and American English from Late Modern through Present-day periods. *The Corpus of Global Web-Based English* (GloWbE) in (26c), *The Oxford English Dictionary* (OED3 online) in (26d), and *The Old Bailey Corpus* in (26e) are used for reference. *The TV Corpus* and *The*

Movie Corpus are used for the additional surveys shown in tables 8.5 and 8.6 in the appendix.

(25) a. American English part of *A Corpus of Late Modern British and American English Prose* (COLMOBAENG, 1732–1879), ed. Teresa Fanego, ca. 370,000 words.
b. *The Corpus of Contemporary American English* (COCA, 1990–2015), ed. Mark Davies, ca. 520 million words.
c. *The Corpus of Historical American English* (COHA, 1810–2009), ed. Mark Davies, ca. 400 million words.
d. *Michigan Corpus of Academic Spoken English* (MCASE), 1,848,364 words.
e. *Santa Barbara Corpus of Spoken American English, Parts 1–4* (SBCSAE), eds. John W. Du Bois, Wallace L. Chafe, Charles Meyer, Sandra A. Thompson, Robert Englebretson, and Nii Martey, ca. 249,000 words.

(26) a. *The British National Corpus* (BYU-BNC, 1980s–1993), ed. Mark Davies, ca. 100 million words.
b. *A Corpus of Late Modern English Texts Extended Version* (CLMETEV, 1710–1920), ed. Hendrik De Smet, ca. 15 million words.
c. *The Corpus of Global Web-Based English* (GloWbE), ed. Mark Davies, ca. 1.9 billion words.
d. *The Oxford English Dictionary* (OED3 online), Oxford University Press.
e. *The Old Bailey Corpus. Spoken English in the 18th and 19th Centuries*, eds. Magnus Huber, Magnus Nissel, Patrick Maiwald, and Bianca Widlitzki, ca. 134 million words.
f. *The TV Corpus* (1950–2018), ed. Mark Davies, ca. 325 million words.
g. *The Movie Corpus* (1930–2018), ed. Mark Davies, ca. 200 million words.

3.2 Coding properties

The following coding properties are used to differentiate the three types of constructional variation. In (27), two sentences or clauses are juxtaposed without conjunction. In (28), two clauses are combined by coordinate conjunctions, which sometimes follow either a colon (: *and/but that is all*) or a semicolon (; *and/but that is all*). All of these are full clauses or sentences. The corresponding reduced forms of *is all* in (29) are anacoluthonic either with a period or with a comma. These three coding properties serve to uncover the pathways whereby this particular construction has developed over time.

(27) a. *We were still alive then.* **That is all.** (1991 *ContempFic*: FIC. COHA)
 b. *[...] she admitted. "I am afraid for Roger,* **that is all.***"* (2000 *DemonApostle*: FIC, COHA)
(28) a. *"We're co-workers, we work together now,* **and that is all.***"* (2004 Play:FatPig: FIC, COHA)
 b. *"You will continue to make your hospital rounds, Doctor,* **but that is all.***"* (1979 *Rainbow Man*: FIC, COHA)
(29) a. *Jet assured her. "My mom's just a little upset,* **is all.***"* (1997 *LittleFurPeople*: FIC, COHA)
 b. *Frank Flynn says. "You were lucky* **is all.***"* (2003 *Ploughshares*: FIC, COHA)

4 Survey results

4.1 Diachronic distribution

Figure 8.2 shows the diachronic development of the three types of construction, as explained in (27) through (29) respectively, in the history of American English (last access: 20 September 2017). The coding for the survey is "* is all ." for ",/Ø is all" and I sifted all the examples based on the three sub-constructions shown in section 3.2.

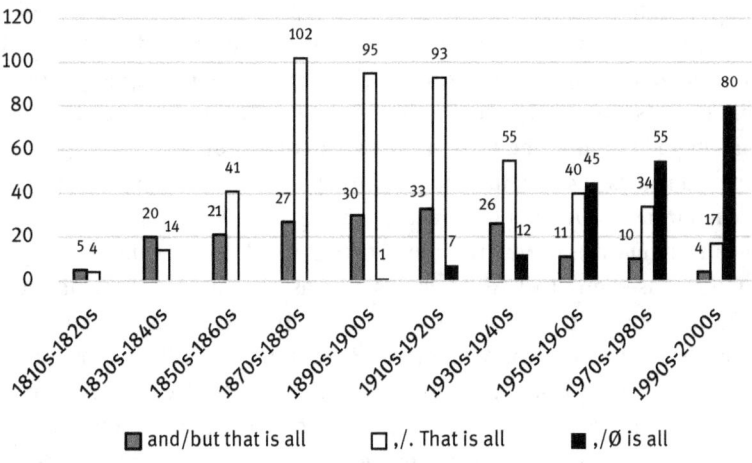

Fig. 8.2: The diachronic distribution of the *is all* constructions in COHA

One interesting finding is that in the mid-nineteenth to the mid-twentieth centuries, two adjacent sentences or clauses began life as a type of coordinate construction with such conjunctions as *and* or *but*, as in (28). It is obvious in terms of token frequency that this construction was preferred over the others. The frequent use of the coordinate construction may have facilitated the constructional reduction in later stages from a full clausal/sentential coordination in (28) through a conjunction-less juxtaposition in (27) to an anacoluthonic construction in (29).

The earliest examples in COHA that illustrate the sentence-final use of *is all* are shown in (30) and (31), while the earliest example in the OED3 online is provided in (32). Note in passing that John Fonte, the author of *Wait until Spring, Bandini* in (32), is an Italian-American novelist who was born and raised in the United States.

(30) "Naw. We're fired off the reservation, **is all**. We got orders to take the herd to hell." (1907 *Rowdy of the Cross L*: FIC, COHA)

(31) "Don't swallow any, **is all**. let's weigh it out, Cash, and see how much it is [...]" (1918 *Cabin Fever*: FIC, COHA)

(32) *Here is a ring I bought you* [...] *Expensive? Naaaw. Three hundred*, **is all**. (1939 *Wait until Spring, Bandini*, OED3 online; Crystal 2017: 171).

This sentence-final usage of *is all* seems not to extend back to the nineteenth century, because the subparts of American English compiled in COLMOBAENG, i.e. 1732–1759 and 1774–1804, include no relevant earlier occurrences. Furthermore, as shown in section 2.2, Crystal (2017: 171) regards the summative function of *is all* in sentence-final position as "a new idiomatic use of *be*" in the twentieth century that "emerged in colloquial North American English – an elliptical form of 'that is all' or (less commonly) 'that was all'". It thus seems that the sentence-final *is all* emerged around the turn of the twentieth century. Notice in passing that the past tense use *was all* in sentence-final position is very infrequent: one example each from COHA and COCA (accessed 20 September 2017).

Table 8.1 summarizes the distributional patterns of the three constructions in British English based on CLMETEV, which serves as an indicator of the different rates of change between these regional varieties of English. Two points are worth mentioning. One is that clausal/sentential coordination without conjunctions is predominant (cf. the corresponding periods in figure 8.2). The fact that juxtaposed constructions are found earlier than their corresponding coordinate constructions in the corpus calls for further examination of the constructional development and variations. However, the other point is more relevant to this study: in British English, no corresponding examples of the sentence-final *is all* in (30) through (32) can be found in the last subpart of CLMETEV, i.e. 1850–1920. Therefore, this anacoluthonic expression *is all* is most likely to be an innovation in American English, which presumably has then spread to other varieties of English (see Mair 2009: 22 for a similar diffusion of *be like*).

Tab. 8.1: The distributional pattern of the three constructions in CLMETEV

Period	1710–1780	1780–1850	1850–1920	Total
and/but that is all	0 (0%)	12(24%)	24 (14.5%)	36 (16.1%)
,/. That is all	8 (100%)	38 (76%)	141 (85.5%)	187 (83.9%)
,/Ø is all	0 (0%)	0 (0%)	0 (0%)	0 (0%)
Total	8 (100%)	50 (100%)	165 (100%)	223 (100%)

All in all, the sentence-final use of *is all* turns out to be an innovation in American English, which stems from an adjacent use of two sentences or clauses with or without conjunctions. In Systemic Functional Grammar (Halliday 2004; Halliday and Matthiessen 2014), the sequential use of a lexico-grammatical item is called "co-text" and properly interpreted only in a relevant stretch of discourse, as mentioned previously. Viewed from the perspective of grammaticalization, it comes as no surprise that such a sequence has been repetitively utilized in discourse as in figure 8.2 and gradually integrated into one anacoluthonic construction in American English as in (24). According to this present survey, in the first two decades of the twentieth century, British English does not witness the emergence of the anacoluthonic usage of *is all*; however, it can be attested in the second half of the twentieth century, as shown in the next section.

4.2 Synchronic distribution

The difference in the diachronic development and distributional variation is reflected in the synchronic situation in British and American English. Table 2 makes a summary of the distributional pattern of the three constructions in BYU-BNC and COCA; the last access to COCA was 17 December 2016. For the main part, American English shows tolerance of the progression of the anacoluthonic use of *is all*, while British English is much more conservative. This survey result also lends support to the idea that the sentence-final *is all* is a case of innovation in American English.

Tab. 8.2: The distributional pattern of the three constructions in BYU-BNC and COCA

	BYU-BNC	COCA
and/but that is all	19 (33.9%)	21 (5.1%)
,/. That is all	30 (53.6%)	83 (20.1%)
,/Ø is all	7 (12.5%)	308 (74.8%)
Total	56 (100%)	412 (100%)

All the examples except one case of *and that is all* are found in the written component of the BYU-BNC corpus (see fn. 3). Generally, anacoluthonic constructions are found to appear prominently in spoken language but not frequently in written language (e.g. Sawada 2016: 166), due to "man-made standards of correctness" (Linell 2005: 77, 163–164); therefore, whether the anacoluthonic *is all* occurs notably in spoken language in American English deserves investigation, see table 8.3:

Tab. 8.3: The distributional pattern of ,/Ø *is all* in COCA (accessed: 22 Sept 2017)

	1990–1992	1993–1995	1996–1998	1999–2001	2002–2004	2005–2007	2008–2010	2011–2013	2014–2015	Total
SPOK	1	1 (1)	1 (1)	0	0	1 (1)	0	0	1	5 1.6%
FIC	26 (15)	29 (15)	32 (12)	44 (13)	37 (15)	41 (13)	29 (12)	25 (9)	24 (8)	287 93.2%
MAG	3 (2)	0	0	2	2	0	1	1	0	9 2.9%
NEWS	0	1	0	3	0	1 (1)	0	1	1	7 2.3%
ACAD	0	0	0	0	0	0	0	0	0	0 0%
Total	30 (17)	31 (16)	33 (13)	49 (13)	39 (15)	43 (15)	30 (12)	27 (9)	26 (8)	308 100%

Table 8.3 demonstrates the distributional patterns of the sentence-final *is all* constructions with or without a comma. For example, looking at the column for 1990–1992 in the table, one can see the number 26 with the number 15 in brackets for the genre of fiction. This means that 26 is the raw frequency of the construction both with comma as in (33) and without comma as in (34), while 15 is only that of the construction without comma. (7) is repeated here as (33):

(33) *"Look, I'm just saying I'm undecided, **is all**."* (2015 *NPR*: SPOK, COCA)

(34) *"Sorry, old sport. It's just sour luck **is all**. Nothing more to be done here."* (2015 *LiteraryRev*: FIC, COCA)

The results of the survey tell us that the sentence-final use of *is all* shows a skewed distribution towards the genre of fiction that is not necessarily categorized as part of spoken language. It is true that the examples found in COCA are all used in conversational parts in each literary work, which may reflect more or less the spoken-ness of the expression, although it is rarely witnessed in spoken genre in table 8.3. If it is an actual colloquial use that is conventionalized in conversation, we would be more likely to use or encounter the expression there. In fact, Crystal (2017: 172) clearly states that "I find myself using it quite often, these days, though never, until now, in a book." However, one indisputable fact is that we cannot find any crucial examples in either SBCSAE or MCASE, which suggests that further extensive and careful research should be required to see whether Crystal's (2017) observation serves as a general picture of Present-day American English. Otherwise, such observations will lead to "spoken language bias" (Uppstad 2005; see the appendix for some relevant survey results).[8]

5 Summary and discussion

5.1 The importance of sequentiality on the pragmatics–grammar interface

Hopper and Traugott (2003: 175–184) set forth a cline of clause integration as follows:

(35) parataxis   >   hypotaxis   >   subordination
    −dependent   +dependent   +dependent
    −embedded   −embedded   +embedded
    (Hopper and Traugott 2003: 178)

---

8 Hundt and Mair (1999) point out that some genres are "fast" (i.e. readily open to innovation), while others are so "slow" that innovations take longer to penetrate them. The relation between "fictional dialogue" and "actual conversation" should thus be explored in my future studies. I express my gratitude to one anonymous reviewer for this comment.

To put it simply, parataxis is a clausal complex chained by a coordinate conjunction as in (28), while hypotaxis is a clausal complex chained by e.g. a subordinating conjunction; the whole clause can be realized as adverbial clauses with *after, since, when*, etc. in English and with certain inflections of or suffixes attached onto verbs e.g. *-nagara, -tari,-te/de*, etc. in Japanese (e.g. Hopper and Traugott 2003: 181; Bisang 1995: 155, 166). Subordination is a clausal complex in which one clause is syntactically embedded as seen in *that*-complementation in English.

In the case of the sentence-final *is all*, the usage can be considered to have changed from parataxis directly to subordination, because examples with clear subordinating conjunctions are extremely infrequent. The following (36) is an exceptional case in my database, but it can be included as part of subordination due to the non-restrictive use of the relative pronoun *which*. In other words, the anacoluthonic use of *is all* seems to have emerged directly from its paratactic use as in (37). (30) is repeated as (37).

(36) *This one, a trumpet, comes out of the Naught,* **which is all**. (Victor Hugo 1833: *By order of the king*: FIC, COHA)

(37) *"Naw. We're fired off the reservation,* **is all**. *We got orders to take the herd to hell."* (1907 *Rowdy of the Cross L*: FIC, COHA)

This development may probably be influenced by or move in tandem with the development of a set of similar expressions in sentence-final position, such as *and all* (which is a very popular locution in Salinger's works above)[9], and more likely [...], *is what I'm saying*, which starts to emerge in almost the same period (Shibasaki 2017b; see section 5.2 below). In fact, McConvell (1998: 302) regards the anacoluthonic amalgamation of sequenced clauses as in (38) as "*is*-marking of subordinate clauses".

(38) a. *That can't be a very welcome outcome, is that rates will now rise.* (Political commentator, ABC TV; McConvell 1998: 302; Calude 2008: 112)

b. *That was what I was talking about, is that they do already do that.* (Student; McConvell 1998: 302; Calude 2008: 112; see Shibasaki 2018)

More importantly, these examples do not only show us one way of syntactic dependence, integrating one clause into the other; they also show us that

---

[9] The expression *and all* is used as a general extender in the NP *and all* construction, as (i): "You mean about my flunking out of Pencey *and all*?" (J. D. Salinger 1951: *The Catcher in the Rye*, 2)

"pragmatically background material attaches to pragmatically foregrounded material" (Lehmann 2008: 211) in that the former can be elaborated linguistically or retained, for example, as a full clause, while the latter may be reduced, for example, as an anacoluthonic clause or a pragmatic marker, as witnessed in the case of *is all* (see Brinton and Kolbe-Hanna 2018 for a similar observation; see figure 8.1). Such a reduced form is not a performance error but a signpost for an interlocutor to expect the end of an utterance, albeit deviating from impeccable grammatical construction (see *expectancy grammar* in Oller 1976; *projector* in Hopper and Thompson 2008; see Shibasaki 2018 for another case study).[10]

The emergent structure in (37) appears to be an exception to the norm and may also deviate from such a theoretical framework as shown in (35). Considering this, anacoluthonic constructions may be formed from a linear sequence of clauses rather than in a hierarchical fashion, which has the potential to ease grammatical constraints to the full extent possible and to realize constructions as addressed in (7), (15) and (37). (39) shows a cline of clausal integration for the anacoluthonic *is all* construction based on the examples summarized in figure 8.2. As addressed in section 2.3, the expanded expression *that's all* plus a relative clause in (39a) is much less frequent, although it can be attested side by side with its non-expanded expression *that's all*; so it is notated in parentheses. Note that the direction of change in (39) is not absolute but shows a general path of change based on the survey results.

(39) a. [...]$_{sentence}$ And *that's all/that is all* ([...]$_{relative\ clause}$)
     b. [...]$_{sentence}$ Ø *that's all/that is all*
     c. [...]$_{clause}$, *that's all/that is all*
     d. [...]$_{clause}$, *is all*
     e. [...]$_{clause}$ *is all*

In the early nineteenth century, the first three constructions (39a) through (39c) compete with each other in terms of frequency. However, the overall course of events in figure 8.2 shows that sequenced sentences move towards stylistic

---

10 What has been discussed on the emergence of anacoluthonic constructions has some bearing on iconicity principles that have been formulated to see the degree of tightness between interpropositional relations: the degree of morphosyntactic tightness reflects the degree of semantic-pragmatic tightness (e.g. Lehmann 1988, 2008; Givón 1990: 826). For example, Foley and Van Valin (1984: 271) state that "the strongest semantic relations will be expressed in the most tightly linked syntactic configurations."

simplification via a gradual formal reduction, which can be described as follows. The direction of change goes from (39a) to (39e) over time as shown in figure 8.2. Two independent sentences chained by coordinate conjunctions come to undergo a series of formal reductions, firstly with the loss of conjunctions (39b), secondly with the loss of sentence boundaries (39c), producing the anacoluthonic construction without the demonstrative subject (39d), finally giving rise to the tightest integration of the preceding clause and the following elements without even a comma between them as in (39e). The directional character of this constructional change appears to go hand-in-hand with the cross-linguistic pathway of change in (35).[11]

Taking into account the emergence of anacoluthonic constructions addressed in Lambrecht (1988) and Shibasaki (2018), one can argue that sequenced clauses serve to facilitate the tightening of their relations semantically and pragmatically and then enable the integration of their morphosyntactic structures. In other words, whether in spoken or in written registers, the specifiable linear sequence of clauses in particular pragmatic conditions, i.e. co-text (Halliday 2004: 5; introduced in section 1; Traugott 2003: 624; pointed out in footnote 4) comes into play in this change.

5.2 Why infrequent constructions can survive

So why can such an infrequent construction as *is all* survive over a century? One might wonder whether other factors than sequentiality or co-text play determining roles in this particular case. As is often the case with constructional analyses, I assume that constructions occurring in a similar discourse-syntactic position have a fair chance of developing in a network, forming a cluster of constructional variants, in order to keep a linguistic ecosystem working at the end of an utterance. In fact, Hoffmann (2005: 140–165) provides evidence that low-frequency expressions hold the potential to gradually become more conventional by analogy with their corresponding high-frequency expressions.

For example, all the constructions shown in (39) have not competed with each other but have developed in a cluster in the twentieth century, see figure 8.2. In addition, another anacoluthonic construction in clause- or sentence-final position that started to come into wide use, i.e. *is what I'm saying*, may have

---

[11] See Shibasaki (2017b) for an analysis of this construction from the perspective of constructionalization (Traugott and Trousdale 2014). For other sentence/clause final elements see Hancil et al. (2015) and Haselow (2016).

formed a part of a constructional taxonomy "*is*-marking of subordinate clauses" (McConvell 1998: 302; see Hancil et al. 2015 and Haselow 2016 for positions closer to mine). Once we take into account Hilpert's (2013: 210) remark that constructional research into the realm of discourse, from a historical perspective, is relatively scant, what the present study contributes to this research field is, I believe, worth consideration (see Shibasaki 2018: 301–304 for an in-depth discussion).

5.3 Innovation in American English and the interplay between spoken and written mediums

Finally, I will show some cases of linguistic innovations in American English, including the emergence of the sentence-final *is all*, that are considered to have spread to other varieties of English, suggesting that language-external factors – e.g. political and economic aspects of a language – are worth an in-depth examination from a broader perspective than taken in this study.

Mair (2009: 22) states that the quotative *be like* construction is an innovation in American English, which is subsequently introduced into Australian and Canadian English with the same innovative function (see Schweinberger 2015 and Amador-Moreno 2015 for the function of *be like* and its related expressions in Irish English). Aijmer (2013: 3) thus suggests that "'new' pragmatic markers (or uses of pragmatic markers) travel quickly to other varieties" in reference to Mair (2009).

Another quickly spreading construction in English today is 'the NP is (that),' which Schmid (2000) regards as a type of shell noun construction, i.e. a set of clausal constructions that express speaker stance such as *the thing is (that)* and *the problem is (that)*. Among shell noun constructions, the OED3 online tells us that the determiner-less *fact is (that)* and *the bottom line is (that)* both originate from American English. The following (40) and (42) are how the OED3 online describes these two shell noun constructions, while the corresponding examples (41) and (43) added to the descriptions are excerpted from my preceding studies on them.

(40) Uses emphasizing the truth of an assertion, esp. in fixed phrases.

    (a) The (honest) truth. Frequently in *the fact is* with *that*-clause, esp. asserting something surprising, unwelcome, or controversial, or making an admission; also *colloq.* (orig. *U.S.*) without *the*.
    (OED3 online, s.v. *fact* A. n. 8. C.)

(41) "He'd do the marketing best, now, of all of us. He knows just where everything is. **'Fact is**, we want him in the family pretty much all the time." (1852 *Hills of the Shatemuc*: FIC, COHA; Shibasaki 2015)

(42) The fundamental and most important or determining factor; the essence, the point, the crux of the argument; the final analysis, conclusion, or outcome, esp. after a debate. (OED3 online, s.v. *bottom line*, 2. Orig. U.S. a)

(43) **The bottom line is that** invention is much more like falling off a log than like sawing one in two. (1982 *Sci. Amer.* Oct. 14/2, OED3 online; Shibasaki 2018: 290)

As regards the loss of the determiner *the* in *the fact is (that)*, we can recall what was discussed in section 4: American English has more potential to facilitate change in form (and perhaps function as well) than British English as in table 8.2 (section 4.2). One can see a similar tendency in Late Modern English as in table 8.1 (section 4.1). *The fact is (that)* can be found in the eighteenth century and becomes conventionalized as a construction through repeated use; in the nineteenth century, it starts to elide the determiner *the* as in (41). Worth mentioning about (41) is that the shell noun *fact* is not used as a bare nominal but it clearly leaves a trace of the gradual loss of the determiner *the* in the apostrophe ('): *the fact is > 'fact is > fact is*. The other shell noun construction *the bottom line is (that)* is newly derived in the last two decades of the twentieth century; therefore, it has not fully undergone the loss of the determiner *the* (but see Shibasaki 2018 for details). Nevertheless, since this construction has already spread into all the other regional varieties of English in the *Corpus of Global Web-Based English* (*GloWbE*, accessed on 22 Nov. 2017), the political and economic impact of the U.S. on other varieties of English and other languages is clear.[12]

The fact that the written component of English comes to reflect the spoken over time, as in (41), gives partial support to the hypothesis of 'colloquialization' shown in (44).

(44) a. away from a written norm which is elaborated to a maximal distance from speech and towards a written norm that is closer to spoken usage, and

---

[12] The spread of informal and colloquial American English slang (e.g. *awesome, dude, asshole*, etc.) among other English varieties can be a good indicator of the political and economic impact of the U.S. I am grateful to one reviewer for this suggestion. See the appendix tables 8.4–8.6.

b. away from a written norm which cultivates formality towards a norm which is tolerant of informality and even allows for anti-formality as a rhetorical strategy (Mair 2006: 187)

As shown in table 8.3 (section 4.2), the sentence-final *is all* construction or a pragmatic marker rarely occurs in spoken registers if at all but mostly in portions of dialogue included in fiction. While advocacy of "written language bias" often strikes the eye of linguists (Linell 2005), there is still some possibility that written language components become incorporated slowly but surely into the realm of spoken language components. What I emphasize here is that there is scope for further study on a grammatical continuum or the interplay between spoken and written mediums not only in one English variety but across regional varieties of English (cf. the two views, i.e. the "sameness of speech and writing" and the "differentness between speech and writing" summarized in Leech 2000).

The sentence-final *is all* construction has not yet been attested in a large number of English varieties, but it can be expected to spread on a global scale from American English to a wider range of English varieties in years to come. All in all, the rise of anacoluthonic constructions turns out to be interwoven with both the historical development and the socio-pragmatics of the language.

Acknowledgements

I would like to express my gratitude to the following researchers: Laurel J. Brinton and Daniela Kolbe-Hanna for their attention to my original paper given at *ISLE4* and their kindness in sharing with me their paper given at the *DiPVaC4* (*Discourse-Pragmatic Variation & Change* 4, Helsinki, 20 May 2018), my two anonymous reviewers for their support and constructive criticism, Kristin Bech and Ruth Möhlig-Falke for giving me the opportunity to contribute to the thought-provoking thematic volume, and Heather Oumounabidji for her last-minute input. Any remaining inadequacies are all my own. Note that this study is a research presentation financially supported by Grant-in-Aid for Scientific Research (C) project (PI: Reijirou Shibasaki, No. 16K02781 and No. 19K00693) and Grant-in-Aid for Scientific Research (B) project (PI: Ryoko Suzuki, No. 17KT0061), the Japan Society for the Promotion of Science.

References

Aijmer, Karin. 2013. *Understanding pragmatic markers*. Edinburgh: Edinburgh University Press.
Amador-Moreno, Carolina P. 2015. "There's, like, total silence again, roysh, and no one says anything": Fictional representations of 'new' pragmatic markers and quotatives in Irish English. In Carolina P. Amador-Moreno, Kevin McCafferty & Elaine Vaughan (eds.), *Pragmatic markers in Irish English*, 370–389. Amsterdam: John Benjamins.
Ando, Sadao. 1969. *Eigo Gohoo Kenkyuu* (Studies in English Phraseology). Tokyo: Kenkyusha.
Ando, Sadao. 2005. *Gendai Eibunpoo Koodi* (Lectures on Modern English Grammar). Tokyo: Nan'undo.
Bisang, Walter. 1995. Verb serialization and converbs: Differences and similarities. In Martin Haspelmath & Ekkehard König (eds.), *Converbs in cross-linguistic perspective: Structure and meaning of adverbial verb forms – Adverbial participles, gerunds*, 137–188. Berlin: Mouton de Gruyter.
Brinton, Laurel J. 2017. *The evolution of pragmatic markers in English: Pathways of change*. Cambridge: Cambridge University Press.
Brinton, Laurel J. & Daniela Kolbe-Hanna. 2018. "It's just a little weird, is all" – The development and use of sentence-final is all. Paper given at the conference *Discourse-Pragmatic Variation & Change 4* (DiPVaC4), Helsinki, Finland, May 28–30, 2018.
Bybee, Joan. 2015. *Language change*. Cambridge: Cambridge University Press.
Calude, Andreea S. 2008. Demonstrative clefts and double cleft constructions in spontaneous spoken English. *Studia Linguistica* 62 (1). 78–118.
Catford, John C. 1965. A linguistic theory of translation: An essay in applied linguistics. Oxford: Oxford University Press.
Costello, Donald P. 1959. The language of 'The Catcher in the Rye'. *American Speech* 34 (3). 172–181.
Corminboeuf, Gilles. 2012. Des *apo koinou* aux constructions louches. In Marleen Van Peteghem, Peter Lauwers, Els Tobback, Annemie Demol & Laurence De Wilde (eds.), *Le verbe en verve: Réflexions sur la syntaxe et la sémantique verbales*, 215–231. Gent: Academia Press.
Crystal, David. 2017. *The story of BE: A verb's-eye view of the English language*. Oxford: Oxford University Press.
Fischer, Olga. 2007. *Morphosyntactic change*. Cambridge: Cambridge University Press.
Foley, William & Robert D. Van Valin Jr. 1984. *Functional syntax and Universal Grammar*. Cambridge: Cambridge University Press.
Follett, Wilson. 1966. *Modern American usage*. New York: Hill & Wang.
Follett, Wilson. 1998. *Modern American usage*, 2nd edn. New York: Hill & Wang.
Fujii, Kenzo. 2006. *Amerika no Eigo: Gohoo to hatsuon* (American English: Phraseology and Pronunciation). Tokyo: Nan'undo.
Givón, Talmy. 1990. *Syntax*, volume II. Amsterdam: John Benjamins.
Halliday, Michael A. K. 2004. *An introduction to functional grammar*. London: Arnold.
Halliday, Michael & Christian Matthiessen. 2014. *Halliday's introduction to functional grammar*, 4th edn. London: Arnold.
Hancil, Sylvie, Alexander Haselow & Margje Post (eds.). 2015. *Final particles*. Berlin: De Gruyter Mouton.
Haselow, Alexander. 2016. A processual view on grammar: macrogrammar and the final field in spoken syntax. *Language Sciences* 54. 77–101.

Hilpert, Martin. 2013. *Constructional change in English*. Cambridge: Cambridge University Press.
Himmelmann, Nikolaus P. 2004. Lexicalization and grammaticalization: Opposite or orthogonal? In Walter Bisang, Nikolaus P. Himmelmann & Björn Wiemer (eds.), *What makes grammaticalization?*, 21–42. Berlin: Mouton de Gruyter.
Hoffmann, Sebastian. 2005. *Grammaticalization and English complex prepositions: A corpus-based study*. London: Routledge.
Hook, Julius N. & Ernst G. Mathews. 1958. *Modern American grammar and usage*. New York: Roland.
Hopper, Paul J. 2011. Emergent grammar and temporality in interactional linguistics. In Peter Auer & Stefan Pfänder (eds.), *Constructions: Emerging and emergent*, 22–44. Berlin: De Gruyter.
Hopper, Paul J. & Sandra A. Thompson. 2008. Projectability and clause combining in interaction. In Ritva Laury (ed.), *Crosslinguistic studies of clause combining*, 99–123. Amsterdam: John Benjamins.
Hopper, Paul J. & Elizabeth C. Traugott. 2003. *Grammaticalization*, 2nd edn. Cambridge: Cambridge University Press.
Hundt, Marianne & Christian Mair. 1999. "Agile" and "uptight" genres: The corpus-based approach to language change in progress. *International Journal of Corpus Linguistics* 4(2). 221–242.
Joyce, Patrick W. 1910. *English as we speak it in Ireland*. London: Longmans, Green, & Co. (reprinted by Wentworth Press, 2016)
Lambrecht, Knud. 1988. There was a farmer had a dog: Syntactic amalgams revisited. *Berkeley Linguistics Society* 14. 319–339.
Leech, Geoffrey N. 2000. Grammars of spoken English: New outcomes of corpus-oriented research. *Language Learning* 50. 675–724.
Lehmann, Christian. 1988. Towards a typology of clause linkage. In John Haiman & Sandra A. Thompson (eds.), *Clause combining in grammar and discourse*, 181–225. Amsterdam: John Benjamins.
Lehmann, Christian. 2008. Information structure and grammaticalization. In Elena Seoane & María José López-Couso (eds.), *Theoretical and empirical issues in grammaticalization*, 207–229. Amsterdam: John Benjamins.
Linell, Per. 2005. *The written language bias in linguistics: Its nature, origins and transformations*. London: Routledge.
Mair, Christian. 2006. *Twentieth-century English: History, variation and standardization*. Cambridge: Cambridge University Press.
Mair, Christian. 2009. Corpus linguistics meets sociolinguistics. In Antoinette Renouf & Andrew Kehoe (eds.), *Corpus linguistics: Refinements and reassessments*, 7–32. Amsterdam: Rodopi.
McConvell, Patrick. 1998. *To be* or double *be*? Current changes in the English copula. *Australian Journal of Linguistics* 8. 287–305.
Mencken, Henry L. 1948. *The American language, supplement II*. New York: Alfred A Knopf.
Oller, John W. Jr. 1976. Evidence for a general language proficiency factor: An expectancy grammar. *Die Neueren Sprachen* 75. 165–174.
Oxford English Dictionary (OED3 online). Oxford: Oxford University Press.
Phillipps, Kenneth C. 1978. *The language of Thackeray*. London: Andre Deutsch.
Rissanen, Matti. 1991. Spoken language and the history of do-periphrasis. In Dieter Kastovsky (ed.), *Historical English syntax*, 321–342. Berlin: Mouton de Gruyter.

Sawada, Shigeyasu. 2016. *Kotoba no Jissai: Hanashi kotoba no koozoo* (The truth about language: The structure of spoken language). Tokyo: Kenkyusha.
Schmid, Hans-Jörg. 2000. *English abstract nouns as conceptual shells: From corpus to cognition*. Berlin: Mouton de Gruyter.
Schweinberger, Martin. 2015. A comparative study of the pragmatic marker *like* in Irish English and in south-eastern varieties of British English. In Carolina P. Amador-Moreno, Kevin McCafferty & Elaine Vaughan (eds.), *Pragmatic markers in Irish English*, 114–134. Amsterdam: John Benjamins.
Shibasaki, Reijirou. 2015. Gendai Amerika Eigo no Nijuu Kopyura koobun (Double copula constructions in Present-day American English). In Minoji Akimoto, Hirofumi Aoki & Mitsuru Maeda (eds.), *Nichi Eigo no Bunpooka to koobunka* (Grammaticalization and constructionalization in Japanese and English), 147–180. Tokyo: Hituzi Syobo Publishing.
Shibasaki, Reijirou. 2017a. Clause combining and integration at right periphery of utterance:…, *is what I'm saying* in American English. Paper presented at the 15th International Pragmatics Conference, Belfast, Northern Ireland, 16–21 July 2017.
Shibasaki, Reijirou. 2017b. Amerika Eigo ni okeru hakaku koobun (Anacoluthonic constructions in American English). In Midori Amano & Naoko Hayase (eds.), *Koobun no imi to hirogari* (Constructional meaning and its extension), 201–221. Tokyo: Kurosio Publishers.
Shibasaki, Reijirou. 2018. Sequentiality and the emergence of new constructions. In Hubert Cuyckens, Hendrik De Smet, Liesbet Heyvaert & Charlotte Maekelberghe (eds.), *Explorations in English historical syntax*, 285–308. Amsterdam: John Benjamins.
Steffensen, Sune Vork & Alwin Fill. 2014. Ecolinguistics: The state of the art and future horizons. *Language Sciences* 41. 6–25.
Traugott, Elizabeth C. 2003. Constructions in grammaticalization. In Brian Joseph & Richard Janda (eds.), *The handbook of historical linguistics*, 624–647. Oxford: Blackwell.
Traugott, Elizabeth C. 2008. 'All that he endeavoured to prove was…': On the emergence of grammatical constructions in dialogic contexts. In Robin Cooper & Ruth Kempson (eds.), *Language in flux*, 143–177. London: Kings College Publications.
Traugott, Elizabeth C. & Graeme Trousdale. 2014. *Constructionalization and constructional change*. Oxford: Oxford University Press.
Uppstad, Per H. 2005. Written language skills and the notion of 'lexicon'. In Per H. Uppstad (ed.), *Language and literacy: Some fundamental issues in research on reading and writing*, 143–158. Department of Linguistics and Phonetics, Centre for Languages and Literature, Lund University.

Texts

Salinger, Jerome David. 1951. *The Catcher in the Rye*. Boston, MA: Little, Brown and Company.
Salinger, Jerome David. 1953. *Nine Stories*. Boston, MA: Little, Brown and Company.
Salinger, Jerome David. 1963. *Raise High the Roof Beam, Carpenters*, in *Raise High the Roof Beam, Carpenters and Seymour: An Introduction*. Boston, MA: Little, Brown and Company.

Appendix

Tab. 8.4: The survey results of the sentence-final *is all* construction in *GloWbE* (accessed: 22 Nov. 2017)

	US	CA	GB	IE	AU	NZ	IN	PK	SG	MY	PH	HK	ZA
FREQ	50	10	19	7	8	8	1	1	1	1	2	1	5
Word (M)	386.8	134.8	387.6	101.0	148.2	81.4	96.4	51.4	43.0	41.6	43.2	40.5	45.4
Per mill.	0.13	0.07	0.05	0.07	0.05	0.10	0.01	0.02	0.02	0.02	0.05	0.02	0.11

* The corpus search of occurrences of "is all." is summarized in table 8.4. I sifted all the examples; the figures end up showing the numbers of ", is all."

Tab. 8.5: The survey results of the sentence-final *is all* construction in *The TV Corpus* (accessed: 1 March 2019)

	1950s	1960s	1970s	1980s	1990s	2000s	2010s	US/CA	UK/IE	AU/NZ	Misc
FREQ	2	4	6	14	35	137	290	433	45	9	1
Word (M)	2.0	8.9	8.8	15.0	31.5	87.5	172.4	265.8	53.2	5.1	2.1
Per mill.	0.98	0.45	0.68	0.93	1.11	1.56	1.68	1.68	0.85	1.75	0.47

* All the examples of UK, IE, AU, NZ, and other varieties of English except one found in 1966 in UK/IE appear after 2000. The other examples are all from American English.

Tab. 8.6: The survey results of the sentence-final *is all* construction in *The Movie Corpus* (accessed: 1 March 2019)

	1930s	1940s	1950s	1960s	1970s	1980s	1990s	2000s	2010s	US/CA	UK/IE	AU/NZ	Misc
FREQ	1	1	11	9	16	15	58	113	130	310	29	5	10
Word (M)	6.6	9.8	10.6	9.1	10.1	14.1	24.6	51.2	63.3	153.3	28.9	3.4	13.9
Per mill.	0.15	0.10	1.04	0.99	1.58	1.06	2.36	2.21	2.05	2.02	1.00	1.48	0.72

Elena Seoane
The role of context in the entrenchment of new grammatical markers in World Englishes

Abstract: This study explores the role of context in the alleged entrenchment of the adverbs *yet, just* and *(n)ever*, among other adverbial elements, as markers of the perfect in World Englishes (Miller 2000; Brown and Miller 2017), from the perspective of Usage Based Theory (Bybee 2006, 2013) and taking data from seven components of the *International Corpus of English* (ICE, Greenbaum 1996). The probabilistic analysis of the results show that all the micro-level contextual factors analyzed (verbal form, verb type and polarity) determine variation and change in this domain of grammar, in combination with two of the three macro-level contextual features analyzed, namely type of perfect meaning and register (see Seoane 2017). Mode, however, turns out not to be a valid predictor in the entrenchment of adverbials, which questions previous work using differences between speech and writing as a proxy for ongoing change in ICE. The results of this contextualized approach to grammatical change leads me to advocate for usage-based, onomasiological and statistically-modelled approaches to grammatical variation, in which register variability must necessarily be taken into consideration (Biber and Gray 2016), independent of mode.

1 Introduction

Miller (2000) and Brown and Miller (2017) argue that the adverbs *just, (n)ever* and *yet* are becoming markers of perfect meaning in spoken English at the expense of the semantic weakening and reduction in the use of *have* + past participle periphrasis (henceforth PrPf).[1] These adverbs, they argue, are on their way to becoming obligatory in newly entrenched constructions expressing resultative (e.g. *She*

---

[1] I am grateful to the editors of this volume and to two anonymous reviewers for their helpful, detailed comments. I am also grateful to Cristina Suárez-Gómez for her work on the data retrieval and analysis. For generous funding I thank the Spanish Ministry of Economy and Competitiveness (grants FFI 2014-53930-P and FFI 2017-82162-P).

Elena Seoane, University of Vigo, Department of English, French and German, Vigo, Spain, elena.seoane@uvigo.es

https://doi.org/10.1515/9783110682564-009

hasn't warned him yet), recent-past (*She has just written it*) and experiential (*She's never been there*) perfect meaning (Miller 2000: 334). They go on to claim that there are grounds for considering examples such as these to be separate constructions rather than separate interpretations of the perfect, but that insufficient attention has been paid to this issue (Brown and Miller 2017: 245–254), especially based on naturally occurring linguistic data (Miller 2000: 339).

Variation in the expression of the perfect has been a topic of considerable interest, initially with variation in the two major L1 varieties, British and American English (cf. the corpus-based studies in Elsness 2009, and Hundt and Smith 2009, among others), and more recently in World Englishes (WEs). Some studies here focus on individual varieties (Davydova 2013 on Singapore English; Seoane 2016 on Jamaican English; Van Rooy 2016 on Black South African English; Werner and Fuchs 2017 on Nigerian English), others on geographically-related varieties (Seoane and Suárez-Gómez 2013; Suárez-Gómez and Seoane 2013 on Asian Englishes) and others on comparisons between a large number of varieties (e.g. Davydova 2011; Werner 2013, 2014; Yao and Collins 2013). Much of this research adopts a semasiological perspective, comparing the use of the present perfect and the preterite (see Engel and Ritz 2000; Biewer 2008; Van Rooy 2009; Werner 2013, 2014, 2016; Davydova 2011; Hundt and Smith 2009; Yao and Collins 2012, 2013; Yerastov 2015; most articles in Werner, Seoane, and Suárez-Gómez 2016; Werner and Fuchs 2017). An onomasiological perspective, which examines all the forms that are used in contexts expressing perfect meaning, has also been taken (Seoane and Suárez-Gómez 2013; Suárez-Gómez and Seoane 2013; Seoane 2016, 2017; Suárez-Gómez 2017b). In these latter studies the role of adverbials in the expression of perfect is addressed, but only briefly.

This study takes an essentially function-to-form (i.e. onomasiological) orientation, since it aims to examine the role of context in the entrenchment of *just*, *(n)ever*, *yet* and other adverbials as markers of perfect meaning independent of the verb form concerned (i.e. not only *have* + past participle forms), and perfect meaning can thus only be detected by reading through the texts themselves. The theoretical framework adopted is Usage Based Theory (UBT, see Bybee 2006, 2011, 2013 among others), since it allows for the incorporation of both micro- and macro-level contextual factors (van Dijk's 2008 terms), and this is especially relevant in multilingual settings such as those dealt with here (Adger and Trousdale 2007: 268, 273; Trousdale 2010: 128; Geeslin and Long 2014: 139). Moreover, UBT provides a useful means of conceptualizing the degree of integration of *just*, *(n)ever* and *yet* as perfect markers, since it accounts for the progressive entrenchment of grammatical elements in the mental grammar of speakers, depending on the degree of exposure to such elements (or exemplars) in real social and historical contexts (see Fischer

2007: 324). Such language contexts can be captured by means of corpus-based studies such as the present one, which follows a variationist design to investigate proportional preferences in different varieties and contexts.

As just noted, this study is corpus-based and uses seven components of the *International Corpus of English* (ICE, Greenbaum 1996). Together with the Inner Circle or L1 variety ICE-GB, British English, used mainly as a reference or benchmark variety, it uses all six complete available ICE corpora representing Asian and African L2s. As Schneider (2018: 5) points out, these are the continents where the "main manifestations" of Outer Circle World Englishes are to be found.[2] These include the following ICE Outer Circle or L2 varieties. First, four varieties from South and South-East Asia: ICE-SIN, Singapore English (SinE), ICE-HK, Hong Kong English (HKE), ICE-PHIL, Philippines English (PhilE) and ICE-IND, Indian English (IndE). Second, two components from Africa: ICE-NIG, Nigerian English (NigE), and ICE-EA, East-African English (EAE), which comprises Kenyan and Tanzanian English.[3] The total number of words is c. seven million (c. one million per variety).

The varieties under analysis are all the result of colonization. The countries where they are spoken were exploitation colonies established mainly in the nineteenth century under British or American administrative control, which involved extended interactions with indigenous populations for a long period of time, giving rise to new varieties of English. In Asia, expansion started in 1600 with the foundation of the East Asia Company. Singapore, the most anglicized country, became a colony in 1819 and in 1842, after the Opium Wars, Hong Kong was ceded to the British Empire. In 1858 India became a Crown colony and in 1898 the only American colony in Asia was established, the Philippines. In all these countries English was transmitted through newly founded schools and was thus associated

---

[2] Another Asian ICE corpus, ICE-Sri Lanka, has been excluded, since only the written part is available.

[3] ICE-EA differs from the other ICE components in various ways. Firstly, as mentioned, it contains two different varieties of English, those spoken in Tanzania and Kenya. Secondly, the two components are not balanced, since the Tanzania one is smaller, and the internal proportion of written and spoken texts for each variety is different from one another and from the general ICE proportion (60% spoken and 40% written). The Tanzania component contains 615,513 words and only 213,801 of them are spoken (34.7% instead of 60%), and the Kenya component contains written texts (401,863 words), spoken material (289,625) and a third category, 'written as spoken', with 100,207 words. The total for Kenya is therefore 791,695 words (49% spoken + written as spoken). This difference between ICE-EA and the other ICE components jeopardizes comparability, as do chronological gaps within and among components and cultural differences in the conception of registers, as is mentioned in section 3.3 below.

with elitist and public roles. The varieties of English they speak now, however, are not elitist colonial remnants. In the last decades, English has expanded to new functions and contexts of usage, they are often (co)official and widely used as second languages, and increasingly as first languages as well. In Africa, the spread of English also began in the seventeenth century, but the British colonies of Nigeria, Kenya and Tanzania were set up in the nineteenth century. Nigeria became a British colony in 1861, and Nigerian English is widely used today for internal purposes (education, business, media) as a second language. In Tanzania the role of English is more limited and more restricted to "high" domains because the colonial presence was lighter and shorter, and also due to the nationalist language policy promoting Swahili as the national language. Kenya became a British colony in 1885 and in the second half of the twentieth century, unlike in Tanzania, Kenyan English spread widely to new internal functions (Schneider 2007, 2018).

According to the Dynamic Model of Postcolonial Englishes (Schneider 2003, 2007), which takes into consideration the colonization type, the identity rewriting of speakers across different diachronic stages in the evolution of the given variety and the associated linguistic changes, these L2s are in the developmental stages set out in figure 9.1 below.

a. SinE has progressed to stage four, endonormative stabilization. It is a nativized and stabilized variety that is beginning to be recognized as a local standard and is said to be on its way to developing into a first-language variety (see Foley 2001; Pakir 2001; Schneider 2007: 160).

b. According to Schneider (2007: 135–139), HKE is still in phase three (nativization), while according to Setter, Wong, and Chan. (2010: 116) it is already moving towards phase four. As an anonymous reviewer points out, the current political situation has given rise to a massive rise of the influence of Mandarin. This might indeed halt the evolution of HKE, even though the "mainlandization" that this phenomenon represents, however, is still subject to rejection, especially among the youth.

c. PhilE is in phase three, and, according to Schneider (2007: 143), external pressure is likely to stall any further developments beyond this stage.

d. IndE is in phase three, nativization, but also shows early symptoms of phase four, both as regards attitudes towards the local standard variety and in terms of literary creativity, which is indicative of a nativized variety (Schneider 2007: 171–172).

e. EAE includes Kenyan English which, like NigE, has been in phase three since the late 1940s (Schneider 2007: 192–197), and Tanzanian English, which "has not moved far into phase three" (Schneider 2007: 199).

f. NigE has been in phase three since the late 1940s (Schneider 2007: 204–210).

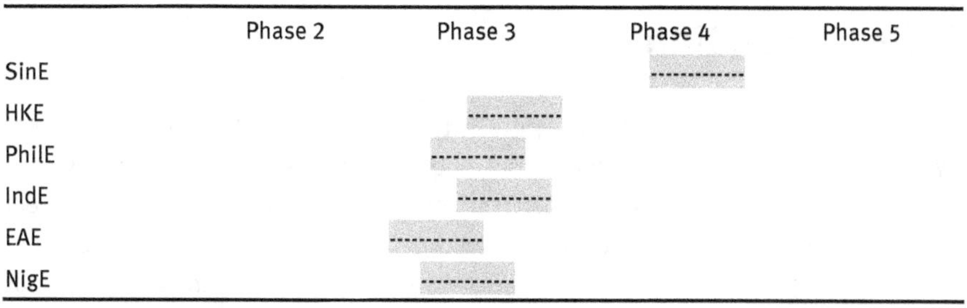

	Phase 2	Phase 3	Phase 4	Phase 5
SinE			-------	
HKE		-------		
PhilE		-------		
IndE		-------		
EAE	-------			
NigE		-------		

Fig. 9.1: Developmental phase of the L2s under study according to Schneider's (2003, 2007) Dynamic Model

An analysis of the results will also take into account the macro-level extralinguistic context, in that the L2 varieties under scrutiny have emerged in situations of language contact and are set in multilingual contexts. Contact with local languages is determinative in shaping them, "usually via the process of second language acquisition of English by indigenous people" (Schneider 2018: 1), and for this reason processes of Second Language Acquisition (SLA) are also considered. These two conditions, language contact and SLA processes, have been shown to make language susceptible to mechanisms such as the principle of transparency and processes of simplification and increasing isomorphism (Thomason 2001; Szmrecsanyi and Kortmann 2011; Schneider 2013), which might account in part for the entrenchment of the adverbials under consideration here as perfect markers.

A register approach to this issue is offered in Seoane (2017), which examines register differences found in L1, L2 and ESD (English as a Second Dialect) varieties of English regarding the role of adverbial support in the expression of perfect meaning. The present study examines a more restricted set of varieties of English and fits a regression model to probe the combined contribution of a wider range of contextual factors. After a brief explanation of the data selection in section 2, section 3 offers a general overview of the data (section 3.1) and concentrates on the description of potentially significant factors in the entrenchment of adverbials; these comprise not only structural contextual factors, such as verbal form, verb type and polarity (section 3.2), but also the inter-discursive relationship between spoken and written texts and between registers, as well as the type of perfect meaning expressed (Section 3.3). Section 4 describes the probabilistic analysis applied to the variables and provides an interpretation and discussion of the results. Finally, section 5 provides some conclusions.

2 Data selection

As noted in the introduction, the approach to the study of the entrenchment of *just, (n)ever* and *yet* as perfect markers is one of function-to-form. In other words, the data are retrieved according to their meaning: only contexts expressing perfect meaning (independent of the form the verb takes) are used. For the same reason, all adverbials expressing perfect meaning were also included in the study and not only *just, (n)ever* and *yet*. 10 high-frequency verbs were selected on the basis of an initial study on the expression of perfect meaning in WEs, which showed that these are the verbs which appear with perfect meaning most frequently in the ICE corpus (Seoane and Suárez-Gómez 2013). This list of verbs excludes *be, have* and *do* since their rate of occurrence as primary auxiliary verbs is extremely high and hence the process of filtering out irrelevant forms would be excessively time consuming.[4] The ten verbs, then, are *come, finish, get, give, go, hear, see, say, tell* and *think*. I extracted all the occurrences of such verbs, which amounted to c. 110,000 tokens. These were manually pruned by reading the contexts and identifying perfect meaning. Coordinated verb phrases (e.g. example (7) below, *the youths have never seen or heard*) are counted as two tokens. A total of 7,374 valid tokens were thus found. As expected, the selection of relevant examples was far from easy. Of particular difficulty was the semantic discrimination of examples (see section 3.3), which entailed the careful reading of generous amounts of surrounding context in order to clarify the time frame in which the action took place. It is important to note that I carefully excluded all tokens expressing perfect meaning that belong to extra-corpus material (interviewers, speakers of a different variety of English); they are annotated with <X> in the corpus.

As mentioned in the introduction, after an overview of the data (section 3.1) the study describes several contextual factors and their combined probabilistic effect on the presence of adverbials to express perfect meaning. The underlying hypothesis, therefore, is that a combination of (all or some of) these contextual factors determines the presence of these adverbials and their potential entrenchment as perfect markers.

---

[4] An anonymous reviewer argues that selecting a number of verbs reduces the claim that the study is onomasiological. Another way of approaching the topic from a function-to-form perspective would involve reading the corpus and including all verbs found with perfect meaning. The manageable number of verbs with perfect meaning that we need (between two and three thousand, since these are examined qualitatively) would be found in a relatively small section of the corpus, which would render comparisons between varieties, modes and registers impossible.

3 Data description

3.1 General overview of the data

Table 9.1 below provides the raw numbers and percentages of tokens expressing perfect meaning for each variety, with a specification of the form of the verb.

Tab. 9.1: Form and regional distribution of the verbs expressing perfect meaning

	BrE	HKE	SinE	IndE	PhilE	NigE	EAE	TOT
PrPf	723	941	664	975	541	700	796	5340
	82.4%	69.3%	65.0%	77.0%	65.0%	68.0%	80.0%	72.4%
Preterite	108	333	307	239	261	303	172	1723
	12.3%	24.5%	30.0%	19.0%	31.3%	29.4%	17.3%	23.4%
Be+Pple	41	35	27	22	26	14	12	177
	4.5%	2.6%	2.6%	1.7%	3.1%	1.3%	1.2%	2.4%
Base form	3	24	11	2	–	6	1	47
	0.3%	1.8%	1.1%	0.2%		0.6%	0.1%	0.6%
Past Pple	1	15	11	14	2	1	6	50
	0.1%	1.1%	1.1%	1.1%	0.2%	0.1%	0.6%	0.7%
Other	1	9	2	6	3	7	9	17
	0.1%	0.7%	0.2%	0.5%	0.4%	0.7%	0.9%	0.2%
TOTAL	877	1357	1022	1258	833	1031	996	7374

Table 9.1 indicates that in both L1 and L2 varieties of English, the envelope of variation is much wider than that traditionally acknowledged in grammars of English (e.g. Quirk et al. 1985: 189–197; Huddleston and Pullum et al. 2002: 139–148) which mention the PrPf periphrasis and, only marginally, the preterite. The preterite, illustrated in (1) below, is reasonably frequent in all varieties, as also noted by Elsness (2009) and Hundt and Smith (2009) for American English. Other forms registered in table 9.1 are clearly productive in the corpus, such as the periphrasis with *be* as an auxiliary (2), the base form (3), the past participle alone (4), and finally some other forms, which are considered to be either performance errors or transcription mistakes, given their marginal frequency (5).

(1) *I **heard** there's a nice big bar open up in Wanchai* (ICE-HK S1A-063)[5]

(2) *And today I think if I have mentioned somewhere in my article recently which **is gone** down by forty-two percent* (ICE-IND S1b-054)

(3) *I went the more they started the crisis I already **tell** them let them move* (ICE-NIG con_58)

(4) *It's opposite to that C I I L only no You never **seen** that place Yeah yeah I forgot the name* (ICE-IND S1A-016)

(5) *Like I've always **tell** myself, as long as I've done my best, I won't rebuke myself* (ICE-SIN W1B-003)

As for the presence of adverbials in the expression of perfect meaning, table 9.2 and figure 9.2 below show their distribution by geographical variety. As mentioned in the methodology section, adverbials of time here include not only *just, (n)ever* and *yet*, but also prepositional phrases, noun phrases and other adverbs that indicate the time frame in which the action takes place, in order to compare the entrenchment of *just, never* and *yet* with that of other potential candidates to function as perfect markers (see section 3.3).

---

5 This very first example may serve to illustrate the role of context in the decision to consider an example as expressing or not perfect meaning. It takes place in a conversation about clubs and bars that the speakers have heard of and / or have visited. The perfect meaning of the action of *hearing* is derived from the fact that the action took place at some undetermined point on the past and, crucially, it has present relevance for the conversation that they are engaged in. Notice also the vacillation between past and present in the last intervention of speaker A (*is was*). Speakers are annotated as A and Z, but Z's words are extra-corpus material (not in italics below).
A: *It I believe it's a kind of uh tourist attraction in Hong Kong now Besides the Peak uh*
Z: Uh ha Uh uhm uhm uhm Uh ha Uh Uh uh Yeah so uh Yeah probably would be Uh I'm in down full I got uh Oh what I like I go I'm used to same the places I know Because Uhm uhm I'm exploring some of the places.
A: *Same as in Wanchai I **heard** there's a nice big bar open up in Wanchai Right across the Banana It's downstair in the basement Have you been there.*
Z: Is that one uh the Big Apple.
A: *Is that what it's call.*
Z: Uh yeah that would be Yeah I have been there I think so.
A: *Yeah **Is** it **was** it good*

Tab. 9.2: Number and percentage of adverbial absence and presence by geographical variety

	BrE	HKE	SinE	IndE	PhilE	NigE	EAE	TOTAL
Adv Absent	636	1004	733	1000	628	802	745	5548
	72.5%	74.0%	71.7%	79.5%	75.4%	77.8%	74.8%	75.2%
Adv Present	241	353	289	258	205	229	251	1826
	27.5%	26.0%	28.3%	20.5%	24.6%	22.2%	25.2%	24.8%
TOTAL	877	1357	1022	1258	833	1031	996	7374

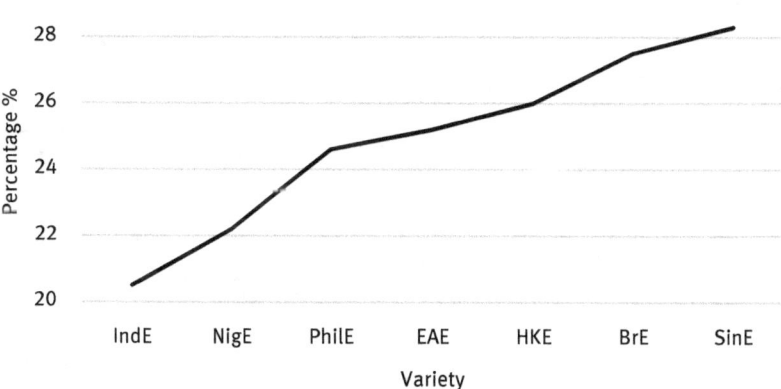

Fig. 9.2: Presence of adverbial per variety

The general data in table 9.2 indicate that verbs expressing perfect meaning take adverbial support in more than 20% of cases, and that this tendency is more pronounced in the L1 variety, BrE, than in L2s, with the sole exception of SinE, where the percentage (28.3%) is very similar to that of BrE (27.5%).

3.2 Structural contextual factors: Verbal form, verb type, polarity

This section turns to a description of contextual factors that have been mentioned in the literature as having an effect on the presence / absence of adverbials in the expression of perfect meaning (Seoane and Suárez-Gómez 2013; Seoane 2017). These factors, together with those in section 3.3, constitute potential predictors of the entrenchment of the adverbials in question, which will be statistically modelled in section 4. Table 9.3 below examines the distribution of verbal forms expressing perfect meaning with adverbial support by form and variety.

The data in table 9.3 seem to lend (weak) support to Miller (2000) and Brown and Miller's (2017) hypothesis in that in BrE the proportion of adverbial support with PrPf forms is high (25.4%), as they predict, or at least is higher than in L2s. However, more notable is the high proportion of adverbial support in preterite contexts, especially in BrE, HKE and EAE. For example, BrE exhibits 25.4% of adverbial support with PrPf forms and 45.4% in preterite forms. In other words, adverbials seem to appear more often with non-canonical forms, such as the preterite. These results, however, remain descriptive at this point and will be statistically tested in section 4.

Tab. 9.3: Distribution of contexts with adverbial support per verbal form in all varieties

	BrE	HKE	SinE	IndE	PhilE	NigE	EAE	TOT
Have + Pple	184 / 723 25.4%	231 / 941 24.5%	149 / 664 22.4%	136 / 975 13.9%	117 / 541 21.6%	139 / 700 19.9%	158 / 796 19.8%	1114 / 5340 20.9%
Preterite	49 / 108 45.4%	98 / 333 29.4%	118 / 307 38.4%	112 / 239 46.9%	81 / 261 31.0%	81 / 303 26.7%	81 / 172 47.1%	620 / 1723 36.0%
Be+Pple	6 / 41 14.6%	5 / 35 14.3%	7 / 27 25.9%	3 / 22 13.6%	5 / 26 19.2%	2 / 14 14.3%	3 / 12 25.0%	31 / 177 17.5%
Base form	1 / 3 33.3%	8 / 24 33.3%	8 / 11 72.7%	2 / 2 100%	–	4 / 6 66.7%	1 / 1 100%	24 / 47 51.1%
Pple	0 / 1 0.0%	6 / 15 40.0%	5 / 11 45.5%	1 / 14 7.1%	1 / 2 50.0%	0 / 1 0.0%	4 / 6 66.7%	17 / 50 34.0%
Other	1 / 1 100%	5 / 9 55.6%	2 / 2 100%	4 / 6 66.7%	1 / 3 33.3%	3 / 7 42.9%	4 / 9 44.4%	20 / 37 54.1%
TOTAL	241 / 877 27.5%	353 / 1357 26.0%	289 / 1022 28.3%	258 / 1258 20.5%	205 / 833 24.6%	229 / 1031 22.2%	251 / 996 25.2%	1826 / 7374 24.8%

The next variable considered concerns the interface between lexis and syntax and is meant to examine whether particular verbs facilitate the use of adverbial support.

Table 9.4 below shows the proportion of adverbial support per verb, with specification of the number of examples with an adverbial / total number of verb tokens, and in brackets the percentage of verb forms with an adverbial. Table 9.4 and the following ones group together all L2s so as to observe general tendencies on the effects of context, which might otherwise be lost due to the low number of examples.

Tab. 9.4: Distribution of adverbials per lexical verb

	BrE	L2s	Total
think	8/22 (36.4%)	60/144 (41.7%)	68/166 (41.0%)
hear	33/95 (34.7%)	120/649 (18.5%)	153/744 (20.6%)
see	53/171 (31.0%)	291/1098 (26.5%)	344/1269 (27.1%)
say	42/141 (29.8%)	334/1148 (29.1%)	376/1289 (29.2%)
get	19/65 (29.2%)	136/333 (40.8%)	155/398 (38.9%)
finish	8/29 (27.6%)	82/215 (38.1%)	90/244 (36.9%)
tell	10/42 (23.8)	119/570 (20.9%)	129/612 (21.1%)
come	24/105 (22.9%)	204/888 (23.0%)	228/993 (23.0%)
go	25/117 (21.4%)	146/777 (18.8%)	171/894 (19.1%)
give	19/90 (21.1%)	93/675 (13.8%)	112/765 (14.6%)
TOTAL	241/877 (27.5%)	1585/6497 (24.4%)	1826/7374 (24.8%)

Think is the verb with the highest percentage of adverbial support in both L1 and L2 varieties of English: 36.4% of all the examples of *think* take adverbial support in BrE and this percentage rises to 41.7% in L2 varieties, thus approaching half of all instances there. Examples like (6) below illustrate the strong connection between *think* with perfect meaning and the presence of an adverbial. Also frequent in BrE is the association between two verbs with the senses *hear* and *see* and the presence of adverbials (34.7% and 31% of cases here, respectively), both illustrated in (7). For L2s, the most frequent verbs collocating with adverbials to express perfect meaning (after *think*) are *finish* (38.1%) and *get* (40.8%, see examples (8) and (9)). Section 4 checks the statistical validity of these differences.

(6) since I was a little girl I've always **thought** of being an entrepreneur (ICE-NIG con_29)

(7) Although both of their parents (my wife and I) are Nyakyusa, the youths **have never seen** or **heard** (leave alone eaten) of Ikifuge – a delicious mashed sweet-potato (ICE-EA pphumanit)

(8) we **haven't finished** yet That's your problem (ICE-PHI S1A-076)

(9) he will be two on the 3rd of Dec , we all well over here , I **have** not **gotten** any job since I came bcos of the kind of my visa we are always given (ICE-NIG sl_02)

We now move on to examine polarity; Miller (2000: 337) and Brown and Miller (2017: 427–428) show that some clauses containing a PrPf form can only be acceptable in negative polarity contexts or if an adverbial is present. In (10) below, these two factors converge:

(10) ?*He has wanted a career in business* vs *He has never wanted a career in business*

An analysis of the distribution of adverbials in positive and negative contexts yields the results set out in Table 9.5, which shows the number of forms with an adverbial / the total number of forms, plus the percentage of adverbial forms, in brackets.

Tab. 9.5: Distribution of adverbials according to context polarity

	BrE	L2s	Total
Positive	211/788 (26.8%)	1234/5680 (21.7%)	1445/6468 (22.3%)
Negative	30/89 (33.7%)	351/817 (43.0%)	381/906 (42.1%)
TOTAL	877	6497	7374

The results in table 9.5 might be seen as corroborating Brown and Miller's (2017: 247–248) intuition that negative polarity contexts and the presence of adverbials privilege the use of present perfect meaning. However, the fact that almost half of the negative polarity contexts contain *never* (see example (10) above) undermines the force of these results. More interesting are the statistically significant differences observed for this variable between L1 and L2 varieties (X^2 *p_value* < 0.5). As we know, negative contexts are structurally and cognitively more complex than positive ones (e.g. Rohdenburg 2006: 149–150, 2015), and L2 varieties resort to adverbial support in negative contexts more frequently than BrE (43% in L2s vs 33.7% in BrE). This is closely related to the extralinguistic, macro-level context in which these varieties develop, situations of language contact, which often entail "a tendency to increase explicitness of linguistic encoding"

(Schneider 2013: 145). In other words, L2s often exhibit an increase in isomorphism with the aim of achieving transparency, a one-to-one correlation between form and meaning, and thus of avoiding ambiguity or miscommunication (see Leufkens's 2015 in-depth discussion on transparency). This search for transparency via increased isomorphism and even redundancy is also typical of learning processes in SLA contexts, which also characterize L2s.

3.3 Discursive factors: Mode, type of perfect meaning, and register

This section deals with predictors derived from the discursive context in which language takes place: oral vs written communicative exchange (*mode*), communicative intention (emphasis on results of the action, how recent the news is, etc.; that is, type of perfect meaning) and differences in audience, formality, extralinguistic setting, social function (*register*).

Starting with mode, Miller (2000) and Brown and Miller (2017) claim that it is in spoken English that the entrenchments of particular adverbials is taking place, but the preliminary results in table 9.6 do not seem to corroborate this for the ICE corpora. Here, the proportion of forms with an adverbial is practically the same for spoken and written BrE and L2s:

Tab. 9.6: Proportion of forms with adverbial support per mode

	BrE	L2	Total
Spoken	191/698 (27.4%)	1273/5191 (24.5%)	1464/5889 (24.9%)
Written	50/179 (27.9%)	312/1306 (23.9%)	362/1485 (24.4%)

Within contextual features, previous studies have also shown that for the study of perfect meaning it is crucial to examine the behaviour of the four broad types of perfect meaning independently (Seoane and Suárez-Gómez 2013: 13–16). The most widely recognized distinction is between resultative, experiential, recent-past (or hot news) and persistent situation perfect meaning, illustrated in (11) to (14) below (see Comrie 1976; see also Dahl 1999: 290–291; Dahl and Hedin 2000: 385–388; Miller 2000: 327–331; Huddleston and Pullum et al. 2002: 143–145). As mentioned in section 2, in order to discriminate subtypes of perfect meaning it was necessary to read large amounts of context, which helped me interpret the actual meaning of the verb and be consistent with the semantic classification of examples. Around 5% of the examples posed quite a semantic dilemma, especially between the resultative and experiential readings.

(11) *Because those people* **have not yet been given** *a chance to act in that capacity* (ICE-IND S1A-057)

(12) *Then, retention is also important, you must store a mental representation of what you* **have seen** (ICE-HK W1A-004)

(13) *This has been Talking Point, Alright Doctor Chua you've just* **heard** *uhm from a few calls Do you think that that's a fair assessment* (ICE-SIN S1B-029)

(14) *So I and I don't think I intend to stop because I see that it* **has** *really* **given** *me uh a lot of peace a lot of tranquility a lot of security uh uh and it has brought me closer I think to God* (ICE-PHI S1A-054)

First, some general results:

Tab. 9.7: Subtypes of perfect meaning in BrE and L2 varieties

	BrE	L2	Total
Resultative	548 (62.5%)	3906 (60.1%)	4454 (60.4%)
Recent past	169 (19.3%)	1479 (22.8%)	1648 (22.3%)
Experiential	146 (16.6%)	1022 (15.7%)	1168 (15.8%)
Persistent situation	14 (1.6%)	90 (1.4%)	104 (1.4%)
TOTAL	877	6497	7374

Table 9.7 shows that resultative meaning is by far the most frequent meaning of the perfect in the ICE components analyzed, with values at around 60%, making it the prototypical meaning of the perfect.

Figure 9.3 below shows the distribution of adverbials per perfect meaning. Given the relatively low number of occurrences expressing persistent situation, with percentages barely higher than 1% (see table 9.7), figure 9.3 focuses exclusively on the other three meanings. It describes the relationship between type of perfect meaning and adverbial use: the prototypical resultative meaning is predominantly expressed independently of adverbial support, whereas the expression of recent past and, to a lesser extent, experiential meaning, show a notable dependence on adverbial support. As for differences between BrE and L2s, these are in tune with the general finding that adverbials are more frequent in BrE in the three types of meaning (see table 9.7). Section 4 will provide the statistical relevance of this factor.

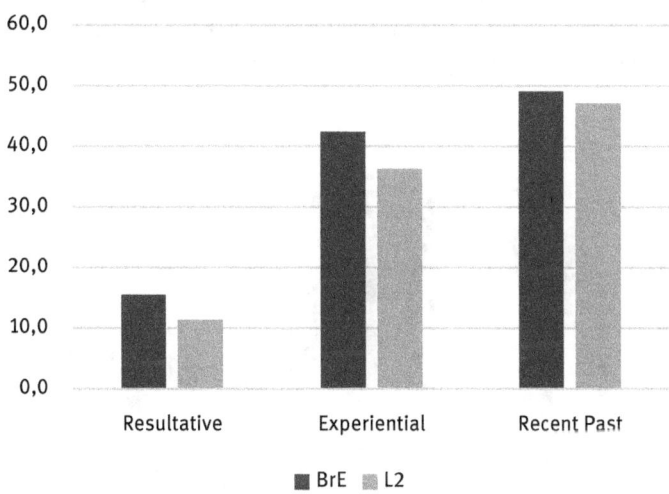

Fig. 9.3: Distribution (percentages) of adverbial support per meaning and variety

As noted in section 3.1, the analysis is not restricted to *just*, *(n)ever* and *yet*, but includes all adverbial expressions which specify the time frame of the action. As for the alleged predominance of *yet* (82 tokens) for the expression of resultative meaning predicted by Brown and Miller (2017: 245–248), this is not confirmed in the ICE corpus, since *already* (158 instances) is more frequent with this meaning.[6] Other adverbials for the expression of resultative meaning include *now* (34) and *today* (28), among others. Recent-past meaning is found frequently expressed with *just*, the adverb which takes the lead among adverbials with 272 examples,

---

[6] I am grateful to an anonymous reviewer who points out that *already* has acquired aspectual functions in L2 varieties such as SinE. The proportion of *already* with respect to the total number of adverbials is however similar or lower in L2s as compared with the L1 under study here, BrE. The distribution of *already* per corpus is the following. Within L2s, in HKE *already* represents 10.2% of all adverbials (36 out 353). In IndE *already* represents 7.4% of all adverbials (19 out of 258). In PhilE *already* is 12.1% of all adverbials (26 out of 215). In SinE *already* is 10.4% of all adverbials (30 out of 289). In EAE it is 5.6% of all adverbials (14 out of 251) and finally in NigE it is 4.4% of all adverbials (10 out of 229). As mentioned, the proportions are similar or lower than in BrE, where *already* represents 12.4% of all adverbials (30 out of 241).

as predicted in Miller (2000) and Brown and Miller (2017). Other adverbs expressing recent past are *now* (165), *today* (107), *this* + point on time (75), *in* + period of time (57) and *recently* (46). Finally, for the expression of experiential meaning, there is there is a clear predominance of *(n)ever*, with 302 occurrences, as Miller (2000) and Brown and Miller (2017) also state. Other adverbials are also registered, among them *since* (15 examples), *for* + period of time (13), and *so far* (7).

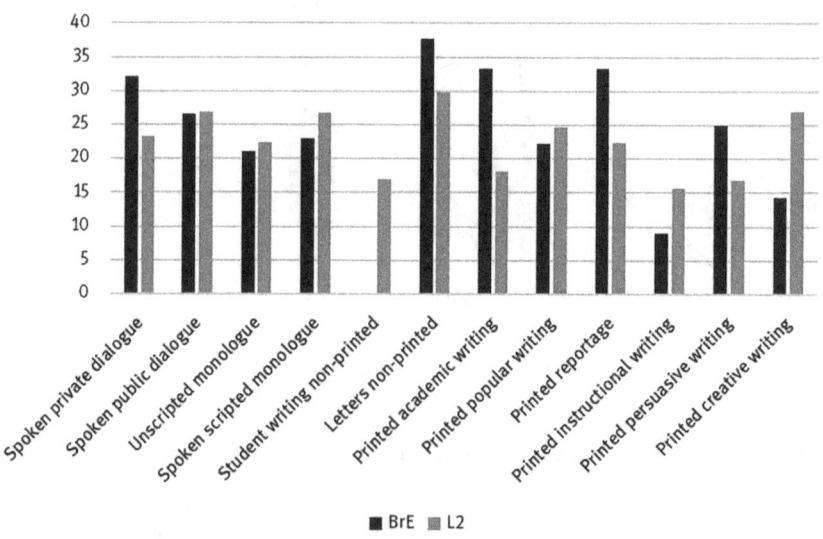

Fig. 9.4: Percentage of adverbial support per register

Figure 9.4 examines the interrelation between register and presence of an adverbial. Spoken registers are the first four on the left in the figure. It has been pointed out that some of the registers are heterogeneous due to cross-cultural differences in the interpretation of text types and decisions related to the compilation of the different components, and hence comparison of the same register between varieties is at times problematic (Mukherjee and Schilk 2012: 191; Hundt 2015: 383–385; Schaub 2016: 269). However, I believe that ICE remains a valid and indeed unparalleled corpus for the observation of general patterns of variability across registers, which is a methodologically necessary step in the study of linguistic variation (see Biber 2012; Biber and Gray 2013, 2016).

Whereas table 9.2 above shows that in the corpus as a whole 24.8% of the examples expressing perfect meaning take adverbial support, figure 9.4 shows how this proportion can oscillate between 0%, the level for non-printed student writing and 37%, for non-printed BrE social and business letters (29 examples with adverbial support out of 78), this despite the fact that both are non-printed written registers.

4 Data analysis

A multivariate approach via a regression analysis was considered to predict the presence/ absence of adverbial adjusting for different potential covariables. Analyses were performed using regression techniques based on generalized linear regression models (GLM, Nelder and Wedderburn 1972; McCullagh and Nelder 1989). Thus, a GLM regression model was considered with a binomial response distribution (using a logit function link) to investigate the factors that can affect the presence/absence of adverbial support. This model is expressed as follows:

(log(Adverbial) ~ Variety, Form, Lexical Verb, Polarity, Mode, Meaning, Register) (Model 1)

where *Adverbial* (Presence vs Absence) is the response variable and *Variety* (BrE vs L2 varieties), *Form, Lexical Verb, Polarity, Mode, Meaning and Register* are the covariates. Statistical analyses were performed using mgcv package (Wood 2017) of the open-source R software (R Core Team 2016). The results obtained are summarized in table 9.8 below.

All the variables analyzed, except for *mode*, have a significant effect on the choice between absence and presence of an adverbial to express perfect meaning. Starting with *variety*, BrE shows a significantly higher proportion of adverbials than L2 varieties: the probability of finding an adverbial in BrE is 35.3% higher than in the L2s under analysis (odds ratio 1.353; Confidence Interval with 95% (IC 95% in table 9.8: [1.131, 1.646]).

The covariate *form* is also statistically significant. More specifically, the preterite forms have a lower probability (62.6%) of being used with an adverbial than the present perfect form; the base form, on the contrary, takes adverbial support significantly more frequently than the PrPf. The model shows that *lexical verb* is also a significant predictor of adverbial presence and absence. Taking the verb *come* as reference level, *finish* and *get* disfavour presence of an adverbial (the probability of finding them with an adverbial expressing perfect meaning is 66.6% and 67% lower than for *come*), whereas *tell* favours it (the probability rises to 41.2%).

Tab. 9.8: Summary of the estimated linear effects for model 1 together with Odds Ratio (OR) and 95% Confidence Intervals (CI) for the estimated OR (*p-values* < 0.05 in bold type)

Predictor	Estimate	Std. Error	z-value	P-value	OR	CI 95% (OR)
Intercept	-0.881	0.128	-6.878	**< 0.001**		
Variety (Reference Level: *L2*)						
BrE	0.302	0.091	3.277	**0.001**	1.353	(1.131, 1.646)
Form (Reference Level: *Present Perfect*)						
Preterite	-0.469	0.084	-5.733	**< 0.001**	0.626	(0.531,0.737)
Be + past participle	0.233	0.192	1.214	0.224	1.262	(0.866,1.839)
Base Form	-1.492	0.4966	-3.005	**0.002**	0.225	(0.084,0.595)
Participle	0.604	0.326	1.851	0.064	1.829	(0.965,3.456)
Other	0.103	0.376	0.276	0.783	1.108	(0.530,2.316)
Lexical verb (Ref. Level: *Come*)						
Go	-0.068	0.123	-0.549	0.582	0.934	(0.734,1.188)
Give	-0.193	0.126	-1.539	0.123	0.824	(0.644,1.05)
Finish	-0.406	0.198	-2.046	**0.040**	0.666	(0.451,0.982)
Hear	0.001	0.126	0.010	0.991	1.001	(0.781,1.281)
Tell	0.345	0.132	2.609	**0.009**	1.412	(1.090,1.829)
Think	-0.369	0.240	-1.535	0.124	0.691	(0.431,1.106)
See	-0.051	0.110	-0.463	0.643	0.950	(0.765,1.178)
Get	-0.400	0.166	-2.393	**0.016**	0.670	(0.484,0.928)
Say	-0.113	0.113	-0.997	0.318	0.893	(0.715,1.114)
Polarity (Ref. Level: *Negative*)						
Positive	-1.261	0.09	-14.761	**< 0.001**	0.283	(0.239,0.335)
Mode (Ref. Level: *Spoken*)						
Written	0.041	0.079	0.518	0.604	1.042	(0.891, 1.215)
Meaning (Ref. Level: *Resultative*)						
Experiential	1.295	0.081	15.823	**< 0.001**	3.651	(3.117, 4.282)
Recent past	2.144	0.007	29.047	**< 0.001**	8.534	(8.417, 6.651)
Persistent situation	3.413	0.264	12.924	**< 0.001**	30.356	(18.093, 50.929)

Predictor	Estimate	Std. Error	z-value	P-value	OR	CI 95% (OR)
Register (Ref. Level: *Spoken private dialogue*)						
Spoken public dialogue	-0.247	0.09	-2.732	0.006	0.781	(0.654, 0.931)
Unscripted monologue	0.261	0.095	2.728	0.006	1.298	(1.077, 1.563)
Spoken scripted monologue	-0.014	0.1115	-0.123	0.902	0.986	(0.793, 1.227)
Student writing non-printed	0.408	0.244	1.675	0.093	1.504	(0.932, 2.425)
Letters non-printed	-0.191	0.139	-1.375	0.169	0.826	(0.629, 1.085)
Printed academic writing	1.337	0.22	6.064	<0.001	3.808	(2.473, 5.806)
Printed popular writing	-0.579	0.215	-2.686	0.007	0.560	(0.367, 0.854)
Printed reportage	0.304	0.197	1.541	0.123	1.355	(0.921, 1.993)
Printed instructional writing	1.067	0.275	3.877	<0.001	2.907	(1.696, 4.982)
Printed persuasive writing	-0.011	0.241	-0.045	0.964	0.989	(0.617, 1.583)
Printed creative writing	0.262	0.177	1.481	0.139	1.300	(0.918, 1.838)

Other conditions found to determine the use of adverbials are *polarity*, *meaning* and *register*. Negative polarity contexts are 71.7% more likely to take adverbial support than positive polarity ones. As for *meaning*, experiential, recent past and persistent situation perfect meaning strongly favour adverbial support as compared to resultative meaning, which is the reference level (p-value <0.001). The variable *register* is also seen to play a role in the entrenchment of adverbials, in that, taking spoken private dialogue as reference level, spoken public dialogue and printed popular writing have a statistically significant lower probability of being found with an adverbial (78.1% and 56% less probable, respectively), whereas unscripted monologue, printed academic writing and printed instructional writing favour adverbial presence (their probability of being found with an adverbial, compared to *come*, is 29.8%, 80.8% and 90.7% higher, respectively).

In the regression model, the variable *mode* turned out not to have a significant effect on adverbial presence (p-value 0.604). Therefore, differences between written and spoken registers do not seem to be responsible for the selection of adverbials to express perfect meaning.

4.1 Interpretation and discussion

The presence of adverbials denoting perfect meaning, which would indicate a potential entrenchment of such adverbials as perfect markers, is significantly more frequent, as already mentioned, in BrE than in L2 varieties and contexts (see table 9.8). From a UBT perspective we can formulate a tentative hypothesis regarding this finding: the degree of the entrenchment of adverbials as perfect markers in mental grammars depends on the degree of exposure to exemplars of such a use, and this is naturally lower in L2s developed in multilingual contexts. This difference between BrE and L2s largely corroborates Miller's (2000) and Brown and Miller's (2017) hypothesis in that adverbials act as perfect markers in BrE in particular, whereas the same cannot be said about L2s, where the proportion of adverbials is significantly lower.

Another finding that partially validates their hypothesis is that adverbials tend to collocate with the PrPf more often than with its stronger competitor, the preterite, which is an indication of the close semantic and contextual correlation between perfect verb form and perfect-meaning adverbial. As for the statistically significant more frequent presence of adverbials with base forms in the corpus (which occur mainly in L2 varieties, see table 9.3), this is understood as the need to overtly and explicitly express present perfect meaning with a verb form that does not express tense or aspect.

Lexical verb also plays a role in the entrenchment of adverbials for the expression of perfect meaning, especially in the case of *finish*, *get* and *tell* in comparison with *come*, the reference level. As for lexical semantics, *finish* and *get* are two activity verbs (according to Biber et al.'s 1999: 360–364 taxonomy) and disfavour the use of adverbials, whereas *tell*, a communication verb, favours the presence of an adverbial. This would tie in nicely with one of the postulates of UBT theory, which suggests that semantics does not determine the syntactic behaviour of verbs, but that each verb has its own unique syntactic print or set of collocational patterns which is stored as such in our mental grammars. However, other activity and communication verbs in the data do not show such strong effects on the choice of adverbial and therefore the effect of lexical semantics will be further explored in future research.

Negative polarity contexts, which are cognitively more complex than positive ones, favour the presence of adverbial support (especially in L2 varieties, see table 9.5). This tendency to adopt adverbials in negative environments can be interpreted as a strategy for fostering transparency, especially in L2s, in that explicit elements which are functionally relevant, such as adverbials indicating the time frame of the action, are preferred in complex contexts, as seen in other linguistic phenomena (see, e.g., Súarez-Gómez 2017a). This variable shows the effects of the macro-level, situational context on L2s, in that these show maximized explicitness of linguistic coding in complex environments, which leads to the use of one-to-one pairings between form and meaning (e.g. preterite + adverbial marker of perfect meaning) and even redundant patterns, as would be the case with PrPf forms + perfect-meaning adverbial. Hence, I am alluding here to the intersection between micro-level context factors (polarity) and macro-level context ones (contact settings, SLA processes), which shapes syntactic variation and change.

Two interpretations are possible for the fact that mode, that is, differences between spoken and written texts in the use of adverbials as perfect markers, is not a significant predictor. On the one hand, it has been argued that spoken language tends to represent more progressive tendencies in language, whereas written language is more conservative and only follows spoken innovations at a later and slower pace, leading McWhorter (2001: 17), for example, to claim that, "most written language is an artificial representation, omitting the signs of change which the real language, the spoken one, is full of". If this is the case, then the hypothesis that I am testing in this study is not confirmed, since the use of adverbials is practically the same in both modes, and thus there is no progressive entrenchment at work. On the other hand, these results may also indicate that using differences between spoken and written data to examine diachronic change is not methodologically valid, and that the cause of variation in this realm is found in other contextual factors. From this evidence it follows that studies using differences between spoken and written language as a proxy for diachronic differences (e.g., Collins 2009a, 2009b; Van der Auwera, Noël and De Wit 2012) do not necessarily yield reliable data, since other factors, such as register, might skew their findings. In fact, several studies have contradicted the common belief that "spoken language is *ceteris paribus* more progressive than written language" (Van der Auwera, Noël and De Wit 2012: 8), and have claimed that writing and speaking are "different grammatical enterprise(s)" and hence that their study needs to be undertaken separately (see Fox 2007: 299, 315). In relation to the hypothesis that I am testing, the entrenchment of adverbials cannot be said to take place predominantly in spoken text-types, since differences between spoken and written texts are not significant.

All categories of the factor type of perfect meaning favour the presence of an adverbial except for resultative meaning, which strongly disfavours it. Resultative meaning, being the most frequent and prototypical, does not seem to require adverbial support to convey its meaning. There is a twofold implication for this result: (i) adverbial support is necessary with rarer perfect meanings, which are more difficult to process, and thus adverbials would again be contributing to provide further explicitness and to ease comprehension; and (ii) the entrenchment of perfect markers would be taking place in the expression of experiential meaning and in the expression of recent-past perfect meaning, but would not be confirmed for the predominant meaning of the perfect, that is, the resultative one, contra Miller (2000) and Brown and Miller's (2017) hypothesis.

The results for the effect of register confirm that there is no divide between spoken and written texts, nor between printed and non-printed written texts, and that the topics covered do not determine the use of adverbials either: printed academic writing, which favours presence of an adverbial, discusses exactly the same disciplines as printed popular writing, which disfavours the use of adverbials, namely humanities, social sciences, natural sciences and technology. Other factors to be determined in future research must condition variation according to register, and they probably have to do with register-internal factors such as communicative purpose, social setting and intended audience. The crucial role of register in grammatical variation has been shown before, for example by Biber and associates, who in numerous works demonstrate that there are systematic differences in the patterns of linguistic variation between registers and sub-registers (Biber 2012; Biber and Gray 2013, 2016). Other studies have also found that register variation is indeed a strong predictor for variation: for example, the multivariate analysis of genitive variation in Szmrecsanyi and Hinrichs (2008: 307), register differences overriding geographical ones in Hundt and Smith's (2009: 57) study of present perfect forms in BrE and AmE, and modals being confronted with genre-dependent variability in Mair (2015: 214). In this study register is also seen to mediate in grammatical variation in ways that clearly deserve further research. Future explorations will deal with the clear intersection between type of perfect meaning and register (see Seoane 2017), since meaning is a powerful predictor for the presence/absence of adverbials. Another intersection is that between mode and register: whereas mode does not play a role in the choice of adverbials, some spoken and some written registers (but not all of them) affect the response variable. This will also need further analyses.

5 Conclusions

This study set out to explore the role of contextual features in the consolidation of the adverbs *just*, *(n)ever* and *yet* as perfect markers, as hypothesized by Miller (2000) and Brown and Miller (2017). The potential consolidation of adverbs is understood in terms of UBT, in such a way that the process would entail the progressive entrenchment of these adverbials as markers of perfect meaning in the mental grammar of speakers. The data for the study were extracted from the ICE corpus, thus allowing for the exploration of a wide range of different spoken and written registers in L1 and L2 varieties. This makes it possible to confirm whether such an ongoing process of entrenchment has filtered through to other Present-Day varieties of English and the potential influence of registers on language variation (Biber and Gray 2013, 2016).

The onomasiological analytical approach adopted allows us to demonstrate that the envelope of variation for the expression of perfect meaning is much wider than is usually recognized. The entrenchment of adverbials as perfect markers, therefore, should not be confined to PrPf forms but should examine all contexts conveying perfect meaning. This inclusive, holistic perspective also led me to examine all adverbial elements expressing perfect meaning, which has helped to confirm the relative entrenchment of *just* and *(n)ever* but not of *yet*, which is surpassed by *already* for the expression of resultative meaning.

The effect of contextual factors was analyzed using a GLM regression model with a binomial response distribution (see table 9.8). The results here show that rates of adverbial use are higher in the L1 variety analyzed, which is explained in terms of L2s having more limited exposure to exemplars of the use of particular adverbials as perfect markers.

The structural contextual factors on the micro-level that potentially motivate the distribution of adverbial markers in the corpus, namely the verbal form expressing perfect meaning, the lexical verb concerned, and the polarity of the clause (see section 3.2), are all predictors of adverbial presence/absence. The regression analysis shows that the entrenchment of adverbials as perfect markers is not as frequent with the preterite as it is with PrPf forms. This seems to validate the initial hypothesis that there is frequent use of adverbials of time associated with the expression of perfect meaning. Examination of the verbs that most frequently take adverbial support has led to the general conclusion that lexical factors condition the use and distribution of adverbials. The precise role played by lexical semantics, however, cannot be determined here and needs further analysis.

Negative polarity was confirmed to facilitate the presence of adverbials as makers of perfect meaning, though the results are to some extent undermined by the fact that *never* is both an adverbial perfect marker and a negative one (see table 9.5). More interesting in regard of this contextual variable is that negative contexts are structurally and cognitively more complex than positive polarity ones, which tend to call for more explicit forms of expression (i.e. with adverbial presence). This has been linked to the fact that our corpus contains a large number of L2 examples (6,497) which occur in contact-language contexts which often show increased isomorphism in complex structural environments such as negative ones.

The discursive factors that have been considered are mode, type of perfect meaning, and register (described in section 3.3). No significant differences are found between the spoken and the written mode, which calls into question the validity of studies using differences between spoken and written English as a proxy for diachronic change. However, type of perfect meaning is a strong contextual factor in the entrenchment of adverbials as perfect markers.

Since mode, topic and printed/non-printed differences do not model register variation in the choice of adverbial, the differences observed between registers are interpreted as having to do with register-internal factors, such as social function, intended audience and communicative purpose, which materialize in particular discourse conventions and thus serve to model syntactic variation (Bybee and Hopper 2001: 3; Neumann 2013: 16; Seoane 2017). This is in line with Bybee and Hopper's (2001: 3) conception of changes in structure "as an on-going response to the *pressure of discourse* rather than as a pre-existent matrix" (my emphasis). In other words, grammatical change is largely determined by context as captured in a broad conception of register. Thus, any approach to synchronic and diachronic grammatical variation must include and control for register variability.

The initial research question of this study concerned the role of context in the potential entrenchment of adverbials as perfect markers. This study has shown, in brief, (i) that there is a complex interplay of structural and contextual factors interacting to shape grammatical variation with independence of mode, and (ii) that the hypothesis by Miller (2000) and Brown and Miller (2017) that *just, (n)ever* and *yet* are becoming perfect markers in spoken BrE is only partially confirmed and in light of this study it would need to be refined as follows. Firstly, the potential entrenchment of adverbials adduced can be seen in BrE as they predicted, but not – or not yet – in L2 varieties. Secondly, only *just* and *(n)ever* are pervasive for the expression of recent past and experiential perfect meaning respectively; *yet*, however, is surpassed by *already* for the expression of resultative meaning. Thirdly, the entrenchment of adverbials does not take place in all types of perfect meaning, but only in the less prototypical and frequent ones, namely recent past and experiential meaning. Fourthly, the entrenchment of adverbs is not confined to the spoken language, since no significant differences were found for mode.

From a methodological perspective, I hope to have shown that attempts at rigorous descriptions of grammatical variation need to combine both a detailed qualitative analysis of the data (manual filtering, interpretation and grammatical analysis of all individual instances) and a quantitative analysis applying statistical modelling to the variation.

References

Adger, David & Graeme Trousdale. 2007. Variation in English syntax: Theoretical implications. *English Language and Linguistics* 11 (2). 261–278.
Biber, Douglas. 2012. Register as a predictor of linguistic variation. *Corpus Linguistics and Linguistic Theory* 8 (1). 9–37.
Biber, Douglas & Bethany Gray. 2013. Being specific about historical change: The influence of sub-register. *Journal of English Linguistics* 41. 104–134.
Biber, Douglas & Bethany Gray. 2016. *Grammatical complexity in academic English. Linguistic change in writing*. Cambridge: Cambridge University Press.
Biber, Douglas, Stig Johansson, Geoffrey Leech, Susan Conrad & Edward Finegan. 1999. *The Longman grammar of spoken and written English*. London: Longman.
Biewer, Carolin. 2008. South Pacific Englishes – unity and diversity in the usage of the present perfect. In Terttu Nevalainen, Irma Taavitsainen, Päivi Pahta & Minna Korhonen (eds.), *The dynamics of linguistic variation: Corpus evidence on English past and present*, 203–219. Amsterdam: John Benjamins.
Brown, Keith & Jim Miller. 2017. *A critical account of English syntax*. Edinburgh: Edinburgh University Press.
Bybee, Joan. 2006. From usage to grammar: The mind's response to repetition. *Language* 82 (4). 711–733.
Bybee, Joan. 2011. Usage-based theory and grammaticalization. In Heiko Narrog & Bernd Heine (eds.), *The Oxford handbook of grammaticalization*, 69–78. Oxford: Oxford University Press.
Bybee, Joan. 2013. Usage-based theory and exemplar representations of constructions. In Thomas Hoffman & Graeme Trousdale (eds.). *The Oxford handbook of construction grammar*. 49–69. Oxford: Oxford University Press.
Bybee, Joan & Paul J. Hopper. 2001. Introduction to frequency and the emergence of linguistic structure. In Joan Bybee & Paul J. Hopper (eds.), *Frequency and the emergence of linguistics structure*, 1–26. Amsterdam: John Benjamins.
Collins, Peter. 2009a. *Modals and quasi-modals in English*. Amsterdam: Rodopi.
Collins, Peter. 2009b. Modals and quasi-modals in World Englishes. *World Englishes* 28 (3). 281–292.
Comrie, Bernard. 1976. *Aspect*. Cambridge: Cambridge University Press.
Dahl, Östen. 1999. Perfect. In Keith Brown & Jim Miller (eds.), *Concise encyclopedia of grammatical categories*, 30–37. Oxford: Elsevier.
Dahl, Östen & Eva Hedin. 2000. Current relevance and event reference. In Östen Dahl (ed.), *Tense and aspect in the languages of Europe*, 385–401. Berlin: Mouton de Gruyter.
Davydova, Julia. 2011. *The present perfect in non-native Englishes. A corpus-based study of variation*. Berlin: Mouton de Gruyter.
Davydova, Julia. 2013. Detecting historical continuity in a linguistically diverse area. The present perfect in modern Singapore English. In Joana Duarte & Ingrid Gogolin (eds.), *Linguistic super-diversity in urban areas – Research approaches*. [Hamburg Studies on Linguistic Diversity], 193–225. Amsterdam: John Benjamins.
Dijk, Teun A. van 2008. *Discourse and context. A sociocognitive approach*. Cambridge: Cambridge University Press.

Elness, Johan. 2009. The present perfect and the preterite. In Günter Rohdenburg & Julia Schlüter (eds.), *One language. two grammars? Differences between British and American English*, 228–245. Cambridge: Cambridge University Press.

Engel, Dulcie & Marie-Eve Ritz. 2000. The use of the present perfect in Australian English. *Australian Journal of Linguistics* 20 (2). 119–140.

Fischer, Olga. 2007. *Morphosyntactic change. Functional and formal perspectives*. Oxford: Oxford University Press.

Foley, Joseph. 2001. Is English a first or second language in Singapore? In Vincent B. Y. Ooi (ed.), *Evolving identities. The English language in Singapore and Malaysia*, 12–32. Singapore: Times Academic Press.

Fox, Barbara. 2007. Principles shaping grammatical practices. *Discourse Studies* 9. 299–318.

Geeslin, Kimberly & Avizia Y. Long. 2014. *Sociolinguistics and second language acquisition*. London: Routledge.

Greenbaum, Sidney. 1996. *Comparing English worldwide: The International Corpus of English*. Oxford: Clarendon Press.

Huddleston, Rodney & Geoffrey K. Pullum. 2002. *The Cambridge grammar of the English language*. Cambridge: Cambridge University Press.

Hundt, Marianne. 2015. World Englishes. In Douglas Biber & Randi Reppen (eds.), *The Cambridge handbook of English corpus linguistics*, 381–400. Cambridge: Cambridge University Press.

Hundt, Marianne & Nicholas Smith. 2009. The present perfect in British and American English: Has there been a change, recently? *ICAME Journal* 33. 45–63.

Leufkens, Sterre. 2015. Transparency in Language. A Typological Study. Utrecht: LOT. Utrecht University, PhD dissertation. http://dare.uva.nl/document/2/155071 (accessed 15 June 2017).

Mair, Christian. 2015. Cross-variety diachronic drifts and ephemeral regional contrasts. An analysis of modality in the extended Brown family of corpora and what it can tell us about the New Englishes. In Peter Collins (ed.), *Grammatical change in English world-wide*, 119–146. Amsterdam: John Benjamins.

McCullagh, Peter & John A. Nelder. 1989. *Generalized linear models* (Monographs on Statistics and Applied Probability) 2nd ed. London & New York: Chapman and Hall.

McWhorter, John. 2001. *The word on the street. Debunking the myth of "pure" Standard English*. New York: Basic Books.

Miller, Jim. 2000. The perfect in spoken and written English. *Transactions of the Philological Society* 98 (2). 323–352.

Mukherjee, Joybrato & Marco Schilk. 2012. Exploring variation and change in New Englishes: Looking into the International Corpus of English (ICE) and beyond. In Terttu Nevalainen & Elizabeth C. Traugott (eds.), *The Oxford handbook of the history of English*, 189–199. Oxford: Oxford University Press.

Nelder, John A. & Wedderburn, Robert W.M. 1972. Generalized Linear Models. *Journal of the Royal Statistical Society* 135 (3). 370–384.

Neumann, Stella. 2013. *Contrastive register variation: A quantitative approach to the comparison of English and German*. Berlin: Mouton de Gruyter.

Pakir, Anne. 2001. The voices of English-knowing bilinguals and the emergence of new epicentres. In Vincent B. Y. Ooi (ed.), *Evolving identities. The English language in Singapore and Malaysia*, 1–11. Singapore: Times Academic Press.

Quirk, Randolph, Sidney Greenbaum, Geoffrey Leech and Jan Svartvik. 1985. *A comprehensive grammar of the English language*. London: Longman.
R Core Team. 2017. *R: A language and environment for statistical computing*. R Foundation for Statistical Computing. Vienna: Austria. https://www.R-project.org/
Rohdenburg, Günter. 2006. The role of functional constraints in the evolution of the English complementation system. In Christiane Dalton-Puffer, Nikolaus Ritt, Herbert Schendl & Dieter Kastovsky (eds.), *Syntax. style and grammatical norms: English from 1500–2000*, 143–166. Frankfurt: Peter Lang.
Rohdenburg, Günter. 2015. The embedded negation constraint and the choice between more or less explicit clausal structures in English. In Mikko Höglund, Paul Rickman, Juhani Rudanko & Jukka Havu (eds.), *Perspectives on complementation: Structure. variation and boundaries*, 101–127. Houndmills: Palgrave Macmillan.
Rooy, Bertus van. 2009. The shared core of the perfect across Englishes: a corpus-based analysis. In Thomas Hoffman & Lucia Siebers (eds.), *World Englishes: Problems – Properties – Prospects*, 309–330. Amsterdam: John Benjamins.
Rooy, Bertus van. 2016. Present perfect and past tense in Black South African English. In Valentin Werner, Elena Seoane & Cristina Suárez-Gómez (eds.), *Reassessing the present perfect. Corpus studies and beyond*, 149–168. Berlin: Mouton De Gruyter.
Schaub, Steffen. 2016. The influence of register on noun phrase complexity on varieties of English. In Christoph Schubert & Christina Sanchez-Stockhammer (eds.), *Variational text linguistics: Revisiting register in English*, 251–270. Berlin: Mouton de Gruyter.
Schneider, Edgar W. 2003. The dynamics of New Englishes: From identity construction to dialect birth. *Language* 79 (2). 233–281.
Schneider, Edgar W. 2007. *Postcolonial English: Varieties around the world*. Cambridge: Cambridge University Press.
Schneider, Edgar W. 2013. English as a contact language: The "New Englishes". In Daniel Schreier & Marianne Hundt (eds.), *English as a contact language*, 131–148. Cambridge: Cambridge University Press.
Schneider, Edgar W. 2018. World Englishes. *Oxford Research Encyclopedia of Linguistics*. Oxford: Oxford University Press. DOI: 10.1093/acrefore/9780199384655.013.27
Seoane, Elena. 2016. The perfect in creole-related varieties of English: The case of Jamaican English. In Valentin Werner, Elena Seoane & Cristina Suárez-Gómez (eds.), *Reassessing the present perfect. Corpus studies and beyond*, 195–221. Berlin: Mouton de Gruyter.
Seoane, Elena. 2017. Modelling morphosyntactic variation in World Englishes from a register perspective. *Miscelanea: A Journal of English and American Studies* 55. 109-133.
Seoane, Elena & Cristina Suárez-Gómez. 2013. The expression of the perfect in East and South-East Asian Englishes. *English World-Wide* 34 (1). 1–25.
Setter, Jane, Cathy Wong & Brian Chan. 2010. *Hong Kong English*. Edinburgh: Edinburgh University Press.
Suárez-Gómez, Cristina. 2017a. The role of transparency and language contact in the structural nativization of relative clauses in New Englishes. *English World-Wide* 38 (2). 212–238. (DOI 10.1075/eww.38.2.05sua)
Suárez-Gómez, Cristina. 2017b. The coding of perfect meaning in African, Asian, and Caribbean Englishes. *English Language and Linguistics*. First View (DOI org/ 10.1017/S1360674317 000508)
Suárez-Gómez, Cristina & Elena Seoane. 2013. 'They have published a new cultural policy that just come out': Competing forms in spoken and written New Englishes. In Kristin Bech &

Gisle Andersen (eds.), *English corpus linguistics: Variation in time. space and genre*, 163–182. Amsterdam & New York: Rodopi.

Szmrecsanyi, Benedikt & Lars Hinrichs. 2008. Probabilistic determinants of genitive variation in spoken and written English: A multivariate comparison across time, space, and genres. In Terttu Nevalainen, Irma Taavitsainen, Päivi Pahta & Minna Korhonen (eds.), *The dynamics of linguistic variation. Corpus evidence on English past and present*, 291–309. Amsterdam: John Benjamins.

Szmrecsanyi, Benedikt & Bernd Kortmann. 2011. Typological profiling: Learner Englishes versus indigenized L2 varieties of English. In Joybrato Mukherjee & Marianne Hundt (eds.), *Exploring second-language varieties of English and learner Englishes: Bridging a paradigm gap*, 167–187. Amsterdam: John Benjamins.

Thomason, Sarah G. 2001. *Language contact. An introduction*. Edinburgh: Edinburgh University Press.

Trousdale, Graeme. 2010. *An Introduction to English sociolinguistics*. Edinburgh: Edinburg University Press.

Van der Auwera, Johan, Dirk Noël & Astrid De Wit. 2012. The diverging need (to)'s of Asian Englishes. In Marianne Hundt & Ulrike Gut (eds.), *Mapping unity and diversity worldwide: Corpus-based studies of New Englishes*, 55–75. Amsterdam: John Benjamins.

Werner, Valentin. 2013. Temporal adverbials and the present perfect/past tense alternation. *English World-Wide* 34 (2). 202–240.

Werner, Valentin. 2014. *The present perfect in World Englishes: Charting unity and diversity*. Bamberg: University of Bamberg Press.

Werner, Valentin. 2016. Rise of the undead? BE-perfects in World Englishes. In Valentin Werner, Elena Seoane & Cristina Suárez-Gómez (eds.), *Re-Assessing the present perfect*, 259–294. Berlin: Mouton de Gruyter.

Werner, Valentin & Robert Fuchs. 2017. The present perfect in Nigerian English. *English Language and Linguistics* 21 (1). 129–153.

Werner, Valentin, Elena Seoane & Cristina Suárez-Gómez. 2016. *Re-assessing the present perfect*. Berlin: Mouton de Gruyter.

Wood, Simon N. 2017. *Generalized additive models: An introduction with R*. (2nd edn). London & New York: Chapman and Hall.

Yao, Xinyue & Peter Collins. 2012. The present perfect in World Englishes. *World Englishes* 31 (3). 386–403.

Yao, Xinyue & Peter Collins. 2013. Functional variation in the English present perfect: A cross-varietal study. In Kristin Bech & Gisle Andersen (eds.), *English corpus linguistics: Variation in time. space and genre*, 91–111. Amsterdam: Rodopi.

Yerastov, Yuri. 2015. A construction grammar analysis of the transitive *be* perfect in present-day Canadian English. *English Language and Linguistics* 19 (1). 157–178.

Martin Konvička
Paradigms, host classes, and ancillariness

A comparison of three approaches to grammatical status

Abstract: In this article, I assess three distinct functionalist approaches to grammatical status and discuss their commonalities as well as their differences. Fundamental to all analyzed proposals is the strict distinction between the expression and content side of the linguistic sign and the view that the functional properties of linguistic elements are primary in defining grammar. Some models work with deictic properties unique to grammatical elements, whereas others focus on the discursive behaviour of grams. The one point of convergence between these diverging proposals is, as I will argue, their reliance on the obligatoriness of grammatical structures. Furthermore, I compare how the individual models deal with the concept of gradable grammaticality and on what grounds, if at all, they discern different degrees of grammaticality.

1 Defining grammar

Every functionally-oriented[1] linguist has a more or less concrete idea of the purpose grammar serves and how to discern grammar from non-grammar.[2] Unfortunately, as Boye and Harder (2012: 1) rightly point out, "[i]t seems as if there has been a feeling that we all know what a grammatical expression is, and because of this the distinction has remained pre-theoretical and intuition-based".

---

1 The attribute *functional* is understood here as an umbrella term defined both in terms of what it is and what it is not. The former approach to functionalism serves as an overarching term for schools of thought such as cognitive, constructional, discourse and usage-based linguistics. The latter approach refers to any approach that is not formal.
2 I would like to thank the anonymous reviewers for their invaluable feedback that helped to rid the first version of this paper of some major flaws. I am also indebted to a number of colleagues and friends whose helpful questions and critical comments significantly contributed to improving the final version of the text. In this regard, I am especially grateful to Kristin Bech and Ruth Möhlig-Falke for their support. All remaining shortcomings are entirely my own.

Martin Konvička, Free University Berlin, English Department, Berlin, Germany,
martin.konvicka@fu-berlin.de

https://doi.org/10.1515/9783110682564-010

In this contribution, I will focus on three attempts that go beyond intuition-based definitions with the aim to provide robust theoretical foundations for the concept of grammatical status. I will look for commonalities and differences among these proposals in order to establish a better understanding of the notion of grammar in contemporary functional linguistics. In particular, I will look for answers to the following two questions: first, how is grammatical status defined within the model in question? Second, how does the model deal with the concept of gradable grammaticality?[3]

For the purposes of this paper, I will focus on the grammaticalization studies of the last four decades as the centrepiece of modern theory regarding grammatical status and grammatical change. Paradoxically, theoretical considerations about the nature of grammatical status within grammaticalization studies are scarce, as the following early comment by Himmelmann (1992: 2) illustrates: "Work in grammaticalization also hardly ever makes explicit the concept of grammar underlying a given investigation". Not much has changed since that time; thus Diewald (2011: 452) and Boye and Harder (2012: 1) could not but reiterate the original critique. The aforementioned scholars, unhappy about the theoretical foundations of the study of grammar, have all posited proposals regarding a theory of grammatical status.

Furthermore, although there seems to be a consensus that grammaticality is a gradable quality (but cf. Andersen 2006), "no one – to our knowledge – has attempted to specify what it means to be more or less grammatical", as Nørgård-Sørensen, Heltoft and Schøsler (2011: 21) point out. This means that apart from the still missing definition of the fundamental distinction between grammar and lexicon, we are also facing an open question of gradable grammaticality.

The lack of any satisfactory definition of the concept of gradable grammaticality is, however, not surprising if we consider the origins of the notion. The idea that grammatical elements can be hierarchically ordered on a cline was introduced in Kuryłowicz (1965: 69). As von Mengden (2016: 124–126) showed, however, Kuryłowicz's introduction of the concept was probably a mere by-product resulting from an inadvertent combination of Kuryłowicz's (1964) work on Indo-European inflectional categories and of the older tradition of grammaticalization research. The far-reaching implications for our understanding of grammar in the form of the concept of degrees of grammaticality will be addressed in this paper.

The functional approaches discussed in this paper, namely those of Himmelmann (1992), Diewald (2010), and Boye and Harder (2012), are all located

---

[3] With *gradable grammaticality* I mean the wide-spread concept of discriminating, mainly based on formal criteria, among different degrees of grammaticality.

somewhere between the two following theoretical positions. On the one hand, there is the structuralist/generative approach, in which a clear distinction is made between grammar and lexicon. This approach is represented by, for example, Roberts and Roussou (2003). The other pole of the continuum is occupied by constructional models such as the one by Traugott and Trousdale (2013), which seemingly discards the central distinction between lexicon and grammar. Describing language as a network of constructions stored in the constructicon (Goldberg 2006: 64) might seem to render the question of a theory of grammatical status irrelevant. However, even Traugott and Trousdale (2013) recognize the differences between contentful and procedural constructions, categories that correspond by and large with the traditional distinction between lexicon and grammar. This division, resembling Ullman's (2001) model, in which a distinction is made between procedural and declarative meaning, does not, however, provide sufficient criteria for defining procedural constructions.

Before proceeding to the individual models, one crucial point of the debate deserves clarification. Implicitly or explicitly, all of the models are defined against the backdrop of Lehmann's ([1982] 2015) parametric model of grammaticalization. Based on a set of six parameters, Lehmann's model, simplified for the purposes of this paper, is based around the central tenet that the form and function of an expression are tied together. The idea is schematically represented by means of a grammaticality cline (Hopper and Traugott 2003: 7) in (1).

(1) content item > grammatical word > clitic > inflectional affix

In line with the conceptual unity of form and function, the cline combines in itself functional changes (*content item > grammatical word*) as well as formal developments (*clitic > inflectional affix*). These two halves are by some, such as Traugott (2002: 27), seen as two separate, albeit connected, processes: primary and secondary grammaticalization (but cf. Breban 2014).

Linking the grammatical function of an expression to its form has at least the following two adverse effects. First, if applied consistently the link leads to false predictions language-internally. Not all grammatical expressions are recognized as such, while some lexical ones meet the formal criteria. Although the present perfect auxiliary in (2a) does not show any signs of coalescence, it is a grammatical word. It is true, however that the auxiliary *have* can be cliticized (2b), but the question arises whether the clitic really is more grammatical than the formally unreduced form (see Askedal 2008: 47). Furthermore, an example such as (2c) shows us how unreliable the formal diagnostics can be because lexical expressions can be reduced as well.

(2) a. *I have got a bicycle.*
 b. *I've got a bicycle.*
 c. *I've a bicycle.*

Using formal criteria as diagnostics of grammatical status therefore works only because we already know in advance that the expression at hand is grammatical. In that case, however, the changes in form do not serve as an indicator, but as a mere *a posteriori* confirmation of grammatical status.

Second, causally linking the form and the function of an expression also poses cross-linguistic difficulties. The languages of the world do not employ morphological means to express grammatical categories in the same fashion (see Bisang 2004: 116–117). Some languages, such as English (3a), use an analytic construction in those contexts in which languages such as Czech (3b) prefer a more synthetic construction.

(3) a. *Did you use to sing?*
 b. *Zpí-váv-al-s?*
   sing-ITER-PST-2SG
   'Did you use to sing?'

Following the logic behind the concept of grammaticality clines such as the one in (1), which posits that more bound expressions should be recognized as more grammatical, we would have to recognize the Czech construction (3b) as more grammatical than the English one (3a). As von Mengden (2016: 139) remarks, consistently following this argument would ultimately lead to "the language typology of the early nineteenth century, when analytic languages were seen as less developed".

Alternatively, to avoid the aforementioned unwanted implications, we would have to limit such a theory of grammatical status based on the conceptual unity of form and function to a specific language. We would have to adjust the relevance of the connection between form and function depending on the language at hand. A form-based model of grammatical status would have to work slightly differently in an analytic language such as English (3a) than in a language with rich morphology such as Czech (3b). Ideally, however, a theory of grammatical status should be valid cross-linguistically.

The search for a functional definition of grammatical status, as becomes obvious from the language-internal and cross-linguistic reasons sketched above, is intertwined with the question of gradable grammaticality. Only a small group of researchers, most notably Andersen (2006), wholly abandon the concept, while the majority more or less explicitly still retains it. If the concept is retained, the question arises how this notion is integrated with the general definition of grammatical status in light of these language-internal and cross-linguistic consistency criteria.

Against this backdrop introducing the challenges of establishing a model of grammatical status, the present discussion of the various models will revolve around the following three central questions. First, how do the models at hand define grammatical expressions as opposed to lexical ones? Second, how do these models deal with the notion of gradable grammaticality? Third, how broadly or narrowly do the models understand grammar?

The models discussed in the present contribution should not be understood as always mutually exclusive. Rather, in many ways they in fact complement each other. The present discussion of the three proposals serves a twofold function. First, as correctives with respect to other existing models of grammar. Second, as genuine attempts to better understand the role that grammar plays in the architecture of human language.

2 A deixis-based approach

First, we will turn to the model proposed by Diewald (1991, 1999, 2008, 2010). The reason for analyzing her contribution first is chronological but, more importantly, it stands out in comparison with the remaining two in terms of the chosen approach to grammatical status. In Diewald's model, the definition of grammatical expressions is not based on the discursive behaviour of grams, but rather on their distinct deictic properties.

The model is built upon "the concept of deixis as the focal criterion for defining grammar" (Diewald 2010: 37). Three types of deictic relations (4) are relevant for the description of grammatical expressions.

(4) a. Strong deictic relation
 b. Weak deictic relation
  i. Syntagmatic weak deictic relation
  ii. Paradigmatic weak deictic relation

While all three aforementioned kinds of deictic relations are found in grammatical expressions, only some of them are diagnostic of grammatical status. Strong deixis and syntagmatic weak deixis are found in lexical expressions as well. Only the third type of deixis is unique to grammatical expressions and will therefore be at the centre of the present discussion. In order to describe the model, however, the two other types of deictic relations have to be briefly addressed as well.

According to Diewald (2011: 458–459), deictic relations consist of a source, a path and a goal. Prototypically, the source of the deictic relation is the speaker, while the goal is the speech event. This is prototypically illustrated by the *strong deixis*. A classic example (Diewald 2011: 459) presents the grammatical category of tense, illustrated by the preterite form *wrote* in (5a). By using the past tense, the speaker establishes a strong deictic relation between the time of the event at hand, i.e. *writing dozens of letters*, and the time of utterance. Contrary to the present tense (5b), the preterite signals that "the narrated event is distant" (Diewald 2011: 459) temporally speaking. The source is the speaker, the goal is the narrated event and the path is the distance between the former and the latter.

(5) a. *She wrote dozens of letters.*
     b. *She writes dozens of letters.*

The same deictic relation, however, can also be observed in lexical expressions, as the examples in (6) show. The element *here* in (6a) expresses a comparable deictic relation in spatial terms as the present tense in (5b) does in temporal terms, namely that the location denoted by *here* is not distant from the speaker. In (6b), on the other hand, the location of the cat is specified as being distant from the speaker.

(6) a. *The cat is lying here.*
     b. *The cat is lying there.*

The second type of deictic relation that Diewald (1991: 28, 54–58, 2010: 40) employs in her model are the *weak deictic relations*. Rooted in the traditional distinction between the syntagmatic and paradigmatic organization of linguistic signs, weak deictic relations can be of two kinds: syntagmatic and paradigmatic.

Syntagmatic weak deictic relations occur between individual expressions realized in a given syntagm. Two examples, taken from Diewald (2010: 43), are given in (7). The pronoun *it* and its anaphoric antecedent *the cat* in the preceding sentence are connected by a weak deictic relation (7a). Similarly, in (7b) a weak deictic relation connects the two clauses by means of the conjunction *but*.

(7) a. *The cat tried to get back into the house. It jumped onto the window sill and pressed itself against the pane.*
     b. *She wanted to make a call, but she could not find her mobile.*

Different from the cases of strong deictic relations in (5) and (6), weak deictic relation in (7) is established between two syntagmatically ordered linguistic signs and not between the speaker and another location. As has been said earlier, the strong and syntagmatic weak deictic relations are both not unique to grammatical expressions. Clearly lexical elements such as the nouns *mother* or *daughter* and adverbs *down* or *in the front* are also tied to other linguistic signs (Diewald 2010: 44). This means that although syntagmatic weak deictic relations do characterize grammatical expressions, they cannot be used as diagnostics of grammatical status.

Diewald's model is therefore centred around the second kind of weak deictic relations: the weak deictic relations on the paradigmatic axis. This type should, unlike weak deixis on the syntagmatic axis, be unique to grammatical signs. It pertains to the relations between linguistic signs organized in a paradigm.

It is important to note that Diewald does not understand paradigms in the traditional narrow sense of *inflectional paradigms*. Rather, similar to Nørgård-Sørensen, Heltoft and Schøsler (2011: 45), the essence of a paradigm lies not in its formal properties, but in the "alternations between members of a limited set of complex signs". These alternations among the individual paradigm members are ensured, according to Diewald, by the existence of weak deictic relations among them.

As an illustration, I will use the traditional example of the inflectional paradigm of the German masculine noun *der Tag*, as discussed by Diewald (2010: 24). A paradigm with periphrastic constructions or word order variables would not be different in principle.

Each paradigm, as outlined in Diewald's (2010: 45) model, has one unmarked member constituting the zero point of the paradigmatic weak deictic relation. In the case of the inflectional paradigm of the German noun phrase *der Tag* in (8), it is the nominative case (8a). The other members of the paradigm, in this case the oblique cases (8b), (8c), and (8d) are marked. Against this backdrop, the deictic path is established between the marked and unmarked member.

(8) a. nominative case, *der Tag*
b. accusative case, *den Tag*
c. genitive case, *des Tages*
d. dative case, *dem Tag(e)*

In the introductory section of the present paper, I asked two questions. The first pertains to how grammar is defined in the individual models. The second question is how those models approach gradable grammaticality.

As far as the first question is concerned, it is the weak deictic structure of paradigms that discriminates grammatical expressions from lexical ones in Diewald's model. The paradigmatic weak deictic relation among the members of a paradigm is closely linked to the parameters of paradigmaticity (Lehmann [1982] 2015: 141–146) and paradigmatic variability (Lehmann [1982] 2015: 146–152) or obligatoriness, which is defined as the lack of paradigmatic variability. Obligatoriness and paradigmaticity are, according to Diewald (2010: 22), "two sides of the same coin." Obligatoriness, as an implication of paradigmatic ordering, will be discussed in more detail below.

As to the second question of defining gradable grammaticality, Diewald takes an unorthodox approach to the issue. Rather than linking the degrees of grammatical status to the formal properties of the grams in question, such as bondedness or phonetic reduction, the model links gradable grammaticality to the different types of deictic relations discussed earlier. Because the three kinds of deictic relations are not mutually exclusive, they are "present in a grammatical item to varying degrees" (Diewald 2011: 461).

This can be explained using the example of the preterite (9a). As discussed earlier, tense is an example of a grammatical expression that establishes a strong deictic relation. At the same time, however, the preterite is also in a paradigmatic weak deictic relation with other possible tense realizations given in (9b) and (9c).

(9)   a. *She wrote dozens of letters.*
      b. *She writes dozens of letters.*
      c. *She will write dozens of letters.*

In a similar vein, the examples in (10) show a combination of syntagmatic and paradigmatic weak deixis expressed by the conjunctions *but* or *although*. On the one hand, the conjunctions connect the two clauses by means of a syntagmatic weak deictic relation, while on the other hand, each individual conjunction stands in a weak paradigmatic relation to other conjunctions that could have been used instead, but were not.

(10) a. *She wanted to make a call, but she could not find her mobile.*
      b. *She wanted to make a call, although she could not find her mobile.*

Although the concept is merely touched upon and not elaborated in much detail, Diewald (2011: 461) suggests that "deictic categories [represent] the semantically richer, less grammaticalized stages and highly abstract, intra-paradigmatic oppositions [represent] older, more grammaticalized stages". Before continuing with a discussion of the various combinations of deictic relations in grammatical expressions, a note about the above quote is in place. Although it is only a short passage, Diewald connects the degrees of grammaticality not only with the type of deictic relations, but also with the semantic content of a given gram. Much like Lehmann's ([1982] 2015: 131) parameter of integrity, Diewald links the degree of grammaticality also with the level of desemanticization. Less grammatical(ized) grams are semantically richer, while more grammatical(ized) items have a more abstract meaning. More grammatical(ized) items are, furthermore, older and represented by intra-paradigmatic (see intra-paradigmatic variability in Lehmann [1982] 2015: 147) rather than strong deictic relations.

As any grammatical item is inherently involved in a paradigmatic weak deictic relation to the remaining members of its paradigm, four logical combinatorial deictic possibilities emerge. First, a combination of paradigmatic weak deixis and strong deixis (9). Second, a combination of paradigmatic weak deixis with syntagmatic weak deixis (10). Third, a combination of paradigmatic weak deixis together with strong as well as syntagmatic weak deixis. Finally, the presence only of paradigmatic weak deixis. Whether all of these combinations are equally plausible and how evenly they are distributed would be a question of possible further empirical research.

With respect to paradigmatic weak deictic relations, or in other words paradigmatic ordering, as the defining feature of grammatical status, it has to be noted that it is not unproblematic for at least two reasons. First, looking at the examples in (11), I want to argue that even linguistic signs in the lexical domain are arranged in paradigmatic or paradigm-like relations. A case in point could be antonyms, synonyms or near-synonyms.

(11) a. *The dog is outside.*
　　 b. *The mutt is outside.*
　　 c. *The hound was outside.*

Just as the verb *is* in examples (11a) and (11b) is in a paradigmatic weak deictic relation with its past-tense form *was* in (11c), it can also be said that the nouns *dog* (11a), *mutt* (11b) and *hound* (11c) are paradigmatically linked together. The difference is, of course, the degree of paradigmatic variability (see Lehmann [1982] 2015: 146). On the other hand, both the nominal paradigm and the verbal paradigm have marked as well as unmarked members. In case of the nominal paradigm, *dog* is presumably the unmarked member, while the present tense of the copula is the unmarked member in the verbal paradigm.

Second, as Boye and Harder (2012: 4) point out, paradigm membership is arguably also a property of all the lexical verbs in (12). Verbs that allow a bare infinitive as complement, such as *see* (12a) or *hear* (12b), are members of a paradigm. Verbs such as *persuade* (12c), which do not allow a bare infinitive as a complement, are not members of that particular paradigm but form a different one, as shown by the fact that (12c) is not a well-formed sentence. If we accept this, paradigmatic weak deictic relations cannot be taken to be a diagnostic of grammatical status.

(12) a. *I saw him run.*
b. *I heard him run.*
c. **I persuaded him run.*

Another criticism of Diewald's model pertains to its static nature. If we disregard the potential issue concerning the fact that paradigmatic relations might not be unique to grammatical expressions, we are still faced with the question of the development of paradigmatic weak deictic relations. The different kinds of deictic relations linked with different types of linguistic signs enable a synchronic description. A dynamic, diachronic perspective is, however, missing.

Furthermore, as we saw earlier in the discussion, paradigmatic ordering is closely linked with obligatoriness. In Lehmann's parametric model, obligatoriness pertains to grammatical categories and it is understood as the "converse equivalent of 'transparadigmatic variability'" (Lehmann [1982] 2015: 148). That means that the speaker cannot leave the grammatical category in question unspecified. A case in point given in Lehmann ([1982] 2015: 14) is the category of number in Latin. Every single noun is always either singular or plural. Nouns unspecified for number are not possible, which means that number is an obligatory category in Latin. In Turkish, on the other hand, number is not obligatory because there are also contexts where nouns can remain unspecified.

In Diewald's approach to grammatical status, obligatoriness is understood slightly differently. First of all, it is understood as a property of paradigm members, not of categories. Second, Diewald distinguishes two types of obligatoriness: *language internal* and *communicative obligatoriness* (Diewald and Smirnova 2010: 100).

Both obligatoriness types are linked to the concept of paradigmatic weak deixis and to paradigmatic organization of linguistic signs. The two obligatoriness types describe the conditions under which a language speaker is obliged to select a particular member of a paradigm over the others. In the case of language-internal obligatoriness, the selection of a paradigm member is steered by the linguistic co-text, whereas communicative obligatoriness describes the selection of a paradigm member steered by the communicative intentions of the speaker instead.

Language-internal obligatoriness is illustrated by (13). The verbal suffix -s has to be realized because the verb *own* is used in the third person singular. The realization of the suffix is therefore dependent on the internal rules of grammar. Diewald paraphrases this type of obligatoriness as follows: "*If form x, then form y*" (Diewald and Smirnova 2010: 100). In this sense, Diewald's language-internal obligatoriness comes close to Lehmann's ([1982] 2015: 148) obligatoriness defined as the lack of paradigmatic variation.

(13) *He own-s a bike.*

In (14), however, we see a different situation. The choice between the active voice (14a), the *be* passive (14b) and the *get* passive (14c) does not depend on any language-internal rules as was the case in (13). Rather, the choice of the passive over the active construction and the further choice of one of the passive constructions over the other depends on the speaker's communicative goals and can be paraphrased in the following way: "*If intention x, then form y*" (Diewald and Smirnova 2010: 101).

(14) a. *He got a promotion.*
  b. *He was promoted.*
  c. *He got promoted.*

This brings us back to the question of whether paradigmatic ordering really is unique to grammatical expressions. Using the examples in (11) (repeated here as (15)), I argue that lexical elements also enter into paradigmatic weak deictic relations. The argument becomes even stronger against the backdrop of the concept of communicative obligatoriness. Depending on the communicative intentions of the speaker, they can choose from the different possibilities to refer to a 'dog'. Just as the active voice (14a) is presumably the unmarked member of the voice paradigm in (14), so is the noun *dog* (15a) the unmarked member in the lexical paradigmatic structure in (15). It does not mean that communicative obligatoriness does not pertain to grammatical expressions, but it means that it applies to lexical expressions as well.

(15) a. *The dog is outside.*
  b. *The mutt is outside.*
  c. *The hound was outside.*

Diewald's proposal regarding obligatoriness as one of the defining properties of grammatical expressions has been criticized by Boye and Harder (2012: 5) for arguably not covering all non-controversial grammatical expressions, and they suggest noun classifiers, gender distinctions and derivational affixes, such as the English ending *-ing*, as examples. This criticism, however, seems unwarranted. Irrespective of the size of a given paradigm, even if it has only one member, this member would still, by weak deictic means, "encode [...] its position in the paradigm itself" (Diewald 2010: 44). Following the principles of communicative obligatoriness, one can argue that the use of the derivational suffix *-ing* is steered by the communicative intentions of the speakers. As I said earlier, however, this is not something pertaining only to grammar.

In sum, what we have seen as a proposal for defining grammar, based on the deictic relations within a paradigm, offers a theory of grammatical status that does not suffer from the shortcomings caused by the conceptual unity of form and function discussed in the introduction. Although Diewald's deixis-based model of grammatical status is a valuable addition to the discussion about the nature of grammar, its reliance on paradigmatic ordering may still not be sufficient to discern grammatical signs from lexical ones. Apart from the concept of paradigmatic weak deictic relations, the model discussed in the current section also recognizes one further key feature of grammatical elements. Grammatical signs, Diewald (2010: 40) writes, "do not have the potential to refer independently; they have to be combined with a lexical entity". The realization that grammatical elements are structurally dependent on others underlies the two remaining models.

3 Discourse-based approaches

3.1 Himmelmann (1992)

Embedded in the tradition of emergent grammar (Hopper 1987, 1988), Himmelmann's (1992) model is premised on the discursive properties of linguistic signs from grammatical ones. The focus on the discursive behaviour of grams connects Himmelmann's approach to Boye and Harder's (2012) proposal. The latter model is analyzed in more detail in the following section, but points of convergence will be highlighted already in the present section. The model explicitly focuses on the dynamics of grammaticalization (see Himmelmann 1992: 2) and does not limit itself to a static description of the differences between lexical and grammatical expressions. Although Himmelmann's model is only a sketch and not all details are fleshed out, it still represents a valuable contribution to the discussion of grammatical status.

The central tenet of the proposal is the primacy of discourse above any preconceived language system. Any regularities are the product of frequent repetition in discourse. Any linguistic structure therefore exists only *a posteriori* and any *a priori* ideas about grammar – or about lexicon – have to be rejected (see Hopper 1987: 144). This is in line with Becker's (1988) concept of *languaging*, that is, of language in constant flux.

In Himmelmann's model, every linguistic sign either enjoys the status of a full sign or has a reduced status. In the latter case, the linguistic sign in question can occur only in combination with at least one other full sign. The status of a linguistic sign is, however, not always stable and can change over time if the right conditions are met.

Let us start with an idealized scenario in which two linguistic signs of the same status appear repeatedly alongside each other. Given the two options regarding their sign status described earlier, there are three possible developmental pathways for the two signs. First (16a), the status of two cooccurring signs remains unchanged. Second (16b), it is possible that the two linguistic signs eventually fuse, resulting in one new linguistic sign. Finally (16c), one of the two erstwhile equal signs eventually loses its full status and becomes structurally dependent on the other sign which retained its status.

(16) a. Full sign A + full sign B > full sign A + full sign B
 b. Full sign A + full sign B > full sign C
 c. Full sign A + full sign B > full sign A + reduced sign B

Examples of the processes in (16a) and (16b) are provided in (17a) and (17b) respectively. While (17a) shows repetition in discourse without consequences, (17b) is an example of univerbation.

(17) a. *we sing* > *we sing*
 b. Old English *dæges eage* 'day's eye' > Present-day English *daisy*

To illustrate the process in (16c),[4] let us look at the well-researched grammaticalization of the English *going to*-V-future construction (see Hopper and Traugott

---

[4] Boye and Harder, whose model is discussed in the following section in more detail, refer to processes of the type (16c) as *ancillarization* (Boye and Harder 2012: 22). The expression undergoing this process gradually loses its ability to be discursively primary and becomes *ancillary*.

2003: 1) which is also comparable with other instances of auxiliarization. The first step in the process, here schematically simplified, is the cooccurrence of two full verbs *go* and *marry* in (18a). The verbs are independent of each other and both have the status of a full sign. In the second step, however, as indicated in (18b), the relationship between the two erstwhile independent signs changes, because it allows for the interpretation of one of them as an auxiliary while the other one retains its original full verb status. Apart from this reading, the older interpretation as in (18a) is also still possible. That changes, however, in (18c) when the auxiliary status of *go* is the only viable interpretation left.

(18) a. *I am going to the church to marry David.*
 b. *I am going to marry David.*
 c. *I am going to enjoy the wedding.*

The gradual shift from (18a) to (18c), a process of the type (16c), starts off with two erstwhile independent, full linguistic signs and leads to a diminished dependent status of one of them. In other words, one of the verbs, in this case the finite form of the verb *to go*, in this particular construction loses its ability to occur on its own and has to cooccur with another verb as a result. The diminished status of grammatical signs is the result of frequent enough repetition in discourse. The loss of full status and the ability to occur on its own in discourse leads to the obligatory cooccurrence of grams with lexemes. This group of signs that can cooccur with the gram is termed *carrier class* (Himmelmann 1992: 18). In later works, they are called *host classes* (Himmelmann 2004: 32) instead.

In Himmelmann's (1992: 16) terms, processes such as (16a) and (16b) would count as instances of lexicalization,[5] while (16c) is an example of grammaticalization. The two processes can be distinguished by comparing their input with their output. Whereas grammaticalization involves a discursively independent sign becoming discursively dependent on a host class, lexicalization leaves the status of the sign in question either unchanged or the sign becomes discursively independent. This line of reasoning and connecting the grammatical or lexical status of an expression to its discursive behaviour in relation to cooccurring expressions is reminiscent of Boye and Harder's (2012: 7) conception of grammaticalization as a process whereby an expression becomes discursively secondary.

An ancillary expression is restricted in its discursive behaviour and needs to be accompanied by a another, discursively primary expression.
5 What is meant by the process in (16a) is the fact that the combination of signs is repeatedly used in discourse. The fact that nothing changes is only one possible outcome.

One further important aspect of Himmelmann's model (1992: 22), already briefly mentioned earlier, is the notion of *carrier* or *host classes*. To get back to the example in (18b), the grammatical element *going to* does not become dependent only on one particular full sign, in this case *marry*. Rather, the grammatical element becomes dependent on a larger class of expressions, i.e. *host classes*. As a result, not only can *am going to* be combined with *marry* (18b), but also with other verbs such as *enjoy* (18c). These carrier or host classes can be compared to the more traditional parts of speech with which they, however, do not necessarily overlap.

To summarize, the present model of grammar and grammaticalization has one major advantage in comparison with the deixis-based model, discussed in the preceding section, in that it incorporates the dynamics of language change. Whereas in Diewald's proposal the mechanism of change from strong deixis to weak deixis is not described, Himmelmann's emergentist model offers an answer with its changing relations of linguistic signs to other cooccurring signs. In terms of Diewald's proposal, the distinction between grammatical and lexical signs can be explained by their differing syntagmatic relations rather than paradigmatic ones.

Against this backdrop, two crucial aspects of Himmelmann's proposal should be stressed. First, not all linguistic signs are equal, discursively speaking. There are full signs that can occur on their own and there are linguistic signs of diminished status that have to cooccur with others. Second, the obligatory cooccurrence of grammatical signs with a member of their host classes becomes crucial. This is in fact an aspect connecting Himmelmann's proposal to Diewald's model, although it is not highlighted in either of them.

To better understand the connection between the two models, let us turn to the simple example given in (19).

(19) *Judy like-s to sing.*

Against the backdrop of Diewald's approach, as discussed in the previous section, agreement between the subject and the verb based on grammatical number is responsible for the obligatory use of the verbal suffix *-s* in *sings*. Using the paraphrase from Diewald and Smirnova (2010: 100) we can say something like: *if third person singular, then -s*.

If we now look at Himmelmann's proposal, I would like to argue that Diewald's concept of language-internal obligatoriness is to a certain extent a mirror image of Himmelmann's dependence of grammatical signs on their host classes. On the one hand, Diewald argues that a given member of a grammatical paradigm is chosen based on a preceding form. In Himmelmann's model, on the other hand, the grammatical expression that obligatorily cooccurs with an expression of undiminished status constrains this expression by virtue of its host class, as the examples in (20) illustrate. The dependent grammatical expression *gonna* requires that one member of its host class, in this case a full verb such as *enjoy* in (20a), must cooccur with it. The phrase *the event* does not belong to the host class of *gonna* and cannot cooccur with it, which explains the ungrammaticality of (20b).

(20) a. *I'm gonna enjoy the event.*
    b. **I'm gonna the event.*

Having addressed the question of defining grammar in Himmelmann's model, let us now briefly turn to the question of gradable grammaticality. The binary division between full and diminished signs does not seem to allow for any distinction of degrees of grammaticality. Nevertheless, Himmelmann (1992: 12) quotes Kuryłowicz (1965) and uses such formulations as "degree of grammaticalization" (Himmelmann 1992: 8), "later stage of grammaticalization" (Himmelmann 1992: 25) or writes "that a prepositionally expressed DATIVE is different from one that in inflectionally expressed in that it is less grammaticalized" (Himmelmann 1992: 10).

This would suggest at least an implicit adherence to the idea of gradable grammaticality. At the same time, however, Himmelmann (1992: 25) recognizes that these formal changes are not diagnostics of grammatical status. He admits that some grammatical expressions coalesce while others do not and emphasizes the typological differences among languages in this regard. It seems, therefore, that the implicit presence of gradable grammaticality is more likely due to terminological traditions than to any central role of the concept in his model.

Concluding, both the reliance on discursive behaviour and the dependence of diminished grammatical linguistic signs on host classes consisting of full lexical signs are tenets present in this model as well as in the recent one proposed by Boye and Harder (2012). Although the two models show some striking commonalities, Boye and Harder (2012) do not quote any work by Himmelmann at all and nothing seems to suggest that they have been influenced by his model. The commonalities between them are therefore probably merely coincidental.

3.2 Boye and Harder (2012)

Like Himmelmann's proposal, Boye and Harder's (2012) theory of grammatical status also presupposes the primacy of discourse before structure, so these two models can be subsumed under the umbrella term *discourse-based approaches*. Boye and Harder's approach is understood to be usage-based (see von Mengden and Coussé 2014 for a discussion of the term) and embedded, moreover, in a wider cognitive approach to language, represented by Relevance Theory (Nicolle 1998; Wilson and Sperber 1993) and Cognitive Grammar (Langacker 2008). Following Sperber and Wilson's cognitive relevance model, utterances consist of conceptual and procedural types of information. To give just one example, a noun such as *house* conveys the conceptual information 'house', whereas grams such as *-s* and *the* in *the house-s* convey procedural information to help process the conceptual information. Despite the similarities, the link between Boye and Harder's discursively primary and secondary expressions and Sperber and Wilson's conceptual and procedural information is not straightforward. Nicolle (1998: 6) points out that discourse connectives such as *so* and *after all* convey procedural meaning, but are nevertheless not grammatical.

Against this backdrop, the centrepiece of the model is the notion of discourse prominence. This is not understood as something exclusively linguistic, but as a general cognitive principle of prioritizing incoming information. Some cognitive input is analyzed as more important in relation to the rest. In terms of linguistic signs, being discursively prominent means, simply put, to be assessed as more important than the other signs cooccurring in the discourse.

Whereas lexical expressions may or may not, in actual communication, convey the main point of a linguistic message, grammatical expressions (morphemes, words, constructions) are conventionally specified as noncarriers of the main point, serving instead an ancillary communicative purpose as secondary or background elements (Boye and Harder 2012: 6–7). Discourse prominence is, however, not a static property that is inherently assigned to a specific sign. Rather, discourse prominence is a scalable quality and the prominence of a given expression can be determined only in relation to the prominence of at least one other expression. This also means that it is not possible to establish the discursive status of a sign in isolation and that context is always of central importance.

If the speakers recognize a given expression as discursively prominent, this expression is recognized as discursively primary compared to other signs in its syntagm. The rest of the syntagm is in turn, by definition, discursively not prominent and therefore ancillary in relation to the discursively primary sign. Up to this point, Boye and Harder's approach resembles Himmelmann's, inasmuch as it posits two types of elements participating in discourse as well – discursively primary or full and discursively secondary or diminished. There are, however, at least two important differences. The first relates to the role of repetition in discourse. The second is the dynamic nature of discourse prominence in Boye and Harder's model.

Whereas in Himmelmann's model frequent repetition in discourse is the reason why one linguistic sign becomes structurally dependent on another one, in the model presented by Boye and Harder (2012: 2) conventions and changes of conventions are the motor of this development. Along the lines of Itkonen's (2008a, 2008b) concept of intersubjectivity, Boye and Harder (2012: 8) understand convention as the reflection of "a state of coordination between members of a community that goes beyond individual instances of linguistic communicative interaction". It is only by convention that an expression is seen as being discursively prominent. Conventions are the result of usage and usage is at the same time affected by existing conventions. However, conventions do not render non-conventional usage impossible. On the contrary, non-conventional usage can give rise to new conventions. This represents a step away from the purely frequency-based viewpoint in Himmelmann's proposal.

Boye and Harder also point out that discourse prominence is always dependent on the context of the utterance. An expression discursively primary in one context can be discursively secondary in another and vice versa. To illustrate this, Boye and Harder use a musical metaphor in which they compare discursively secondary elements to second violins in an orchestra. Second violins are exactly the same violins as first violins, but due to the organization of the orchestra their position is not so prominent.

To be able to test whether a given expression is discursively primary, Boye and Harder (2012: 14–15) employ two tests: the nonfocalizability test and the nonaddressability test. They are based on the hypothesis that, under normal circumstances, it is not possible to focalize discursively secondary expressions and that discursively secondary expressions cannot be addressed by questions such as *how?, when?, where?* and others.

An example of nonaddressability of discursively secondary expressions is provided in (21). While we can easily use the question *who?* to address the subject *the tortoise*, the question *what?* to address the object *a strawberry* or the question *what does the tortoise do?* to address the verb *eats*, we cannot use any question of this type to address the suffix *-s* of the verb or the articles *the* or *a*.

(21) *The tortoise eats a strawberry.*

Similarly, discursively secondary elements can, under normal circumstances, not be focalized. Only discursively primary expressions can be focalized, as (22) demonstrates.

(22) a. *The TORTOISE eats a strawberry.*
      b. *The tortoise EATS a strawberry.*
      c. *The tortoise eats a STRAWBERRY.*

The only exceptions to the above-mentioned are situations in which contrastive, metalinguistic stress is used to emphasize a given grammatical device as opposed to other members of its paradigm. The grammatical expressions that are usually in the background become discursively primary in these contexts. An example is given in (23) where speaker A erroneously uses the verb without the suffix -s, which is subsequently pointed out by B by focalizing that grammatical expression.

(23) A: *The tortoise eat a strawberry.
B: The tortoise eatS a strawberry.

Discourse prominence is, as has been said earlier, not a static property of a particular expression, but depends on the context. To give an example, the lexical sign *red* in (24a) is discursively primary because it is the most important piece of information in the utterance. The very same adjective in (24b), however, is discursively secondary in relation to the head of the noun phrase in question, i.e. in this case the noun *bicycle*. Moreover, discursively secondary expressions are not necessarily secondary only in relation to discursively primary expressions, but also in relation to other discursively secondary expressions. For example, the indefinite article *a* in (24b) is less discursively prominent within the noun phrase and has to be seen as discursively secondary in relation to *red bicycle*.

(24) a. *The bicycle is red.*
b. *This is a red bicycle.*

The examples in (24) show that non-controversial lexical elements such as *red* can sometimes be discursively prominent and sometimes discursively secondary. Grammatical expressions such as the articles *the* and *a* or the copula *is*, on the other hand, are under normal circumstances not capable of becoming discursively primary. This asymmetry is the centrepiece of Boye and Harder's model, and helps to distinguish lexical from grammatical elements. While lexical expressions can be either discursively primary or secondary, grammatical expressions can only be discursively secondary. This is because of the *ancillariness* of grammatical expressions. That means that grammatical expressions have to cooccur together with other, discursively more prominent expressions. They cannot be used independently on their own. This is a concept comparable to the host class dependence in Himmelmann's (1992) model.

As is apparent from examples such as (24), lexical expressions are not defined in terms of inherent high prominence. Examples of metalinguistic contexts such as (23) demonstrate that grammatical expressions cannot be defined in terms of inherent low prominence either. Rather, both are defined in terms of having or lacking the potential to be discursively primary or, in other words, to be the main point of an utterance. As the examples above show, however, both grammatical and lexical expressions have the potential to become discursively primary, albeit in the case of grammatical elements under particularly specific circumstances.

Although there certainly seems to be a strong correlation between the grammatical status of an expression and its lack of discursive prominence, the latter does not always indicate the former. As we saw in the case of the focalizability test in (23), even grammatical expressions can sometimes be focalized. The addressability test, on the other hand, seems to be a more robust indicator of ancillariness. Examples such as (25) could, however, potentially problematize even the criterion of addressability because they show that the perception of discourse prominence can differ depending on the interlocutor. Speaker A intended *you know* as a discourse particle and did not assign high discourse prominence to it. Speaker B, however, interpreted that same particle as discursively primary, contrary to A's original intentions.

(25) A: *He's a divorcé, you know.*
B: *I didn't.*
A: *It's not a big deal for those people.*[6]

Although (25) does not represent a pure counterexample of nonaddressability, examples like this show that in ambiguous contexts expressions intended as discursively less prominent can nevertheless be reanalyzed as discursively prominent. That makes it possible to address expressions originally intended as unaddressable.

The discourse prominence of pragmatic markers such as *you know* or *I think* is in fact discussed by Boye and Harder (2012: 16). They conclude that these expressions are undoubtedly grammatical, implying that the diverging perception of discourse prominence as shown in (25) should not be possible. This demonstrates that even though the discourse prominence of a given expression is conventional (Boye and Harder 2012: 8), it is also always open to interpretation to a certain degree.

---

6 *A therapist, a comic book, and a breakfast sausage.* Young Sheldon. Season 1, episode 4. Original air date 16 November 2017. Episode script available online: https://www.springfieldspringfield.co.uk/view_episode_scripts.php?tv-show=young-sheldon-2017&episode=s01e04 (accessed 1 June 2018).

Having discussed the question of grammatical status, we can now turn to the second question, pertaining to the concept of gradable grammaticality. Boye and Harder (2012: 32) criticize earlier treatments of degrees of grammaticality on account of their lacking the necessary theoretical basis and rather reflecting the scholars' own preconception about grammar. In their model, the concept of gradable grammaticality based on formal criteria is retained. However, a theoretical explanation based on discursive prominence or lack thereof is also provided. Their proposal (Boye and Harder 2012: 33) provides theoretical foundations, lacking in other extant models, for treating affixes as more grammatical than clitics and enables the retention of a grammaticality cline such as (26).

(26) full verb > auxiliary > clitic > affix

Boye and Harder argue that the essential problem underlying any claims about gradable grammaticality is "the absence of a theory of what it means to be grammatical" (Boye and Harder 2012: 33). They are definitely right in saying that a theory of grammatical status is a desideratum in the study of grammar, grammaticalization and grammatical change in general. I would, however, like to argue that the concept of gradable grammaticality is flawed even if understood against the backdrop of Boye and Harder's theory of grammatical status.

As I already discussed in the introduction, the concept of gradable grammaticality is problematic for several reasons, irrespective of the theory of grammatical status at hand. Firstly, as was pointed out in connection with Bisang's (2004) research on East and mainland Southeast Asian languages, the emphasis on the conceptual unity of form and function reduces the cross-linguistic validity of any theory of grammatical status. Second, the link between form and function does not always hold, even from the perspective of a single language (Askedal 2008: 47; Popova 2017; see section 1).

Boye and Harder (2012: 33) explain that the formal properties often associated with grammatical status, such as the phonetic reduction of *going to* (27a) to *gonna* (27b), are potentially due to the discursively secondary status of those expressions.

(27) a. *She is going to call her.*
b. *She's gonna call her.*

On the one hand, this approach to gradable grammaticality is based on a theoretical basis which is an undisputed progress compared to earlier models. According to the logic of Boye and Harder's proposal, a bound form is less likely to carry the most important information of the utterance. The more bound a certain expression is, the less probable it is that that expression will be used discursively primary. An expression that is seen as conventionally ancillary is in turn more prone to formal changes as well.

On the other hand, Boye and Harder (2012: 33) also say that the formal criteria usually connected to a more grammatical status cannot be taken as diagnostics of that status. They emphasize that "[i]t cannot be taken for granted that showing more symptoms is always equivalent to being more grammatical" (Boye and Harder 2012: 33). This remark brings us back to the criticism of gradable grammaticality expressed in the introductory section of this article. Boye and Harder have definitely succeeded in providing a theoretical backing for the concept of gradable grammaticality. The problematic aspects of the concept, however, do not disappear even with such a backing. It follows, moreover, that if the formal criteria cannot serve as diagnostics of the degree of grammaticality, as Boye and Harder (2012: 33) themselves admit, we can only consider these criteria once we establish the grammatical status of the expression at hand. In terms of Boye and Harder's (2012: 7) model, this means that we have already established that the expressions in question are by convention ancillary and discursively secondary. In other words, by using formal criteria to discern between different degrees of grammaticality, we regress to the approach to grammatical status Boye and Harder originally set out to supersede.

In (28a) the reduced form *'ve got* is supposedly more grammatical than its non-reduced form *have got* due to the higher degree of boundedness it shows. The same reductive processes, however, can also affect lexical constructions as illustrated by (28b), but in this case the formal change does not affect its functional status. Looking at the obvious asymmetry, the question arises as to why formal changes lead to a more grammatical status in grammatical expressions, but not to a more lexical status in lexical ones? From a logical point of view, we have two options. Either admit that formal criteria are not reliable in determining the functional status of any expression and stop using them, or start distinguishing among degrees of lexicality, in other words among more and less lexical lexemes for the sake of consistency. I would like to argue for the former possibility.

(28) a. *I have got a turtle.* > *I've got a turtle.*
b. *I have a turtle.* > *I've a turtle.*

Boye and Harder have demonstrated that formal criteria are not best suited to discern lexical expressions from grammatical ones. If that is the case, the question logically poses itself as to why these formal criteria would be suitable for discerning different grades of grammaticality. Therefore, I argue that if we know how problematic a concept of gradable grammaticality is, it is only consistent to abandon that concept altogether. Boye and Harder (2012: 32) in fact refer to Andersen (2006) as an example of someone who has already given up the link between form and function behind gradable grammaticality. It should be noted, however, that I do not want to argue that we should not be interested in formal changes at all. Rather, I would like to argue that we gain more when we start looking at formal and functional changes separately.

4 Discussion and concluding remarks

The aim of this paper was to consider three existing proposals for a theory of grammatical status in the tradition of grammaticalization studies. The point of departure was the realization that a definition of grammar is often missing even though it should be at the heart of every work on grammaticalization. During the last couple of decades, it has gradually become obvious that the most common grammatical model for the purpose of grammaticalization research, Lehmann's ([1982] 2015) parametric model, is in a number of aspects insufficient. Although some progress has definitely been made, the answer to the question of how to define grammar still remains a desideratum.

The proposals made thus far can be divided into two groups. On the one hand, there are Himmelmann's (1992) and Boye and Harder's (2012) models, which are based on differing discursive properties of grammatical and lexical expressions. On the other hand, Diewald explains the difference between lexical and grammatical expressions by virtue of their differing deictic properties. These, however, ultimately boil down to a paradigmatic ordering of grammatical elements.

For both Himmelmann (1992), and Boye and Harder (2012), grammatical expressions are understood as reduced or restricted as far as their discourse possibilities are concerned. According to Himmelmann, lexical signs are full signs that can lose their full status over time. Consequently, the reduction of the full status has to be compensated for, so grammatical signs come to be obligatorily accompanied by full signs.

Boye and Harder, on the other hand, propose that the difference in discursive properties manifests itself in the possibility for lexical expressions to become discourse prominent and by the lack of the potential for discourse prominence in grammatical expressions. Lexical expressions are flexible and can be prominent parts of the discourse, depending on the context, whereas grammatical expressions lack this ability and are always discursively secondary in relation to a lexical expression.

In contrast to the former group, Diewald's model builds on the various deictic properties of grammatical and lexical expressions. Grammatical signs are not seen as diminished in any way, but as having different deictic properties to the lexical ones. Linguistic signs form a continuum with strong deixis on the one end and paradigmatically interpreted weak deixis on the other. Typical lexical expressions form strong deictic relations, whereas typical grammatical expressions form weak deictic relations to the members of its paradigm. Between these poles there are, furthermore, intermediate forms of lexemes with weak deictic properties and grams capable of strong deixis. Forming a paradigm and maintaining deictic relations to its members is seen as the defining property of grammatical expressions.

Although all three contributions differ in detail and the perspective they take, they nevertheless also have a number of aspects in common. In all three models there is agreement in principle regarding the basic distinction between lexicon and grammar. Moreover, in all three models this distinction is not seen as a binary opposition, but as a continuum. At one end there are prototypically lexical and on the other prototypically grammatical signs. All three models also more or less pre-theoretically agree on the concept of grammar. They do not perceive grammar as a closed set of rules with discourse markers on the periphery but accept a broader concept of grammar that encompasses pragmatic markers as well. Diewald (2011) is particularly explicit in emphasizing this position. Furthermore, in all three models the so-called *a priori* grammar postulate is rejected (Hopper 1988) and grammar is not seen as the prerequisite of discourse but as its product.

Although the proposals presented here differ in a number of aspects, they are not incompatible. Rather, they represent three complementary approaches to the issue of describing the nature of grammatical signs. Most alike are the proposals by Himmelmann and by Boye and Harder, both of which build on the conventionalization of the discursive properties of linguistic signs. By means of frequent usage in combination, certain expressions can lose their full sign status, following Himmelmann, or become discursively secondary by convention, following Boye and Harder.

The discussion in this article has also demonstrated the limits of these models. Himmelmann's and Boye and Harder's models are dynamic in that they explain how the respective discursive properties come about. By contrast, Diewald's model provides only a synchronic look at the differences in the deictic properties of linguistic signs. It is therefore not clear how lexical expressions change their strong deictic relations in order to become weak deictic and thus grammatical. Furthermore, it is also unclear whether paradigmatic relations, taken by Diewald to be the definitional properties of grammar, are indeed limited to grammatical expressions. Similarly, Boye and Harder have on the one hand definitely demonstrated a very strong correlation between discourse prominence and grammaticality. On the other hand, grammatical expressions do not always lack discourse prominence. There are a number of reasons why it is plausible that grammar is not the main point of an utterance and thus discursively primary, but there is also evidence to the contrary.

Lack of discourse prominence and weak deictic relations both hint at one aspect of grammaticality that has so far not been fully covered in the literature, namely, the relation between grammatical and lexical expressions. Boye and Harder use the adjective *ancillary* to describe the discursive role of grams because they can only function in combination with a lexical expression. This structural relation is also implicitly present in Himmelmann's proposal. Grammatical linguistic signs by virtue of their diminished sign status must cooccur with other signs. In other words, grammatical signs must *obligatorily* cooccur with other signs. This is also recognized by Popova in the closing statement of her treatise on the disparity of form and function in Bulgarian and Macedonian:

> There are important correlations between being grammatical and having certain formal properties. [...] Overall, however, [...] in looking at grammatical constructions there is a need to go beyond the degree of grammaticalization of the function word and to look at properties like paradigmaticization, generality and obligatoriness. (Popova 2017: 28)

Whereas paradigm membership (Diewald 2010) and general or abstract meaning (Boye and Harder 2012: 5) have been shown to be potentially problematic because these properties are not necessarily unique to grammar, obligatoriness of grammatical categories seems promising. Being implicit in Diewald's model and explicit in Himmelmann's, as well as in Boye and Harder's proposals, the idea that grams are structurally dependent and therefore obligatorily realized connects all three proposals discussed in the present paper.

Apart from the search for a definition of grammaticality, the second question I tried to answer in this paper was related to the concept of gradable grammaticality. The majority of approaches to grammaticalization and grammar change in general assume that some grams are more grammatical than others. The degrees are usually based on the formal properties of the grams in question. Grams realized as affixes are considered more grammatical than grams realized as free words or clitics. As a number of scholars have repeatedly demonstrated, however, this conceptual unity of form and function in the form of grammaticality clines is problematic. The formal changes linked to grammatical status are not exclusive to grammatical expressions and they are problematic from a cross-linguistic perspective as well.

Each of the three models discussed in this paper tackle gradable grammaticality differently. First, Diewald's deixis-based model does not include any formal criteria to establish grammatical status at all. In passing, however, Diewald (2011: 461) mentions the possibility to distinguish different degrees of grammaticality on the basis of the distinct combinations of deictic relations they can possibly enter into. Second, Himmelmann's model does not explicitly work with gradable grammaticality either. His proposal for a theory of grammatical status focuses solely on the differences in the discursive behaviour of lexical and grammatical expressions. Formal changes affecting grammatical expressions are in his model treated separately from functional changes. Third, Boye and Harder base their theory of grammatical status on discourse prominence, which does not directly involve the formal aspect of any expression. At the same time, however, they uphold the tradition of formally defined degrees of grammaticality. Although Boye and Harder's model explains why discursively secondary expressions are susceptible to phonetic attrition, semantic bleaching and coalescence, it does not follow why these reductive processses should increase the degree of grammatical status but at the same time not influence the lexical status in any way. None of the three proposals discussed in the present paper use formal criteria to define grammatical status. Boye and Harder's model, however, exploits formal properties when it comes to the question of gradable grammaticality, even though they at the same time recognize the problematic aspects of the concept of degrees of grammaticality.

Although it has been repeatedly stated how important a theory of grammatical status is for our understanding of grammar and grammaticalization (Himmelmann 1992: 2; Diewald 2011: 452; Boye and Harder 2012: 1), contributions solely dedicated to this topic have been rare. The present paper has offered a comparative analysis of the three main models of grammatical status proposed in the context of grammaticalization studies in the last three decades. Focusing on the principles the individual models employ to define grammatical status as well as how the models approach the concept of gradable grammaticality, the present paper maps the strengths and shortcomings of the extant proposals and tries to point out the points of convergence that could prove valuable for further research.

References

Andersen, Henning. 2006. Grammation, regrammation, and degrammation: Tense loss in Russian. *Diachronica* 2. 231–258.

Askedal, John Ole. 2008. 'Degrammaticalization' versus typology. Reflections on a strained relationship. In Thórhallur Eythórsson (ed.), *Grammatical change and linguistic theory. The Rosendal papers*, 45–79. Amsterdam: John Benjamins.

Becker, Alton J. 1988. Language in particular: A lecture. In Deborah Tannen (ed.), *Linguistics in context: Connecting observation and understanding. Lectures from the 1985 LSA/TESOL and NEH Institutes*, 17–35. Norwood, NJ: Ablex.

Bisang, Walter. 2004. Grammaticalization without coevolution of form and meaning: The case of tense-aspect-modality in East and mainland Southeast Asia. In Walter Bisang, Nikolaus P. Himmelmann & Björn Wiemer (eds.), *What makes grammaticalization? A look from its fringes and its components*, 109–138. Berlin: Mouton de Gruyter.

Boye, Kasper & Peter Harder. 2012. A usage-based theory of grammatical status and grammaticalization. *Language* 88 (1). 1–44.

Breban, Tine. 2014. What is secondary grammaticalization? Trying to see the wood for the trees in a confusion of interpretations. *Folia Linguistica* 48 (2). 469–502.

Diewald, Gabriele. 1991. *Deixis und Textsorten im Deutschen*. Tübingen: Niemeyer.

Diewald, Gabriele. 1999. *Die Modalverben im Deutschen: Grammatikalisierung und Polyfunktionalität*. Tübingen: Niemeyer.

Diewald, Gabriele. 2008. Grammatikalisierung, Grammatik und grammatische Kategorien. In Thomas Stolz (ed.), *Grammatikalisierung und grammatische Kategorien*, 1–32. Bochum: Brockmeyer.

Diewald, Gabriele. 2010. On some problem areas in grammaticalization studies. In Ekaterini Stathi, Elke Gehweiler & Ekkehard König (eds.), *Grammaticalization: Current views and issues*, 17–50. Amsterdam: John Benjamins.

Diewald, Gabriele. 2011. Grammaticalization and pragmaticalization. In Bernd Heine & Heiko Narrog (eds.), *The Oxford handbook of grammaticalization*, 450–461. Oxford: Oxford University Press.

Diewald, Gabriele & Elena Smirnova. 2010. *Evidentiality in German: Linguistic realizations and regularities in grammaticalization*. Berlin: Mouton de Gruyter.

Goldberg, Adele E. 2006. *Constructions at work. The nature of generalizations in language*. Oxford: Oxford University Press.

Himmelmann, Nikolaus P. 1992. *Grammaticalization and grammar*. Köln: Institut für Sprachwissenschaft, Universität zu Köln.

Himmelmann, Nikolaus P. 2004. Lexicalization and grammaticalization: Opposite or orthogonal? In Walter Bisang, Nikolaus Himmelmann & Björn Wiemer (eds.), *What makes grammaticalization? A look from its fringes and its components*, 21–42. Berlin: Mouton de Gruyter.

Hopper, Paul J. 1987. Emergent grammar. In Joe Aske, Natasha Beery, Laura Michaelis & Hana Filip (eds.), *Berkeley Linguistics Society. Proceedings of the Thirteenth Annual Meeting, February 14–16, 1987: General session and parasession on grammar and cognition*, 139–157. Berkeley, CA: Berkeley Linguistics Society.

Hopper, Paul J. 1988. Emergent grammar and the a priori grammar postulate. In Deborah Tannen (ed.), *Linguistics in context: Connecting observation and understanding. Lectures from the 1985 LSA/TESOL and NEH Institutes*, 117–134. Norwood, NJ: Ablex.

Hopper, Paul J. & Elizabeth Closs Traugott. 2003. *Grammaticalization*. 2nd edn. Cambridge: Cambridge University Press.

Itkonen, Esa, 2008a. Concerning the role of consciousness in linguistics. *Journal of Consciousness Studies* 15 (6). 15–33.

Itkonen, Esa, 2008b. The central role of normativity in language and linguistics. In Jordan Zlatev, Timothy P. Racine, Chris Sinha & Esa Itkonen (eds.), *The shared mind. Perspectives on intersubjectivity*, 279–305. Amsterdam: John Benjamins.

Kuryłowicz, Jerzy. 1964. *The inflectional categories of Indo-European*. Heidelberg: Winter.

Kuryłowicz, Jerzy. 1965. The evolution of grammatical categories. *Diogenes* 51. 55–71.

Langacker, Ronald W. 2008. *Cognitive grammar. A basic introduction*. Oxford: Oxford University Press.

Lehmann, Christian. 1982. *Thoughts on grammaticalization. A programmatic sketch*. Köln: Institut für Sprachwissenschaft, Universität zu Köln.

Lehmann, Christian. 2015. *Thoughts on grammaticalization*. 3rd edn. Berlin: Language Science Press.

Nicolle, Steve. 1998. A relevance theory perspective on grammaticalization. *Cognitive Linguistics* 9 (1). 1–35.

Nørgård-Sørensen, Jens, Jens Heltoft & Lene Schøsler. 2011. *Connecting grammaticalisation*. Amsterdam: John Benjamins.

Popova, Gergana. 2017. Constructions, grammatical status and morphologization. *Studies in Language* 41 (1). 1–32.

Roberts, Ian & Anna Roussou. 2003. *Syntactic change: A minimalist approach to grammaticalization*. Cambridge: Cambridge University Press.

Traugott, Elizabeth Closs. 2002. From etymology to historical pragmatics. In Donka Minkova & Robert Stockwell (eds.), *Studies in the history of the English language*, 19–49. Berlin: Mouton de Gruyter.

Traugott, Elizabeth Closs & Graeme Trousdale. 2013. *Constructionalization and constructional changes*. Oxford: Oxford University Press.

Ullman, Michael T. 2001. The declarative/procedural model of lexicon and grammar. *Journal of Psycholinguistic Research* 30 (1). 37–69.

Von Mengden, Ferdinand. 2016. Functional changes and (meta-)linguistic evolution. In Muriel Norde & Freek Van de Velde (eds.), *Exaptation in language change*, 121–162. Amsterdam: John Benjamins.

Von Mengden, Ferdinand & Evie Coussé. 2014. The role of change in usage-based conceptions of language. In Evie Coussé & Ferdinand von Mengden (eds.), *Usage-based approaches to language change*, 1–19. Amsterdam: John Benjamins.

Wilson, Deirdre & Dan Sperber. 1993. Linguistic form and relevance. *Lingua* 90 (1-2). 1–25.

Hendrik De Smet
The motivated unmotivated

Variation, function and context

Abstract: Variation occurs when a language has two or more ways of achieving the same communicative goal. Cases of variation have been approached in very different ways by two different groups of linguists. Variationists assume that variation is natural and common. On this view, change is due to naturally occurring variation interacting with language-external forces. Functionalists assume that variation is anomalous. On this view, change may reflect a language-internal drive to eradicate variation. In this paper, it is argued that these conflicting views can be reconciled by considering how variation functions in the broader context of the grammar. Drawing on a case study into the prepositional complements following emotion adjectives, it is proposed that variation (as Variationists maintain) is natural and that languages have no intrinsic tendency to reduce variability. Nevertheless, the synchronic availability and historical development of specific variants is (as Functionalists maintain) also internally motivated, typically by analogical relations.

1 Introduction

Variation occurs whenever a language has two or more ways of achieving the same communicative goal. In (1), for example, the prepositions *with*, *by*, *at*, *in*, *about* and *over* all do a roughly similar job marking the external source or cause of the emotional state denoted by *disappointed*.

(1) a. *The local residents were bitterly disappointed **with** the decision.* (BNC)
 b. *Although I will be better off, I am very disappointed **by** the outcome.* (BNC)
 c. *Stephen was disappointed **at** what he took to be a refusal.* (BNC)
 d. *He felt deeply disappointed **in** Eleanor's visit.* (BNC)
 e. *I'm real disappointed **about** the letter.* (BNC)

Hendrik De Smet, University of Leuven, Department of Linguistics, Leuven, Belgium, hendrik.desmet@kuleuven.be

f. *Gray said everyone at the club is deeply disappointed **over** the current situation but they [are] all trying to put it right.* (BNC)

In linguistic practice, such situations of variation may occasion very different responses. In what follows, I will compare two approaches, which – taken to their extremes – offer incompatible interpretations of variation.

According to one tradition – the Variationist tradition – variation as in (1) above is widespread and natural. Seen from this perspective, "language is inherently variable" (Tagliamonte 2012: 3; see also Labov 1972). A Variationist is therefore likely to regard the examples in (1) as typical of what language is like – the different examples make up just one of many variable contexts in Present-day English. Once recognized as being in variation, the Variationist might go on to determine whether the available options are constrained by speaker lect or register, and (if so) whether those constraints reflect ongoing language change. However, according to another tradition – which I will refer to here as the Functionalist[1] tradition – variation is never or rarely semantically neutral. On this view, "a difference in syntactic form always spells a difference in meaning" (Bolinger 1968: 127; see also Haiman 1980; Goldberg 1995). This view goes back all the way to Humboldt's one-meaning-one-form principle, and has been given firm theoretical grounding in Saussurean Structuralism. Backed by almost two centuries of linguistic theorizing, then, a Functionalist will probably object to the examples in (1) constituting a case of genuine variation. They would go on to argue that the different prepositional complements following *disappointed* come with different shades of meaning and are, as a result, not strictly interchangeable.

These different views are linked to different understandings of language change. On the Functionalist side, one finds expressed the idea that languages, in principle, strive to maintain or restore isomorphism over time (e.g. Dik 1988; Anttila 1989; Geeraerts 1997: 105). Even though the role of isomorphism in language change is regularly called into question (Lass 1998: 342–352; Croft 2000: 68), Functionalist thinking holds its ground in historical linguistics as a set of implicit assumptions. On the one hand, the literature abounds with claims that one form disappears or undergoes functional change *because* it is functionally equivalent to another (see De Smet et al. 2018 for examples and more elaborate discussion). On the other hand, some work in Grammaticalization Theory banks

---

[1] The term *Functionalist* is not used here with reference to any specific language model or research tradition (e.g. Functional Grammar, Westcoast Functionalism or Systemic Functional Grammar) but simply to group those linguists who assume that formal contrasts are necessarily meaningful.

on the idea that the diachronic success of new forms may be due to their being different from established forms – for instance, in being more expressive (Haspelmath 1999).

On the Variationist side, there is a more articulate model of language change. As Poplack (2011: 211) puts it: "The standard variationist construal of change involves the progressive increase of one of a set of variant expressions of a meaning or function until it ousts its competitors from the grammatical sector." This "ousting" is believed to happen not so much to restore isomorphism – variation, after all, is perfectly natural – but because variation is "potentially unstable" (Montgomery 2007: 111). Speakers may at any time attribute social meaning to the variation around them and, as a result, develop selectional preferences for one variant or another. Such preferences are primarily motivated by speakers' social ties and aspirations as individuals, but they can eventually lead to shifting usage preferences at the community level, amounting to language change proper (Labov 1972).

Even if this contrast somewhat caricaturizes the two approaches to variation, the tension it highlights is real enough.[2] This is not to say that no attempts have been made towards reconciliation – there have been several, some of which will be discussed below – or that individual researchers must necessarily choose sides – many do not. Even so, the incompatibility between the two approaches is fundamental enough to raise serious questions about how language is organized and how it changes. This incompatibility makes it difficult for linguists working in different frameworks to take each other's data seriously, despite calls to the contrary (e.g. Mufwene 1994). In fact, it has regularly given rise to open tension between more Variationist-leaning and more Functionalist-leaning work.

This tension is the main focus of the present paper, which aims to offer another attempt at reconciliation. The approach taken here is to explore an alternative perspective that tries to put variation and its function in the context of the broader grammatical system. Specifically, it is argued that both variation and functional motivation can only be meaningfully interpreted by taking into account the system that "generates" the variants involved (see also De Smet et al. 2018). In what follows, section 2 starts by examining Variationist and Functionalist approaches more closely, further exploring the tension between them. Section 3 considers two earlier attempts at resolving the tension. However, as argued in section 4, these attempts inevitably raise new issues. Section 5 then outlines a

---

[2] As one reviewer pointed out, there is another tension that may need reconciling, between the Variationist approach to syntax and the work done by formal syntacticians who analyze dialectal variation in terms of "the parameters provided by Universal Grammar" (Cornips and Corrigan 2005: 3). This tension, however, is not the topic of this paper.

way of addressing those issues, illustrating and supporting the argument with a case study into the area of variation illustrated in (1) above, that is the prepositional phrase complements following emotion adjectives in general, and *disappointed* in particular. Section 6 rounds off with concluding remarks.

2 Conflict

The tension described above is an old one. The Variationist tradition is grounded in work on phonological variation (Labov 1972), where semantics simply does not come into play. When Variationist thinking and methodology are extended into the domain of the lexicon or grammar, the neutrality of meaning becomes less self-evident. As Lavandera (1978) puts it:

> *Laughing* and *laughin'*, or /gard/ and /gaːd/ can more convincingly be shown to be used to say referentially the same thing than any pair of postulated synonymous syntactic constructions such as *The liquor closet was broken into* vs. *They broke into the liquor closet*. (Lavandera 1978: 175)

The way out has been to assume that between lexical or grammatical variants semantic differences may well exist but they have no truth-conditional value. Labov (1978) argues that grammatical variants have the same "referential" or "representational" meaning. In an often-quoted position statement, Sankoff (1988) develops this view further, proposing that whatever semantic differences exist between variants can be neutralized in context:

> While it is indisputable that some difference in connotation may, *upon reflection*, be postulated among so-called synonyms whether in isolation or in context [...], there is no reason to expect these differences to be pertinent every time one of the variant forms is used. Indeed the hypothesis underlying the study of syntactic variation within a framework similar to that of phonological variation is that for certain identifiable sets of alternations, these distinctions come into play neither in the intentions of the speaker nor in the interpretation of the interlocutor. Thus we say that *distinctions in referential value or grammatical function among different surface forms can be neutralized in discourse*. Moreover, this is the fundamental discursive mechanism of (nonphonological) variation and change. (Sankoff 1988: 153, emphases in the original)

There is little doubt that Sankoff (1988) here distances himself from Functionalist thinking, as is clear from the following:[3]

> [T]wo different lexical items or structures can almost always have some usages or contexts in which they have different meanings, or functions, and it is even claimed by some that this difference, though it may be subtle, is always pertinent whenever one of the forms is used. The contrary viewpoint is adopted here, however. (Sankoff 1988: 153)

In later Variationist work, this anti-Functionalist undertone sometimes becomes amplified. A striking example is Poplack's (2015) portrayal of Functionalism as being akin to the practices of prescriptive grammarians. Functionalists and prescriptivists alike, she argues, have a knack for correctly identifying variant expressions but then typically fail to acknowledge them as such. Rather, they revert to often dogmatic and poorly-informed attempts "to imbue each form with a privative context of occurrence, whatever it may be, so long as it is distinct from that of its counterpart(s)". Other authors voicing scepticism or even hostility towards Functionalism include Mair (2003), Noël (2003), Bresnan and Nikitina (2009) or Torres Cacoullos and Walker (2009). All take as their starting assumption the Variationist idea that variation is natural and therefore neither has nor requires a functional explanation.

Predictably, more Functionalist-leaning authors have reacted to this. Romaine (1981), for instance, has been quick to point out that building a theory of variation and change on the truth-conditional side of meaning alone is likely to miss much of what may be driving grammatical change. Her comments anticipate later work revealing the central involvement of textual and interpersonal meanings as well as the role of pragmatic inferencing in grammaticalization. Leaving this line of argumentation aside, however, of special interest here are attempts to incorporate (non-truth-conditional) aspects of meaning in the analysis of variation, using otherwise Variationist methods.

One way of doing this is by adding functional parameters to the statistical models describing the variation, factoring in semantic features of the contexts in which variants occur (e.g. Rosenbach 2002). Another technique is to perform various types of collocational analyses. Gries and Stefanowitsch (2004), for example,

---

[3] Here, too, Sankoff echoes Labov (1978: 8), who expresses veiled scepticism of the Functionalist position (which he refers to as "formalist") when he writes: "It is good that there should be these two opposing imperialisms. The sociolinguist, intent on social variation, might miss some of the subtle differentiations that grammar can make. The formal linguist, insensitive to social variation, may create differences that are as idiosyncratic as the New York City woman who said to me, 'The little ones are my [veɪzɨz]; the big ones are my [vɑzɨz]'".

show that the English dative alternation is highly sensitive to verb lemma. Verbs like *give, tell* or *show* strongly favour the ditransitive construction, whereas verbs like *bring, play* or *take* strongly favour the prepositional dative construction.

Although some obscuring of the boundaries between Variationist and Functionalist theory and practice seems to be going on here, there is still striking disagreement as to how the results are to be interpreted. Perhaps the difficulty is that meaning always has to be approached indirectly, through contextual clues. For example, it has been shown that the English *s*-genitive is preferred over the *of*-genitive when the relation expressed is one of inalienable possession (Rosenbach 2002). This is one reason why *Sue's lungs* tends to be favoured over *the lungs of Sue*. Yet, even though inalienable possession is a semantic category, it does not follow that the *s*-genitive somehow marks inalienable possession. There is no contradiction in using *Sue's lungs* to refer to the pair of lungs Sue is dissecting in biology class. The same could be said of collocational evidence, which may point to semantic differences between variants but does not actually identify those differences.

This, then, leaves room for interpretation. Gries and Stefanowitsch (2004), once they have made clear that their collostructional analysis reveals "subtle differences between *seemingly* synonymous constructions" (emphasis added), go on to conclude that "many alternations are much more restricted than has hitherto been assumed" (Gries and Stefanowitsch 2004: 97). Similarly, Colleman, writing on the dative alternation in Dutch, maintains that collocational analysis can "provide the basis for [...] empirically valid generalizations about the semantic parameters driving the dative alternation" (Colleman 2009: 593). But others, despite adopting similar techniques, are more cautious. Collocational differences between variants or associations to different semantic contexts may, for instance, reflect entrenched habits or persistent usage patterns rather than semantically driven choices (Noël 2003: 369; Torres Cacoullos and Walker 2009; Poplack and Torres Cacoullos 2015: 277; Blas Arroyo and Schulte 2017). This brings to mind Sankoff and Thibault's (1981) foresighted suggestion that the conflict between Functionalist and Variationist thinking may well prove difficult to resolve on strictly empirical grounds.

3 A compromise

Can Variationist and Functionalist approaches be reconciled then? Several solutions have been suggested, the common denominator of which is that the conflict between Variationist and Functionalist perspectives may actually matter less than appears at first sight.

At the Variationist end, we must again turn to Sankoff (1988). Even as he goes against Functionalist thinking in introducing the concept of neutralization-in-discourse, Sankoff does not go so far as to reject Functionalism altogether. His position is best characterized as agnostic, treating both his own Variationist view and the Functionalist view as hypotheses:

> [T]his notion [of neutralization-in-discourse] must remain a hypothesis, as must its antithesis – that at every use of a form its full complement of distinctions is somehow brought into play by the speaker and/or hearer. (Sankoff 1988: 154)

Ultimately, Sankoff does not seek to justify the Variationist approach by demonstrating the existence of functional equivalence between variants. Instead, he looks for justification in the observation of 'weak complementarity' (Sankoff and Thibault 1981; see also Schwenter and Torres Cacoullos 2010: 14; Tagliamonte 2012: 16). Weak complementarity means that the prevalence of one form in a lect or register negatively correlates with the occurrence of another form. Given such a correlation and given some degree of functional similarity, it is only reasonable to conclude that the forms are in variation and are potentially subject to change, with one form replacing the other – no matter their exact semantic specifications. Sankoff (1988: 155) even speculates that variation may involve not only variant forms for (roughly) the same function, but also variant functions (see also Lavandera 1978: 179–180). In other words, speakers can differ in how they say things as well as in the things they say. As long as there is weak complementarity, the Variationist approach is vindicated.

At the Functionalist end, there is openness to the idea that a language may offer alternative coding options, if not quite for the same meaning, at least for the same language-external state of affairs to be linguistically represented (Langacker 1987; Taylor 2002). As Langacker puts it:

> Grammatical structure is based on conventional imagery, which reflects our ability to construe a conceived situation in alternate ways. The full conceptual or semantic value of a conceived situation is a function of not only its content [...], but also how we structure this content with respect to such matters as attention, selection, figure/ground organization, viewpoint, and level of schematicity. In regard to all of these we are capable of making adjustments, thereby transforming one conceptualization into another that is roughly equivalent in terms of content but differs in how this content is construed. (Langacker 1987: 138)

For example, the transitive and intransitive constructions in (2a)–(2b) can be used to describe the same scene. The variants highlight different aspects of the scene and meet different information-structural demands, but the scene itself does not impose either one of the construals the variants express. It is the speaker who chooses to construe the scene in whichever way meets his or her communicative goals or, simply, first comes to mind.

(2) a. *The defendant **dropped** the gun* (1966, Google Books)
      b. *the gun **dropped** to the floor.* (1967, Google Books)

From this, it is a small step to Croft (2010). Like Variationists, Croft looks for the origins of change in naturally occurring variation. Inspired by the notion of construal, he finds variation in the many options speakers have to verbalize the same experience. Croft argues that this type of variation is far more extensive than is generally recognized. To show this, he describes the variation in speakers' retellings of the *Pear Story* film.[4] Even though the speakers in question are not only describing the same scenes, but share the same overall discourse goal, variation is the norm. Consider, for instance, some variant descriptions in (3), from Croft (2010: 10–11):

(3) a. *he comes off of the ladder*
      b. *he comes down with a load of pears*
      c. *and he comes down*
      d. *climbs down the ladder*

The extent of the variation implies that language not only offers speakers numerous ways to verbalize one and the same experience, but also leaves them considerable freedom to choose between them:

> Any single situation may be verbalized in multiply different ways. Because of the fundamental indeterminacy of communication – due to the fact that speakers cannot read each other's minds, speakers must rely on their own unique histories of prior uses of the linguistic forms, and every situation being communicated is unique – different verbalizations of the same experience are communicatively more or less equivalent, or at least not a priori distinguishable. (Croft 2010: 42)

This indeterminacy, according to Croft, gives rise to the variation over which socially-driven selection mechanisms can subsequently operate, leading to the

---

4 The *Pear Story* is a short film made in 1975, showing a narrative sequence of events but without dialogue or other linguistic support. As part of an experimental study (see Chafe 1980), the film has been shown to speakers of different languages, who have been asked to retell the story. The study provides a rare opportunity for observing different speakers independently creating a linguistic representation of the same experience.

propagation or loss of specific variants over time.⁵ Again the message is that variants may well enter into competition without necessarily having complete semantic equivalence.

4 New problems

The solutions discussed above suggest that the discrepancy between Variationist and Functionalist perspectives is only an apparent one. Fundamentally, there need be no conflict. If variants are interpreted as near-synonyms, the Variationist concedes that variants are not exact synonyms, while the Functionalist concedes that variants may be interchangeable in some contexts. Each can attend to their own business without getting in the other's way. Still, even though a position along the lines of Sankoff (1988) or Croft (2010) may be preferable to a tug-of-war between more extreme Functionalist or Variationist views, there are problems left that need addressing. The following focuses on two general problem areas, one mainly relevant to the Functionalist approach, the other to the Variationist approach.

4.1 Motivation

One of the basic intuitions driving Functionalist thinking is that the structure of language is more or less optimally adapted to its function, which is first and foremost communication (Nuyts 2007: 548). The isomorphic principle is one reflex of this underlying idea. Isomorphism states that for a communicative code to be clear and efficient, forms should be reliably associated with meanings, with a one-to-one mapping as the optimum. Many meanings mapped to one form would cause ambiguity, while many forms mapped to one meaning would needlessly burden memory.

The question, then, is how to account for violations of isomorphism. Ideally, from a Functionalist point of view, these are still explicable as somehow being functionally motivated. Indeed, in one respect, one-to-many mappings have already been recognized to have a functional advantage over one-to-one mappings. Without polysemy, the linguistic code would lack the flexibility to adapt to new situations. Croft therefore reformulates the isomorphic principle as follows:

---

5 Mufwene (1994: 202–203) offers a similar, though anecdotal example of grammatical variation. Interestingly, he too suggests that individual preferences may be the primary drive of speaker choice here.

> Polysemy is both economically and iconically motivated [...]. The set of related meanings can be thought of as a connected region in conceptual space [...]. The actual iconic correspondence between meaning and form is between a single form and a single region in conceptual space [... T]he larger the region, the fewer total words necessary to cover the conceptual space, and the more economically motivated the form-meaning correspondence. (Croft 2002: 106)

However, the other type of violation – synonymy, or near-synonymy – is harder to account for. Variation brings redundancy to the communicative code that may, from a Functionalist perspective, lack an obvious communicative advantage. At best, variants offer different construals, which can explain their distributional preferences, but as Taylor (2002: 281) recognizes, such alternate construals may be no more than functional "luxuries" that a language could just as easily do without. At worst, semantic differences are so subtle that even Functionalists themselves fail to identify or agree on the semantic contrasts encoded by pairs of variants. Once the Functionalist admits to widespread near-synonymy, the question arises how to account for it in functional terms. In brief, where is the motivation in variation?

4.2 Delimitation

Variationists may be less concerned with motivation, but must face an issue that is arguably even thornier. Weak complementarity supports but also challenges Variationist practice and thought. As a phenomenon, it is common in diachronic data. With time, the frequency of one form goes up, just as the frequency of another goes down. If the forms belong to the same semantic domain, it is sensible to assume, with Sankoff (1988), that they are in variation. However, complementarity may prove to be weak indeed.

Consider the diachronic relation between English *must* and *have to* as expressions of deontic necessity, as in (4). Historically, *must* has been on the decline while *have to* has been on the rise (Myhill 1995; Biber 2004; Leech et al. 2011).

(4) a. '*You* **must** *get something inside you,*' *insisted Sukey bossily,* '*and you too, Daisy.*' (BNC)
b. *I mean, there must be meetings you* **have to** *go to.* (BNC)

However, the rise of *have to* does not match the decline of *must* in magnitude, nor do their respective timings exactly align (Biber 2004). Furthermore, a score of other potentially rivalling expressions also need to be factored into the equation. Those include other modals and semi-modals like *be to, had better, need (to), ought (to), shall* and *should,* not to mention lexical alternatives (Leech et al. 2011:

114). Some of the other variants, moreover, feature in other alternations as well. For example, *must* is also a marker of epistemic necessity, alternating with epistemic adverbs and parentheticals, while *shall* varies with *will* and *going to* as a marker of future tense. Finally, if this is not bewildering enough, *must* and *have to* are also semantically different and to some extent syntactically complementary (Coates 1983; Myhill 1995). Even if such differences need not sit in the way of variation and change, as both Sankoff (1988) and Croft (2010) propose, there is the non-trivial question of how much difference between alleged variants can be tolerated before they cease to be variants? In sum, if we open the door to near-synonymy or mere functional relatedness, determining what Variationists call "the envelope of variation" – that is, the range of contexts in which variants actually vary – may often turn out to be an intractable problem. For a Variationist analysis, this is not a promising starting point.

When variation eludes circumscription in terms of discrete variables, I will refer to it here as *hypervariation*. Drawing attention to this type of variation, Van de Velde (2014) speaks of many-to-many mappings between forms and functions: any single form can realize many functions and any single function can be realized by many forms. As Van de Velde points out, many-to-many form-function mappings are a recurrent organizational principle in complex systems (see also Kuhle 2014). It is found, for instance, in physiology, animal behaviour and neural architecture. In terms of language variation, many-to-many mappings imply that a linguistic variable can subsume a range of variants and each of those variants may in turn be subsumed under a range of other variables. In other words, different envelopes of variation may be connected (Brook 2018).

To the extent that the problem of hypervariation is a methodological one, its consequence is that Variationist studies of grammatical variation mostly focus on a smaller subset of variations that allow an acceptable degree of delimitation. In the end, variation must be delimited syntactically or lexically, as well as semantically (Labov 1978; Sankoff and Thibault 1981). For example, the variation between *that* and zero in (5) is delimited by the syntactic context of a matrix predicate and a finite complement clause. The variation between a ditransitive and a prepositional dative construction in (6) is delimited lexico-grammatically by the presence of a verb that can select for two arguments and the overt expression of those arguments in context. This type of variation can be characterized as *choice-dependent*: a prior syntactic or lexical choice creates a variable context with a limited set of semantically equivalent options.

(5) a. *I **knew that** you would want them back* (BNC)
    b. *We **knew** you were there.* (BNC)

(6) a. *Here, **give me the phone**. I'll deal with it!* (BNC)
　　b. *The phone was handed over to Erika, who confirmed the trip and then **gave the phone to her mother*** (BNC)

The study of choice-dependent variation in grammar is perhaps not in itself problematic. In fact, phonological variation is likewise circumscribed by phonological, morphological or lexical structure. However, it should be clear that a considerable amount of variation in grammar is much less readily captured.

That said, let me also speculate that even though hypervariation primarily poses a methodological problem, it may have a theoretical sting. As Variationists assume that variation has the potential of turning unstable (Montgomery 2007: 111; see section 1 above), it follows that variation must be potentially stable and that change happens when externally triggered. As Deumert and Mesthrie (2000: 116) put it, "all change is preceded by variation but not all variation leads to change". This characterization, however, may be primarily one of narrowly circumscribed choice-dependent variation. Choice-dependent variation can be stable because it exists in what is a relatively closed system, barred from extensive interaction with other variations. In hypervariation, by contrast, variation and change may stand in a different relation. In the situation of interlocking variables that characterizes hypervariation, change can easily run rampant, as it will have complex ripple effects beyond the grammatical context in which it first starts. If so, in hypervariation, instability is likely to be the rule rather than the exception. Moreover, in hypervariation, many changes may be happening without a language-external trigger or drive, but simply in response to other ongoing changes.

5 Grammatical context

The problems raised above do not have ready and easy solutions. However, one way to approach them is to analyze variation in relation to its broader grammatical context (see Aaron 2010). Taking into account grammatical context is the obvious first step to describing and understanding hypervariation, but it can also offer insight into the linguistic motivation underlying variation.

To show this, the following sections return to the variation illustrated above, involving the various prepositional phrase complements that can mark the external source of emotion following *disappointed* and other emotion adjectives. As a first step, the variation in this domain of grammar is described on a synchronic basis, using data from the *British National Corpus* (BNC). The domain is subject to hypervariation, defying the usual descriptive methods. The variation is therefore described using a network-inspired model. This shows just how pervasive and intricate variation can be, challenging both Variationist and Functionalist approaches. Next, the diachrony of one specific variable context is turned to by tracing the history of the prepositional phrase complements of *disappointed*. Using data from the *Hansard Corpus* (HC), it is shown that this context has a long history of variation and change. However, when this history is seen against the background of the broader grammatical system of adjective complementation, it also becomes clear that – despite what may appear to be excessive variation and random diachronic fluctuation – there is still good reason to believe in linguistic motivation underlying both variation and change.

5.1 Describing hypervariation

In English, predicatively used emotion adjectives optionally combine with prepositional phrase complements (henceforth PP-complements) to mark the source of emotion. Studies of complementation are often cast in terms of the "matching-problem" (Noonan 1985), asking which predicate types pattern with which complement types. The same literature reveals various factors that determine likely matches, including semantic and syntactic factors but also historical and extra-linguistic factors (see De Smet 2013 for an overview). The matching problem applies also to emotion adjectives and PP-complements. Predictably, it turns out that different adjectives combine with different PP-complements, as shown in (7).

(7) a. *He was **sorry about** the outcome of an affray that he had not started and in no way wanted.* (BNC)
    b. *This wedding is what he's been **afraid of**.* (BNC)
    c. *Instead of the clarity and precision of Newtonian mechanics, we have to be **content with** a more fuzzy account of affairs.* (BNC)

Also predictably, many adjectives allow more than one PP-complement, as shown in (8)–(9) (and see also (1) above). The alternative options are usually not pure synonyms, but their meanings are similar enough to allow variation into the system.

(8) a. *Lisner wrote to me that John was **excited about** my plans […]* (BNC)
    b. *I was **excited at** the thought of seeing her again.* (BNC)
    c. *There can be little doubt that Picasso was **excited by** the work that Braque brought back to Paris from l'Estaque* (BNC)

(9) a. *Companies that are* **confident about** *their ability to learn may even prefer some ambiguity in the alliance's legal structure.* (BNC)
b. *The last Hercules crash was more than 20 years ago and the base say they remain* **confident in** *the safety of the transporter plane.* (BNC)
c. *It is easy to be tolerant of members of other races if one is* **confident of** *one's own standing in society* (BNC)

Even when the general syntactic template is kept constant to predicative adjectives and their PP-complements, the variation defies easy delimitation.[6] For example, as (8)–(9) show, *about*-complements can alternate with *at*-complements and *by*-complements following *excited*, but they potentially alternate with *in*-complements and *of*-complements following *confident*. These interlocking patterns of variation are typical of hypervariation.

The first step to dealing with hypervariation is obviously to describe it. To do this for the grammatical subsystem of emotion adjectives and their PP-complements, data were extracted from the BNC. This was done in two rounds. In a first round, a query was run retrieving any forms of the verb *be* (i.e. having 'VB' as part of their pos-tag), followed by an adjective (i.e. any form tagged 'AJ0'), followed by any of the forms *at, about, by, in, of, over* or *with*. The results were randomly filtered down to a 5% sample (n=3,361). The sample was manually analyzed to identify all emotion adjectives with a source-complement. This produced a list of 97 adjectives, which formed the input to the second query. The second query retrieved all instances of any of the 97 adjectives previously identified, again preceded by a form of *be* (i.e. having 'VB' as part of the pos-tag) and followed by any of the forms *at, about, by, in, of, over* or *with*. This produced a second concordance (n=17,592). The concordance was manually checked for any remaining false positives, eventually retaining a data set with 15,595 instances. The two-step procedure was meant to keep manual analysis manageable, as well as to reduce dependence on the pos-tagging of the corpus.[7]

---

[6] The emotional state of an experiencer participant and its external source or trigger can of course also be expressed by other means, including verbs (e.g. *the authorities deeply regretted the outcome* (BNC)) and verbal idioms (e.g. *she felt anger at his unfeeling attitude* (BNC)). Note also that the complement of an emotion adjective can be expressed by other means than a PP (e.g. *He was upset that Daisy was gone* (BNC)). Needless to say, all of this only complicates matters further. For the sake of the argument developed here, however, it suffices to focus on emotion adjectives and their PP-complements.

[7] The search procedure is a compromise between precision and recall. The first sample-based query dramatically improves precision for the second query. At the same time, recall is optimized in that the procedure is predominantly bottom-up, rather than starting from preconceived lists

A word is in order on the manual part of the analysis, which excluded false positives from the data sets produced by the two queries. Hits in the data set were retained as relevant if they contained an adjective and a PP, with the adjective describing an emotional state, and the PP its cause. An "emotional state" was understood as a mental state involving positive or negative valence (e.g. *content* vs *ashamed*) and/or increased or lowered arousal (e.g. *amazed* vs *bored*) felt in relation to a person, object or situation. While these dimensions fall far short of capturing the full meanings of the adjectives involved, they allow reasonably principled discrimination between emotion adjectives (e.g. *confident, horrified, obsessed,* etc.) and other adjectives (e.g. *adept, aware, capable, certain, unwell,* etc.). In case of doubt, adjectives were initially retained in the data set, but if all instances for a given adjective were doubtful, the adjective was eventually deleted from the data set. One recurrent coding issue involved the distinction between participial adjectives and verbs. Here, an inclusive policy was adopted: only if the verbal reading was the only option, was an instance excluded from the data set.

The final data set provides a detailed (if not exhaustive) picture of which emotion adjectives pattern with which PP-complements in the English represented by the BNC. The patterning proves to be extremely complex, however, and requires visualization for efficient description. To this end, a network plot was created, as shown in figure 11.1 below, which captures as much of the information available in the data set as possible. The nodes in the network are the adjectives and prepositions found in the data set. The size of the nodes is proportional to the log-transformed frequency of the forms (within the data set). Forms with fewer than 50 occurrences were excluded from the plot. The links between the nodes reflect co-occurrence patterns between adjectives and prepositions. The weight of the links is proportional to the transitional probability for the adjective to be followed by the preposition (again, as calculated within the data set). Links with a transitional probability below 2% were excluded from the plot.[8] Finally, the colour coding for the adjectival nodes reflects the degree to which adjectives are loyal to a single type of PP-complement, from yellow for maximal loyalty to

---

of adjectives. However, recall is not completely optimal. In two respects, the procedure is *not* bias-free. First, the list of prepositions was compiled on the basis of introspection. Second, high-frequency adjectives had a better chance of making it into the final selection. The frequency bias is a defendable sacrifice, however, since it would in the end be difficult to properly describe the combinatorial behaviour of low-frequency adjectives anyway.

8 A transitional probability of 2% corresponds to the lowest-frequency link (n=1) for the lowest-frequency node (n=50) that can be included in the plot. This way, lower-frequency adjectives are treated with the same descriptive granularity as higher-frequency adjectives.

Fig. 11.1: Emotion adjectives and their PP-complements in Present-day English (BNC)

red for maximal promiscuity.⁹ The layout of the plot was calculated using the Fruchterman-Rheingold algorithm.

Without going into the details, the following observations can be made from figure 11.1. Clearly, variation is the rule. High-loyalty adjectives are a minority, with only 13 (or 23%) of the 56 adjectives depicted being exclusively linked to a single PP-complement type. Bear in mind that this is necessarily an

---

9 The loyalty measure is calculated as the standard deviation for the transitional probabilities between an adjective and all of the seven PP-complement types in the data set. A maximally loyal adjective occurs with only one PP-complement type, so the standard deviation is calculated over one transitional probability at 100% and six others at 0%, giving a standard deviation of 37.8. As an adjective patterns with more prepositions, its transitional probabilities become more evenly distributed over the different PP-complement types, so the standard deviation drops. A maximally promiscuous adjective would have the same transitional probability of 14.3% for each of the seven PP-complements, giving a standard deviation of 0.0.

overestimation of adjectival loyalty, due to the limitations of the corpus and of how the data are visualized in figure 11.1. For example, the share of maximally loyal adjectives drops further if those combinations are taken into account that have a lower than 2% transitional probability, such as the ones illustrated in (10).

(10) a. *he stared down at his Saturday suit and was **afraid at** the new possibility that he had become a man set in his ways, upset by change.* (BNC)
b. *What it is that teachers are **dissatisfied about** we will return to later.* (BNC)
c. *I am **interested by** the idea of the tempo that flows naturally.* (BNC)

We can also look at this from the point of view of the PP-complements. Consider, for example, the patterns of alternation that arise from PP-complements occurring with the same emotion adjectives. With seven PP-complement types, there are 21 conceivable binary alternations. Figure 11.1 shows that, of these, almost every alternation is actually attested in the context of at least one adjective. The only pair of PP-complements that is not seen to alternate with any of the adjectives in figure 11.1 is *of*-complements and *with*-complements. But even this alternation is in fact well-attested when combinations with a less than 2% transitional probability are taken into account, as illustrated in (11)–(12).

(11) a. *well I was pleased, I was **pleased of** it* (BNC)
b. *He tested the noose with his foot. He pulled hard at it until he was **pleased with** it.* (BNC)

(12) a. *I could see he was **ashamed of** what he was doing* (BNC)
b. *they were **ashamed with** what they had done* (BNC)

Observe further that variation is not only widespread, it is also very intricate, in that distributional overlaps are typically partial. With any specific adjective, alternating PP-complements may alternate only some of the time. For instance, although *thrilled* selects both *with*-complements and *at*-complements, it would be much easier to replace *with* by *at* in (13a) than in (13b).

(13) a. *two years on experts are **thrilled with** the results.* (BNC)
b. *The twins had been **thrilled with** the computer, of course* (BNC)

Partial overlap is also what characterizes the more general distributional patterns. Essentially every PP-complement can alternate with every other PP-complement in at least some contexts, but none of the PP-complements pattern identically and most do not even pattern very similarly. For most alternating pairs of PP-complements, it is clear from figure 11.1 that the distributional overlap is restricted to a relatively small subset of adjectives. For instance, *of*-complements and *in*-complements only alternate as potential complements to *confident* (see (9) above); *of*-complements and *over*-complements only alternate following *optimistic*, etc. The pair of complements whose distribution is most similar is *at*-complements and *by*-complements. But even for this pair distributional overlap is incomplete: a small group of emotion adjectives pattern with *at*-complements but not with *by*-complements, including *angry, ashamed, furious, happy* and *unhappy*.

Finally, apart from being prone to variation, the behaviour of emotion adjectives and PP-complements also shows some other striking tendencies. First, the many cases of partial overlap between variants are of course suggestive of semantically-motivated patterning, with semantically related adjectives distributing in similar ways. For example, adjectives denoting *fear* (*afraid, frightened, scared, terrified*) tend to favour *of*-complements; adjectives denoting a more or less stable state of mild positive emotion (*comfortable, content, happy, satisfied*) tend to favour *with*-complements; adjectives denoting sudden surprised agitation (*alarmed, astonished, shocked, stunned, surprised*) tend to take *at*-complements, etc. Second, morphologically related antonyms like *satisfied* and *dissatisfied* or *happy* and *unhappy* show similar distributional preferences. Presumably, the distributional behaviour of the stem carries over to that of the derived form. Third, there is also a syntactic or at least formal regularity. All of the adjectives combining with *by*-complements are formally past participles. This is no coincidence, as there is only a thin line between predicatively used adjectival past participles and verbal passives, which typically pattern with *by* as marker of the agent role in a passive clause.

These observations link back to the preceding theoretical discussion. Judging from the behaviour of emotion adjectives and PP-complements, the Variationist approach will find itself ratified in the abundance of variation, but it may be challenged by the interlocking character of the alternation patterns. Functionalist thinking may find semantic differences between variants hinted at in their diverging distributional preferences, but would be challenged by the striking degree of tolerance to variation.

5.2 Motivation

While far from exhaustive, the above description goes some way towards putting variation in its grammatical context. At least, we can now focus on a more narrowly circumscribed pocket of variation and interpret the variation found there against the background of a more extensive system. Doing so, variation and change can be seen in a somewhat different light, revealing some of the linguistic motivation underlying it.

By way of example, let us turn to the most promiscuous of emotion adjectives – *disappointed*, as seen in figure 11.1 above – and add the diachronic dimension to the picture. In the BNC data set described above, *disappointed* combines with *with*-complements (31%), *by*-complements (28%), *at*-complements (22%), *in*-complements (16%) and *about*-complements (3%), and (as shown by (1f) above) it is marginally attested with *over*-complements as well. To describe how this distribution evolved over time, use was made of the *Hansard Corpus* (henceforth HC). The HC consists of the written records of parliamentary debates in the British Houses of Parliament, covering (approximately) the last two centuries. The HC was queried for all instances of *disappointed* immediately followed by *about, at, by, in, of*,[10] *over* or *with*. The data for every second decade were retained and manually analyzed to remove false positives. This eventually produced a diachronic data set covering the two centuries represented by the HC, made up of 11 synchronic "slices", starting with the 1800s, 1820s, 1840s, etc., containing all instances of *disappointed* followed by a PP-complement marking the source of disappointment (n=5,553). The share of the different complement types within this data set is plotted over time in figure 11.2 below.

What can be learned from this? It is obvious from figure 11.2 that *disappointed* has (as far as the data set goes) been a promiscuous adjective from the start and has over a period of two centuries shown no noticeable inclination towards mending its ways. A standardized loyalty score[11] has been superimposed on the plot, confirming this general impression. The loyalty score rises somewhat in periods during which a single PP-complement dominates the distribution (*in*-complements in the 1800s, *at*-complements in the 1880s, *with*-complements in the 1920s, *by*-complements in the 2000s) but there is no overall trend towards increasing or, for that matter, decreasing loyalty. This is despite the fact that there has actually been a lot of change going on. The distributional profile of *disappointed* by the 2000s has changed markedly compared to what it looked like in the 1800s. Yet, the ideal of one-to-one mappings between form and function

---

10 As it turns out, *disappointed* is sometimes followed by an of-PP, but in this use *disappointed* means 'deprived of' (e.g. suddenly those who invested a large amount of capital in mills and the cultivation of the soil were **disappointed of** the fruits of their enterprise before they could get their first returns (1848, HC)). Examples like this were eventually not retained, as *disappointed* is not an emotion adjective here.

11 The loyalty score was calculated as explained in section 5.1, footnote 9, and then standardized so that maximal loyalty corresponds to 1 (= exclusive selection of a single PP-complement) and minimal loyalty to 0 (= equal selection rates for all PP-complements).

remains about equally far removed. The history of *disappointed*, then, is far from supporting the idea that languages might strive to get rid of variation over time. It could be countered that the variants might be expressing useful functional contrasts, but in light of the constant turn-over in the preferred PP-complement type – from *in*, to *at*, to *with*, to *by* – this too is, at face value, doubtful.

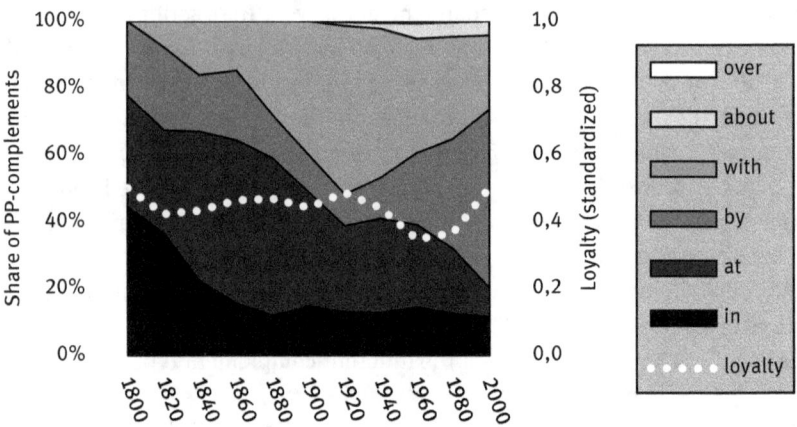

Fig. 11.2: The PP-complements of *disappointed* over time (HC)

While this again confirms the naturalness of variation, there is something remarkable about the variation. The distributional behaviour of *disappointed* in Present-day English was found to be extreme, in that *disappointed* has the lowest loyalty score of all of the 56 adjectives documented in the BNC data set. It is therefore somewhat surprising that this property is diachronically stable. After all, extreme values tend, statistically, to be short-lived. One could say that *disappointed* just seems to be the kind of adjective that attracts variation. But this comes down to saying that there must be a linguistic property of *disappointed* or of the overall system of PP-complementation with emotion adjectives that is responsible for the variation observed. In terms of the matching problem, one could speculate that the set of PP-complements just does not offer an ideal match for *disappointed* – or that it offers too many acceptable matches.

This need not be far-fetched. As an emotion adjective, *disappointed* has a comparatively complex semantic structure, as it involves negative feelings towards an object that had fostered positive feelings of hope or anticipation before but somehow failed to meet expectations. Such a complex semantic structure makes it difficult to semantically relate *disappointed* to other emotion adjectives. That is, it contains elements of meaning also found in the semantics of other adjectives, such as an implicit change of state (as in *upset*), an element of surprise (as in *alarmed*), and an element of negative feeling (as in *unhappy*), but it is nevertheless semantically dissimilar from any of those adjectives. As a result, it defies semantic classification and, by the same token, semantically-based PP-complement selection. In other words, *disappointed* may well have a sensible linguistic excuse for being promiscuous.

If it is reasonable to suspect linguistic motivation in the prolonged state of extreme variability characterizing the distributional behaviour of *disappointed*, it also makes sense to see linguistic motivation in at least some of the specific changes that the distributional behaviour of *disappointed* underwent. Given no very strong propensity towards any specific PP-complement type, changes taking place elsewhere in the system may be enough to tilt the balance in favour of one complement type or other in the context of *disappointed*. For example, the modest rise in *about*-complements from the 1920s to 1960s echoes an overall rise of *about*-complements with emotion adjectives and a more general simultaneous increase in the frequency of *about* across the board.[12] This means that the appearance of *about*-complements with *disappointed* is really no coincidence. *About*-complements became more strongly entrenched, hence more easily available for selection, and *disappointed* – never picky when it comes to complement selection – welcomed the newcomer.

As another example, the increasing use of *by*-complements with *disappointed* could be linked to changes in the semantics of the corresponding verb *disappoint*. As an emotion adjective, *disappointed* marks a state resulting from dashed hopes or frustrated anticipation. As a verb, however, *disappoint* is polysemous. It can take an animate object and then typically has a causative meaning, 'cause (someone) to feel disappointed', as in (14a). But it can also take an inanimate object and mean 'fail to live up to (hopes, expectations)' or 'defeat, frustrate (plans)', as in (14b)–(14c).

---

12 An automatic query in the HC for *about*, preceded by any of the adjectives found to combine with *about*-complements in Figure 1 above, shows that emotion adjectives with *about* were very infrequent before 1860 (with normalized frequencies below 2pmw), began to rise slowly from the 1860s onwards to just under 10pmw in the 1910s, then rose sharply between the 1910s and 1970s, to level again around 160pmw in the 1980s to 2000s. This development parallels an overall simultaneous rise in the frequency of *about* in the HC, from 316pmw in the 1800s to 882pmw in the 1910s (steady but slow increase), then suddenly to 2,729pmw in the 1970s (sharp rise), to end at 2,876pmw in the 2000s (stabilization).

(14) a. *There is one omission in the address which I own has a great deal **disappointed** me* (1805, HC)
b. *Would the commons of England disregard the opinions, and **disappoint** the expectations of the people?* (1805, HC)
c. *the bill could properly be denominated inefficient, because it was professedly to raise 27,000 men immediately, and it had wholly **disappointed** this design* (1805, HC)

In Present-day English, the causative use in (14a) is most common, but in 19th-century English the non-causative uses in (14b)–(14c) dominated. That the causative use became the default meaning of the verb *disappoint* implies that the semantic link between the passive form of the verb and the emotion adjective was strengthened (increasingly, the subject of the adjective aligns to the patient argument of the verb). As adjective and passive verb gravitated towards each other, the PP-type common to both began to receive stronger grammatical support and the frequency of *by*-complements with *disappointed* increased.

In sum, the history of *disappointed* gives little occasion to believe that the language system strives to maintain subtle semantic contrasts or to suppress needless variation. In that respect, language appears to have no drive towards functional optimization. Nevertheless, the history of *disappointed* suggests that both variation and change may arise for system-internal reasons. This in turn points to the kinds of linguistic motivation that really underlie the use of near-synonymous variants. At least in part, the use of specific variants with *disappointed* and other emotion adjectives is motivated by the network of associative relations between complex patterns, such as the semantic similarity relations between emotion adjectives, the morphological relations between adjectives and the forms from which they are derived, or the formal relation between past participial adjectives and passives. Broadly speaking, such relations can be labelled analogical, because they primarily depend on similarity. Motivation then resides in the fact that, by analogy, similar treatment is given to similar things. Because this is a form of cognitive efficiency (see Rosch 1978), it is fundamentally a functional principle.

6 Concluding remarks

The preceding discussion does not – and was not meant to – offer a conclusive analysis of the system of emotion adjectives and PP-complements. For this particular domain of grammar, the corpus analysis gives a detailed picture of where variation occurs, but without delving into the various factors that drive the selection of specific variants. It also hints at semantically motivated patterning, but without going into any great detail. What I hope the discussion makes clear, however, is how Variationist and Functionalist approaches might both benefit from taking into account grammatical context, and how this can eventually also help to reconcile both types of approach.

Even in the face of rampant variation, there is no reason to give up the Functionalist premise that linguistic structure is motivated by the function it serves. Only, what is motivated in variation is sometimes just the existence of the variants – not the semantic contrasts they code. While such contrasts will always exist, they need not be the *raison d'être* of the variation. Rather, variants can be thought of as coding solutions speakers come up with as they draw on their grammatical resources. Speakers apply these resources by analogy. Patterns successfully relied on in the past can be reused in similar situations, which is how semantic patterning can arise. For example, a speaker may select *with*-complements with *furious* because they are used to doing so with *angry* – but if the fury is one that flares up suddenly, the same speaker may instead analogize to *shocked, horrified, appalled* or *alarmed* and select an *at*-complement. Or a speaker may select one or other PP-complement with *furious* simply based on the choice they had made or had been exposed to previously. Exactly what traces in linguistic memory a speaker will call on in making a linguistic choice is unpredictable and whatever patterning emerges from such choices may at some point be suspended again (see Hopper 1987). This does not make semantic patterning any less real, but it does imply that semantic patterning can be just a by-product of linguistic choice – not its primary purpose.

Variation, then, arises because grammars offer multiple near-equivalent solutions to the same coding problem. In choosing a PP-complement with *furious*, a speaker can look to *angry*, or to *shocked*, or to any previous use of *furious* itself. Even if variation observed in a given grammatical context appears redundant or excessive, each of the individual variants is likely to be a grammatically well-motivated structure, because they are somehow analogous to coding solutions that have been relied on under similar circumstances.

One could wonder why the grammar over-generates solutions – one solution would do, why have many? First, having an abundance of solutions may offer an advantage, particularly to the speaker, who faces the problem of efficiently coding experience into an intelligible linguistic form. Just as a (coding) solution is more effective if it can be depended on to solve more than one problem, as in cases of polysemy, it is generally easier to solve a (coding) problem if it allows more than one solution, as in cases of variation.

Second, many linguistic subsystems are parasitic on their elements' core functions. The PP-complements with emotion adjectives are a case in point. In all likelihood, prepositions do not grammaticalize because they are so useful at coding specific shades of emotional meaning. Rather, let us assume prepositions typically grammaticalize for the sake of marking spatial relations. When speakers need to link a cause to an emotion adjective, they turn to PP-complements as a usable resource, but because the demands of coding human emotions are not the forces that have shaped this particular resource, the available form-function mappings may be less than optimal. After all, there is no reason why the divisions of labour that work well for coding spatial relations should work also for coding the causes of emotional states. In other words, even if a choice is semantically motivated, it can be a compromise at the same time – a good fit but imperfect nonetheless.

Once the linguistic motivations for variation are better understood, it becomes easier to see the linguistic motivations of change. Language change is sometimes equated with the social propagation of a linguistic variable. However, in a system that exhibits hypervariation, instability is likely to be inevitable and perpetual, because any change in one variable context will also affect other variable contexts, in an unending cascade of linguistic causes and consequences. This is of course not to deny that social forces can interact with this, or that innovations, in order to become conventionalized, must spread across a speech community. But those facts do not preclude the possibility that the structure of grammar itself creates conditions that may be favourable or unfavourable to specific changes, or that change in one domain may interact with developments in other areas of the language. Variation and change are so interwoven that if there is linguistic motivation in variation, there must also be linguistic motivation in change.

Acknowledgements

I would like to thank the editors of this volume and two anonymous referees for their comments on an earlier version of this paper. I am also grateful for the useful feedback from Pierre Swiggers and the participants to the *Gradience and Constructional Change* workshop held in Edinburgh in November 2017.

References

Aaron, Jessi. 2010. Pushing the envelope: Looking beyond the variable context. *Language Variation and Change* 3. 191–222.

Anttila, Raimo. 1989. *Historical and comparative linguistics*. Amsterdam: John Benjamins.
Biber, Douglas. 2004. Modal use across registers and time. In Anne Curzan & Kimberly Emmons (eds.), *Studies in the history of the English language II: Unfolding conversations*, 189–216. Berlin: Mouton de Gruyter.
Blas Arroyo, José Luis & Kim Schulte. 2017. Competing modal periphrases in Spanish between the 16th and the 18th centuries. *Diachronica* 34. 1–39.
Bolinger, Dwight. 1968. Entailment and the meaning of structures. *Glossa* 2. 119–127.
Bresnan, Joan & Tatiana Nikitina. 2009. The gradience of the dative alternation. In Linda Uyechi & Lian Hee Wee (eds.), *Reality exploration and discovery: Pattern interaction in language and life*, 161–184. Stanford: CSLI Publications.
Brook, Marisa. 2018. Taking it up a level: Copy-raising and cascaded tiers of morphosyntactic change. *Language Variation and Change* 30. 231–260.
Chafe, Wallace (ed.). 1980. *The Pear Stories: Cognitive, cultural, and linguistic aspects of narrative production*. Norwood, New Jersey: Ablex.
Coates, Jennifer. 1983. *The semantics of the modal auxiliaries*. London: Routledge.
Colleman, Timothy. 2009. Verb disposition in argument structure alternations: A corpus study of the Dutch dative alternation. *Language Sciences* 31. 593–611.
Cornips, Leonie & Karen P. Corrigan (eds.). 2005. *Syntax and variation: Reconciling the biological and the social*. Amsterdam: John Benjamins.
Croft, William. 2000. *Explaining language change: An evolutionary approach*. London: Longman.
Croft, William. 2002. *Typology and universals*. Cambridge: Cambridge University Press.
Croft, William. 2010. The origins of grammaticalization in the verbalization of experience. *Linguistics* 48. 1–48.
De Smet, Hendrik. 2013. *Spreading patterns: Diffusional change in the English system of complementation*. Oxford: Oxford University Press.
De Smet, Hendrik, Frauke D'hoedt, Lauren Fonteyn & Kristel Van Goethem. 2018. The changing functions of competing forms: Attraction and differentiation. *Cognitive Linguistics* 29. 197–234.
Deumert, Ana & Rajend Mesthrie. 2000. Language variation and change. In Rajend Mesthrie, Joan Swann, Ana Deumert & William L. Leap (eds.), *Introducing Sociolinguistics*, 114–147. Amsterdam: John Benjamins.
Dik, Simon C. 1988. Isomorfisme als functioneel verklaringsprincipe. *GLOT* 11. 87–106.
Geeraerts, Dirk. 1997. *Diachronic prototype semantics*. Oxford: Oxford University Press.
Goldberg, Adele E. 1995. *Constructions: A construction grammar approach to argument structure*. Chicago: University of Chicago Press.
Gries, Stefan T. & Anatol Stefanowitsch. 2004. Extending collostructional analysis: A corpus-based perspective on 'alternations'. *International Journal of Corpus Linguistics* 9. 97–129.
Haiman, John. 1980. The iconicity of grammar. *Language* 56. 515–540.
Haspelmath, Martin. 1999. Why is grammaticalization irreversible? *Linguistics* 37: 1043–1068.
Hopper, Paul J. 1987. Emergent grammar. *Proceedings of the Berkeley Linguistics Society* 13. 139–157.
Kuhle, Anneliese. 2014. Language as tool: The analogy to primate cognition. *Language & Communication* 34. 1–16.
Labov, William. 1972. *Sociolinguistic patterns*. Philadelphia: University of Pennsylvania Press.
Labov, William. 1978. Where does the sociolinguistic variable stop? A response to Beatrice Lavandera. *Working Papers in Sociolinguistics* 44. 7–23.

Langacker, Ronald W. 1987. *Foundations of Cognitive Grammar*, vol. 1: *Theoretical prerequisites*. Stanford: Stanford University Press.

Lass, Roger. 1998. *On explaining language change*. Cambridge: Cambridge University Press.

Lavandera, Beatriz R. 1978. Where does the sociolinguistic variable stop? *Language in Society* 7. 171–182.

Leech, Geoffrey, Marianne Hundt, Christian Mair & Nicholas Smith. 2011. *Change in contemporary English: A grammatical study*. Cambridge: Cambridge University Press.

Mair, Christian. 2003. Gerundial complements after *begin* and *start*: Grammatical and sociolinguistic factors, and how they work against each other. In Günther Rohdenburg & Britta Mondorf (eds.), *Determinants of grammatical variation in English*, 329–345. Berlin: Mouton de Gruyter.

Montgomery, Michael. 2007. Variation and historical linguistics. In Robert Bayley & Ceil Lucas (eds.), *Sociolinguistic variation: Theories, methods, and applications*, 110–132. Cambridge: Cambridge University Press.

Mufwene, Salikoko S. 1994. Theoretical linguistics and variation analysis: Strange bedfellows? In Katharine Beals, Jeannette Denton, Robert Knippen, Lynette Melnar, Hisami Suzuki & Erica Zeinfeld (eds), *Papers from the 30th Regional Meeting of the Chicago Linguistic Society*, Vol 2: *The parasession on variation in linguistic theory*, 202–217. Chicago: Chicago Linguistic Society.

Myhill, John. 1995. Change and continuity in the functions of the American English modals. *Linguistics* 33. 157–211.

Noël, Dirk. 2003. Is there semantics in all syntax? The case of accusative and infinitive constructions vs. *that*-clauses. In Günther Rohdenburg & Britta Mondorf (eds.), *Determinants of grammatical variation in English*, 329–345. Berlin: Mouton de Gruyter.

Noonan, Michael. 1985. Complementation. In Timothy Shopen (ed.), *Language typology and syntactic description*, vol. 2: *Complex constructions*, 42–110. Cambridge: Cambridge University Press.

Nuyts, Jan. 2007. Cognitive Linguistics and Functional Linguistics. In Dirk Geeraerts & Hubert Cuyckens (eds.), *The Oxford handbook of Cognitive Linguistics*, 543–565. Oxford: Oxford University Press.

Poplack, Shana & Rena Torres Cacoullos. 2015. Linguistic emergence on the ground: A variationist paradigm. In Brian MacWhinney & William O'Grady (eds.), *The handbook of language emergence*, 267–291. Oxford: Wiley-Blackwell.

Poplack, Shana. 2011. Grammaticalization and linguistic variation. In Bernd Heine & Heiko Narrog (eds.), *The Oxford handbook of grammaticalization*, 209–224. Oxford: Oxford University Press.

Poplack, Shana. 2015. Pursuing symmetry by eradicating variability. Keynote lecture presented at *New Ways of Analysing Variation* 44, Toronto, 22–25 October.

Romaine, Suzanne. 1981. On the problem of syntactic variation: A reply to Beatrice Lavandera and William Labov. *Working Papers in Sociolinguistics* 82 1-38.

Rosch, Eleanor. 1978. Principles of categorization. In Eleanor Rosch & Barbara B. Lloyd (eds.), *Cognition and categorization*, 27–48. Hillsdale, NJ: Lawrence Erlbaum.

Rosenbach, Anette. 2002. *Genitive variation in English: Conceptual factors in synchronic and diachronic studies*. Berlin: Mouton de Gruyter.

Sankoff, David. 1988. Sociolinguistics and syntactic variation. In Frederick J. Newmeyer (ed.), *Linguistics: The Cambridge survey*, vol. 4: *Language: The socio–cultural context*, 140–161. Cambridge: Cambridge University Press.

Sankoff, David & Pierrette Thibault. 1981. Weak complementarity: Tense and aspect in Montreal French. In Brenda B. Johns & David R. Strong (eds.), *Syntactic change*, 205–216. Ann Arbor: Department of Linguistics, University of Michigan.

Schwenter, Scott A. & Rena Torres Cacoullos. 2010. Grammaticalization paths as variable contexts in weak complementarity in Spanish. In James W. Walker (ed.), *Aspect in grammatical variation*, 13–26. Amsterdam: John Benjamins.

Tagliamonte, Sali A. 2012. *Variationist Sociolinguistics: Change, observation, interpretation*. Oxford: Wiley-Blackwell.

Taylor, John R. 2002. Near synonyms as co-extensive categories: 'High' and 'tall' revisited. *Language Sciences* 25. 263–284.

Torres Cacoullos, Rena & James A. Walker. 2009. The present of the English future: Grammatical variation and collocations in discourse. *Language* 85. 321–54.

Van de Velde, Freek. 2014. Degeneracy: The maintenance of constructional networks. In Ronny Boogaart, Timothy Colleman & Gijsbert Rutten (eds.), *Extending the scope of Construction Grammar*, 141–179. Berlin: De Gruyter.

María José López-Couso
Grammar in context: On the role of hypercharacterization in language variation and change

Abstract: Hypercharacterization (Lehmann 2005) or accretion (Kuteva 2008) is a widely attested cross-linguistic phenomenon which involves the accumulation of apparently "redundant" linguistic material in the marking of one category within the same structure. In this study I examine a number of cases of structural hypercharacterization in the history of English, focusing on the domain of syntax and paying attention to the motivations and functions of hypercharacterized forms and constructions. The selected case studies include the development of "strengthened" adverbial subordinators (e.g. *for because, like as if*), the occurrence of resumptive pronouns in subject extraction contexts, and the use of so-called "double-locative overlap constructions" and their relevance for the grammaticalization of existential *there*. These three examples show that hypercharacterization is interesting not only in and of itself, but also because of its great significance for language variation and language change.

1 Introduction

A recurrent concept in linguistic theory and description is attrition, a process which typically involves the reduction and eventual loss of linguistic material at the phonological level (phonological attrition or erosion) or the loss of lexical or referential meaning at the semantic level (semantic attrition or bleaching).[1] Though acknowledging that attrition is a rather pervasive feature in language change (hence its relevance to, for example, grammaticalization processes),

---

[1] I gratefully acknowledge the financial support of the European Regional Development Fund and the following institutions: the Spanish Ministry of Science, Innovation, and Universities (grant FFI2017-86884-P) and the Autonomous Government of Galicia through its Directorate General for Scientific and Technological Promotion (grants ED431D 2017/09 and ED431B 2017/12). I am also grateful to the editors of the volume and to two anonymous reviewers for their valuable comments on an earlier version of this study.

María José López-Couso, University of Santiago de Compostela, Department of English and German, Faculty of Philology, Santiago de Compostela, Spain, mjlopez.couso@usc.es

https://doi.org/10.1515/9783110682564-012

languages sometimes show the opposite tendency towards increased complexity through the accumulation of apparently "redundant" linguistic material in the marking of one category within the same structure, which brings about multiple determination of form and function. In recent years, growing attention has been directed to this widely attested cross-linguistic phenomenon, variously termed as "hypercharacterization" (Lehmann 2005), "pleonasm" (Lehmann 2005; Sornicola 2006), or "accretion" (Kuteva 2008), among other labels, all of which refer to a range of (seemingly) disparate and unrelated patterns observed at different levels in the linguistic system, from phonology and lexis to morphology and syntax.

Hypercharacterization phenomena are interesting not only in and of themselves, but also – and especially – because they provide appealing instances of linguistic competition between alternatives (i.e. between variants with and without accrued material) and because they may result in the emergence of new constructions. In this context, the aim of this study is to look into relevant instances of structural hypercharacterization in the history of English, focusing in particular on the domain of syntax. The study is organized as follows: section 2 introduces the notion of hypercharacterization or accretion, and presents evidence for the type of phenomena normally subsumed under these labels from different linguistic domains and from different languages worldwide. Attention is paid here to the potential motivations for the occurrence of hypercharacterization and to the functions of hypercharacterized forms and constructions, both at the communicative level and at the level of grammatical change. Section 3, in turn, is devoted to the discussion of three case studies of structural hypercharacterization in the history of English syntax: (i) "strengthened" adverbial subordinators (section 3.1); (ii) the occurrence of resumptive pronouns in complementation structures involving subject extraction (section 3.2); and (iii) the use of so-called "double-locative overlap constructions" and their relevance for the grammaticalization of existential *there* (section 3.3). The article closes with some remarks on the significance of hypercharacterization for language variation and change (section 4).

2 Defining and explaining hypercharacterization

As mentioned in section 1, attrition is a familiar concept in linguistics. In situations of language contact, for example, the usual possibility for morphosyntactic paradigms which interact is attrition, so that it is generally agreed that contact favours the reduction of linguistic complexity (but see below). Similarly, loss of phonetic substance (or erosion) and semantic attrition (or semantic bleaching) are changes typically identified in grammaticalization processes. Already in

Meillet's (1912) ground-breaking article "L'évolution des formes grammaticales", grammaticalization is characterized by a weakening in the phonological form of the item and a bleaching of its meaning. Likewise, a good number of the definitions of grammaticalization offered over the last few decades also refer to attrition as a crucial component of grammaticalization processes.

There is, however, a second possibility, namely the addition of linguistic material through a process known as hypercharacterization (Lehmann 2005), accretion (Kuteva 2008), or pleonasm (Lehmann 2005; Sornicola 2006). By way of illustration, consider example (1) below (see Kuteva 2008: 190), from Ngemba, a language spoken in Cameroon, which signals the relative-clause construction through the concurrent use of five different markers, namely a relative conjunction, a complementizer, pronoun-retention, a verbal suffix, and a sentential definitizer.[2]

(1) nyung **wá bah** a-keshung-**ne** mung wa **la** a kung atsang.
    man REL BAH he-TNS.beat-NE child DET LA he enter into.prison
    'The man who beat the child went to prison.'

Further manifestations of hypercharacterization are not difficult to identify across languages. A classic example is found in the expression of definiteness in some Scandinavian languages (see, among others, Dahl 2004, 2009): while Danish marks definiteness either by means of the preposed free definite articles (*den, det, de*), as in (2a), or by the enclitic article suffixed to the noun, as in (2b), in Swedish (2c) and in Norwegian (2d) both article forms can be used together in definite noun phrases containing prenominal modifiers.

(2) a. **det** stor-e hus   c. **det** stor-a hus-**et**
       DEM big   house   DEM big   house-DEF
       'the big house'   'the big house'

    b. hus-**et**   d. **det** stor-e hus-**et**
       house.DEF   DEM big   house-DEF
       'the house'   'the big house'

Another interesting case of hypercharacterization in syntax concerns the use of expletive subject pronouns in languages which mark person on the verb (see Lehmann 2005; Sornicola 2006). In Latin as well as in several modern Romance languages, overt subjects are not required, since grammatical information on

---

[2] Of these five markers, only the complementizer -*bah* is optional.

person is already conveyed in the verb inflection, as in Italian *viviamo* and Spanish *vivimos* 'we live'. However, side by side with these basic unmarked forms, there also exist the hypercharacterized emphatic variants *noi viviamo* and *nosotros vivimos*, which contain a subject pronoun as the surplus element. Interestingly, in written standard French the subject pronoun has become obligatory, so that "the reinforcement of the subject reference no longer functions at the communicative level, but merely at the syntactic level" (Lehmann 2005: 137).

Perhaps the most appealing question that comes to mind when dealing with accretion phenomena concerns the motivations and functions of accrued forms and constructions. This issue becomes especially relevant if we consider that accretion apparently goes against the principle of linguistic economy and represents a clear violation of one of the maxims of Grice's Cooperative Principle, namely the Maxim of Quantity: "Make your contribution as informative as is required (for the current purposes of the exchange)" and "Do not make your contribution more informative than is required" (Grice 1975: 45).

Kuteva (2008) provides a convenient summary of various potential motivations for the accumulation of linguistic material within the same structure. One possible explanation is the so-called residual quirk theory: "a novel structure appears but the old one continues to exist, so that the two are used together within the same expression" (Kuteva 2008: 190). This would account, for instance, for the stacking together in the noun *children* of two formative elements for the expression of pluralization, namely -(e)r and -en. In such cases, as Lehmann (2005: 141) explains, "in a diachronic perspective, the two concurrent markers are not on the same level. There is an inner marker which for some reason does not quite do the job, and an outer marker which is currently productive and which speakers feel should appropriately appear on such a word form".

Accretion may also result from the application of necessary adjustments in situations of language contact. As mentioned above, language contact has recurrently been mentioned as a factor favouring the reduction of linguistic complexity, therefore predicting that high-contact languages or varieties are characterized by low complexity (see, e.g., Dahl 2009: 42). It seems, however, that language contact may also lead to increased complexity. An example is found in colloquial Singapore English relative clauses of the type *The man who sell icekachang one gone home already*, which combine the Standard English *wh*-relativizer in clause-initial position with the postponed relative pronoun *one* modelled on Chinese (Alsagoff and Ho 1998: 133). Similarly, at the level of lexis, language users may deliberately accumulate linguistic material, in order to make sure that when using a recently borrowed word or expression, they will be understood. Typical examples of this strategy, to which Crystal (1995: 60) refers as "explain yourself", are found in the use of synonymic doublets of the type *animate or gyue courage to* in the Early Modern English example in (3), which couples a Romance borrowing (here the verb *animate*, adopted from Latin into English in the late fifteenth century) with a paraphrase in English (*give courage to*), which was added by Thomas Elyot as a kind of contextual glossing which helped in the decoding process of a then unfamiliar word.

(3) *whiche that prince did nat for lacke of iugement, he beinge of excellent lernyng, as disciple to Arystotell: but to thentent that his liberalite emploied on Cherilus, shoulde* **animate or gyue courage to** *others moch better lernid, to contende with hym in a semblable enterprise.* (1534, Thomas Elyot, *The Boke named The Governour*)

A similar formation is *suppose or wene*, shown in (4) and (5) from Early English Books Online (EEBO), where a "difficult" word (the French loan *suppose*, which entered English in the mid-fourteenth century) is coordinated with the Old English verb *wenan* ('think, imagine') in a mutually defining pair.

(4) *Fourthly / neyther they also are of right opynyon: whiche* **suppose or wene** *y^t theyr selues may not obteyn any thyng by praier, but yf they come worthely to praye /* (EEBO, 1534, *A Prymer in Englyshe, with certeyn prayers & godly meditations, very necessary for all people that vnderstonde not the Latyne tongue*)

(5) *Euen lykewyse as thou thy selfe (if I be nat begyl [...]d) wolde be lesse discontēted with him / which sholde* **suppose or wene** */ that thou arte nat borne:* (EEBO, 1534, *A playne and godly exposytion or declaratio[n] of the co[m]mune crede [...]*)

On other occasions, however, the repetition or accumulation of linguistic material cannot be attributed to any apparent functional reason. As discussed by Haiman and Ourn (2009: 568–569), Southeast Asian languages like Khmer make extensive use of verbatim repetition of a form to convey, among other meanings, pluralization or intensification; for example, *cruuk l'aaw l'aaw* (literally 'pig good good') means 'very good pig'. However, in addition to such instances of referential repetition, where plurality or intensity are represented iconically by means of the literal duplication of the word in question, Khmer also frequently couples a word with a near-synonym as a result of what Haiman and Ourn (2009) call "decorative or non-referential symmetry". In Khmer this process of doubling, which is particularly common in the formulaic registers, applies to both content words like nouns, verbs, and adjectives, as in (6a–b), and to function words like prepositions and conjunctions, as in (7a–b).

(6) a. *kdav*   *un*   'warm'
       warm   warm
    b. *lumnew* *thaan*   'residence'
       residence residence

(7) a. *baeu*   *prawseun* / *prawseun* *baeu* 'if'
       if   if   if   if
    b. *prawkaawp* *daoj*   'with'
       with   with

In examples like (6) and (7), hypercharacterization has little or no referential function, but is used for purely aesthetic or ornamental purposes in order to make one's speech more stylish and elegant and less harsh (see Haiman and Ourn 2009: 583).[3] Synonymic doublets with an elaborative or ornamental function can also be found in English at various points in history (see the Present-day English phrases *last and final, rules and regulations, let or hindrance, in this day and age,* etc.), though they seem to have been particularly common in the Renaissance period, when they became a major feature of literary language (Adamson 1999: 559). In the early sixteenth century, "the use of doublings had become the hallmark of the aureate style favoured by Caxton and his press" (Adamson 1999: 557), and at the end of the century, doubling had become so common that tripling was sometimes required.

The examples of hypercharacterization or accretion adduced in the preceding paragraphs demonstrate that the phenomenon is rather pervasive in languages and that the accumulation of synonymous linguistic material may result from different motivations and may also have different effects. Along these lines, it may be worth examining whether the motivation for the use of the hypercharacterized forms and structures discussed in section 3 responds, for example, to the iconic principle that "more of the same form stands for more of the same meaning" (Lakoff and Johnson 1980: 128) or whether determinants of a different kind lie behind the formation of such apparently redundant patterns.

---

[3] It is perhaps this kind of ornamental hypercharacterization that fits better Kuteva's (2008) description of accretion as the accumulation of "frills".

3 Exploring structural hypercharacterization in the history of English syntax

As seen in the preceding section, hypercharacterization or accretion is a relatively common phenomenon in languages at different linguistic levels. In this section I explore three instances of structural hypercharacterization in the history of English syntax, namely "strengthened" adverbial subordinators, resumptive pronouns in extraction contexts, and so-called "double-locative overlap" constructions. As will become apparent from the discussion that follows, the three selected case studies illustrate how hypercharacterized forms and constructions play crucial roles in the domains of language variation and language change.

3.1 On "strengthened" adverbial subordinators

A characteristic feature of one-word adverbial subordinators in the history of English is their high degree of syntactic and semantic polyfunctionality (see, among others, Hansen and Nielsen 1986: 243–265; Kortmann 1997: 289–336). Syntactically, a considerable number of adverbial subordinators do not serve exclusively this function; semantically, many adverbial subordinators can signal more than one interclausal relation in the adverbial semantic space. The proportion of "general-purpose" and polysemous adverbial subordinators was much higher in Old English than in later stages (see Kortmann 1997: 306, table 10.6, and 315, table 10.7, for syntactic and semantic polyfunctionality, respectively). For example, as regards syntactic or categorial polyfunctionality, most of the forms which served as adverbial subordinators at this early stage were used as adverbs and/or as prepositions as well, and some of them also performed other functions.[4] By way of illustration, table 12.1 below provides the different roles of some common Old English polyfunctional items.

---

[4] Even the conditional connective *ȝif*, which is considered by Braunmüller (1978: 104) one of the very few "genuine Proto-Germanic conjunctions" in a Germanic language, was not restricted in Old English to its use as an adverbial subordinator, since it could also be employed as a [+wh] complementizer with the meaning 'whether'.

Tab. 12.1: Polyfunctionality of Old English adverbial subordinators

	Conjunction	Adverb	Preposition	Other functions
ær 'before / formerly'	✓	✓	✓	
butan 'but / without'	✓	✓	✓	
nu 'now that / now'	✓	✓		✓ (interjection)
oþ 'until'	✓		✓	
siþþan 'since / after'	✓	✓	✓	
swa 'so'	✓	✓		✓ (pronoun)
þa 'when / then'	✓	✓		✓ (pronoun)
þeah 'though / however'	✓	✓		
þonne 'when / then'	✓	✓		

The list of polyfunctional forms with a subordinating function in table 12.1 is by no means comprehensive; other one-word items such as þanon ('whence / thence'), þær ('where / there'), þenden ('while / meanwhile'), and þider ('whither / thither') also belong to this category (see Mitchell 1985: §2418). As seen in table 12.1, the highest degree of overlap is found between the subordinating and the adverbial functions. Supporting quantitative evidence for this fact is provided by Kortmann (1997). In his data adverbs represent the preferred categorial source of Old English adverbial subordinators (32.4%; see Kortmann 1997: 305, table 10.5), and 37.8% of the items in his inventory of adverbial conjunctions also functioned as adverbs (Kortmann 1997: 306, table 10.6). It is only from Middle English onwards that English developed "special-purpose" or syntactically monofunctional adverbial subordinators (see Kortmann 1997: 310) and that the inventory of adverbial subordinators experienced a decrease in syntactic and semantic polyfunctionality and an increase in functional differentiation and semantic precision (see Fischer 1992: 287; Kortmann 1997: 291, 314–315). For instance, the semantic streamlining of adverbial subordinators in the course of history is evinced by the progressive reduction over time in the proportion of semantically polyfunctional subordinators, which dropped from 64.9% in the Old English period to 44.4% in Present-day English (see Kortmann 1997: 315, table 10.7; 334, table 10.18).

The most immediate problem arising from the high degree of overlap between adverbial subordinators and adverbs in Old English is that of potential ambiguity between the two functions in particular contexts. Although element order, punctuation, and metrical stress in the poetry have been suggested as possible clues helping in disambiguation (see, for example, Mitchell 1984; 1985: §§2444–2449, 2536–2560), it must be admitted that "[f]requently it cannot be determined which we have" (Mitchell 1985: §2418).[5] Thus, while word order can be a valuable and reliable guide in the prose, since most adverbs favoured verb-second order and conjunctions favoured verb-final order, this was by no means a regular rule; for example, clauses introduced by *ær*, *nu*, and *siþþan* often showed verb-final order also when these polyfunctional items were used adverbially (see Mitchell 1985: §2539; Traugott 1992: 220).

Interestingly, Old English also made use of further strategies to mark polyfunctional items such as those in table 12.1 as unambiguously belonging to the category of adverbial subordinators. Among these we find the addition of the subordinating markers *þe* and *þæt*, as in *þonne þe*, *nu þæt*, *þider þe*, etc. (see Mitchell 1985: §2424; Traugott 1992: 220–222), and (more importantly for the purposes of the present study) the doubling of the conjunction, as in *swa swa*, *þa þa*, *þær þær*, *þider þider*, and *þonne þonne* (see Mitchell 1985: §2424). Illustrative examples of these two strategies are given in (8) and (9).

(8) **Þider ðe   Stephanus forestop   ðider folgode   Paulus**
    where   PART Stephen   went before there followed Paul
    'Where Stephen went before, there Paul followed'
    (ÆCHom i. 52. 5; from Mitchell 1985: §2471)

(9) **Ðaða hi   ealle hæfdon þysne ræd   betwux   him gefæstnod, þa**
    when they all   had   this decision between them confirmed then
    becom Godes   grama ofer hi   ealle
    came   God's   anger over them all
    'When they all had confirmed this decision among themselves, God's anger came over them all'
    (ÆCHom i. 10. 28; from Mitchell 1985: §2539)

While the first of these patterns remained in later stages as a useful way of indicating subordinator status (see Kivimaa 1966; Watts 1982; Beal 1988; Fischer 1992: 293–295; Kortmann 1997: 308–311; Rissanen 1997, 1999: 303–304), the Old English strategy of doubling, which is related to accretion or hypercharacterization as defined in section 2, is not attested in post-Old English times. However,

---

[5] Mitchell (1984: 272–273; 1985: §2423) maintains, however, that phonological differentiation existed in Old English between the conjunctions *ær*, *nu*, *þa*, *þanon*, *þær*, *þeah*, and *þider* and their homonymous adverbial counterparts, between the demonstrative *þæt* and the conjunction *þæt*, as well as between the demonstrative *se* and the relativizer *se*.

the Middle and Early Modern English periods witnessed the emergence of a new pattern which closely resembles the Old English strategy of doubling illustrated in (9) above and which shares with it the unequivocal marking of subordinator status. This strategy produces "polymorphemic subordinators consisting of two adverbial subordinators, each of which alone suffices to express the interclausal relation(s) signalled by the complex (one-word or phrasal) subordinator as a whole" (Kortmann 1997: 312).

A prototypical example of this pattern is the complex subordinator of Condition *an(d) if*, which combines two conditional connectives, namely *and* 'if'[6] and *if* 'if', and which has the same meaning as either of the individual conjunctions on its own (see OED s.v. *if*, conj. and n. 8. b; *and*, conj.¹, adv., and n.¹ II. 13. b; Kortmann 1997: 312).[7] Some examples of this hypercharacterized conditional subordinator are given in (10)–(13).

(10) *Perfor lerne þe byleue leuest me were **And if** any werldly wi3t wisse me coupe.* (c1394 *P. Pl. Crede* 17; OED s.v. *if*, conj. and n. 8. b)

(11) *But **and yf** he wolde haue hythe he myght haue ben here* (PPCME2, CMREYNAR; from Fodor 2010: 300)

(12) *Anodur tyme I shal be as glad to do you pleser **and iff** I kan.* (1482 N. KNYVETON *Let. cMay* in *Cely Lett.* (1975) 145; OED s.v. *and*, conj.¹, adv., and n.¹ II. 13. b)

(13) *Thou know'st 'tis death, **an if** it be reveal'd* (1592 Marlowe, *Jew of M.* (Tauchn.) IV; from Visser 1963-1973: §880)

Occasionally, we also find sequences where the two subordinators occur in the reverse order *if and*, rather than *and if* (see OED s.v. *if*, conj. and n. 8. b). A mid-eighteenth-century example from Henry Fielding's *Tom Jones* is given here as (14).

(14) *"But what's to be done, husband?" "**If an** she be a rebel, I suppose you intend to be-tray her up to the Court".* (1749, Henry Fielding *Tom Jones* II, ii (1840) 154)

---

[6] On the use of the conditional subordinator *and* in the history of English, see Klemola and Filppula (1992), Rissanen (1999: 281), Culpeper and Kytö (2000), and Fodor (2010). Although Mitchell (1985: §§3668–3670) discusses some potential Old English examples, the use of *and* as a conditional subordinator seems to be mostly a Middle English development.

[7] Kortmann (1997: 312) also mentions the Early Modern English conditional subordinator *when if* < *when* 'when, if' + *if* 'if'. However, as is the case with the other strengthened subordinators he cites, he provides no examples of the combination.

The combinations *and if* and *if and* in such examples bear strong formal parallels to the Khmer cases of so-called "decorative or non-referential symmetry" provided in section 2. Note, for instance, the similarity of the English formations discussed here with the Khmer examples in (7a) above; in both cases, the pairs of synonyms involve conditional conjunctions meaning 'if' and both languages allow two alternative word order arrangements.

Together with *an(d) if*, a number of other Middle and Early Modern English formations also belong to the pattern of strengthened subordinators.[8] For example, within the domain of Time relations, the connectives *before ere, before or*, and *or ere* also illustrate accretion, since they derive from the combination of two items with identical meaning: 'before'.[9] Examples of the use of these hypercharacterized subordinators are given in (15) to (18) from the OED.

(15) **Before or** *þei resceyue hem, þei knelen doun.* (c1400 *Mandeville's Trav.* (1839) viii. 83; OED s.v. *ere* conj. C. 1. c)[10]

(16) *What Paul calls his own, was thut he had of old [...]*, **before ere** *he received any from Christ.* (1660 S. FISHER *Rusticus ad Academicos* 98; OED s.v. *before* adv., prep., conj., and n. C. 1. b)

(17) *But this heart shall breake in a 100. thousand flowes* **Or ere** *ile weepe* (1608 W. SHAKESPEARE *King Lear* vii.445; OED s.v. *ere* conj.² C. 1. d)

(18) *His soul shall dwell with him in hell,* **or ere** *yon sun go down!* (1823 J. G. LOCKHART *Calaynos in Anc. Spanish Ballads* xiii; OED s.v. *or* adv.¹, prep., conj.² C. 1. c)

The domain of causal relations also provides instances of hypercharacterized connectives. One of these is *for because* 'because' (see OED s.v. *because* prep. and conj. B. 1. a; *for* prep. and conj. A. 21. e; MED s.v. *bicause* conj. 1; *for* conj. 1), which combines two conjunctions, *for* and *because*, with the same meaning 'because',

---

8 In addition to the forms discussed in detail in this section, Kortmann (1997: 300, 312, 371) mentions in passing the following mergers as borderline cases of strengthened subordinators: concessive *although* (< *al* 'although/even/all' + *though* 'though/however'), and temporal *until* (< Old Norse *unz* 'until' + Old Norse *til* 'until, toward') and *unto* (< Old Norse *unz* 'until' + *to* 'until/to').
9 On temporal clauses introduced by *before, or,* and *ere* in Middle and Early Modern English, see Fischer (1992: 355) and Rissanen (1999: 313).
10 In the OED entry for *ere* conj., examples such as (15) are interpreted in the following way: "with a redundant *ere* (in sense A. 4b), or some equivalent word, belonging to the principal clause, though occasionally standing in the subordinate".

as in (19)–(21).[11] Though Kortmann (1997: 312) considers this combination an Early Modern English development, the MED provides some fifteenth-century examples, a couple of which are given as (19) and (20). Note in the early example in (19) the addition of the marker of subordination þat (see above) to the hypercharacterized subordinator for because.

(19) *And **for because** þat he was so wel with god, þerfore þei worschipe him.* (?a1425(c1400) *Mandev*.(1) (Tit C.16) 109/35; MED s.v. *for* conj. 1)

(20) *The kyng of Fraunce myght none other do thenne, **For be-cavse** he had no power of men.* (a1450 *Parton*. (1) (UC C.188) 3204; MED s.v. *bicause* conj. 1)

(21) *They are much deceiued [...] **for because** the Stellion hath a rustie colour.* (1608 E. TOPSELL *Hist. Serpents* 276; OED s.v. *because* prep. and conj. B. 1. a)

A similar formation involves the strengthened subordinator *for why* (see OED s.v. *forwhy* adv. and conj. B. 1. a; *why* adv. (n. and int.) V. 8. c), shown in (22) and (23).

(22) *But no man that hath ony rayson in his hede ought not to counseyll you the same, **for whi** the daunger is there grete.* (1490 CAXTON tr. *Foure Sonnes of Aymon* (1885) ix. 202; OED s.v. *forwhy* adv. and conj. B. 1. a)

(23) *'Why, Dame,' said the hostler,[...]'as for what he was like I cannot tell, [...] **for why** I never saw un.'* (1821 SCOTT *Kenilworth* I. xi. 281; OED s.v. *why* adv. (n. and int.) V. 8. c)

In addition to the interclausal relations of Condition, Time, and Cause, strengthened subordinators can also be identified in the domain of Comparison. Consider, for instance, the marker *ascaunce(s)* 'as if, as though', which results from the combination of Middle English *as* 'as, as if' and Old French *quanses, canses, cansez, quanse* 'as if' (see OED s.v. *askances*, conj. and adv. A; MED s.v. *ascaunce* (adv. & conj.) 1), as shown in (24) and (25).

(24) *They walkid to & fro..**as skaunce** þey knewe nauȝte.* (c1460 (?c1400) *Beryn* (Nthld 55) 1797; MED s.v. *ascaunce* (adv. & conj.) 1)

---

[11] On the history of causal connectives, in particular *for* and *because*, see Wiegand (1982), Rissanen (1989; 1999: 305–307; 2006: 135–136), Fischer (1992: 345–347), Traugott (1992: 252–255), Molencki (2008, 2012), and Uchida and Iyeiri (2017), among others.

(25) *Keeping a countenance **ascanses** she vnderstood him not* (a1586 SIR P. SIDNEY *Arcadia* (1590) ii. xvi. sig. Z6ᵛ; OED s.v. *askances* conj. and adv. A)

Comparison seems to be a particularly fruitful domain for the emergence of strengthened connectives. Besides *ascaunce(s)*, the conjunction *like* has been found to occur at different points in the history of the language in various complex connectives, all of which represent cases of hypercharacterization. Although the subordinator *like* is attested already in the fifteenth century introducing clauses of Similarity, its comparative use with the meaning 'as if' developed in Early Modern English (see Romaine and Lange 1991: 271, note 7; Rissanen 1999: 316; López-Couso and Méndez-Naya 2012a: 177; 2012b: 314–315). It then gained ground in Late Modern English, when it became strongly criticized by prescriptive grammarians, a stigmatization which still continues in the present day (see, among others, Quirk et al. 1985: §15.50; Huddleston and Pullum et al. 2002: 1158). Most interestingly for the purposes of the present discussion, in Middle English and Early Modern English *like* occurred mainly as part of a number of complex subordinators also involving *as* (see Fischer 1992: 358; Kortmann 1997: 371, note 159; Rissanen 1999: 316), including *like as*, *as like*, *like as if*, and *like as and*, all meaning 'as if'. Some examples are given in (26)–(29).

(26) *It seemed **like as** a new light broke in on my soul.* (1847 A. BRONTË *Agnes Grey* xi. 173; OED s.v. *like* adj., adv., conj., and prep. P1. a)

(27) *To [...] bere a candell brennynge in procession [on Candlemas day]. **As lyke** they wente bodely with our lady.* (1499 *Mirk's Festialis* (de Worde) i. f. cxiiᵛ/2); OED s.v. *like* adj., adv., conj., and prep. P1. a)

(28) *It was **like as if** I never saw what sin was before; how real and how dreadful.* (1882 *Wesleyan-Methodist Mag.* July 548/2; OED s.v. *like* adj., adv., conj., and prep. P1. b)

(29) *To haue the rule of his body, landes & goodes, that his wife chyldren and seruauntes, haue laboured for all their lyfe tyme, to be so taken, **lyke as and** it were extorcion* (1523 J. FITZHERBERT *Bk. Surueyeng* xiii.f.26; OED s.v. *like* adv., prep., and conj. P1. c)

Although the various strengthened subordinators discussed in the preceding paragraphs belong to different individual types of interclausal relations within the adverbial semantic space as classified by Kortmann (1997), namely Condition,

Time, Cause, and Comparison,[12] they nevertheless share a number of features which make them form a far more homogeneous group than appears at first sight. On the one hand, in *an(d) if, before ere/or, or ere, for because/why, ascaunce(s)*, and *like as if* and variants, the first element in the respective combinations (*and, before, or, for, as*, and *like*) are polyfunctional items, which can serve functions other than that of subordinators of Condition, Time, Cause, and Comparison. For instance, some of these items (*and, for, or*) also had a coordinating function, which can be held responsible, at least in part, for the gradual decline over time of their subordinating use. As Rissanen (1989: 8; 1999: 307) puts it, causal *for* shifted from subordinator to coordinator, once the Late Middle English innovation *because* grammaticalized. Similarly, Fischer (1992: 355) explains how subordinating *or* rapidly disappeared, once *before that* was introduced in Late Middle English, "presumably because it is easily confused with the co-ordinating conjunction". Be that as it may, it cannot be denied that through hypercharacterization these polyfunctional connectives make their subordinating role overt and explicit and are, therefore, less prone to potentially ambiguous readings than their plain counterparts. Hence, our hypercharacterized subordinators crucially differ from the Khmer "decorative" formations discussed in section 2 above, which, though bearing striking formal similarities with the English formations, clearly depart from them functionally. In other words, the hypercharacterized English subordinators *an(d) if, before ere/or, or ere, for because/why, ascaunce(s)*, and *like as if* are more closely related to instances of Crystal's (1995: 60) "explain yourself" strategy, where hypercharacterization clearly responds to a mechanism which serves the function of making yourself understood (see section 2).

Moreover, all the hypercharacterized conjunctions under discussion in this section came to life in the course of Middle English or Early Modern English. In this respect, then, they bear witness to the crucial relevance of the medieval period in the configuration of the inventory of English clause-connecting devices, as well as to the description of Early Modern English as "essentially a period of experiment and transition" (Kortmann 1997: 302). In this context, hypercharacterized subordinators could easily fit in the category of "ephemera" in the domain of adverbial subordination as defined by Kortmann (1997: 301), i.e. "items which

---

12 With the exception of the connectives *before ere, before or*, and *or ere*, which belong to the network of temporal relations (more specifically, to the domain of Posteriority 'before'), the remaining subordinators discussed here belong to the (cognitively more complex) network of CCC relations. This could be taken as indicative of the existence of a potential relation between degrees of cognitive complexity and the emergence of the hypercharacterized subordinators at issue in this section.

are rarely documented and did not survive the language period in which they came to be used as adverbial subordinators".[13] In fact, the combinations *for because*, *for why*, *before or*, or *ere*, and *askances* are described in the OED as obsolete or archaic, *before ere* as archaic and rare, and *and if* as archaic and confined to regional dialects from the South-west of England, where it can still occur in its reduced form *nif* (see also Visser 1963–1973: §880), as shown in (30).

(30) *Then Golding's 'Ovid' is in Everyman's lib. &* **nif** *you want a readin list ask papa.* (1963 W. C. WILLIAMS Paterson (new ed.) III. 138; OED s.v. *nif* conj.²)

In turn, *like as if* was characterized as "now somewhat *rare*" in the second edition of the OED (1989) and appears as "now *nonstandard*" in the third edition, where the entry was updated in June 2016. It seems, however, that the combination is becoming quite popular in the contemporary language, especially in speech and informal style. (31) and (32) are two examples from internet discussion forums.

(31) *It seems* **like as if** *the intermediate div is the input for another dropdown and the return value is empty,* (05/09/2017)

(32) *It looked* **like as if** *the hotel was short on staff and just trying to manage although the breakfast wasnt that busy.* (22/01/2018)

It could be argued that, as happens in so-called "*like*-parentheticals" (see López-Couso and Méndez-Naya 2014: 52–53), in cases like (31) and (32) the connective *like* has become bounded to the verb to such an extent that verb and conjunction have come to be apprehended as a single chunk. Hence, the need is felt for an explicit marker introducing the subordinate clause. If this is so, the "revival" of the *like as if* combination in Contemporary English may well respond to motivations similar to those identified in other recent cases of accretion, like that of the so-called "double copula construction" (Andersen 2002), "reduplicative copula construction" (Curzan 2012), or "2-B construction" (Tuggy 1996), exemplified in (33a–b).

(33) a. *The thing* **is is** *that we haven't told John yet.* (from Tuggy 1996: 712)
b. *The problem* **is is** *that they didn't say anything about it.* (from Tuggy 1996: 712)

---

13 On ephemeral concessive connectives, see Blanco-García (2017).

It seems, therefore, that the motivations for the occurrence of the hypercharacterized formation *like as if* in the contemporary language are probably far from those which prompted the emergence of the combination in medieval times. Nevertheless, the occurrence of examples such as (31) and (32) in Contemporary English proves the recurrent use of accretion in the domain of clause connectives in the history of the English language.

3.2 On the use of resumptive pronouns in complement clauses with subject extraction

Another syntactic pattern which illustrates accretion is so-called extraction contexts with resumptive pronouns, i.e. with pronouns that fill the gap left by an absent relativized noun phrase. In both Old English and Middle English, relative clauses introduced by the invariable relativizers *þe* and *þat* allowed the relativized position to be filled by a resumptive personal pronoun, mostly one in the third person, as shown in (34)–(37).

(34) *Eadig bið se   wer, **þe** **his** tohopa bið to Drihtne*
     blessed is the man   that his   hope   is in the-Lord
     'Blessed is the man whose hope is in the Lord'
     (*King Alfred's Old English prose translation of the first fifty psalms*, Psalm 39; from O'Neill 2001: 148)

(35) *Swa bið eac þam   treowum **þe him**   gecynde bið up heah*
     so   is   also to-those trees   PT to-them natural is   up high
     to standanne
     to stand
     'So it is also with trees to which it is natural to stand up straight'
     (*Bo* 25.27.20; from Traugott 1992: 229)

(36) *It was a king bi are dawes, **þat** in **his** time were gode lawes He dede maken, and ful wel holden;*
     'There was a king in former days, in whose time there were good laws which he caused to be made and to be well kept;'
     (*Havelok* 27–29; from Ogura 2017: 193)

(37) [...] *it was þat ilk cok, /* **þat** *petre herd* **him** *crau,* [...]
'it was that very cock, which Peter heard crow'
(*Cursor* (Vesp) 15995–6; from Fischer 1992: 309)

Instances of this kind, which can be described as involving accretion or hypercharacterization, coexisted at these early stages with the counterpart construction without pronoun resumption. Compare (37), from the Cotton Vespasian manuscript of the *Cursor Mundi*, with (38), which shows the same extract in the Trinity manuscript:

(38) *þis was þe same cok:* **þat** *petur herde* **Ø** *crowe* (Cursor (Trn))

The pattern with no pronoun resumption seems to have been the preferred variant in Early English. Mitchell (1985: §2198), for instance, argues that the combination of the indeclinable particle *þe* and a personal pronoun in relative clauses was not common in the Old English period: it occurred in just five per cent of *þe* clauses in the poetry and was even less frequent in the prose.

Different interpretations have been adduced in the literature for the occurrence of the less common variant with the resumptive pronoun as in constructions of the type shown in (34) to (37) above. Mustanoja (1960: 202), for example, refers to reasons of emphasis as (at least partly) responsible for the existence of such hypercharacterized structures in Middle English. However, he also mentions that the combination of the relativizer and the pronoun in the same clause serves a clear syntactic purpose, inasmuch as it indicates the case of the relativizer which, being an invariant particle, is not case-marked. Similar explanations are provided by Traugott (1992: 229) for Old English and by Fischer (1992: 308–309) for Middle English. In Traugott's words, "the pronoun fills the gap and specifies the relativised NPs clause-internal role as subject or object, etc." (Fischer 1992: 229). This explains why the frequency of resumptive pronouns in relative clauses of this kind is reduced from Late Middle English onwards, once the *wh*-pronouns, which have overt case marking, became established in the relativizer system (Fischer 1992: 309). Along similar lines, Curme (1931: 205ff.)[14] and Ogura (2017: 180ff.) maintain that the construction helps "to make the grammatical relations clear" (Curme 1931: 206) and they emphasize its cohesive function, since the pattern helps "to make the meaning of the passage as clear as possible" (Ogura 2017: 194). Moreover,

---

14 Curme (1931) refers to the pattern under discussion here as the "double determinative" construction.

following Sells (1984),[15] McCloskey (2006), and Asudeh (2012), Bartnik (2013) characterizes constructions with resumptive pronouns in Old English relative clauses introduced by *þe* as "processing artifacts", that is, as devices which are not licensed by the grammar, but which facilitate language production in cases which present a processing challenge for the speaker.

It seems, however, that the variation between relative constructions with no resumptive pronouns and their hypercharacterized counterparts with pronoun resumption had a far-reaching relevance and important consequences in language change beyond the relative clause system itself. An additional domain in English grammar where the existence of the pattern illustrated in (34)–(37) also had major implications is the complementation system, more specifically the distributional patterns of the two major complementizers *that* and zero across time in so-called subject extraction contexts.

Subject extraction involves the removal of a noun phrase subject from its place within the subordinate clause and its insertion higher in the syntactic hierarchy by a process of relativization, topicalization, or the like. It is this process of raising of the subject from the sub-clause into the matrix that triggers the obligatory selection of the zero complementizer in present-day standard English.[16] This is shown by the unacceptability of (39b) and (40b) as paraphrases of (39a) and (40a).[17] It seems that avoidance of ambiguity is the main reason for the impossibility to use the *that* complementizer in such cases (see, among others, Langendoen 1970: 102–103; Bolinger 1972: 32; Quirk et al. 1985: §§15.4, note d; 17.63; Bergh and Seppänen 1994; Huddleston and Pullum et al. 2002: 953): the use of *that* in these contexts could lead to a wrong parsing of the sequence, since the complementizer *that* could be misinterpreted as the subject of the verb phrase in the sub-clause immediately following (*is* and *will be sent* in (39) and (40), respectively).

(39) a. *The reduction product depended not on the current (the factor which Faraday's law teaches us Ø is so crucial to electrochemistry) but on the voltage* (from Huddleston 1971: 179).

---

15 Sells (1984) uses the label "intrusive pronoun" instead of "resumptive pronoun".
16 The *that* + gap sequence can nevertheless be found in some American English dialects (see Bergh and Seppänen 1994: 136, fn. 2).
17 While the use of zero is compulsory in subject extraction contexts, the complementizer *that* is allowed in cases where the push-down *wh*-element realizes a function other than that of subject. Consider in this connection (i) below, where the relativizer *which* functions as the object of *send* and the presence of the noun phrase subject *John* in the sub-clause prevents misinterpretation:
(i) *I will read the memo (which) Pat hopes (**that**) John will send you* (from Quirk et al. 1985: §17.63).

b. *[...] *the factor which Faraday's law teaches us **that** is so crucial to electrochemistry* [...]

(40) a. *I will read the memo (which) Pat hopes Ø will be sent to you.* (from Quirk et al. 1985: §17.63)

b. **I will read the memo (which) Pat hopes **that** will be sent to you.*

Subject extraction contexts constitute a good illustration of diachronic change. Judging from the data available for earlier stages, zero-clauses in subject extraction contexts were by no means obligatory in the Old English period, but merely an alternative to *that*-clauses. An example of the use of the complementizer *that* is given in (41), while (42) illustrates the use of zero in a similar context and with the same complement-taking predicate, namely the utterance verb *secgan* 'say'.

(41) Đonne   wæs   Biise   Eastengla   biscop,   þe   we sægdon   **þætte**
     then   was   Bise   of-the-East Angles   bishop   that we said   that
     in þæm   foresprecenan   seonoþe   wære.
     in the   aforementioned   synod   was
     'Then Bise, who we have said was present in the aforementioned synod, was bishop of the East Angles.'
     (*Bede* 280.12; from Mitchell 1985: §1980)

(42) ða   getriewan   friend   þonne ic   secgge   Ø   sie   ðæt   deoryrðeste   ðing
     the true   friend   again I   say   be   the   dearest   thing
     ealra   þissa   weoruldgeslða
     of-all   this   worldly prosperity
     'The true friend I say again is the most precious of all these worldly things'
     (King Alfred's *Boethius*; from Seppänen and Bergh 1996: 46)

A similar state of affairs seems to hold for Middle English, where sequences with the zero complementizer, as in (43)–(44), coexisted with constructions featuring the overt complementizer *that*, as shown in (45)–(46):

(43) *Y pray ʒow alle* [...] *þat ʒe charge neuer body with oþe þat ʒe suppose Ø wyl be for swore.* (c1303 Mannyng, *Handl. S.* 2790; from Visser 1963–1973: §547)

(44) *þe toþer, þat ʒe seyen Ø is blasfemye of me.* (*Wyclifite Sermons*, i.166.36; from Warner 1982: 170)

(45) *þa namen hi þa hi wenden **þat** ani god hefden* (Peterborough Chronicle, MCXXXVII, line 161)

(46) *I am he that thou knowe **that** dyd doo destroye Rome* (Caxton, Charles the Grete 52.30; from Curme 1912: 379)

Bergh and Seppänen (1994: 134, table 3) show that it is in the course of the Middle English period that zero gains ground at the expense of *that* in environments with subject extractions; while in Old English *that*-clauses represent 87% of the total number of instances of the type under discussion in their data, the percentage falls to 30% in Middle English. The decline of the overt complementizer in such constructions seems to have been particularly noticeable in the time span 1250–1350. Interestingly, the zero complementizer experienced a much quicker growth in sequences involving subject extractions than in complement constructions with no extraction. Even with high-frequency predicates, such as *know*, *think*, *say*, and *tell*,[18] Rissanen's (1991: 279) figures for zero in Late Middle English are much lower: 14% and 34% for the periods 1350–1420 and 1420–1500, respectively. As Rissanen puts it, "the most dramatic overall increase takes place in the second half of the sixteenth and in the early seventeenth century, when the frequency of zero jumps from around 40 per cent to around 60 per cent" (Rissanen 1991: 279).

The special behaviour of subject extraction contexts as regards *that*/zero distribution is also corroborated by Warner's (1982) results from the Wyclifite Sermons: while the overall occurrence of zero in the data amounts to only 3.6% of the cases (Warner 1982: 169), when the subject of the complement clause is removed by topicalization or relativization, zero is mandatory, except in a couple of isolated examples after the complement-taking predicate *wite* 'know' (Warner 1982: 170). One of these is given here as (47).

(47) *For þese þat God woot **þat** shal be saved,* [...] (Wyclifite Sermons, i.166.36; from Warner 1982: 170)

The frequency of *that* in subject extraction environments decreases rapidly at the end of Middle English, in such a way that in Early Modern English zero can be

---

18 High-frequency predicates have been identified in the extensive literature on complementation as zero-favouring, both for Present-day English and for earlier stages. See, among many others, Huddleston (1971: 179), Bolinger (1972: 18ff.), Elsness (1982: 11ff.; 1984: 522–523), Warner (1982: 171), Fanego (1990: 145), Rissanen (1991: 284–285), and López-Couso (1996: 276–278).

said to have taken over completely. In Bergh and Seppänen's material for this period *that* represents just 4% of the total number of relevant instances (1994: 139).[19] No occurrences of *that* in subject extraction contexts are attested in their Late Modern English data.

In addition to the two patterns discussed so far, with either the *that* complementizer or its zero counterpart, subject extraction contexts also allowed in earlier English a third alternative pattern, which, interestingly, involves hypercharacterization or accretion. In this variant construction, the extraction site in the complement clause is occupied by a resumptive pronoun immediately following the *that* complementizer, thus yielding sequences of the type shown in (48) to (50) below from Old, Middle, and Early Modern English, respectively:[20]

(48) *in þære cirican   seo cwen   gewunade   hire gebiddan, þe*
     in that church   the queen   was-accustomed-to   her prayers   that
     we ær   cwædon þæt   heo   cristen   wære
     we   before said   that she   Christian was
     'In that church the queen, who we have said was a Christian, was accustomed to say her prayers'
     (*Bede* 62.4; from Mitchell 1985: §1980)

(49) *Her sorrowe that she contynually made for her right dere frende blonchardyn,* **that** *for the loue of her she trowed* **that he** *had other be lost or ded.* (Caxton, *Blanchardyn and Eglantine* 120.11; from Curme 1912: 379)

(50) [He] *asked [...] what hee shoulde doe to a woman* **whome** *hee suspected* **that she** *hadde falsified hir fayth* (1567 Painter, *Pal. Pleas.* II, 92; from Visser 1963–1973: §547)

Structures of this type, which are regarded as deviant in contemporary standard English, "since they introduce a double pronominalization of the antecedent" (Quirk et al. 1985: §17.63), were particularly frequent in the earliest periods of the language (see Bergh and Seppänen 1994: 139, table 5) and it is not until after 1500

---

19 Subject extraction is already a knock-out context in the Shakespearean corpus used by Fanego (1990: 148, fn. 14) and in the works of John Dryden examined by López-Couso (1996: 273).
20 Occasional instances of resumptive pronouns after the zero complementizer are also found in Middle English, as shown in the following Chaucerian example:
(ii) *þis is he,* **which** *þat myn uncle swer'th* **he** *mot be ded.* (c 1374 Chaucer, *Troil.* II, 654; from Visser 1963–1973: §547)

that the pattern fell into disuse in the standard language (Seppänen and Bergh 1996: 47). More importantly for the purposes of this study, the pattern "complementizer *that* + resumptive pronoun" was still used to some extent in Middle English, precisely at the time when, as seen above, the change-over from *that* to zero as the default complement-clause link had already taken place in the non-resumptive pattern. Although this may be merely coincidental, it may also be the case that accretion was responsible for the delayed generalization of the complementizer zero in hypercharacterized subject extraction constructions involving a resumptive pronoun, in contrast to the pattern lacking resumption (i.e. that not showing hypercharacterization), where the complementizer zero was perfectly well established before the end of the Middle English period.

3.3 On the relevance of "double-locative overlap constructions" for the grammaticalization of existential *there*

As shown in the preceding sections, hypercharacterization phenomena provide appealing instances of linguistic competition between alternatives, such as the variation between single and strengthened adverbial subordinators (see section 3.1) or the alternation found in subject extraction contexts between constructions with and without resumptive pronouns (see section 3.2). Hypercharacterization may also be relevant for the discussion of processes of language change, inasmuch as the existence of hypercharacterized constructions may result in the emergence of new grammatical structures. One of such cases involves the grammaticalization of existential *there*.

Although non-locative explanations have occasionally been given for the origin of existential *there* (see, for example, Davidse 1992), the most likely source for the so-called dummy *there* is the distal deictic adverb *there*, 'in/at that place'. According to the locative account (see Bolinger 1977: 91–92; Breivik 1983, 1997: 32; Traugott 1992: 217–219; Johansson 1997; Pfenninger 2009: 49–53, among others), the split of the existential *there* from the spatial deictic *there* presumably started in pre-Old English times (see Breivik 1977: 346), though the grammaticalization of the *there*-existential pattern was not complete until much later. As shown by Breivik (1983: 278, 319) and López-Couso (2006: 182), existentials with *there* gradually replaced *there*-less existentials, which were particularly frequent in Early Old English, until the former became the default pattern from Late Middle English onwards (see Breivik 1983: 320-321).

Since Old English and Middle English represent crucial periods in the process of grammaticalization of existential *there*, in López-Couso (2011) I explored the developmental relation between deictic *there* and existential *there* in Early English. In particular, my aim was to identify potential parallels between the development of the existential marker in the history of the language and its acquisition by English-speaking children, which has been investigated in depth by Johnson (1999, 2001, 2005). Using longitudinal data from seven children in the CHILDES archive (MacWhinney 1995), Johnson shows that children first produce *there* deictics before producing utterances which allow both a deictic and an existential reading and, eventually, clear instances of existentials (Johnson 1999: 95–114, 2001: 131–134). The following examples from the speech of Naomi, one of the children in CHILDES, illustrate the developmental stages identified by Johnson in the process of acquisition:[21]

(51) a. *There's diaper.* (Naomi 1;8)

b. *There some for Mommy.* (Naomi 2;0)

c. *There's a fox in the box.* (Naomi 2;5)

d. *There's a lollipop right there.* (Naomi 2;4)

e. *There was a big kangaroo.* (Naomi 2;9)

f. *There's not enough room.* (Naomi 2;11)

Naomi's earliest uses of *there* correspond to the source deictic construction (51a) and are often accompanied by perceptual cues such as pointing gestures or directed gazing, which help the addressee to identify the referred object in a particular location. At the age of 2;0, however, Naomi starts producing overlap utterances (51b), which share properties of both the deictic and the existential constructions and therefore allow the two readings. Contexts of this kind are labelled "overlap deictics" by Johnson (1999: 84–85), i.e. statements where *there* serves the function of informing the addressee of the existence of something by pointing it out. Overlap deictics such as (51b), where *there* conveys both an existence-informing meaning and a deictic meaning, seem to pave the way for the ontogenetic grammaticalization of the existential *there*. However, in Johnson's view, it is overlap utterances of the type shown in (51c–d) that play a more decisive role in the emergence of unambiguous *there*-existentials in Child English. These "double-locative overlap deictics", to use Johnson's terminology (1999:

---

21 The age range of Naomi's data in CHILDES is 1;1–5;1.

85), show the co-occurrence in the same clause of *there* and another locative expression (*in the box* in (51c) and *right there* in (51d)). Interestingly, instances of this kind can be said to illustrate accretion or hypercharacterization as defined in the present study, since they show double (maybe redundant) specification of the location of what is pointed out (*a fox* and *a lollipop* in (51c) and (51d), respectively). As such, they invite the child to seek a distinct, "non-locative function for the initial deictic *there*" (Johnson 1999: 104; see also 85, 112), thus favouring and facilitating the reanalysis of *there* as an existential marker. The final stage is represented by clear existentials of the type in (51e–f), which start occurring in Naomi's speech at the age of 2;9, only after the child produces several overlap deictics, including the hypercharacterized double-locative overlaps.

Similar developments to the one outlined above for Naomi are shown by the other six children in CHILDES examined by Johnson, and for most of them the overlap stage, where hypercharacterized "double locatives" belong, precedes the production of unambiguous existentials (see Johnson 1999: 101–111 for relevant instances).[22]

As seen above, in Child English the evidence for the constructional grounding of existentials in deictics is indeed robust. My examination of the prose texts of the Old and Early Middle English sections of the Helsinki Corpus (López-Couso 2011) suggests that the diachronic process of grammaticalization of *there*-existentials with the verb *be* follows a parallel developmental pathway to that attested in L1 acquisition. On the one hand, as in early child speech, the existential pattern is historically grounded in the deictic, via an intermediate stage corresponding to overlap utterances which share features of both the locative and the existential constructions. On the other hand, and most importantly for the purposes of this study, double-locative overlaps seem to have played a crucial role in the historical development of *there*-existentials, just as they do in Child English. Examples (52)–(56) summarize the various stages in the diachronic grammaticalization of the existential pattern with *there*.

(52) **ðar** was se cing gehaten Sæbyrht. Ricolan sunu.
 there was the king called Sæbyrht Rocola's son
 'There was the king named Sæbyrht, the son of Ricola.'
 (HC; O2, Two of the Saxon Chronicles Parallel, R 604.3)

---

22 The only exception in Johnson's data is Abe, who does not produce any instances of the overlap patterns before the first clear existentials. This is probably due to the fact that Abe's corpus has the latest starting age of the seven children (2;4), very close to the age of the first attestations of the existential pattern (2;6) (see Johnson 1999: 100).

(53) Ac þa strengstan weras wuniaþ on þam lande & micele
    but the strongest men live in the land and great
    burga **ðær** synd & mærlice geweallode:
    cities there are and splendidly walled
    'But the strongest people live in the land and there are large and splendidly fortified cities there:'
    (HC; O3, *The Old Testament, Numbers* 13.29)

(54) & Iohannes fullode on Enon wið Salim forðam þe **þær**
    and John baptized in Eon with Salim because there
    wæron manega wætro & hi togædere comun & wæron gefullode.
    were many waters and they together came and were baptized
    'And John was baptizing in Aenon near Salim, because there was much water there and people were coming and were being baptized.'
    (HC; O3, *West-Saxon Gospels, John* 3.23)

(55) for **þær** wæs an forehus æt þære cyrcan duru.
    for there was a porch at the church door
    'for there was a porch at the church door.'
    (HC; O4, *An Old English Vision of Leofric, Earl of Mercia*, 31)

(56) Ah **þer** nis butan an godd þur hwam witerliche
    but there not-is but one god through whom certainly
    ha alle weren iwrahte [...]
    they all were created
    'But there isn't but one god by whom they all were created [...]'
    (HC; M1, *The Katherine Group*, 22)

The similarities of the developmental path shown here with Naomi's examples in (51) above are certainly striking. Originally a distal deictic adverb ('in/at that place'), as in (52), *þær* started occurring in overlap deictics, such as those in (53) and (54), where it can be read both as a locative (i.e. 'the cities in that land are large and walled'; 'water was abundant in Aenon') and as an existential (i.e. 'there are great and fortified cities in that land'; 'there was much water in Aenon'). Hypercharacterized double-locative overlap constructions of the type shown in (55) served as bridging contexts (Heine 2002) in the process of change, just as they do in the ontogenetic development of existential *there* summarized above. Given that in this example location is already specified by means of the prepositional phrase *æt þære cyrcan duru* ('at the church door'), the cooccurrence of *þær* and this spatial expression in the same clause may have prompted the reanalysis of the originally deictic *þær* as an existential marker. As in the case of Child English, it is only after overlap deictics and, in particular, hypercharacterized constructions of the double-locative overlap type are firmly consolidated in the system that unambiguous existentials (see (56)) start occurring in significant numbers in the data. The distribution of the overlap deictic, double-locative overlap deictic, and unambiguous existential constructions in the Helsinki Corpus data examined in López-Couso (2011) is summarized in figure 12.1.[23]

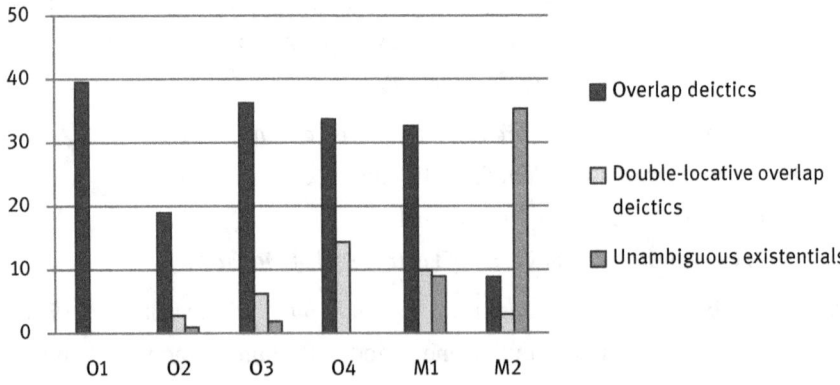

Fig. 12.1: Distribution of the overlap deictic, double-locative overlap deictic, and existential constructions in the prose texts of the Old and Early Middle English sections of the *Helsinki Corpus*. Normalized frequencies per 100,000 words (data from López-Couso 2011: 93, table 2). Periodization: O1 = –850; O2 = 850–950; O3 = 950–1050; O4 = 1050–1150; M1 = 1150–1250; M2 = 1250–1350.

As seen here, overlap deictics of the type illustrated in (53) and (54) above clearly predominate from subperiod O1 (–850) to subperiod M1 (1150–1250). In turn, double-locative overlap constructions such as (55), which occur only sporadically in O2 (850–950), gradually become more common in Late Old English (subperiods O3 and O4). Interestingly, the decrease in the transition from Old to Middle

---

[23] The texts analyzed amounted to 551,738 words.

English of such overlap utterances, which invite the existential interpretation but for which the deictic reading cannot be totally discarded, runs parallel to the rise in frequency of uses of *there* which are incompatible with the locative interpretation (see (56) above). Note that the existential reading becomes the default interpretation only in subperiod M2 (1250–1350), thus paving the way for the grammaticalization of the *there*-existential pattern and for the final split between locative *there* and existential *there*.

4 Concluding remarks

By focusing on three case studies selected from the domain of syntax, namely strengthened adverbial subordinators, pronoun resumption in extraction contexts, and "double-locative overlap constructions" with *there*, the present study has shown the relevance of hypercharacterization phenomena in language variation and change and their pervasive presence in various levels of the linguistic system and in different kinds of linguistic contexts.

The strengthened subordinators *an(d) if, before ere/or, or ere, for because/why, ascaunce(s)*, and *like as if* (and variants) examined in section 3.1 prove the recurrent application of hypercharacterization in the domain of adverbial clause connectives in the history of English. It has been shown that the main motivation for hypercharacterization in the Middle and Early Modern English formations studied here is the avoidance of potential ambiguity, in cases in which the need is felt for an explicit indication of the subordinating function of a polyfunctional conjunction. The discussion also paid attention to the fact that hypercharacterization can affect one and the same adverbial subordinator at different points in time along its recorded history and can serve additional purposes beyond its primary disambiguating effect. As seen in section 3.1, it seems that the "revived" use of *like as if* with the predicates *seem* and *look* in the contemporary language responds to determinants of a different kind than those at work in earlier English. In such cases, the conjunction *like* has become fused to the preceding verb in such a way that the sequence verb + *like* is apprehended as a single chunk by speakers, who therefore require the sub-clause to be signalled by another subordinator with the same meaning and function (*as if*).

The disambiguating role of hypercharacterization can also be identified in the use of resumptive pronouns filling the gap left by a relativized noun phrase (see section 3.2). More importantly, the use of resumptive pronouns in complement constructions involving subject extraction suggests that hypercharacterization may also be held responsible for the slowing down of the replacement of the complementizer *that* by the complementizer zero in subject extraction contexts over the course of the Middle English period.

Finally, the evidence adduced in section 3.3 from so-called double-locative overlap constructions reveals that linguistic accretion may also play a crucial part in grammaticalization processes, such as the emergence and consolidation of existential *there*. The diachronic data presented in this section suggest that double-locative overlap deictics had a significant role in the grammaticalization of *there*-existentials in the Late Old English and Early Middle English periods, just as they do in the ontogenetic grammaticalization of the construction in Child English.

All in all, the foregoing discussion has shown that hypercharacterized forms and constructions resulting from accretion realize important functions in linguistic systems, both at the communicative level and at the level of grammatical structure, and that structural hypercharacterization may have different motivations and also different effects. As has become clear from the individual discussions of the three case studies considered in this article, hypercharacterization or accretion is much more than the mere addition of "redundant", "superfluous", "useless", or "functionless" material. In other words, as Kuteva (2008) proposes, what from a static synchronic point of view may seem to be unnecessary "frills" of phonological and morphosyntactic material can be plausibly explained as the result of predictable language change – as well as language variation – phenomena. On the basis of in-depth analysis of diachronic data from English, in this study I have shown that in at least three concrete areas of English syntax (strengthened adverbial subordinators, pronoun resumption in extraction contexts, and "double-locative overlap constructions" with *there*), accretion or hypercharacterization plays a crucial role.

References

Adamson, Sylvia. 1999. Literary language. In Roger Lass (ed.), *The Cambridge history of the English language, vol. III, 1476–1776*, 539–653. Cambridge: Cambridge University Press.

Alsagoff, Lubna & Chee Lick Ho. 1998. The relative clause in colloquial Singapore English. *World Englishes* 17 (2). 127–138.

Andersen, Gisle. 2002. Corpora and the double copula. In Leiv Egil Breivik & Angela Hasselgren (eds.), *From the COLT's mouth ... and others'. Language corpora studies in honour of Anna-Brita Stenström*, 43–58. Amsterdam & New York: Rodopi.

Asudeh, Ash. 2012. For a unified theory of resumption. In Alain Rouveret (ed.), *Resumptive pronouns at the interfaces*, 121–188. Amsterdam: John Benjamins.

Bartnik, Artur. 2013. Dative resumptive pronouns in Old English þe relatives. In Marcin Krygier (ed.), *Of fair speche, and of fair answere*, 61–65. Frankfurt/Main: Peter Lang.

Beal, John. 1988. Goodbye to all 'that'? The history and present behaviour of optional 'that'. In Graham Nixon & John Honey (eds.), *An historic tongue. Studies in English linguistics in memory of Barbara Strang*, 49–66. London & New York: Routledge.

Bergh, Gunnar & Aimo Seppänen. 1994. Subject extraction in English: The use of the *that*-complementizer. In Francisco Fernández, Miguel Fuster & Juan José Calvo (eds.), *Papers from the 7th International Conference on English Historical Linguistics*, 131–143. Amsterdam: John Benjamins.

Blanco-García, Cristina. 2017. Ephemerality in concessive subordinators. Evidence from the history of English. In Sofía Bemposta-Rivas, Carla Bouzada-Jabois, Yolanda Fernández-Pena, Tamara Bouso, Yolanda J. Calvo-Benzies & Iván Tamaredo (eds.), *New trends and methodologies in applied English language research III: Synchronic and diachronic studies on discourse, lexis and grammar processing*, 59–81. Bern: Peter Lang.

Bolinger, Dwight. 1972. *That's that*. The Hague: Mouton.

Bolinger, Dwight. 1977. *Meaning and form*. London: Longman.

Braunmüller, Kurt. 1978. Remarks on the formation of conjunctions in the Germanic languages. *Nordic Journal of Linguistics* 1. 99–120.

Breivik, Leiv Egil. 1977. A note on the genesis of existential *there*. *English Studies* 58. 334–348.

Breivik, Leiv Egil. 1983. *Existential* there. *A synchronic and diachronic study*. Bergen: Department of English.

Breivik, Leiv Egil. 1997. *There* in space and time. In Heinrich Ramisch & Kenneth Wynne (eds.), *Language in time and space: Studies in honour of Wolfgang Viereck on the occasion of his 60th birthday*, 32–45. Stuttgart: Franz Steiner Verlag.

Crystal, David. 1995. *The Cambridge encyclopedia of the English language*. Cambridge: Cambridge University Press.

Culpeper, Jonathan & Merja Kytö. 2000. The conjunction *and* in Early Modern English: Frequencies and uses in speech-related writing and other texts. In Ricardo Bermúdez-Otero, David Denison, Richard M. Hogg & C. B. McCully (eds.), *Generative theory and corpus studies: A dialogue from 10 ICEHL*, 299–326. Berlin: Mouton de Gruyter.

Curme, George O. 1912. A history of English relative clauses. *The Journal of English and Germanic Philology* 11 (3). 355–380.

Curme, George O. 1931. *Syntax*. Boston: Heath.

Curzan, Anne. 2012. Revisiting the reduplicative copula with corpus-based evidence. In Terttu Nevalainen & Elizabeth Closs Traugott (eds.), *The Oxford handbook of the history of English*, 211–221. Oxford: Oxford University Press.

Dahl, Östen. 2004. *The growth and maintenance of linguistic complexity*. Amsterdam: John Benjamins.

Dahl, Östen. 2009. Increases of complexity as a result of language contact. In Kurt Braunmüller & Juliane House (eds.), *Convergence and divergence in language contact situations*, 41–52. Amsterdam: John Benjamins.

Davidse, Kristin. 1992. Existential constructions: A systemic perspective. *Leuvense Bijdragen* 81. 71–99.

EEBO = *Early English Books Online*. https://quod.lib.umich.edu/e/eebogroup/

Elsness, Johan. 1982. *That* v. zero connective in English nominal clauses. *ICAME News* 6. 1–45.

Elsness, Johan. 1984. *That* or zero? A look at the choice of object clause connective in a corpus of American English. *English Studies* 65. 519–533.

Fanego, Teresa. 1990. Finite complement clauses in Shakespeare's English, I and II. *Studia Neophilologica* 62. 3–21; 129–149.

Fischer, Olga. 1992. Syntax. In Norman Blake (ed.), *The Cambridge history of the English language, vol. II, 1066–1476*, 207–408. Cambridge: Cambridge University Press.
Fodor, Alexandra. 2010. Another subordinator, *an't* please you: A diachronic study of conditional *and*. In Alaric Hall, Olga Timofeeva, Ágnes Kiricsi & Bethany Fox (eds.), *Interfaces between language and culture in medieval England. A festschrift for Matti Kilpiö*, 289–306. Leiden & Boston: Brill.
Grice, H. Paul. 1975. Logic and conversation. In Peter Cole & Jerry L. Morgan (eds.), *Syntax and semantics 3: Speech acts*, 41–58. New York: Academic Press.
Haiman, John & Noeurng Ourn. 2009. Decorative symmetry in ritual (and everyday) language. In Roberta Corrigan, Edith A. Moravcsik, Hamid Ouali & Kathleen Wheatley (eds.), *Formulaic language. Volume 2. Acquisition, loss, psychological reality, and functional explanations*, 567–587. Amsterdam: John Benjamins.
Hansen, Erik & Hans Frede Nielsen. 1986. *Irregularities in Modern English*. Odense: Odense University Press.
Heine, Bernd. 2002. On the role of context in grammaticalization. In Ilse Wischer & Gabriele Diewald (eds.), *New reflections on grammaticalization*, 83–101. Amsterdam: John Benjamins.
Huddleston, Rodney. 1971. *The sentence in written English: A syntactic study based on an analysis of scientific texts*. Cambridge: Cambridge University Press.
Huddleston, Rodney & Geoffrey K. Pullum et al. 2002. *The Cambridge grammar of the English language*. Cambridge: Cambridge University Press.
Johansson, Stig. 1997. A corpus study of existential clauses: Register variation and discourse function. In Terttu Nevalainen & Leena Kahlas-Tarkka (eds.), *To explain the present. Studies in the changing English language in honour of Matti Rissanen*, 303–318. Helsinki: Société Néophilologique.
Johnson, Christopher R. 1999. *Constructional grounding: The role of interpretational overlap in lexical and constructional acquisition*. University of California, Berkeley, PhD dissertation.
Johnson, Christopher R. 2001. Constructional grounding: On the relation between deictic and existential *there*-constructions in acquisition. In Alan Cienki, Barbara J. Luka & Michael B. Smith (eds.), *Conceptual and discourse factors in linguistic structure*, 123–136. Stanford: CSLI Publications.
Johnson, Christopher R. 2005. Developmental reinterpretation in first language acquisition. Paper presented at the Symposium *Exemplar-based models in linguistics*, 79th meeting of the Linguistic Society of America, Oakland, January 2005.
Kivimaa, Kirsti. 1966. *Þe and Þat as clause connectives in Early Middle English with especial consideration of the emergence of the pleonastic Þat*. Helsinki: Societas Scientiarum Fennica.
Klemola, Juhani & Markku Filppula. 1992. Subordinating uses of *and* in the history of English. In Matti Rissanen, Ossi Ihalainen, Terttu Nevalainen & Irma Taavitsainen (eds.), *History of Englishes: New methods and interpretations in historical linguistics*, 310–318. Berlin: Mouton de Gruyter.
Kortmann, Bernd. 1997. *Adverbial subordination. A typology and history of adverbial subordinators in European languages*. Berlin: Mouton de Gruyter.
Kuteva, Tania. 2008. On the frills of grammaticalization. In María José López-Couso & Elena Seoane (eds.), *Rethinking grammaticalization. New perspectives*, 189–217. Amsterdam: John Benjamins.
Lakoff, George & Mark Jonhson. 1980. *Metaphors we live by*. Chicago: University of Chicago Press.

Langendoen, D. Terence. 1970. The accessibility of deep structures. In Roderick A. Jacobs & Peter S. Rosembaum (eds.), *Readings in English transformational grammar*, 99–104. Waltham, MA: Ginn & Company.
Lehmann, Christian. 2005. Pleonasm and hypercharacterisation. In Geert Booij & Jaap van Marle (eds.), *Yearbook of morphology 2005*, 119–154. Dordrecht: Springer.
López-Couso, María José. 1996. That/zero variation in Restoration English. In Derek Britton (ed.), *English historical linguistics 1994*, 271–286. Amsterdam: John Benjamins.
López-Couso, María José. 2006. On negative existentials in Early English. In Leiv Egil Breivik, Sandra Halverson & Kari E. Haugland (eds.), *'These things write I vnto thee ...': Essays in honour of Björn Bækken*, 175–187. Oslo: Novus Press.
López-Couso, María José. 2011. Developmental parallels in diachronic and ontogenetic grammaticalization: Existential *there* as a test case. *Folia Linguistica* 45. 81–102.
López-Couso, María José & Belén Méndez-Naya. 2012a. On the use of *as if*, *as though* and *like* in Present-day English complementation structures. *Journal of English Linguistics* 40 (2). 172–195.
López-Couso, María José & Belén Méndez-Naya. 2012b. On the origin and development of comparative complementizers in English: Evidence from historical corpora. In Nila Vázquez-González (ed.), *Creation and use of historical English corpora in Spain*, 311–333. Newcastle upon Tyne: Cambridge Scholars Publishing.
López-Couso, María José & Belén Méndez-Naya. 2014. From clause to pragmatic marker: A study of the development of *like*-parentheticals in American English. *Journal of Historical Pragmatics* 15 (1). 36–61.
MacWhinney, Brian. 1995. *The CHILDES project: Tools for analyzing talk*. Hillsdale, NJ: Erlbaum.
McCloskey, James. 2006. Resumption. In Martin Everaert & Henk van Riemsdijk (eds.), *The Blackwell companion to syntax*, 94–117. Oxford: Blackwell.
MED = Kurath, Hans et al. 1952–2001. *Middle English Dictionary*. Ann Arbor: University of Michigan Press. http://ets.umdl.mich.edu/m/med/
Meillet, Antoine. 1912. L'évolution des formes grammaticales. *Scientia (Rivista di Scienza)* 12 (26, 6). 384–400.
Mitchell, Bruce. 1984. The origin of Old English conjunctions: Some problems. In Jacek Fisiak (ed.), *Historical syntax*, 271–299. Berlin: Mouton de Gruyter.
Mitchell, Bruce. 1985. *Old English syntax*, 2 vols. Oxford: Clarendon Press.
Molencki, Rafał. 2008. The rise of *because* in Middle English. In Masachiyo Amano, Michiko Ogura & Masayuki Ohkado (eds.), *Historical Englishes in varieties of texts and contexts: The Global COE Programme, International Conference 2007*, 201–215. Frankfurt/Main: Peter Lang.
Molencki, Rafał. 2012. The competition between *because* and *forbecause* in Late Middle English. Paper presented at the *17th International Conference on English Historical Linguistics*, University of Zurich, August 2012.
Mustanoja, Tauno F. 1960. *A Middle English syntax. I. Parts of speech*. Helsinki: Société Néophilologique.
O'Neill, Patrick P. (ed.). 2001. *King Alfred's Old English prose translation of the first fifty psalms*. Cambridge, MA: Medieval Academy of America.
OED = *Oxford English Dictionary* Online. http://www.oed.com/
Ogura, Michiko. 2017. Resumptive pronouns in Old English relative clauses. In Jane Roberts & Trudi L. Darby (eds.), *English without boundaries: Reading English from China to Canada*, 180–194. Newcastle upon Tyne: Cambridge Scholars Publishing.
Pfenninger, Simone E. 2009. *Grammaticalization paths of English and High German existential constructions: A corpus-based study*. Bern: Peter Lang.

Quirk, Randolph, Sidney Greenbaum, Geoffrey Leech & Jan Svartvik. 1985. *A comprehensive grammar of the English language*. London: Longman.
Rissanen, Matti. 1989. The conjunction *for* in Early Modern English. *NOWELE* 14. 3–18.
Rissanen, Matti. 1991. On the history of *that*/zero as object clause links in English. In Karin Aijmer & Bengt Altenberg (eds.), *English corpus linguistics. Studies in honour of Jan Svartvik*, 272–289. London & New York: Longman.
Rissanen, Matti. 1997. Optional *that* with subordinators in Middle English. In Raymond Hickey & Stanisław Puppel (eds.), *Language history and linguistic modelling: A festschrift for Jacek Fisiak on his 60th birthday*, 373–383. Berlin & New York: Mouton de Gruyter.
Rissanen, Matti. 1999. Syntax. In Roger Lass (ed.), *The Cambridge history of the English language,* vol. III, *1476–1776*, 187–331. Cambridge: Cambridge University Press.
Rissanen, Matti. 2006. On the development of borrowed connectives in fourteenth-century English: Evidence from corpora. In Ursula Schaefer (ed.), *The beginnings of standardization: Language and culture in fourteenth-century England*, 133–146. Frankfurt/Main: Peter Lang.
Romaine, Suzanne & Deborah Lange. 1991. The use of *like* as a marker of reported speech and thought. A case of grammaticalization in progress. *American Speech* 66. 227–279.
Sells, Peter. 1984. *Syntax and semantics of resumptive pronouns*. University of Massachusetts, Amherst, PhD dissertation.
Seppänen, Aimo & Gunnar Bergh. 1996. Subject extraction in English: Some problems of interpretation. *Studia Anglica Posnaniensia* 30. 45–67.
Sornicola, Rosanna. 2006. Expletives and dummies. In Keith Brown (ed.), *Encyclopedia of language and linguistics*, 2nd edn., vol. 4, 399–410. Oxford: Elsevier.
Traugott, Elizabeth Closs. 1992. Syntax. In Richard M. Hogg (ed.), *The Cambridge history of the English language*, vol. I: *The beginnings to 1066*, 168–229. Cambridge: Cambridge University Press.
Tuggy, David. 1996. The thing is is that people talk that way. In Eugene H. Casad (ed.) *Cognitive linguistics in the redwoods: The expansion of a new paradigm in linguistics*, 713–752. Berlin: Mouton de Gruyter.
Uchida, Mitsumi & Yoko Iyeiri. 2017. *For* and *because*: A comparative study of causal conjunctions in Caxton's *Paris and Vienne* and three French versions of the same text. In Mitsumi Uchida, Yoko Iyeiri & Lawrence Schourup (eds.), *Language contact and variation in the history of English*, 61–79. Tokyo: Kaitakusha.
Visser, Fredericus T. 1963–1973. *An historical syntax of the English language*, 4 vols. Leiden: Brill.
Warner, Anthony. 1982. *Complementation and the methodology of historical syntax*. London: Croom Helm.
Watts, Richard. 1982. The conjunction *that*: A semantically empty particle? *Studia Anglica Posnaniensia* 15. 13–37.
Wiegand, Nancy. 1982. From discourse to syntax: *For* in early English causal clauses. In Anders Ahlqvist (ed.), *Papers from the 5th International Conference on Historical Linguistics*, 385–393. Amsterdam: John Benjamins.

List of contributors

in alphabetical order

Lynn Anthonissen
University of Antwerp & LMU Munich
Linguistics Department
Prinsstraat 13, S.D.214
2000 Antwerpen
Belgium
lynn.anthonissen@uantwerpen.be

Kristin Bech
University of Oslo
Department of Literature, Area Studies
and European Languages
Postboks 1003 Blindern
0315 Oslo
Norway
kristin.bech@ilos.uio.no

Hendrik De Smet
University of Leuven
Department of Linguistics
Blijde-Inkomststraat 21, box 3308
3000 Leuven
Belgium
hendrik.desmet@kuleuven.be

Dagmar Haumann
University of Bergen
Department of Foreign Languages
Postboks 7805
5020 Bergen
Norway
dagmar.haumann@uib.no

Kristin Killie
The Arctic University of Norway
Department of Education
9037 Tromsø
Norway
kristin.killie@uit.no

Martin Konvička
Free University Berlin
English Department
Habelschwerdter Allee 45
14195 Berlin
Germany
martin.konvicka@fu-berlin.de

María José López-Couso
University of Santiago de Compostela
Department of English and German
Faculty of Philology
Avda. Castelao s/n
15782 Santiago de Compostela
Spain
mjlopez.couso@usc.es

Bettelou Los
University of Edinburgh
Linguistics and English Language
School of Philosophy, Psychology and Language Sciences
Dugald Stewart Building
3 Charles Street
EH8 9AD Edinburgh
Scotland, UK
b.los@ed.ac.uk

Thijs Lubbers
c/o Bettelou Los
University of Edinburgh
Linguistics and English Language
School of Philosophy, Psychology and Language Sciences
Dugald Stewart Building
3 Charles Street
EH8 9AD Edinburgh
Scotland, UK
b.los@ed.ac.uk

Belén Méndez-Naya
University of Santiago de Compostela
Department of English and German
Faculty of Philology
Avda. Castelao s/n
15782 Santiago de Compostela
Spain
belen.mendez@usc.es

Ruth Möhlig-Falke
Heidelberg University
English Department
Kettengasse 12
69117 Heidelberg
Germany
ruth.moehlig@as.uni-heidelberg.de

Elena Seoane
University of Vigo
Department of English, French and German
Faculty of Philology and Translation
Praza das Cantigas, Campus CUVI
36310 Vigo
Spain
elena.seoane@uvigo.es

Reijirou Shibasaki
Meiji University
School of Interdisciplinary Mathematical Sciences
4-21-1 Nakano, Nakano-ku
Tokyo 164-8525
Japan
reijiro@meiji.ac.jp

Index

accommodation 116
accretion 333ff., 338f., 341, 343, 347ff., 353f., 356, 360
Accusative-and-Infinitive construction 50f., 129ff., 133, 135, 141, 145, 148, 150
adjective 15ff., 19ff., 23, 25f., 28ff., 36, 38f., 43, 45, 47, 66, 78, 81, 86f., 94ff., 99, 102ff., 107f., 111ff., 118f., 157f., 163ff., 168, 171ff., 178ff., 182
– category of 8, 166, 180, 186
– depictive adjective 172
– emotion adjective 10, 305, 308, 316ff., 328
– inflection of adjectives 98
– predicative use 318
– strong (Old English) 17f., 20ff., 28, 33f., 37f., 45
– weak (Old English) 16ff., 20ff., 25, 27f., 36f., 45
adjective position 15ff., 20, 29, 33, 45
adjective-adverb pairs 165
adjunct 16
adult lifespan 8
adverb 93ff., 99ff., 105, 107, 109f., 112ff., 116ff., 249, 256, 264, 270, 272
– category of 8, 166, 180, 186
– class of 96, 166
– degree adverb 93ff., 99ff., 109ff., 159, 175, 178
– dual-form adverb 8, 157ff., 166f., 171, 173, 181f., 185
– evaluative adverb 193ff., 214
– evidential adverb 9, 193ff., 202, 207ff., 214f., 217
– -ly-marked adverb 158ff., 165, 167ff., 173ff., 177ff., 182ff., 192, 197
– manner adverb 96, 112, 120, 159, 166, 172f., 175, 186, 197, 199
– modal adverb 193ff.
– quantification, adverb of 96
– sentence adverb 191ff., 199ff., 206f., 211, 216f.
– stance adverb 186
– transparent adverb 172f., 186

– zero-marked 158ff., 163ff., 167ff., 173ff.
adverbial 53f., 71, 134, 138, 141, 150, 249f., 253f., 256ff., 267ff.
adverbial clause 208, 210ff.
adverbial relations
– Cause 344, 346
– CCC relations 346
– Comparison 344ff.
– Condition 342, 344ff.
– Time 256, 343f., 346
adverbial subordinator 10
– complex 342, 345f.
– general-purpose/polysemous 339
– one-word 339f., 342
– special-purpose/monofunctional 340
– strengthened 333f., 339, 342ff., 354, 359f.
adverbial suffix -e (Old English) 165
adverbial support 253, 257ff., 267ff., 271

Ælfric 49ff., 53ff., 68, 70ff., 78, 82ff.
– *Catholic Homilies I* 56, 61, 68, 71, 84
– *Catholic Homilies II* 56, 68
– *Lives of Saints* 50, 56, 58ff., 68, 71, 73, 82f., 85
– supplemental homilies 78
– *Treatise on the Bible* 56, 68, 70ff.

alliteration 50, 54
amalgam construction 230
amalgamation 9, 221, 223ff., 238
ambiguity 200, 261, 340, 346, 350, 359
– ambiguity, contextual 164
– ambiguity, grammatical 162, 164, 178, 182
American English 158, 160f., 221, 224ff., 230ff., 241ff., 247, 250, 255, 270
anacoluthon 221ff., 227, 229, 231f., 234ff., 238ff., 243
analogical reasoning 5
analogy 5f., 127, 240, 305, 326f.
Ancrene Riwle 105, 107
AntConc (concordancing software) 57
apposition 16, 27, 44
argument structure 142

argumentative prose 53
Ash, John 181
Asian Englishes 250
assertion 62f.
assertive illocutionary force 9, 192f., 208f., 211f., 217
assonance 54
attrition 333ff.
Australian English 241
authorship 49, 55, 60, 65, 87, 126
auxiliary 66
auxiliary verb 254

backgrounding 59, 64
Bede, *History of the English Church* 56, 69ff., 73, 76ff.
bilingualism 99, 115
Black South African English 250
borrowing 95, 98, 115ff., 120, 130, 135
boundedness 94f., 104, 108, 117, 119
– boundedness, conceptual 180
British English 158, 161, 226, 231, 234f., 242, 250ff., 262, 265, 270, 272
British National Corpus 226, 232, 235f., 316, 318, 323

Canadian English 241
case 70, 78, 83
– accusative 84
– dative 53, 83
– genitive 76, 83f., 310
– nominative 70, 83, 86
Catcher in the Rye (novel) 222f., 225, 238
categoricalness 148f., 151
categorization 127, 193
category marking 10
causative meaning 325
causative verbs 129, 133
chiasmus 51ff.
child language (L1) acquisition 355f., 362, see also language acquisition
chunking 2, 57, 73, 127
clausal word order 15
codification 158ff., 166f., 181f.
coding of experience 311, 319, 327f.
cognitive domain 4
cognitive efficiency 326

cognitive linguistics 2
cohesion 134
collocation 4, 94ff., 103ff., 107f., 113f., 118, 215, 259, 309f.
collocational analysis 309
colloquiality 223, 225, 227, 234, 237, 242
colloquialization 242
collostructional analysis 310, 329
colonization 251f.
communicative purpose 270, 272
comparative 96, 158, 177
competition 313
complementation 334, 350, 352, 363
– adjective complement 317
– matching-problem 317
– prepositional complement 305f.
– prepositional phrase complement 308, 316ff., 326, 328
complementizer 335, 339, 350ff., 360f.
– *that* 350ff., 360
– zero 350ff., 360f., 363f.
conceptualization 2
conjunction 52, 65, 99
– coordinating 78, 86f., 238, 240
– subordinating 66, 238
connective 342ff., 359, 362, 364
construal 311, 314
construction 4
construction grammar 126ff., 142
constructional change 125, 129, 139, 141, 147, 150f., 240
constructional grounding 356
constructional semantics 125, 141, 143
context 1, 3ff., 10f., 44, 93, 110
– bridging context 8f., 110f., 120, 191f., 195, 198ff., 205, 207, 217f., 357
– critical context 191
– grammatical context 316, 322, 327
– isolating context 110
– macro-level context 4, 8, 93f., 99, 119f., 157, 161, 172f., 249f., 253, 260, 269
– micro-level context 4, 7ff., 93, 99, 119, 127, 157, 161, 172f., 216, 249f., 269, 271
– situational context 173
– structural or systemic context 4, 307, 314
– switch context 110f., 113
– theoretical context 1, 5ff., 9ff.

context-absorption 201
contextualization 4, 7, 11, 28f., 45, 51, 249
conventionalization 110ff., 114, 126, 200, 237, 242, 328
Cooperative Principle 336
Corpus of Contemporary American English (COCA) 224, 229, 232, 234ff.
Corpus of Global Web-Based English 231f., 242, 247
Corpus of Historical American English (COHA) 229, 232
Corpus of Late Modern British and American English 230, 232
Corpus of Late Modern English Texts Extended Version 229, 232, 234f.
"correct" English 160, 167
correspondence analysis 7, 55, 65ff., 72ff., 80f., 143
co-text 4, 7, 9, 164, 221, 224, 228, 230f., 235, 240
court scribes, role of 168
Cura Pastoralis 7, 15, 29f., 33, 39, 44ff., 56, 69ff., 73, 76

Danelaw 94, 98, 115, 119f.
data-driven approach 49, 55, 57, 65, 87
dative alternation 310, 315
decategorialization 96
declarative 192, 217
declension (Old English) 15
decontextualization 6, 126
definiteness 15, 39
degree modifier 100, 104, 111f., 117, 120
deictic *there* 354ff., 362
delexicalization 96
deontic necessity 314
depictive construction 163f., 167, 171f., 180
determiner 66
determiner phrase (DP) 82, 84f.
dialects of Middle English 107, 117ff.
Dialogues of Gregory the Great 56, 58ff., 69ff., 73, 76, 82f., 85, 87
Dictionary of Old English (DOE) 101
Dictionary of Old English Corpus (DOEC) 165
didactic genre 78, 86
diffusion 6
direct speech 60

discourse 1, 3f., 6f., 9, 11, 44, 52, 224
discourse analysis 3, 5, 11
discourse function 59, 133f.
discourse referent 86
discourse structure 54, 64, 134f., 150, 210
discourses 3ff., 11
distributional profile 322ff.
domain-general learning/knowledge 2, 127
double object construction 139
double-locative overlap construction 10, 333f., 339, 354ff.
doubling 337f., 341
downtoning function 159
Dynamic Model of Postcolonial Englishes 252

Early English Books Online (EEBO) 139
Early English Prose Fiction corpus 205
Early Modern English 4, 65, 125, 127, 134f., 141, 150f., 165f., 176
East-African English 251
eigenvalue (principal inertia) 69
Eighteenth Century Collection Online (ECCO) 139
Eighteenth-Century Fiction corpus 205
emergent grammar 224, 239
EMMA corpus 8, 129, 139f., 148f.
emotion 96
emotional state 10, 318f.
endonormative stabilization 252
English as a Second Dialect 253
entrenchment 9, 127, 149, 151, 249f., 253f., 256, 258, 267ff., 310, 325
ephemera 346f.
epistemic necessity 315
epistemicity 128, 193f., 196, 214, 315
erosion 333f.
evidentiality 125, 130, 135ff., 141f., 144ff., 151, 193, 196, 216
existential *there* 333f., 354ff.
experiencer 83, 318
experiential perfect meaning 250, 261f., 264, 267, 270, 272
explain yourself strategy 337
expletive 335
exposition 53, 60, 63, 71, 74, 78, 81, 87
expressiveness 95, 99, 109, 119

fictional genre 225, 230, 236f., 243
finite verb 51ff., 60, 63, 131, 134
Fish fork 7, 49, 54f., 58, 87
fixed collocation 97, 179, 185
foregrounding 64, 74, 170f.
forensic linguistics 126
formality 261
free variation 160, 180, 182, 186
frequency 51, 54f., 57f., 61, 63ff., 71ff., 82f., 86, 93f., 100, 103, 105, 107, 109, 118ff., 201, 205, 207, 230, 234, 236, 239f., 319
frequency bias 319
frill 338, 360, 362
Fuller, Thomas 140ff., 147ff., 151
functionalist linguistics 2f., 9f., 305ff., 309ff., 313f., 317, 322, 327
function-to-form approach 250, 254
fuzziness of categories 8, 157, 166, 171, 186

gender, grammatical 98
genericity 138
genre 4, 9, 49, 53, 55, 61, 64f., 78, 81, 86f., 147
given information 15, 17, 19ff., 24ff., 27, 31ff., 36, 38, 45, 86, 127, 132, 134f., 150
Google n-grams 57
grammar 1ff., 7, 44
grammar books 160, 185
grammatical gradability 10
grammaticalization 6f., 9, 95f., 99, 110, 113f., 120, 128, 131, 135, 158, 165, 167, 186, 191, 200, 221, 230, 235, 306, 309, 328
– diachronic 333ff., 354ff., 359f., 362ff.
– ontogenetic 355, 360, 363, see also ontogenesis
grounding 63

Hansard Corpus 317, 323
hearer interpretation 200, 216
Helsinki Corpus 49, 56, 101, 106f., 111f.
homilies 50, 53, 55, 61ff., 68, 71, 73, 80, 84, 86f.
homonymy 341
Hong Kong English 251
host-class expansion 96, 114, 228
hybridization 118, 120

hypercharacterization 10, 333ff., 338f., 341ff., 348ff., 353f., 356, 358ff.
hypervariation 10, 315ff., 328, see also variation
hypotaxis 221, 237f.

iconicity 18, 32, 239, 314, 337f.
idiom principle 2
impersonal verb 53
inalienable possession 310
Indian English 251
indirect speech 60, 62
individual-level reading 15, 20ff., 26f., 31f., 34ff.
inference 196, 200f.
informality 224, 242
information structure 54, 133f., 311
information-rearranging device 150
innateness hypothesis 2
innovation 126, 328
intended audience 270, 272
intensification 93ff., 99, 101, 103, 109f., 112, 118f., 159
– boosting 94, 100, 116
– maximization 94, 100, 104f., 117
intensifier 7, 93ff., 99ff., 105ff., 118ff.
– amplifier 94
– booster 108, 118f.
– maximizer 101, 104, 109, 117
International Corpus of English (ICE) 9, 249, 251
intersubjectification 6
intragenerational change 127
intransitive construction 311
Irish English 226f., 231, 241
is all-construction 9, 221, 224ff., 231, 233, 236, 239, 243, 247
is-marking of subordinate clauses 238, 241
isomorphism/isomorphic principle 253, 261, 272, 306f., 313

Jamaican English 250
Japanese 238

key word frequency 57
knowledge of language 2ff., 6

L'Estrange, Roger 140, 143, 146ff., 151
L1 variety 255, 260, 271
L2 variety 251ff., 255, 257ff., 265, 268f., 271f.
language acquisition 2f., 5, 126, 128, *see also child language (L1) acquisition*
language change 125ff., 151, 249, 305ff., 311f., 315ff., 321, 323, 325f., 328
language contact 93, 95, 99, 115, 131, 226, 253, 260, 269, 334, 336, 361, 364
– with French 98
– with Low German 98
– with Scandinvian 93f., 97ff., 116ff.
language evolution 5
language system 326
Late Modern English 4, 103, 114, 135, 139, 158, 162, 166, 186, 232, 242
"late subject" construction 86
Latin 15f., 29ff., 39ff., 46, 62, 66, 78, 84f., 87, 130ff., 135
Layamon's *Brut* 102, 105, 107
layering 96, 111
lexeme 4
lexical bundle 57
lexical density (type-token ratio) 57
lexicalized compound 178
lifespan change 125, 128, 141, 145ff., 150ff.
linear iconicity 15, 18, 24
linear modification 17
linguistic choice 327
linguistic economy 336
linguistic individual 125ff., 139, 141f., 147, 150f.
linguistic knowledge 126, 128, 150
linguistic memory 327
linguistic variation 4, 9f., 127, 249, 264, 305ff., 311ff., 320ff., 324, 326ff.
locative *there* 354, 356f., 359
Lowth, Robert 157, 160, 167, 181
loyalty score 323f.

main clause 51f., 63f., 74
Mandarin 252
Maxim of Quantity 216, 336
MCASE 232, 237
meaning is choice 5
mediopassive construction 177
mental grammar 4, 126, 128, 250, 268, 271

metaphorization 5
metonymization 5
metre 50, 54, 105, 107, 118, 120
metrical prose 49f., 55, 68
Michigan Corpus of Academic Spoken English 232
Middle English 4, 7, 20, 63, 93f., 97ff., 105ff., 114ff., 119, 125, 131, 134, 150, 158, 165ff.
Middle English Dictionary (MED) 98, 102f., 113ff., 118f.
Milton, John 140, 142, 147ff., 151
mindsay 137, 142
Minimalist Syntax 19
modal construction 175
modal verb 136f., 142, 314
modality 125, 136ff., 141f., 145ff., 193
mode (communicative exchange) 4, 249, 261, 265, 267, 269f., 272, *see also spoken language, written language*
– spoken 267, 269f., 272
– written 267, 269f., 272
modelling 6
modification 15f., 39f., 94, 99, 107, 112, 122, 163, 170f., 179
– attributive 17, 19ff., 28, 31ff., 35ff., 45
– postmodification 105
– postnominal 15ff., 26ff., 32f., 36, 39f., 43ff.
– predicative 17ff., 28, 31ff., 37f., 45
– premodification 85, 112
– prenominal 15ff., 20ff., 26ff., 30ff., 34, 36f., 39f., 43ff.
mood 70
– imperative 70
– indicative 61, 68, 70, 74
– subjunctive 70
motivation 10, 305, 307, 313f., 316f., 322f., 325ff.
Movie Corpus 232, 247
multifactorial analysis 9
multilingual setting 250
multivariate analysis 186, 265, 270
multivariate statistics 66
Murray, Lindley 181

narrative 49, 53, 55, 58ff., 71, 74, 76, 80ff., 87
nativization 252

negation 191, 201, 211, 214
network plot 319
neutralization-in-discourse 311
new information 15, 17, 19ff., 23ff., 31ff., 36, 38, 83, 86, 134
n-gram 49, 55, 57, 59f., 64, 66
– 4-gram 55, 58f., 61f., 64f., 81, 83, 85
– trigram 72ff., 77f., 80ff.
– unigram 55, 66, 68ff., 72f.
n-gramming 55, 57, 62, 64ff., 81, 87
Nigerian English 250ff.
Nineteenth-Century Fiction corpus 205
nominalization 76, 84, 87
Nominative-and-Infinitive construction 8, 125f., 129ff., 145ff.
non-canonical word order 50, 52, 55
non-finite verb 51
non-metrical prose 49, 55
non-standard language use 160
non-standard varieties 161
normative attitudes 158, 185
norsification 8, 93f., 98, 117, 119
noun 76, 81, 83f.
– common noun 66
– proper name 70
noun phrase 7, 15, 23f., 26f., 29f., 38ff., 42, 44ff., 50, 81, 83
– internal structure 81
NP-fronting 131f.
numeral 70f.

object 50ff., 60, 132ff., 150
object-fronting 132
Old Bailey Corpus (OBC) 8, 157f., 162, 164, 167ff., 173f., 179ff., 229ff.
Old English 4, 7, 15ff., 20ff., 26, 28ff., 32, 34f., 38, 40ff., 49ff., 53, 55ff., 63, 68, 81, 88, 97f., 101f., 104, 107, 111, 115f., 118ff., 130, 165f.
Old Norse 8, 93f., 97ff., 115ff.
ontogenesis 355, 358, *see also grammaticalization (ontogenetic)*
orientation, semantic-pragmatic 8, 157, 161, 164, 167, 170ff., 180, 186
– event orientation 170, 172f., 175ff., 180, 182, 186
– object-participant orientation 171f., 177

– participant orientation 170ff., 175ff., 186
– reference-point orientation 171, 175, 179f., 186
– speaker orientation 170, 175f., 186, 193, 202, 209
– state orientation 171, 175, 177ff.
– subject-participant orientation 171, 173, 177, 193f., 214
Ormulum 7, 93f., 97ff., 112f., 115ff.
Orosius 56, 69ff., 73, 76
overlap 340, 355f., 359
overlap deictic construction 355ff., 360
Owen, John 140ff., 147ff., 151
Oxford English Dictionary (OED) 95, 98ff., 102f., 113ff., 118f., 165, 178f., 206, 222, 231f.

paradigmatic integration 110
parallelism 51ff.
paratactic construction 230
parataxis 221, 230, 237f.
Paris Psalter 101
paronomasia 54
participle phrase 44
Part-of-Speech (POS) tagging 55, 64ff., 72ff., 77f., 80ff., 87
passive construction 125f., 129ff., 138, 141, 147f., 150f., 322, 326
passivization 134f.
Paston letters 58
pattern, grammatical 4
PCU verbs 130, 137, 139ff., 147ff.
– cognition verbs 145
– perception verbs 130, 145
– utterance verbs 130, 136ff., 144f., 151
peak marking 54
Penn-Helsinki Parsed Corpus of Early Modern English 135
Penn-Helsinki Parsed Corpus of Middle English 99f., 104, 106
Pennsylvania Dutch 227, 231
perfect marker 9, 249f., 253f., 256, 268ff.
perfect meaning 249f., 253ff., 259ff., 264f., 267ff.
persistent situation perfect meaning 261f., 267
Philippines English 251

phonological variation 308
phrasal status 179
phrasal verb 99
phrasal word order 15
pleonasm 334f.
poetry 96, 105, 107
polarity 249, 253, 257, 260, 267f., 271
– negative 260, 266ff., 271
– positive 267, 271
polyfunctionality, syntactic and semantic 339f.
polysemy 313, 325, 327
postmodification 76, 81, 83f., 87
pragmatic device 62, 64, 88
pragmatic enrichment 112
pragmatic inferencing 309
pragmatic marker 229, 239, 241, 243
pragmatics 3, 5f.
preposition 305, 319f., 328
preposition stranding 82
prepositional phrase (PP) 52f., 76, 81f., 85f.
prescriptivism 158, 166f.
present participle 15f., 39f., 43f.
present participle modifier 7
present perfect 250, 260, 265, 268, 270
presentational *there*-construction 86
pressure of discourse 272
preterite 250, 255, 258, 265, 268f., 271
Priestley, Joseph 181
Principal Component Analysis 66
principle of transparency 253
Proceedings of the Old Bailey 162, 164
productivity 118
projector 239
pronoun 50f., 53, 62, 66, 70, 74, 83
– personal 66
– possessive 66
pronoun resumption 10
punctuation 57, 65, 78, 83, 88
purpose clause 59f., 66, 83

quantifier 66, 78, 81, 87, 126
quotative *be like* construction 241

R (statistical software package) 55, 65, 68, 72, 265
raising 350

rationale clause 60
reanalysis 6, 8f., 191f., 196f., 199f., 207, 209ff., 356, 358
reason clause 63f., 66, 83
recent-past perfect meaning 250, 261f., 264, 267, 270, 272
redundancy 261, 333f., 338, 343, 356, 360
referent tracking 54
register 49, 55, 66, 84, 87, 249, 251, 253f., 261, 264f., 267, 269ff., 306, 311
register variation 249, 270, 272
regression analysis 265, 271
relative clause 81, 83, 208, 211f., 336, 348ff., 360f., 363
– *se þe*-relative 83
– *þe*-relative 83
relativization 348, 350, 352, 359
relativizer 341, 349
– invariable *þat* 348
– invariable *þe* 348
– *wh*-relativizer 336, 350
relexification 116
renewal 95, 97, 109
reportative marker 147, 150f.
residual quirk theory 336
restrictivity 15, 20ff., 27f., 31ff., 45, 208, 210ff., 215, 238
– non-restrictive 83, 86f.
– restrictive 83, 86
resultative construction 163f., 167, 171f., 180
resultative perfect meaning 249, 261ff., 267, 269ff.
resumptive pronoun 333f., 339, 348ff., 353f., 359f., 364
rhematic 18, 20, 22f., 25, 28, 45
rhetorical device 50f.
rule-learning 128
RWeka (software package) 65

saliency 20, 25, 32, 34, 131
Salinger, J.D. 221ff., 226, 238
sampling 72, 81
Santa Barbara Corpus of Spoken American English 232, 237
scope 166f., 170, 191f., 194, 197, 199, 206ff., 214ff., 230, 243
scribal interpolation 185

second-language acquisition 253, 261, 269
Segmented Discourse Representation Theory 64
self-reflexive 94
semantic bleaching 96, 111f., 333ff.
semantic change 128, 136, 325
semantic field 4
semantic prosody 96, 105
semanticization 200f.
sense-making 5
sentence-length 57
sequentiality 221, 237, 239f.
shell noun construction 241f.
simplification 253
Singapore English 250f.
slot-and-filler principle 2
sociolinguistic factors 157, 162, 164, 167, 181f.
– age 147f., 161
– class 161, 167, 181f., 185f.
– education 126, 160f., 167, 181f., 185f.
– gender 161, 167, 181f., 185f.
social network 127f.
social setting 270, 272
sociolinguistics 127
spatial relation 10, 328
speaker intention 200, 216
specialization (semantic) 125, 139, 147, 151
spelling 98, 100
spelling books 160
spoken language 224, 226, 230, 236f., 240ff., 249, 251, 253, 261, 267, 269ff., see also mode (communicative exchange)
spoken language bias 227, 237
stage-level reading 15, 20ff., 26f., 34ff., 39, 45
stance marker 175
Standard English 158, 167, 170
standardization 157f., 160, 162, 166f., 181f., 185
statistical preemption 128
structuralist levels 6
Structuralist linguistics 306
stylometrics, stylometry 7, 49, 55, 65, 126
subclause 52, 63f.
– embedded clause 63

– subordinate clause 63
subject 52ff., 59f., 67, 72, 83, 85f., 132, 134, 136f., 141ff., 148, 150
subject complement 86
subject extraction 333f., 339, 348, 350ff., 359ff., 364
subjectification 6, 96, 197, 199f.
subjectivity 158, 173, 175f., 178, 186, 193, 197
subordinating marker 340f., 346, 359
– þæt 341
– þe 341
subordination 221, 237f.
Subordination Deranking Hierarchy 63
suffix *-līc* (Old English) 165
suffix *-ly* 157f., 160, 165
– derivational 165f.
– inflectional 166
summative function 227f., 234
Swahili 252
symbolic view of grammar 3
symmetry, decorative/non-referential 337, 343, 346
synonymic doublet 337
synonymy, synonymity 308, 310, 313f., 326, 337, 343
syntactic integration 231
Systemic Functional Grammar 9, 224, 235

teenage vernacular 225
temporal adverb (time adverbial) 66, 71
Tense
– past tense 70, 74
– present tense 70
text structuring device 62
text type 49, 59, 62ff., 71, 74, 80f., 87, 264
Thackeray, William Makepeace 225f.
thematic 18ff., 22, 25, 28, 36, 45, 134
theme-rheme 230
to-infinitive 60, 130, 133, 141
topic, topical information 36f., 45, 134, 150
topicalization 350, 352
transitive construction 311
transitivity 135, 208
translation 15f., 29f., 33ff., 40ff., 44f., 50, 53, 62, 71f., 74, 87
transparency 261, 268
truth-conditional value 308

TV Corpus 231f., 247

Universal Grammar 128
usage-based linguistics 2, 126ff.
Usage-Based Theory 249f., 268, 270

usage guides 158, 160, 185

variability 305, 325
variation, *see also hypervariation*
– choice-dependent 315f.
– grammatical 249, 270, 272
– individual 147, 151
– phonological 316
– spelling 57
– stylistic 33, 39, 50, 53ff., 57, 62ff., 86ff., 140, 147, 160, 181
– syntactic 272
variationist linguistics 10, 251, 305ff., 313ff., 317, 322, 327
varieties of English 221, 234, 241ff., 247, 251
Verb Second (V2) 49, 51, 53, 63, 74, 87, 134f., 150
vernacular speech 162
vernacular universal 161
vocative 35

weak complementarity 311
West-Saxon Gospels 15, 29, 35, 56, 68, 70ff.
West-Saxon written standard 57
word length 57
word order 99, 112
– SVO 99, 134, 150
word order variation 15
WordSmith (software tool) 99
World Englishes 9, 249ff., 273
– Inner Circle 251
– Outer Circle 251
'written-as-spoken' language 162, *see also mode (communicative exchange)*
written language 250f., 253, 261, 265, 269ff., *see also mode (communicative exchange)*
written language bias 243
Wulfstan 49, 55f., 61ff., 69ff., 73, 78, 84ff., 88

York English 161
York-Toronto-Helsinki Corpus of Parsed Old English (YCOE) 29, 39, 42, 44, 54ff., 63, 65f., 72, 81

www.ingramcontent.com/pod-product-compliance
Lightning Source LLC
Chambersburg PA
CBHW051556230426
43668CB00013B/1865